DEBTFARE STATES AND THE POVERTY INDUSTRY

D1572144

Under the rubric of 'financial inclusion', lending to the poor – in both the global North and global South – has become a highly lucrative and rapidly expanding industry since the 1990s. A key inquiry of this book is what is 'the financial' in which the poor are asked to join. Instead of embracing the mainstream position that financial inclusion is a natural, inevitable and mutually beneficial arrangement, *Debtfare States and the Poverty Industry* suggests that the structural violence inherent to neoliberalism and credit-led accumulation have created and normalised a reality in which the working poor can no longer afford to live without expensive credit.

The book transcends economic treatments of credit and debt by revealing how the poverty industry is inextricably linked to the social power of money, the paradoxes in credit-led accumulation and 'debtfarism'. The latter refers to rhetorical and regulatory forms of governance that mediate and facilitate the expansion of the poverty industry and the reliance of the poor on credit to augment/replace their wages. Through a historically grounded analysis, the author examines various dimensions of the poverty industry ranging from the credit card, payday loan and student loan industries in the United States to micro-lending and low-income housing finance industries in Mexico.

Providing a much-needed theorisation of the politics of debt, *Debtfare States and the Poverty Industry* has wider implications of the increasing dependence of the poor on consumer credit across the globe, this book will be of very strong interest to students and scholars of Global Political Economy, Finance, Development Studies, Geography, Law, History and Sociology.

Susanne Soederberg is Professor and Canada Research Chair in Global Political Economy at the Department of Global Development Studies, cross-appointed with the Department of Political Studies, Queen's University, Canada.

RIPE Series in Global Political Economy

Series Editors: Jacqueline Best (*University of Ottawa, Canada*), Ian Bruff (*Manchester University, UK*), Paul Langley (*Durham University, UK*) and Anna Leander (*Copenhagen Business School, Denmark*)

Formerly edited by Leonard Seabrooke (*Copenhagen Business School, Denmark*), Randall Germain (*Carleton University, Canada*), Rorden Wilkinson (*University of Manchester, UK*), Otto Holman (*University of Amsterdam*), Marianne Marchand (*Universidad de las Américas-Puebla*), Henk Overbeek (*Free University, Amsterdam*) and Marianne Franklin (*Goldsmiths, University of London, UK*)

The RIPE series editorial board are:

Mathias Albert (*Bielefeld University, Germany*), Mark Beeson (*University of Birmingham, UK*), A. Claire Cutler (*University of Victoria, Canada*), Marianne Franklin (*Goldsmiths, University of London, UK*), Randall Germain (*Carleton University, Canada*) Stephen Gill (*York University, Canada*), Jeffrey Hart (*Indiana University, USA*), Eric Helleiner (*Trent University, Canada*), Otto Holman (*University of Amsterdam, the Netherlands*), Marianne H. Marchand (*Universidad de las Américas-Puebla, Mexico*), Craig N. Murphy (*Wellesley College, USA*), Robert O'Brien (*McMaster University, Canada*), Henk Overbeek (*Vrije Universiteit, the Netherlands*), Anthony Payne (*University of Sheffield, UK*), V. Spike Peterson (*University of Arizona, USA*) and Rorden Wilkinson (*University of Manchester, UK*).

This series, published in association with the *Review of International Political Economy*, provides a forum for current and interdisciplinary debates in international political economy. The series aims to advance understanding of the key issues in the global political economy and to present innovative analyses of emerging topics. The titles in the series focus on three broad themes:

- the structures, processes and actors of contemporary global transformations
- the changing forms taken by governance, at scales from the local and everyday to the global and systemic
- the inseparability of economic from political, social and cultural questions, including resistance, dissent and social movements.

The *RIPE Series in Global Political Economy* aims to address the needs of students and teachers. Titles include:

Debtfare States and the Poverty Industry
Money, discipline and the surplus population
Susanne Soederberg

Currency Challenge
The euro, the dollar and the global financial
Miguel Otero-Iglesias

DEBTFARE STATES AND THE POVERTY INDUSTRY

Money, discipline and the surplus population

Susanne Soederberg

Routledge
Taylor & Francis Group

LONDON AND NEW YORK

First published 2014
by Routledge
2 Park Square, Milton Park, Abingdon, Oxon OX14 4RN

and by Routledge
711 Third Avenue, New York, NY 10017

Routledge is an imprint of the Taylor and Francis Group, an informa business

© 2014 Susanne Soederberg

British Library Cataloguing in Publication Data
A catalogue record for this book is available from the British Library

Library of Congress Cataloging in Publication Data
Soederberg, Susanne
  Debtfare states and the poverty industry: money, discipline and the
  surplus population/Susanne Soederberg.
  pages cm. – (Ripe series in global political economy)
  Includes bibliographical references and index.
  1. Debt – Political aspects. 2. Consumer credit – Political aspects.
  3. Poverty – Government policy. 4. Poor – Finance, Personal.
  5. Financial institutions – Political aspects. I. Title.
  HG3701.S595 2014
  332.7'43 – dc23
  2014004596

ISBN: 978–0-415–82266–4 (hbk)
ISBN: 978–0-415–82267–1 (pbk)
ISBN: 978–1-315–76195–4 (ebk)

Typeset in Bembo and Stone Sans by
by Florence Production Ltd, Stoodleigh, Devon, UK

To all those struggling with and against
the oppression of debt

CONTENTS

ILLUSTRATIONS

Tables

Figures

ACKNOWLEDGEMENTS

Numerous people and organisations have supported me in this book project. I would like to thank the Social Science Humanities Research Council of Canada for their generous financial support through a Standard Research Grant and the Canada Research Chair programme. In many ways, *Debtfare* is an extension of my previous book, *Corporate Power and Ownership in Contemporary Society* (Routledge, 2010) and the *Socialist Register* Workshop, organised by Greg Albo, Leo Panitch and Vivek Chibbers in February 2010, pushed me to think about the connection between corporate power and consumer debt. I also thank the participants of this workshop for their perceptive comments and suggestions, especially Dick Bryan, Ben Fine, Sam Gindin and David McNally. I would also like to acknowledge Jamie Peck and Loïc Wacquant for their insightful and encouraging comments regarding my early formulations of debtfare.

The Social Science Humanities Research Council of Canada, once again, provided generous funding for an interdisciplinary workshop on, *'Repoliticising Debt'*, held at Queen's University, Canada in May 2012 and which I co-organised with my former post-doctoral student, Dr Adrienne Roberts. This workshop, which was comprised of legal scholars, political scientists, sociologists and geographers, facilitated to further consolidate my ideas about money, debt, and the poverty industry. I would like to thank all of the workshop participants, Patrick Bond, Linda Coco, Kate Ervine, Gavin Fridell, Genevieve LeBaron, Randy Martin, Philip McMichael, Katherine Rankin, Sebastian Rioux and Marcus Taylor. A special thanks is due to Adrienne Roberts, who, during her tenure as a post-doctoral student at Queen's University, provided me with stimulating discussions about debt and social reproduction. I would also like to thank Thomas Marois, Paolo Novak and Alfredo Saad Filho for inviting me to present various aspects of this book to the Department of Development Studies at SOAS, University of London. I would also like to acknowledge Teivo Teivainen for inviting me to share my ideas on

Debtfarism with his students and colleagues at the University of Helsinki. It was a privilege to be in the 'Rio de Janeiro of Europe' on two separate occasions!

Many thanks for research assistance goes to several graduate students at Queen's University, namely: Jesse Hembruff, Victoria Henderson, Korey Pasch, Leanne Roderick, Siahra Skelton, and Aída Sofía Rivera Sotelo. I would also like to recognise my colleagues at Queen's University for their encouragement and support throughout this project, especially Alexandre Da Costa, Dia Da Costa, Jayant Lele, Dorothy Lele and Laureen Snider. I would also like to acknowledge Pete Harris at Routledge and RIPE Series Editorial Board for backing this project and, in particular, Ian Bruff for his incisive, generous and constructive feedback, which has greatly improved the manuscript.

Last but not least, I thank my family Sydney Soederberg, Teivo Taylor, Anne and Barry Taylor and Nena Wirth, who have been extremely tolerant and supportive throughout the book-writing process. The biggest gratitude, however, goes to my partner, Marcus Taylor. Marcus, I am forever in your debt!

Finally, I should note that modified versions of Chapters 4 and 8 have appeared as the following articles and I thank the publishers for their permission to reprint adapted versions in this book: 'The US Debtfare State and the Credit Card Industry: Forging Spaces of Dispossession', *Antipode: Radical Journal of Geography*, 45(2), 2013, pp. 493–512 and 'The Mexican Debtfare State: Micro-Lending, Dispossession and the Surplus Population', *Globalizations*, 9(4), 2012, pp. 561–75.

Susanne Soederberg
Kingston, Ontario, Canada
January 2014

ABBREVIATIONS

ABA	American Bankers Association
ABS	Asset-backed Securitisation
AFI	Alliance for Financial Inclusion
APR	Annual Percentage Rate
BAPCPA	Bankruptcy Abuse Prevention and Consumer Protection Act
BIS	Bank for International Settlements
BOP	Base of the Pyramid
CBO	Congressional Budget Office
CETES	*Certificados de la Tesoreria* (Mexican Federal Treasury Certificates)
CFPB	Consumer Financial Protection Bureau
CFSA	Community Finance Service Association
CGAP	Consultative Group to Assist the Poor
CNBV	*Comision Nacional Bancaria y de Valores* (National Banking and Securities Commission, Mexico)
CIDOC	*Fundacion Centro de Investigacion y Documentaria de la Casa, A.C.* Central Foundation for the Investigation and Documentation of Housing (Mexico)
CONAVI	*Comisión Nacional de Vivienda* (National Housing Commission, Mexico)
CONDUSEF	*Comisión Nacional para la Protección y Defensa de los Usuarios de Servicios Financieros* (National Commission for the Defense of Financial Services Users of Mexico)
CRA	Community Reinvestment Act
CRL	Centre of Responsible Lending (United States)
DOE	US Department of Education
EOI	Export Promotion Industrialisation

FDIC	Federal Deposit Insurance Corporation (United States)
FiSCA	Financial Service Centres of America
FOVISSSTE	*Fondo de la Vivienda del Instituto de Seguridad y Servicios Sociales de los Trabajadores del Estado* (State Funds for Housing of the Institute of Security and Social Services for Workers, Mexico)
G20	Group of Twenty
G20 Principles	Group of Twenty Principles for Innovative Financial Inclusion
GLB	Gramm-Leach-Bliley Act also known as the Financial Services Modernization Act of 1999 (United States)
GPFI	Global Partnership for Financial Inclusion
GSE	Government-Sponsored Enterprise
IDB	Inter-American Development Bank
IFC	International Financial Corporation
IMF	International Monetary Fund
Infonavit	*Instituto del Fondo Nacional para Vivienda de los Trabajadores* (Institute of the National Housing Funds for Workers, Mexico)
ISI	Import Substitution Industrialisation
OCC	US Office of the Comptroller of the Currency
OECD	Organisation of Economic Co-operation and Development
PROGRESA	Programa de Educación, Salud y Alimentación
PRWORA	Personal Responsibility Work and Opportunity Act (United States)
MCTF	US Middle-Class Task Force
MFI	Microfinance Institution
MIVs	Microfinance Investment Vehicles
MMW	Minimum Wage (Mexico)
NAFTA	North American Free Trade Agreement
Sallie Mae	Student Loan Marketing Association (United States)
SAPs	Structural Adjustment Policies
SCF	Survey of Consumer Finances (Federal Reserve)
SHF	Mexican Federal Mortgage Company
SLABS	Student Loans Asset Backed Securitisation
SLM Corporation	Privatised Student Loan Marketing Association, as of 1996
SOFOL	*Sociedad Financiera de Objeto Limitado* (Special Purpose Financial Company, Mexico)
SOFOM	*Sociedades Financieras de Objeto Múltiple* (Multiple Purpose Financial Company, Mexico)
TANF	Temporary Assistance for Needy Families (United States)
TILA	Truth in Lending Act (United States)
UN-HABITAT	United Nations Human Settlements Programme
USAID	United States Agency for International Aid

INTRODUCTION

The increasing indebtedness of adults across the globe is not headline-grabbing news these days. Likewise, most readers would not find it surprising that many marginalised people, not least those designated as underemployed or unemployed, have become increasingly reliant on costly payday loans, credit cards and microfinance loans to pay for basic subsistence needs. The fact that student loans in the United States have surpassed $1 trillion[1] and are now higher than all other types of consumer credit (save mortgage debt) is considered by many observers to be an unfortunate, yet indispensable part of obtaining gainful employment after graduating high school. Paradoxically, debt has become the last hope for avoiding, reducing, or at least delaying the pain of marginalisation.

That these statements do not invoke amazement and curiosity attests to the power of the societal structures and processes that have normalised, disciplined and naturalised the reality of pervasive debt, or what I refer to here as *debtfare*. In what follows, I attempt to interrupt the dominant narrative of debtfare by revealing how and why the increasing reliance of the working poor on expensive forms of privately created money (what is conventionally termed 'consumer credit') is a social construction that has been facilitated and reproduced by states and capitalists in the neoliberal era. Briefly, neoliberalism refers to contested, contradictory and complex processes carried out at various scales (global, national, local) by capitalist states through rhetorical and regulative means. These neoliberal processes are not only guided by the preference for market-led, but also entail disciplinary and ideological dimensions (Gill, 1995; Fine, 2002; Peck and Tickell, 2002; Brenner *et al.*, 2010).

Since the 1990s, the types of credit available to those living near or below the poverty line have expanded. Traditional pawnshops and loan sharks now compete with a variety of products designed to serve the under-banked. Lending to the poor has become big business and is now integrated into mainstream financial institutions as opposed to operating on the fringes of the economy (Karger, 2005).

This shift has been referred to by Michael Hudson (1996) as the 'poverty industry' and by Ananya Roy (2010) as 'poverty capital'.[2] Complementary to, but analytically and thematically distinct from, the work of Hudson and Roy, this book explores specific components of the poverty industry, including a focus on the credit card, student loan and payday loan industries in the United States and on the microfinance and housing finance industries in Mexico.

The decision to focus on the United States and Mexico as the primary sites of analysis is driven by a desire not only to examine the particularities of the poverty industry in both a developed and developing world context, but also to explore the cross-cutting relational factors of the industry writ large. Although the United States was not the first country to embrace neoliberalisation – that dubious honour belongs to Chile under the Pinochet regime – the combination of its geopolitical significance (e.g., financial and military power) and the fervour with which the state has implemented and defended neoliberalism has thrown the articulations of debtfarism and the poverty industry into stark relief. Because of its geographical proximity to, and thus particular historical relationship with, the United States, Mexico represents fertile ground to study the coercive and ideological features of the poverty industry in the context of a middle-income country. Through these two case studies, I illustrate the broader power structures and strategies involved in the creation and reproduction of the poverty industry as well as the roles of money, the surplus population and debtfarism therein. Debtfarism and the poverty industry are certainly not exclusive to these two countries and the theoretical framework of this book is intended to provide a launching pad for the pursuit of future studies in different national as well as scalar contexts. The increasing dominance of credit and the new modes of governance embodied in debtfare are salient, yet undertheorised and understudied, features of neoliberalism. This book takes a modest first step in that direction.

To deconstruct the poverty industry in the United States and Mexico, I employ a Marxian lens to complement debates about consumer credit in the wider financialisation, microfinance and consumer studies literature. The approach is three-fold. First, I interrogate the role of money in the poverty industry by locating the roots of its power within the wider dynamics of capital accumulation. This allows me to dispel powerful tropes that normalise and depoliticise debtfare, such as 'financial inclusion' (usually applied in the context of the global South) and the 'democratisation of credit' (used in the context of the global North). I am guided here by a few simple questions: What constitutes 'the financial' into which the poor are urged to voluntary join? What does the democratisation of privately created money backed by the state (otherwise known as 'credit') imply, and who benefits from the expansion of the monetised relations of debt?

Having interrogated the role of money, I move on to reconceptualise the targets of the poverty industry: that is, underemployed and unemployed workers, or what Marx refers to as the surplus population (Marx, 1990). In doing so, I ask why the poverty industry focuses on surplus workers and consider the consequences of their inclusion into 'the financial'. Simultaneously, I interrogate the underlying causes of the poverty of the surplus population in contemporary capitalism. The third and final feature of this study is the exploration and theorisation of the role played by neoliberal states in the facilitation and reproduction of the poverty industry. Here, I am specifically concerned with capturing and explaining debtfare.

As other writers have insisted, the multifaceted and dynamic nature of neoliberalism has yielded specific forms of state intervention to enable the mediation, discipline and normalisation of various social tensions relating to the poor. Jamie Peck (2001), for instance, has drawn on the concept of the 'workfare' state to analyse the commodification and coercive nature of social welfare programmes. Loïc Wacquant (2009, 2010), on the other hand, has coined the term 'prisonfare' to capture the criminalisation of poverty as a way of disciplining the poor. Prisonfare and workfare states are not standalone neoliberal states. Instead, they reflect important and overlapping features of neoliberalism that occur in specific temporal and spatial contexts of capital accumulation. In this same vein, I propose that debtfare is a component of neoliberal state intervention that has emerged to mediate, normalise and discipline the monetised relations that inhabit the poverty industry.

Paralleling the neoliberal insistence that there is no alternative to market-based growth, the rhetorical and regulative features of debtfarism encourage widespread reliance on credit to augment and/or replace the living wage or government benefit cheque. In doing so, debtfarism assists in the recreation of the Gramscian illusion of '*one class, one society*', while foregoing a material compromise with workers (Gramsci, 1971). This compromise does not entail public support for a living wage or social protection from the market. Instead, in the neoliberal era, the pact has been rearticulated in terms of safeguarding market freedoms and equality in order to ensure that all consumers – regardless of their income or lack thereof – may benefit from standards of fairness, competition, transparency and accountability. The 'benefits' of debtfarism are continually framed by what Marx (2005) refers to as the illusion of the 'community of money', a term characterising capitalist society as one based on 'individualism and concepts of liberty, freedom and equality backed by laws of private property, rights to appropriation and freedom of contract' (Harvey 1989: 168). This illusion is further bolstered, for instance, by the seeming neutrality of the legal obligation of debt and claims of consumer protection.

As focal points, money, the surplus population and debtfare are inseparable elements in my analysis of the poverty industry. Together, they inform the following three arguments that run through the length of the book. First, the poverty industry is neither natural nor inevitable. It is constructed and reproduced by powerful capitalist interests and the rhetorical and regulatory features of neoliberal states – in particular, debtfarism. The various aspects of the poverty industry studied in Part II and Part III of this book reveal that the poverty industry is a product of past attempts to overcome barriers to the expansion of capital accumulation. Credit-led accumulation is a specific trend in the attempt to overcome those barriers.

The second strand of my thesis is that surplus workers are not only important sources for the expansion and intensification of credit-led accumulation, but they also represent a necessary condition and vital feature of capital accumulation (Marx, 1990; Clarke, 1994). As discussed in Chapter 2, the surplus population is not a self-reproducing, naturalised feature of capitalism but rather a highly dynamic social relation. As a social relation, the surplus population must be constructed and reconstructed, both biologically and as labour power. By this I mean two things. First, the surplus workers need to be able to reproduce themselves through the acquisition of basic subsistence requirements, including food, shelter, clothing and healthcare (Katz, 2001; Bakker and Gill, 2003; Peterson, 2003; LeBaron and Roberts, 2010). Second, and more broadly, the social reproduction of surplus population hinges on the ability to impose the basic imperative of capitalism: to earn a living based on market-dependence in such a manner that it appears as a natural and inevitable aspect of life, or as the *ordinary run of things* (Marx, 1990; de Angelis, 2007).

The third and final strand of my thesis is that the social power of money, reinforced by the debtfare state's rhetorical and regulative framings, assists in distorting the exploitative, unequal and disciplinary nature of the loan. Here the loan is seen as a voluntary exchange of equivalents between two consenting parties, where class-based power and exploitation are less visible and less politicised than in a wage-labour/employer relation. The debt relation, which lies at the heart of the poverty industry, is also disciplinary in nature, which facilitates the social reproduction of the surplus population as a category of labour power.

In their capacity as debtors, surplus labourers are compelled to continually search for work to meet the repayment schedule of their loans (Harvey, 1989). It is because of the social power of money in capitalism that the social reproduction of labour power in the poverty industry becomes relatively less politicised and explicitly exploitative *vis-à-vis* primary forms of exploitation through wage-labour. Creditor-debtor relations, on the other hand, are captured by what Marx referred to as secondary forms of exploitation by which he means the modification of workers' income through interest rates, late fees and so forth. Aside from extracting interest- and fee-based revenue, secondary forms of exploitation serve not only to distort class-based power, but also to impose market discipline over surplus workers. This does not imply that struggles and tensions are absent in secondary forms of exploitation; but rather that these monetised relations of debt assume different expressions and, due to debtfarist state strategies, often articulate themselves in the realm of exchange in the form of consumer protection and/or the democratisation of credit. As I maintain below and throughout the book, power relations and paradoxes entailed in secondary forms of exploitation can neither be made legible nor understood solely in the realm of exchange.

Given the significance of money as the foundational plank in my analysis, its mystical powers must be problematised. Despite being so obviously central to any understanding of debt, money remains largely ignored in the existing literature. In what follows, I query the reasons for this neglect and explain why filling this gap is essential to a more complete understanding of the emergence, expansion and reproduction of the poverty industry.

Money

> Money is simultaneously everything and nothing, everywhere but nowhere
> in particular, a means that poses as an end, the profoundest and most
> complete of all centralizing forces in a society where it facilitates the greatest
> dispersion, a representation that appears quite divorced from whatever it is
> supposed to represent. It is a *real* or *concrete abstraction* that exists external to
> us and exercises real power over us.
>
> – David Harvey, *The Urban Experience*, 1989: 167

Money organises every aspect of our lives. Everyone needs money to meet basic
reproductive needs such as food, clothing and shelter. Yet money is also secretive
and individualising. As Brett Williams (2004: 55) observes:

> I know a lot more about my friends' sex lives than I do about their finances
> . . . The one thing they will never permit to be known about them, to any
> friend, the only thing that cannot be discussed, is how much money they
> have in the bank . . . Therefore, we have no joint knowledge of how we
> are dealing with the money issues in our lives; each of us faces the problem
> alone.

The individualising, isolating and enigmatic aspects of money, captured by
Williams' observation, can make people feel personally responsible when they do
not have enough money to meet rent or mortgage payments, student loan payments,
childcare expenses, health care costs and/or groceries bills – to the point where
anxiety, fear and helplessness begin to invade and poison their daily lives. The lack
of money, which often results in a state of indebtedness, also serves to intensify socio-
economic inequalities while masking the underlying reasons for them. These features
of money described by Williams are neither neutral nor phenomena that have emerged
from a naturally evolving economy. They are instead historical social constructions
that express particular relations of class-based power in capitalist society.

Why start with money, one might ask?

Money is not only one of the most commonplace features in our everyday lives,
it remains one of the most illusive, especially as concerns the deconstruction and
denaturalisation of debt.[3] So, what is money? At the surface level, the immediate
response to this question may seem straightforward enough. If we rely on the
conventional economic understanding, money is a unit of account, a store of value
and a medium of exchange. These economic meanings of money are pervasive
and taken as common-sense facts. The problem is that few scholars writing in the
areas of consumer credit and financialisation have attempted to move beyond
this conventional definition. In practice, while political economists have defined
the financial system as constituting both the monetary and credit systems, the latter
has generally become the sole focus, resulting in money being taken as a given.

There has been a failure to interrogate the social power of money with the aim of denaturalising its predominant economic meaning and presence in neoliberalism. As discussed above, neoliberalism generally refers to the post-1980 temporal frame that has been marked by credit-led accumulation and neoliberal state interventions supporting a 'pro-corporate, freer-trading, "market order"' (Peck, 2010: 9). Moreover, few academic treatments have sought to understand the intrinsic yet tension-ridden social nature of money. Scholars have instead been content to explore the social and cultural dimensions of money by uncritically grafting their analyses onto existing economic meanings (Zelizer, 1997; cf. Ingham, 2001, 2004). From this perspective, credit and money are seen as things or objects upon which either actors bestow social and cultural meanings, such as respect for contracts, subjectivities, trust and risk/uncertainty or become embedded in social and cultural networks (Granovetter, 1985; Leyshon and Thrift, 1997; Calder, 1999; Francois, 2006; Wennerlind, 2011). Lost is why and how the capitalist mode of production and exchange facilitate the illusion of the power of things over people, particularly the working poor.

These oversights represent a major obstacle to explaining the origins of power, transformation and social reproduction of the monetised relations of debt in the poverty industry. As a corrective, I employ a historical materialist framework to locate the origins of social power of money in the wider context of the dynamics of capital accumulation. A more detailed survey of the existing literature reveals what makes this approach distinct.

The contemporary sources from which we can begin to search for theorisations of money are few and far between. A theory of money is conspicuous in its absence in the otherwise rich and informative debates about consumer society (Calder, 1999; Burton, 2008), financial inclusion and poverty capital such as microfinance (Rankin, 2001; Roy, 2010) and financialisation (Martin, 2002; Peterson, 2003; Langley, 2008; Montgomerie, 2009, 2010; Krippner, 2011). To be fair, the work of these scholars is not driven by the same set of questions as the present study and many of their insights into the subjective understandings and representations of consumer credit have, as I discuss below, helped to make sense of the *social* context in which money operates. However, the question remains as to why scholars avoid a theoretical interrogation of money.

Some of the reasons offered for this avoidance relate to the very traits that make it so important to place money at the heart of our investigation from the start. David Harvey opens his discussion of money in *The Urban Experience* by quoting the French writer, Émile Zola, noting that money 'is very difficult to write a novel about' because 'it is cold, glacial, devoid of interest'. Harvey (1989) goes on to suggest that Marx's lengthy studies on the topic of money 'make for dull reading'.

In her comprehensive survey of consumer culture, Dawn Burton (2008: 29, my emphasis) points out that 'the *cultural* independence and power of money remains largely unquestioned' in the literature, particularly with regard to consumer credit and its role in consumption. As Burton notes, the lack of academic attention paid to the role of credit is accompanied by a dearth of in-depth accounts of the cultural aspects of credit, namely the role of trust and risk in credit relationships (Burton,

2008; Francois, 2006). It is useful to reflect briefly on the reasons given by Burton for this absence.

First, Burton notes that the discussion of credit and by extension finance and financial services, has long been the province of economists. Unfamiliar literature that uses different theoretical approaches and research techniques can be off-putting, especially to scholars who are keen to pursue broader social trends. Burton's second reason for the lack of attention to credit mirrors Harvey's (1989) reflection on the understudied social power of money: it is dull. For Burton (2008: 31), we need to recognise 'the lack of glamour, fun and frivolity of credit compared to other areas of consumption . . . Consumers often find dealing with their finances a rather dull business and researchers may feel the same, too'.

A third factor explaining why so little attention is given to credit concerns its invisibility. Lendol Calder (1999) argues, for instance, that consumer credit has few material artefacts that can be read as text and thus be studied and researched over time. As illustrated by Williams' (2004) observation above, money is considered a private affair and is often not spoken about in public – or private, for that matter. Secrecy as a barrier to the study of credit is clearly a pertinent consideration (Calder, 1999:13–14; Simmel, 2004; Burton, 2008). Issues of confidentiality governing the acquisition and use of credit by consumers are also important obstacles in its study (Calder, 1999: 13).

These are all important and valid points. Theories of money and applied finance *can* seem dull, foreign and private. By leaving these issues unexplored, however, the literature fails to challenge the assumption that money and credit is a natural state of affairs. A historical materialist approach, by contrast, allows us to see how these factors are socially constructed in the wider context of the dynamics of and relations of power inherent to, capital accumulation. We need to recognise that the neglect of the theoretical contemplation of money in the neoliberal era is a reflection of the mysterious character and power of money itself. As such, the deconstruction of money and its connection to credit has not been adequately answered in the literature on financialisation, which has been over-populated by Foucauldian and other post-structuralist analyses that miss the mark in terms of questioning power and its origins. Instead of theorising the social power of money, many theorists of consumer debt have embraced the economic meaning of money and then proceed to complement this treatment by focusing on how ordinary people, social networks and institutions fuse social and cultural meanings onto economistic understandings of money and credit. In doing so, they naturalise the social power inherent to money and its ability to neutralise, individualise, level and normalise highly exploitative and unequal relations of power between people in capitalism.

I take seriously Viviana Zelizer's (1997: 6) suggestion that 'the task of social theory is to explain the uncontested revolutionary power of money'. However, I take Zelizer's impetus in a different direction in order to provide a more complete explanation of power, social transformation, the social reproduction of capitalism and the role of the poverty industry therein.

In the first three chapters of *Debtfare*, I set up a theoretical framework that allows the reader to grasp what the revolutionary power of money means with regard to the poverty industry. Specifically, I address where the power comes from, who or what possesses it, over whom it is wielded and why. I argue that it is precisely the mediation, neutralisation and legitimisation of this power that fuels neoliberal-led capitalism and more specifically, credit-led accumulation. At its core, this power conceals and thus renders as natural the exploitative and unequal social relations inherent to debt. The social power of money, which is rooted in the capitalist mode of production and exchange, is a class-based phenomenon that possesses both temporal and spatial dimensions (Harvey, 1999). This social power is, moreover, deeply intertwined with, and dependent on, capitalist states. In the neoliberal era, where privately created money (credit) dominates, debtfare is the prevailing trope.

Contentions of Marx on money

There is far from a consensus on the theoretical utility of Marx's theory of money in neoliberal capitalism. For economic geographers Andrew Leyshon and Nigel Thrift, who have studied money and credit intensively (from both a Marxist and post-structuralist perspective), there are several limits to a Marxian analysis that weaken its explanatory power, particularly with respect to the rapid growth of credit in the form of what Leyshon and Thrift (1997) refer to as virtual money. Due to changes in the landscape of money, these authors suggest that the Marxian approach needs to be, at the very least, augmented.

All theories require constant reassessing, updating and fine-tuning, if they are to adequately capture the changing nature of social reality that they are designed explain. All too often, however, Marxists have failed to question and thus push forward their frameworks. On the other hand, many scholars have been too quick to dismiss Marx and Marxian accounts on money based on weak charges of economic reductionism and productivism (Langley 2008). In our efforts to move Marxian theorisations of money and credit forward, it is useful to engage with Leyshon and Thrift's criticisms, as this will ultimately serve to clarify and deepen the historical materialist framework that informs this study.

Andrew Leyshon and Nigel Thrift identify four areas in need of revision in what they refer to as the Marxian 'model' of money. It should be noted that the primary target of this critique is the Marxist scholar, David Harvey. The first aspect of Marxian theory that requires modification is the tendency to derive the importance of money in relation to capitalist production. For Leyshon and Thrift, this position is anachronistic, as productive capital has become delinked from the financial system. The way in which this alleged rupture is to be interpreted and explained is crucial to an analysis of money. In short, a key weakness of Marx's theorisation of money is that it is outdated. As Leyshon and Thrift (1997: 55) note, 'all of these drawbacks come from the historically specific nature of Marx's account of money'.

The second change required, according to Leyshon and Thrift (1997: 56), is the role of the state. Marxian theory, they suggest, does not view the state as a major actor in the financial system. Yet, the state is a constant and constitutive feature of the contemporary financial system. Similarly, the third area in need of attention in Marxian analyses of money relates to what Leyshon and Thrift (1997: 56) see as the inability of Marxist theory to make sense of the proliferation of credit and its numerous forms: 'As national and then international markets for credit have grown and coalesced, as the value of speculation has increased and as large-scale movements of money have taken place, so the Marxian model is increasingly revealed as inadequate.'

The fourth weakness is the lack of attention given to the manner in which the financial system sustains itself, despite continual crises and increasing risks and complexity. Leyshon and Thrift (1997: 56) suggest that the reproduction of the financial system is partly due to 'numerous, cross-cutting regulatory systems based upon networks of trust as well as coercion and censure'. For these authors, the history of regulation is vital to explaining the maintenance of the financial system.

Leyshon and Thrift are correct to suggest that the Marxian theorisation of money needs updating, particularly with regard to our study of the poverty industry. However, we need not leave Marx to attend to these limits, given that the core of historical materialism continues to offer the most powerful explanatory framework available to rigorously challenge and deconstruct the dominant economistic account of money. Instead, we can work within the Marxian framework to update and strengthen as well as to contest and clarify the weaknesses identified by Leyshon and Thrift while advancing the three major planks that comprise the historical materialist approach used in this book: the social power of money, the reproduction of the surplus population and debtfare states.

While making important contributions in their own right, Leyshon and Thrift (and many other authors discussed above) are content with relegating the economistic understanding of money and by extension credit, to the economists while focusing on the social and cultural factors of the financial system. Separating the discussion of money from the dynamics of capital accumulation makes it impossible to understand these relations of power in their historical context and thus explain social change. Moreover, vacating the economic forms to study the cultural and social features of credit merely grants economists exclusive and unfettered control over this realm. Given that the charge of economic determinism with regard to Marx's work by Leyshon and Thrift underpins many of the studies on consumer credit, it is helpful to ponder briefly on the meaning of this critique.

With their charge of economic determinism (1997: xv), Leyshon and Thrift incorrectly suggest that the Marxian model makes a clear distinction between the economic sphere (in which money is often confined) and other spheres of life such as the social and cultural onto which the economic sphere is too often unproblematically mapped. Drawing on Timothy Mitchell (2008: 1117), this critique of economic determinism is somewhat curious, given that 'the economy' as an object of power and knowledge is a relatively recent product of socio-technical practice that emerged in the mid-twentieth century. Leaving this anachronism aside, the solution to the alleged claims of Marx's economic determinism is to retain an economic meaning of money and embed it into social and cultural networks of power and trust (cf. Granovetter, 1985).

In Chapter 1, I show that this critique is misguided, since it falsely conflates materialism with economism. In so doing, this critique fails to recognise that Marx's historical materialist method is driven by a rigorous attempt at deconstructing the view that commodities, including money, are social relations that assume specific forms, roles and powers in capitalist society. Marx begins *Capital*, for instance, by trying to understand historically how and why money appears as a thing, yet possesses very real social power over human beings in capitalist society (Marx, 1990, chs 1–3). In so doing, Marx is concerned with explaining how the capitalist market system and money disguise real social relations through the exchange of things (Harvey, 2010a). Understanding money as a social relation within the wider processes of the capitalist mode of exchange and production (as opposed to 'the economy') is thus very different from Leyshon and Thrift's Marxian rendition that 'money is a form of social interaction' (1997: 55–6). Put more succinctly, only a Marxian approach to money will allow us to effectively 'Occupy Economics'.

To set the book on a course guided by historical materialism, my analysis begins and builds on a Marxian treatment of money to understand the relations of power and paradoxes inherent to the poverty industry. In contemporary capitalist societies, we witness the expanding legal rights of creditors supported by the increasingly disciplinary and coercive powers of states. These features assist capitalists in recouping the principal amount and interest of their loan – at any cost, including facilitating the manipulation of the time in which they are able to extract interest from the original outlay through such strategies as asset-backed securitisation. This raises key questions about how we should analyse and explain the production and reproduction of these essential trends in contemporary capitalist societies, particularly as it affects the surplus population. In, what follows, I demonstrate that a Marxian approach still offers the richest answer to these questions as it allows us to fully grasp the inner workings of capitalism. And, in particular, a key feature of contemporary forms of credit-led accumulation: 'The perpetual tendency to try to realise value without producing it' (Harvey, 1974: 254; Duménil and Lévy, 2011; Lapavitsas, 2013). I return to this conundrum in Chapter 2.

Structure of the book

This book is organised into three main parts. Part I lays out the theoretical framework by discussing the significance of money (Chapter 1), credit (Chapter 2) and debtfare states (Chapter 3). Parts II and III draw on several cases of the poverty industry in the United States and Mexico, respectively.

The first three chapters that comprise Part I of *Debtfare* offer a theoretical framework through which we can deconstruct and denaturalise the monetised relations that constitute the poverty industry. The focus of Chapter 1 is the demystification of money from a Marxian perspective. The main argument of this chapter is that while money assumes its appearance as a neutral object or thing, this is a constructivist illusion. To move beyond this fetishism, it is essential that we contextualise and understand the role of money in the wider dynamics of capital accumulation. The two interlinked objectives of this chapter are to problematise economistic treatments of money and to lay a foundation for the further theorisation of credit in Chapter 2. Chapter 1 covers necessary conceptual building blocks for a more potent understanding of debt and the monetised relations of power therein, whereas Chapter 2 outlines and explains the power and paradoxes of credit.

In Chapter 2, I demonstrate why a Marxian theory of money remains the most powerful explanatory framework for theorisations of consumer credit and debt relations. I develop this argument by, first, discussing how credit is a special form of money and thereby assumes similar social powers. In contrast with money, however, credit plays a different role in capital accumulation. As privately created money, that is money manufactured by capitalists, credit serves to absorb the contradictions in the dynamics of capital accumulation. I then posit that a Marxist framework allows us to grasp the nature and role of credit as part of the wider and tension-ridden processes of capital accumulation. It is within these tensions that I begin to theorise the 'silent compulsions' (Marx, 2005) and structural violence that makes the surplus population dependent on the high cost credit that lies at the heart of the poverty industry.

Chapter 3, which comprises the final chapter in Part I of this book, examines the role of neoliberal states in facilitating the construction, expansion and reproduction of the poverty industry. The analytical construction of my approach to the poverty industry in the United States and Mexico emerges from and is rooted in, the social power of credit within the dynamics of capital accumulation. Put another way, my understanding of the capitalist state is a materialist one. I use this approach to discuss the regulatory and rhetorical meanings of neoliberalisation before elaborating four of its relevant features: monetarism, corporate welfarism, workfarism and what I refer to as debtfarism.

Before continuing, a caveat is in order. To my mind, capitalist states play an integral and inseparable role in mediating and facilitating the social power of both money and credit money. For the purpose of clarity, however, I have decided to keep these elements artificially separated in the more abstract discussion that comprises Part I of *Debtfare*. These elements are, however, brought together in the more concrete analyses of debtfarism and the poverty industry in Parts II and III of the book.

Part II of the book opens with a Preface, 'Debtfarism and the Making of the Poverty Industry', which elaborates on the rationale behind the three case studies used to illustrate the poverty industry in the United States – the credit card industry (Chapter 4), the student loan industry (Chapter 5) and the payday loan industry (Chapter 6). The Preface also sets out to explain the significance of the United States to the understanding of the poverty industry writ large. The Preface then briefly historicises the so-called democratisation of credit in the United States and highlights the importance of the consumer protection trope to the expansion and normalisation of the poverty industry.

The Preface to Part III, 'Debtfarism, Development and Dispossession' justifies and elaborates on the significance of the three chapters that comprise the final section and brings the argument in this section in line with the overall aim of the book: namely, to understand the capitalist nature of power and the paradoxes therein, which both constitute and reproduce the poverty industry. The three chapters in this section cover the politics of universalising financial inclusion in the global South (Chapter 7) and case studies on two important features of the poverty industry in Mexico – the microfinance industry (Chapter 8) and housing finance (Chapter 9).

The book concludes by summarising the argument that has sought to reveal and explain the complex and contradictory roles played by debtfarism and the social power of money in the construction of the poverty industry in the United States and in Mexico. It bears repeating that these case studies could not have been conceived without the analytical framing afforded by a historical materialist inquiry into money and capitalist states. It is my hope that readers will find this theoretical approach useful and applicable to other forms of consumer credit as well as other aspects of the changing configuration of class relations in neoliberal capitalism. Indeed, relations of power that have become increasingly defined by the social power of money.

Notes

1 Unless otherwise stated, all sums in this book are in US dollars.
2 Since my analysis explores more than the microfinance industry, I draw on Hudson's term 'poverty industry'; however, my core concerns, analytical framing, and case studies differ from his discussion.
3 As will become clear in the next two chapters, a Marxian understanding of money deconstructs money as a social relation first, before moving to a theorisation of credit (Mandel, 1968; de Brunhoff, 1976; Marx, 1990, 2005; Clarke, 1994; Bonefeld and Holloway, 1995; Harvey, 1999; Itoh and Lapavitsas, 1999; Bryan and Rafferty, 2006; Fine, 2010).

PART I

Theorising money, credit and debtfare states

1

DEMYSTIFYING MONEY

The main objective here is to demystify money from a Marxian perspective, or, what is the same thing, a historical materialist approach. The central argument of this chapter is that money can be viewed as a social relation of power only if it is contextualised within the wider dynamics of capital accumulation. To this end, I have organised the chapter into four main sections. Section One sets out to distinguish between economism (or economic determinism) – with which Marxian theory is conventionally but incorrectly charged – and a historical materialist method of deconstruction. This discussion provides the platform for Section Two, which is aimed at demystifying money as an economic category or thing by drawing on the tools of historical materialism. Section Three elaborates on how inequality and exploitation become distorted in the illusions of equality, freedom and democracy that define capitalist society, or what Marx (2005) refers to as the community of money. Section Four summarises the argument and provides concluding remarks.

Economism versus historical materialism

We begin our analysis of money with the first charge made by Leyshon and Thrift (1997) regarding the Marxian tendency toward economism. Readers will recall from the introductory chapter that economism refers to the reduction of all social and cultural dimensions of life to the economy. Many authors have levied a similar charge against Marx and Marxian approaches in order to hurriedly discredit the vastly complex and rich theory of historical materialism. For many non-Marxian scholars, the corrective to this alleged weakness in Marx has been to accept the standard economic understanding of money and credit, while animating it with social relations and moving away from charges of economism by emphasising the primacy of the social and cultural dimensions of finance.

I maintain, however, that Leyshon and Thrift's first critique is based on a fundamental misreading of Marx. This charge, upon which the rest of the four criticisms are based, rests on a problematic reading of *Capital* (and David Harvey's work, in turn) as an economic text rather than as a materialist critique of classical political economy (Clarke, 1991; Holloway and Picciotto, 1991). As such, Leyshon and Thrift conflate economism with materialism. The difference between the two starting analytical points is not only significant for the study of money and its role in the social relations of debt, but also impedes our ability to break with the world of appearances at the beginning of our analysis (Clarke, 1978).

For Marx, it is important to deconstruct the appearances or illusions of capitalist society, or what he refers to as 'fetishism'. We discuss this term in more detail below. Suffice it to say here that fetishised appearances of money and credit as natural objects, while quite real to all of us, are important for Marx because they hide the relations of domination and exploitation that characterise capitalism. As we will see, Marx deconstructs economic categories such as the commodity and money, for instance, to reveal their inner social content. It is, therefore, imprecise to charge Marx with economism.

For Marx, materialism describes the way societies fulfil their wants and needs.[1] Or, as Harvey (1989: 8) plainly states: 'We need to eat in order to live, think, argue, raise children, fight, enjoy ourselves,' and so on. The manner in which all societies throughout history have accomplished this is based on its mode of production. The way in which the capitalist mode of production is organised masks social relations of power. This veil or disguise is what Marx refers to as fetishism. It is important to stress that while fetishism has different meanings in other academic traditions, it takes on a specific sense in Marx's work (Harvey, 1999, 2010a and b; Marx, 2005).

Fetishism is an illusion that is constructed, yet also real. As Marx suggests in his historical materialist method, because fetishism is a social construction, it can also be dismantled. David Harvey's classic example of fetishism in capitalism is enduring and reveals, once again, why his method of historical materialism is a corrective to economism rather than an extension of it. Harvey begins by asking readers to trace back where their dinner came from in order to become aware of the many people involved in even the simplest of meals. Despite the presence of these people, we consume our meals without knowing anything about them. We know nothing of the conditions of their lives and labour, their joys, discontents and aspirations – all of which remain concealed from us and subordinated to the prices we pay for commodities. For Harvey (1989: 8), 'this masking arises because our social relations with those who contribute to our daily sustenance are hidden behind the exchange of things in the market place'. Marx's objective in *Capital* and his materialist method is to demystify the fetishism of commodities in the market and to build a theory of how commodities are produced, traded and consumed in order to comprehend the technical conditions and social relations that put food on the table. Money, of course, is central to commodity fetishism and therefore the critique of money is intrinsic to the critique of the fetishised relationships that underscore capitalism (Marx, 1990, 2005).

Marx's method is not intrinsically economistic in nature: it does not seek to understand the capitalist mode of production as an economic realm divorced from social considerations. Marxian theory is concerned with understanding how a particular type of social relation gives rise to the power of things over people. As such, it seeks to demystify capitalist society as a naturally occurring and harmonious set of market relations and reveal it as a mode of production marked by silent compulsions and unequal and exploitative relations. Marx devised his historical materialist method to expose and deconstruct economistic representations of capitalist markets as the embodiment of natural harmony in which buyers and sellers voluntarily meet to exchange goods and services. In doing so, Marx sought to reveal that perfectly functioning markets and the invisible hand of rational, competitive and self-interested individuals would not produce an outcome beneficial to all, but would instead make the capital class incredibly wealthy while relatively impoverishing the workers and everyone else (Harvey, 1999; 2010a; Marx, 1990, 2005).

If we fail to employ a historical materialist approach to our investigation of debt, we are left with an economist's view of money and credit in capitalist society – upon which we can construct only complementary, fetishised understandings. What is lost, both analytically and politically, is the ability to understand how and why the social power of money continues (with assistance from states) to promote the illusion of the equality of exchange. This is critical given the extent to which the neoliberal era is marked by privately created money generated by capitalists and extended at very high rates of interest to the surplus population.

Demystifying money

Following Marx, this section will reveal that it is impossible to demystify money as an economic category and thus grasp its social power, by remaining exclusively in the sphere of exchange, i.e., the realm in which consumer credit is largely studied in the financialisation and consumer credit literature. For Marx, the primary reason for this is that one cannot break through the money fetish in the realm of exchange because this sphere operates on the fetishised principle of equivalence. This latter principle, upon which the price system rests, implies that 'the circulation of commodities requires the exchange of equivalents' (Marx, 1990: 160, quoted in Harvey, 1999). For Marx (1990: 168–9), the power of the money fetish in the realm of exchange is its ability to conceal 'the social character of private labour and the social relations between individual workers, by making those relations appear as relations between material objects, instead of revealing them plainly'. Seen from this angle, the power of money dissolves previous social ties and dependencies evident in pre-capitalist communities by becoming the real community (Marx, 2005: 224–5). The community of money, moreover, is characterised 'by individualism and certain conceptions of liberty, freedom and equality backed by laws of private property, rights to appropriation and freedom of contract' (Marx, 2005; Harvey, 1989: 168). It is therefore difficult to grasp the social power of money by beginning with the sphere of exchange.

Marx (1990) begins his demystification of money by identifying a basic assumption that was taken for granted by political economists of his time: Why does one commodity (money) operate as an impartial *numéraire*, so that the relative values of all other commodities can be unequivocally expressed as a price? By interrogating these observations, Marx is interested in revealing how and why capitalist social relations are constructed (and reconstructed). As Harvey suggests, 'money is not established arbitrarily or out of mere convention. The money commodity is produced in the course of history by a specific social process – participation in acts of exchange' (Harvey, 1999: 10).

The revolutionary power of money lies in the fact that, as a commodity, it becomes the direct incarnation of all human labour. In capitalism, Marx notes that people

> relate to each other in their social process of production in a purely atomistic way. Their own relations of production therefore assume a material shape that is independent of their control and their conscious individual action. This situation is evident by the fact that the products of human labour universally take on the form of commodities. The riddle of the money fetish is therefore the riddle of the commodity fetish.
>
> (Marx, 1990: 187; see also Mandel, 1968; de Brunhoff, 1976)

For Marx, the key to solving this puzzle is not to grasp that 'money is a commodity', but rather to discover 'how, why and by what means a commodity becomes money' (Marx, 1990: 183). To tackle this conundrum, Marx urges us to go beyond the sphere of exchange – characterised by illusions of individuality, equality and freedom – in order to understand its connection to the sphere of production, where class relations of inequality become apparent (Marx, 1990). In contrast with other treatments to money in capitalism (Zelizer, 1997; Simmel, 2004; Ingham, 2004), Marx begins his analysis by exploring the circulation of capital (as opposed to money) and the class relations implied therein, which is implied in Marx's inquiry into how a commodity becomes money (Harvey, 1989). This analytical move reveals, as Harvey suggests (1989: 169), 'a deep tension between the individual and equality that the possession of money implies and the class relations experienced in the making of that money'. Marx sought to break through the fetishism of money by developing a labour theory of value. It is to an outline of this theory that we now turn our attention.

Labour theory of value

To understand how a commodity becomes money, Marx identifies three types of value inherent in all commodities: use-value, exchange-value and value (Marx, 1990). Use-value describes the usefulness of a commodity. Without someone needing or wanting a particular commodity (social validity), it cannot enter into the exchange process. The exchange-value, as noted above, is allegedly based on the principal of equivalents. The exchange-value of a commodity is not inherent to it, e.g., a pacific salmon does not swim around with a price on its tail any more than a coffee bean emerges with a price on its husk. As such, the exchange-value (represented by prices) of our salmon or coffee bean implies that a commodity is exchangeable for something else and that something else is revealed only when the commodity is exchanged. An exchange-value must therefore be commensurable to something and reducible to a third thing. For Marx, this commensurability is not found in use-value, but instead in the fact that all commodities are products of human labour. Up to this point, Marx's argument parallels classical political economist, David Ricardo (Itoh and Lapavitsas, 1999).

According to Ricardo, the exchange-value of a commodity (price) is determined by the actual labour time involved in producing the commodity. Marx departs from Ricardo's theory of value on the basis that the type of human labour that is embodied in commodities cannot represent the actual time taken to produce the commodity, as the longer it takes to produce a commodity, the more valuable it would be. For instance, why would you pay more for salmon that took a fisherman longer to catch, when you could get the same fish at half the price from a more efficient and/or skilled fisherman? Indeed, if time were the true measurement of exchange-value, commodities produced by unskilful or lazy workers would therefore be more valuable than other commodities.

To overcome this problem – and thereby distinguish his approach from those of the classical liberal political economists of his time – Marx added to the concept of concrete labour a second type of human labour present in all commodities: abstract labour. Unlike the heterogeneous nature of concrete labour (e.g., tailoring, spinning and weaving), abstract labour captures the homogenous aspects of human labour that forms the value of commodities (Marx, 1990: 137). Put another way, the commonality of all different forms of concrete labour is human labour in general. To anticipate the narrative somewhat, it is important to note that Marx uses the distinction between concrete and abstract labour to understand grasp how the appearance of commodities as things posses value. Marx (1990: 142), for instance, stresses that abstract human labour creates value but is not itself value. Abstract labour becomes value in its coagulated state, in objective form (money). 'The value of the linen as a congealed mass of human labour can be expressed only as an "objectivity" [. . .], a thing which is materially different from the linen itself and yet common to the linen and all other commodities'.

It follows from the above discussion that Marx's understanding of value and its measurement, is defined by abstract human labour, which he refers to as socially necessary labour time. Socially necessary labour time refers to 'the labour-time required to produce any use-value under the conditions of production normal for a given society and with the average degree of skill and intensity of labour prevalent in that society' (Marx, 1990: 129). Socially necessary labour time is determined by a wide range of circumstances such as the workers' average degree of skill, science and its technological application and so forth (Marx, 1990). Socially necessary labour time is, therefore, highly dynamic as well as spatially and temporally specific; definitions of what is 'normal' and 'average' are also, socially constructed by relations of power in capitalist mode of production (Harvey, 1999).

Marx's construction of value is vital to understanding what is *necessarily* concealed by money in its role in exchange-values under capitalism and thereby debunk its natural state, which is, of course, implied when theorists 'just assume' money. Although value is immaterial (abstract), it is *objective* (or, concrete). As Harvey explains, value is a social relation, which you cannot actually see, touch, or feel directly. Yet, this value has an objective presence in that it is represented by money as a measure of value. Money is, therefore, not simply a commodity, but also a symbol or tangible, quantitative expression of value (socially necessary labour time) embodied in price. This monetary representation in the form of prices 'makes value (socially necessary labour time) the regulator of exchange relations. On this view, prices, which are the quantitative expression of exchange-value, are 'the money-name of the labour objectified in a commodity' (Marx, 1990: 195). 'Since money does not reveal what has been transformed into it, everything, commodity or not, is convertible into money. Everything becomes saleable and purchasable' – this ability to hang a price tag on everything and everyone on the planet is a defining feature of the commodification process (Marx, 1990: 229).

Value as socially necessary labour time and its quantitative expression in monetary terms (i.e., prices), is historically specific to the capitalist mode of production. Extracting value from workers is not a natural state of affairs, however. As we will see in the rest of the book, value as socially necessary labour time must instead be reproduced through coercive and ideological means on a continual basis in order to ensure the expansion of value, or, what is the same thing, capital accumulation. What exactly does money conceal? This question is important, if we are to explain and understand the power relations involved in debt as well as their reproduction through state and class relations. Marx's labour theory of value provides us with the answers.

The expansion of value, or capital accumulation (for which money is a material expression), involves complex social processes that are based on inequality, as well as exploitation. Indeed, the augmentation of exchange values is the primary goal of capitalists. The increase of value involves a transformation of money into commodities and back into money plus profit. As Marx (1990: 153–5) notes: 'It is under the form of money that value begins and ends and begins again, every act of its own spontaneous generation . . . Value therefore now becomes value in process, money in process and, as such, capital.' Capital can be formed by converting money and use-values and putting them into circulation in order to make money, to produce surplus value.

The capitalist form of circulation rests upon (and produces) an inequality because capitalists possess more money (values) at the end of the process than they did at the beginning. A problem arises here, however. Values are established by an exchange process, which, as we saw above, rests on the principle of equivalence. How then can capitalists realise an inequality (i.e., profit, or, using Marxian symbols, M^1) through an exchange process, which presupposes equivalence? This query cannot be addressed in the realm of exchange. It is only through the violation of the principle of equivalence (by cheating, robbery, fraud, forced exchanges, robbery and the like) that capitalists can make a profit. The same holds true for interest-generating exchanges. By charging welfare recipients 300 percent interest for a $200 payday loan, payday lenders extract interest to the detriment of the welfare recipient, a process I detail more fully in Chapter 6. Seen from this angle, the rule of equivalence in exchange is in no way offended even though surplus value is produced. In Marxist theory, exploitation refers to the excess of value that labourers embed in commodities relative to the value the labourers require for their own social reproduction (Clarke, 1994; Harvey, 1999). Drawing on Marx, this type of exploitation, which occurs in the realm of production, is referred to in this book as primary exploitation.

The labour theory of value reveals several important points for understanding the social power in money. First and foremost, it unveils the meaning and *necessity* of the money fetish, especially with regard to the illusion of the principal of equivalents. As Marx argues, nature does not produce money, any more than it produces a rate of exchange or a banker (Marx, 2005: 239). As we saw with the creation of wage-labour, money does not emerge from a naturally evolving market: 'The money commodity is produced in the course of history by a specific social process – participation in acts of exchange' (Harvey, 1999: 10). Monetary-based exchange in capitalist society has led to a situation in which producers relate to each other by way of the products they exchange rather than directly as social beings.

Social relationships are therefore expressed as relationships between things (fetishism), while the things themselves exchange according to their value, which is measured in terms of abstract labour (Harvey, 1999: 17). As such, the realm of exchange does not reveal the inherent nature of capitalism. As Harvey (1999: 17, my emphasis) citing Marx (1990), notes:

> The act of exchange tells us nothing about the conditions of labour of the producers, for example and keeps us in a state of ignorance concerning our social relations as these are mediated by the market system. We respond solely to the prices of quantities of use values. But this also suggests that, when we exchange things, 'we imply the existence of value . . . without being aware of it'. *The existence of money – the form of value – conceals the social meaning of value itself.* 'Value does not stalk about with a label describing what it is.'

Too many analyses of financialisation tend to begin and end their discussions by locating money in the realm of exchange, which hides the class character of the social relations in the capitalist mode of production. As I noted in the Introductory Chapter, this assumption leads to the charge from Leyshon and Thrift (1997) that the significance of money cannot be understood via production. Yet, it is only by situating money in the capitalist mode of production that we are able to defetishise money as a social relation. More specifically, it is only by taking this step that we are able to see how and why money which serves as a commodity and as a symbol of value (price) and thereby learn the origins of its power and change (Clarke, 1994; Marx, 2005).

Grasping money as an expression of value necessitates that we understand its role in the realm of production, where, for instance, there are 'entirely different processes that go on in which this apparent individuality, equality and liberty disappear' because 'exchange-value already in itself implies a silent compulsion over the individual' (Harvey, 1999: 28). This is not easily visible in the realm of exchange, but this does not mean that exploitation and inequality are not present in this sphere. We explore these secondary forms of exploitation in the next chapter where I analyse the social power of credit money.

Marx's community of money

Marx's strategy of defetishising money is aimed at critiquing the assumption of classical political economists that values are a self-evident, natural and universal truth. As Marx notes, classical political economists only begin to reflect on money 'after the events [production of value] have taken place and therefore with the results of the process of development ready at hand'. On this view, the value of money is determined by the price of commodities. This perspective cannot grasp what money distorts in capitalist society. 'It is however precisely this finished form of the world of commodities – the money form – which conceals the social character of private labour and the social relations between individual workers, by making those relations appear as relations between material objects, instead of revealing them plainly' (Marx, 1990: 168–9).

The ability of money to conceal inequality and exploitation through its role as the universal equivalent bestows money with revolutionary powers to conceal the power relations involved in the production and exchange of commodities. 'Just as in money every quantitative difference between commodities is extinguished, so too for its part, as a radical leveller, it extinguishes all distinctions' (Marx, 1990: 229–30). As the ultimate objectifier – 'a god among commodities' – money is not only able to largely obliterate subjective connections between objects and individuals, but also reduce personal relations to the 'cash nexus' (Zelizer, 1997: 7). As Simmel (1978: 325 quoted in Harvey, 1989: 166) points out, money 'becomes the frightful leveller – it hollows out the core of things, their specific values and their uniqueness and incomparability in a way which is beyond repair. They all float with the same specific gravity in the constantly moving stream of money'.

It bears repeating here that Marx's understanding of money cannot be understood in isolation from the capitalist mode of production *and* exchange. This is an important point to keep in mind in our study of the poverty industry because money assumes a particular quality in capitalist societies as opposed to pre-capitalist societies thereby entailing historically distinct articulations of power and roles with regard to debt (cf. Mauss, 1967; Graeber, 2011). In capitalism, money is 'a material representative of general wealth, as individualised exchange value, money must be the direct object, aim and product of general labour, the labour of all individuals. Labour must directly produce exchange-value, i.e., money. When labour is wage labour and its direct aim is money, then general wealth is posited as its aim and object. Where money is not itself the community, it must dissolve the community' (Marx, 2005: 224). In the expansion of capital accumulation, money appears more as a 'power external to and independent of the producers' and moreover 'the power which each individual exercises over the activity of others or over social wealth exists in him as the owner of exchange values, of money' (Harvey, 1989: 167). Seen from this view, 'money becomes the mediator and regulator of all relations between individuals; it becomes the abstract and universal measure of social wealth and the concrete means of expression of social power'. Money, Marx re-emphasises, dissolves the community and in doing so 'becomes the *real community*' (2005: 225). This is an important point to keep in mind, as the power of money is further accentuated in the contemporary period of credit-led accumulation (Chapter 2).

Due to its role as the universal equivalent in the production process, the community of money destroys bonds of personal dependency and replaces it with 'objective dependency relations' between individuals who relate to each other through market prices and money and commodity transactions (Marx, 1990: 229). As Harvey (1989: 175) puts it, 'money in our pockets represents our objective bond to the community of money as well as our social power with respect to it'. Individuals are now governed by concrete abstractions (e.g., prices, interest rates, credit ratings, etc.) whereas previously they depended on one another. The increased dependency on concrete abstractions also imply that class-based power is less visible and direct than, for example, in primary forms of exploitation in which workers and capitalist confront one another. In Chapter 2, I, following Marx, designate these forms of exploitation as secondary forms of exploitation by which I mean that workers' income have been modified through consumer credit.

The community of money in capitalism possesses certain meanings, which have been succinctly captured by Harvey (1989: 168):

> The community of money is strongly marked by individualism and certain conceptions of liberty, freedom and equality backed by laws of private property, rights to appropriation and freedom of contract. Such personal freedoms and liberties exist, of course, in the midst of an 'objective bondage' [Simmel, 1978: 300] defined through mutual dependency within the social division of labour and a money economy.

Freedom (i.e., independence from the will of others) is significant in understanding the social reproduction of capitalism. As Harvey notes, 'The owners of money are free (with constraints) to choose how, when, where and with whom to use that money to satisfy their needs, wants and fancies; yet they cannot escape the fact that this freedom is embodied in the objective relations of money (1989: 168).

Marx's attempt to demystify money as the universal equivalent reveals that the liberal concept of freedom of the market is not freedom at all; but instead, a constructed fetishism or an illusion. Harvey (2010a: 42) summarises the fetishised notion of freedom in this regard well:

> Under capitalism, individuals surrender to the discipline of abstract forces (such as the hidden hand of the market made much of by Adam Smith) that effectively govern their relations and choices. I can make something beautiful and take it to market, but if I don't manage to exchange it then it has no

value. Furthermore, I won't have enough money to buy commodities to live. In short, if we are to eat, then we have no choice (silent compulsions) but to sell our labour on the market (Marx and Engels, 1974).

It is worth repeating that the community of money, while real, is a fetishised view of capitalist society. The appearance of the community of money is vital to socially reproduce the inequality and exploitation that underpins capitalism and especially its contemporary forms of credit-led accumulation. Part of this reproduction, is undertaken by scholars, policy-makers and journalists of finance, who not only continually treat money as a 'thing in itself' but also artificially separate the spheres of exchange and production, which can be seen in the dichotomous view of the 'real' economy (production) and financial markets (exchange). These popular assumptions and representations (falsely) exemplify the realm of exchange as embodying equality, freedom and democracy, as is evident in the wider financial inclusion and democratisation of credit agendas promoted by what I refer to as debtfare states. As I discuss in Chapter 3, a key site of the reproduction of the community of money is the capitalist state and, in particular its neoliberal forms of governance such as debtfarism. For now, it is important to emphasise that the social power of money, and by extension the community of money, also possesses important temporal and spatial attributes.

As a commodity, money appears as an external object capable of becoming the private property of an individual, which, in turn, suggests that its social power becomes the private power of private persons (Marx, 1990: 229–30). The social power that attaches to money is without limit. The accumulation of money as unlimited social power is an essential feature of the capitalist mode of production. This is, particularly true in the contemporary, neoliberal period and credit-led accumulation (Harvey, 1999; see also Clarke, 1988; Bonefeld and Holloway, 1995). Once money, as the universal equivalent of all commodities, becomes the representation of all socially necessary labour time, the potential for further accumulation are limitless (Harvey, 1989, 1999). And, with this accumulation of wealth, comes the accumulation of social power. This social (class) power inherent in the very existence of money as a mediator of commodity exchange radically transforms and fixes the meanings of space and time in social life, particularly as these relate to debt and credit relations (Harvey, 1989: 165).

The spatial and temporal dimensions that form part of the social power of money in capitalism are integral to understanding the social reproduction of the community of money. As many authors, including Marx, have demonstrated, space and time are not only important features inherent to the processes of capital accumulation, but also assume particular expressions of power therein (Marx, 1990; Thompson, 1991; Lefebvre, 1991b). As Harvey notes (1989: 165), 'the very existence of money as a mediator of commodity exchange radically transforms and fixes the meanings of space and time in social life'. Harvey's work is particularly useful in understanding the spatial and temporal dimensions within the community of money (Harvey, 1989, 1999). For Harvey, capitalists, who possess money, also possess the power of social control along temporal and spatial lines. 'Money can thus be used to command time (including that of others) and space, while command over time and space can easily be parlayed back into command over money' (Harvey, 1989: 186).

Money functions as a store of value and hence social power. It therefore allows individuals to choose between present and future satisfactions and even allows consumption to be moved forward in time through borrowing (Harvey, 1989: 173). The construction of time as a measurable, calculable and objective magnitude was essential for organising wage labour, but has also had powerful consequences for the credit system. As Harvey (1989: 187) observes: 'Those who can afford to wait always have an advantage over those who cannot.' Similar to time, space is integral to the community of money. Money facilitates transactions 'over otherwise inaccessible distances, an inclusion of the most diverse persons in the same project, an interaction and therefore unification of people' into the community of money (Harvey, 1989: 176).

Concluding remarks

In this chapter, I sought to demystify the common economistic understanding of money as a thing. In doing so, I discussed how Marx's concept of historical materialism moves our understanding of money beyond economism. I demonstrated that a rigorous understanding of the social power inherent to money in capitalism must be, first, understood in the sphere of production, as opposed to the realm of exchange. I revealed that the Marxian approach provides a powerful framework for understanding the social power of money, given its role as the universal equivalent in the capitalist mode of production. In contrast to non-Marxist sociological accounts that seek to represent money as a social relation by virtue of the fact that people interact with *it* and assign meaning to *it*, Marx exposes the unequal and exploitative social power concealed by and reproduced in, the community of money (Marx, 1990, Chs. 1–3; cf. Zelizer, 1997; Ingham, 2004).

Indeed, much of the literature on financialisation and consumer society stops at the realm of exchange without venturing into the wider capitalist relations of production and by extension, accumulation. This is the root of their explanatory weakness in grasping the origins of social transformation, the social power of money and the social reproduction of credit in neoliberal capitalism. A related issue in theorising finance as a separate entity from the social relations of capitalist production is the over-emphasis on finance and its tendencies toward greed-driven speculation, as the primary source of crises and immiseration in contemporary times. While financial speculation and predatory forms of consumer credit have played important and detrimental roles in destabilising societies and dispossessing hundreds of millions of people, there are deeper structural factors involved in neoliberal capitalism that have helped to legitimate, reproduce and stoke the dominance of interest-generating income over productive-based profit since the early 1980s. The silent compulsions identified here will help us to theorise more completely the machinations and paradoxes involved in the social transformation and reproduction of credit-led capitalism from the ground up and therewith lift the veil off of the attributes of democracy, equality and freedom imbued in the social power of money.

Note

1   Unlike other forms of social coordination, the capitalist mode of production is based on the exchange of commodities for profit, which can occur only through the unequal and exploitative relations of class power. As I discuss later in the chapter, these hierarchical and uneven social relations upon which our societies are based and reproduced, albeit in spatially and temporally differentiated ways, is masked by the social power of money and the community of money more generally.

2

THE POWER AND PARADOXES OF CREDIT

In this chapter, I build on the Marxian conceptualisation of the social power of money in such a way so as to facilitate a more complete understanding of credit and its extension to the surplus population. The argument I develop here has two interrelated parts. On the one hand, I suggest that the Marxian theory of money remains the most powerful explanatory framework for theorisations of consumer credit.[1] There are at least two reasons for this. First, a Marxian perspective draws our attention to the fact that credit is a special form of money and thereby assumes social powers similar to money. Unlike money, however, credit plays a different role in capital accumulation. As privately created money – that is, money that is manufactured by capitalists – credit serves to absorb the contradictions in the dynamics of capital accumulation. Second, a Marxist framework allows us to grasp the nature and role of credit as part of the wider and tension-ridden processes of capital accumulation (Harvey, 1999).

On the other hand and building on this particular Marxian perspective of credit, I suggest that the nature of consumer credit to low-income workers and the subsequent expansion of the poverty industry can be explained in the following manner: A key and recurrent issue wracking contemporary forms of capital accumulation has been the over-accumulation problem. The latter refers to the lack of profitable investment sites and thus a surplus of money, combined with the increasing rise of the relative surplus population (Harvey, 1999, 2003). Since the 1990s, a dominant strategy employed by capitalists to absorb the tensions of over-accumulation has been the creation and extension of credit money to low-income workers in exchange for high rates of interest as well as commissions and fees. In this book, I refer to this social phenomenon as credit-led accumulation. Since credit is a form of money, or, more precisely, privately created money, it shares similar illusions to money in terms of freedom, democracy and equality. As we will see later in the book, these fetishisms are embodied in the dominant tropes of the poverty industry such as the democratisation of credit trope, which is dominant in the United States (see Part II) and the financial inclusion rhetoric, which prevails in the global development project (see Part III).

Armed with a historical materialist approach laid out in Chapter 1, we are able to pierce this fetishised surface to grasp that consumer credit is not only infused with class-based power, but also structural violence and silent compulsions. We can also see that solutions based on credit money are inherently paradoxical in nature. Marx warns us that credit acts only to heighten these tensions, which, in turn, spurs the continual drive for increasingly more speculative strategies such as asset-backed securitisation (or, ABS). Briefly, ABS, which played a large role in the 2007–2008 US sub-prime mortgage crisis, transforms illiquid assets (such as sub-prime home mortgages) into tradeable, interest-bearing securities (stocks and bonds) that are then sold to investors (Elul, 2005). In this sense, a Marxian theory of money is essential to understand the expansion of the poverty industry as well as to explain the role of consumer credit in socially reproducing marginality.

The argument in this chapter is developed in five main sections. Section One identifies two key reasons for the theoretical gaps in our knowledge about credit. It then goes on to explain why a Marxian conceptualisation of money and credit in capital accumulation remains a powerful explanatory framework, particularly with regard to some of the key questions driving this book. The subsequent three sections elaborate on key points of a Marxian framework of credit. Section Two examines various tensions of money and thus its limits, in facilitating the expansion of value (capital accumulation). Section Three analyses the nature and role of credit money as a response to the tensions in capital accumulation by elaborating on its similarities and its differences regarding money. In my efforts to connect consumer credit to capital accumulation in order to explain the expansion of the poverty industry, Section Four explores how and why capitalists have employed consumer credit to exploit this ever-growing reserve of labour power in neoliberalism. In doing so, this section serves to bring together money, credit money and the dynamics of capital accumulation to begin to problematise the tensions and exploitative relations in the poverty industry. Section Five provides a summary of the argument advanced here.

Limits to theorising credit

There are at least two analytical weaknesses in both Marxist and non-Marxist scholarship that have hindered rigorous explanations of credit in the contemporary neoliberal era. On the one hand, authors draw on a fetishised understanding of money and, by extension, credit (Martin, 2002; Schwartz, 2009). Seen from the perspective of our discussion in Chapter 1, both money and credit are taken as given and treated as things or objects, devoid of social power and disconnected from the conflict-ridden processes of capital accumulation. On the other hand, there has been a lack of precision regarding the similarities and differences between credit and money. More often than not, both are subsumed under financialisation.

As discussed in the Introduction, it has been convention among many scholars of political economy to define the financial system as constituting both the monetary and credit systems; yet money is pushed aside such that credit – or more often than not, finance – becomes the primary, if not sole, focus. In these analyses, credit appears simply as a resource (thing) to which people, businesses and governments have access – at the discretion of and at a cost established by, others (Germain, 1997: 17).

It follows from this that the emphasis in many discussions tends to focus on the credit system – or, what is often referred to in the literature as the financial system. This system is seen to be comprised of supporting social networks, institutions and regulatory systems (Leyshon and Thrift, 1997, 1999; cf. Mitchell, 2008; Granovetter, 1985) that animate and influence fetishised understandings of credit with subjectivities and performativity (de Goede, 2005; MacKenzie, 2006; Froud et al., 2007; Marron, 2007; Langley, 2008). My point of contention with these analyses is that they end where they should begin. They should not assume credit 'just is', but instead should try to grasp its very existence as a social construct in the context of capitalist society. This is necessary in order to understand that the relations of power underpinning credit cannot be separated from the wider dynamics of capital accumulation, which includes *both* consumption (exchange) *and* production (Harvey, 1999; Fine, 2002).

To be clear, I am not suggesting that post-structuralist perspectives are unhelpful in the study of credit. As we explore the machinations of the social reproduction of credit and its impact on the working poor, analyses of the cultural dimensions of credit (e.g., constructions of trust, uncertainty, subjectivities, etc.) add another layer of explanatory rigour to the fetishised appearances of credit. The point is that a deeper analysis of the roots of power and social reproduction cannot be understood by treating credit in economistic terms. We need to grasp that credit is privately created money and, like money, is therefore a social relation of power. Before elaborating on credit in this way, however, it is helpful to define what I understand by social reproduction.

Briefly, social reproduction refers to the various aspects of (re)constructing capitalist society. These include: biological reproduction, reproduction of the labour force and reproduction of provisioning and caring needs (Katz, 2001; Bakker and Gill, 2003). The ongoing commodification of these social relations and the disciplinary machinations therein, demands that social reproduction be continually reconstructed in order to veil the silent compulsions of the social power of money in the form of credit. Moreover, the regulatory features of credit cannot be a secondary consideration; this is why the following chapter, which discusses debtfare states, tackles issues such as the role and nature of regulation regarding consumer credit.

To put it another way, there exists more below the surface of the credit system than a historical assemblage of regulatory structures, institutions and networks of actors, as is so often depicted in the scholarly literature on financialisation and consumer credit. The origins of power, social transformation and reproduction need to be located in the *materiality* of capitalist society and the tensions therein (see Chapter 1).

To transcend the surface appearances regarding consumer credit, a Marxian theory of money remains the most rigorous basis upon which to build. It allows us to address basic, yet vital, questions that many scholars writing on financialisation have neglected: Why did credit emerge? Why do certain people possess such immense power to deny and/or provide access to credit? And how is this legitimated?

By posing the above questions, I am interested not only in understanding why the economically vulnerable have become increasingly dependent on high-priced consumer credit, but also in identifying the social machinations involved in recreating – that is, normalising, depoliticising and legitimating – the social necessities that compel the working poor to depend on credit as opposed to living wages. My objective is to challenge the institutional tropes and practices upheld by states and international development organisations (e.g., World Bank, IMF, G-20) that assume financial inclusion and the democratisation of credit to be the most efficient method of assisting the poor in the neoliberal era. The point here is that existing analyses of financialisation do not permit us to look deeply and critically at what actually constitutes 'the financial' as in the case of financial inclusion, or 'credit' in the case of the democratisation of credit, which the poor are invited to voluntarily enter (while being structurally coerced to do so). The six case studies in this book clearly reveal the structural violence and silent compulsions inherent to 'the financial' as it relates to the poverty industry.

The second limit in existing approaches to consumer credit has been the preference given to the primacy of the realm of exchange over production in attempts to make sense of the proliferation and social reproduction of the dominance of credit (otherwise referred to in the literature as financialisation or finance-led capitalism). This inevitably leads to the separation of what is often referred to as the 'real' economy (production) from the financial economy. This bifurcation distorts the intrinsic connection between money and credit money, on the one hand and the social power of money and credit money to the wider processes of capital accumulation, on the other. It also results in a neglect of interrogations into how and why the dominance of credit money is constantly recreated and represented as natural, despite the inherent contradiction and social consequences involved in attempting to realise value without producing it (see Chapter 1).

It cannot be stressed enough that my usage of the word *processes* in conjunction with *capital accumulation* implies that the latter is not a static object but instead a complex, highly contradictory, anarchic and dynamic series of actions that are neither inevitable nor natural. I do not employ the fashionable terms financialisation or financialised capitalism in this book for the very reason that these terms serve to facilitate the conceptual imprecision around money, credit and the financial system. The latter, as I understand it, is essentially, albeit not exclusively, comprised of money and credit money as well as institutional and class-based networks. We investigate some of these features in the next chapter and in the several case studies that follow. For now, it is helpful to understand the role and limits of money in the wider processes of capital accumulation.

The role and tensions of money in capital accumulation

As discussed in Chapter 1, the nature and role of money (i.e., real money as in the money commodity or state-backed legal tender) cannot be grasped by remaining in the sphere of exchange, largely because of the illusion of equality, democracy and freedom facilitated in this realm. The primary reason for this is the ability of money to embody yet conceal the presumed equality of exchange surrounding labour power. Instead, Marx argues that to comprehend the revolutionary power of money, it is necessary to enter the realm of production to see how and why money becomes the direct incarnation of all human labour and thereby serves to distort the inequality and exploitative relations involved in creating surplus value, or what Marx refers to as the money fetish (de Brunhof, 1976; Marx, 1976; Rodolsky, 1977). As a commodity, money appears as an external object or thing that is capable of becoming the private property of individuals, who in turn can wield social power over others. In capitalism, this power is class-based: the owners of the means of production (capitalists) have been able to accumulate the vast majority of money. As Marx notes, the accumulation of money is unlimited social power (Clarke, 1988; Harvey, 1999; Marx, 2005). This power has grown exponentially and unevenly in the neoliberal era (Harvey, 2007).

For money to maintain its social power as the universal equivalent, it needs to function as a trusted store of value. This is an extremely important point to keep in mind, as it forms a basic tension in capital accumulation. It bears repeating, however, that while money has a use-value, it does not have intrinsic value (i.e., price). The preservation of the quality of money is difficult to maintain given the inherent tensions in capital accumulation. In Chapter 3, I explain how the power of capitalist states and the role of monetarist forms of intervention become crucial in this regard (Clarke, 1988; Bonefeld and Holloway, 1995; Harvey, 1999; Krippner, 2011; Panitch and Gindin, 2012).

Before turning to key tensions in capital accumulation, it is useful to stress that the drive to accumulate surplus value (profit) is the primary engine that powers growth under capitalism (Marx, 1976; Harvey, 2001). An abbreviated version of the accumulation process in formulaic version may be regarded as: $M-C-M^1$, where M is money, C is a commodity produced by labour using means of production and M^1 is profit. Marx rejected the bourgeois economists' position that growth under capitalism is harmonious in nature; this position holds true in terms of the credit system. Instead, he suggested that due to internal tensions in capitalist society crises will often result from structural barriers to the accumulation of (surplus) value (Clarke, 1994; Harvey, 2001; Fine, 2010).

Three tensions that crop up in accumulation processes are features that capitalism presupposes and depends upon (Harvey, 1999, 2001). First, capitalism does not only require free labour, it also necessitates the presence of an excess labour force, or what Marx refers to as an industrial reserve army, or surplus population. The reserve army facilitates the expansion of capitalist production. To illustrate this point, I draw on a standard expression of the expansion of value (or, what is referred to as surplus value, or profit) in the circulation process of capital:

$$M \rightarrow C\ [LP + MP] \ldots P \ldots C^1 \rightarrow M^1$$

Where M stands for money; C and C^1 for commodities; LP for labour power; MP for the means of production, including machinery, energy inputs, raw materials and partially finished products; P for production; and M^1 for profit (Harvey, 1989: 18). To illustrate, a capitalist purchases labour, or LP (coffee pickers) and machinery (MP) to harvest, process and mill (P) coffee berries for $1,000 (M). This same capitalist then sells the finished product, namely: coffee beans (C^1) to coffee houses for $2,000 ($M^1$). Seen from this angle, there must be regulations in place to increase the supply of labour (liberal migration policies), if the price of coffee is particularly lucrative. On the other hand, regulatory mechanisms must also exist that can decrease the supply of labour when coffee prices tumble. These mechanisms would allow for unemployment and/or the introduction of labour-reducing technology aimed at increasing both the quantity and quality of coffee harvested. Expressed differently, strategies must be in place either to bring down wages below value (a point I return to below) or to increase the productivity of the workers who remain employed.

Second and related, for the expansion of production to occur, a capitalist must be able to purchase the necessary means of production, e.g., machines, raw materials, etc. Third, there needs to be a market to absorb the increasing quantities of commodities produced. People have to need and want coffee (use-value), or at least be encouraged to want and need coffee through the advertising industry. If uses for coffee cannot be found, or if an effective demand (backed by the ability to pay) is not present, then the conditions for capital accumulation disappear (Harvey, 2001: 238–9).

Each of these three tensions presents a potential obstacle to capital accumulation that stands to precipitate a crisis (Harvey, 2001: 239). In Marxian theory, a fundamental stressor that underpins all of these tensions is the tendency to over-accumulate capital (Mandel, 1968; Amin, 1974; Clarke, 1988, 1994; Bonefeld and Holloway, 1995; Harvey, 1999, 2003). While Marx's general laws of capital accumulation are complex and highly dynamic, it suffices here to note that the over-accumulation of capital refers to a situation in which there is a surplus of capital relative to profitable opportunities to employ that capital. This is sometimes accompanied by surpluses of labour (Harvey, 2001; Charnock et al., 2014). As Harvey (2001: 240) argues,

> The various manifestations of crises in the capitalist system – chronic unemployment and underemployment, capital surpluses and lack of invest-ment opportunities, falling rates of profit, lack of effective demand in the

market and so on – can, therefore, be traced to the basic tendency to over-accumulation.

The absence of profitable investment sites, for instance, increases tension on the store of value of money (Clarke, 1988, 1994). As we will see in the next section, the role of credit money plays a vital function in smoothing the tensions of capital accumulation. As a form of money, it also wields immense power – most of which is privately held.

Credit money in capital accumulation: swindler and prophet

The process by which banks create money is so simple that the mind is repelled.
– John Kenneth Galbraith, 1974, quoted in Stanford, 2008: 194

The generalisation of a form of 'money of account', or what Marx refers to as credit money, is designed to alleviate the tensions inherent in capital accumulation (Clarke, 1994; Marx, 2005). Credit money originated in privately contracted bills of exchange and notes of credit, which took on the social form (and powers) of money as soon as they begin to circulate as means of payment (Mandel 1968; Harvey, 1999; Lapavitsas, 2013). Credit serves to ease the strain placed on physical money as store of value, since the quantity of credit money can either be increased or reduced, depending on the required levels needed for circulation. Thus, it facilitates the reproduction of the accumulation process as a whole (Harvey, 1999: 245). This point can be illustrated by returning to the example of coffee production.

To deal with the three points of tension mentioned earlier, our coffee capitalist will have to hoard (save) enough money to purchase the necessary equipment and the cost of labour and to bridge the time until the return of value through production is realised. Even if the coffee capitalist has been able to do this, they will inevitably require more money to deal with the inherent stresses of capital accumulation, including: replacing inefficient technology, absorbing price fluctuations, dealing with a drop in demand, and so forth. The ability of our coffee capitalist to access credit money becomes vital to the smooth flow of attempts to expand value. This example of the significance of credit money to lubricate the wheels of capital accumulation makes an important point: credit money is a necessary condition to deal with the periodic tensions emerging in capital accumulation (Mandel, 1968; Harvey, 1999, 2001).

According to Marx, credit money exists as a lever for expanded reproduction as it realises the internal relation of production and circulation without this internal relation having been performed in real terms (Marx, 1991; Bonefeld, 1995: 189). In doing so, credit money establishes continuity between money tied in production and exchange, where there was none before (Harvey, 2001: 245). However, credit money also accelerates the violent outbreaks of the underlying tensions in capital accumulation (Marx, 1991: 572). As Marx (1991: 572–3) observes:

> The credit system has a dual character immanent in it: on the one hand it
> develops the motive of capitalist production, enrichment by the exploitation

of others' labour, into the purest and most colossal system of gambling and swindling and restricts ever more the already small number of the exploiters of social wealth; on the other hand however it constitutes the form of transition towards a new mode of production. It is this dual character . . . of swindler and prophet.

In what follows, I discuss the role played by credit money in resolving a key tension associated with over-accumulated capital: the constant fluctuations of the size and composition of what Marx refers to as the relative surplus population; that is, the target group for creditors. Before turning to this discussion, however, it is important to parse out the similarities and differences between money and credit money, as well as highlight two types of credit money. This exercise will help to deepen our conceptualisation of consumer credit, as it assists in our understanding of social power and the tensions inherent in credit money itself.

Money and credit money: similarities and differences

As noted above, credit is similar to money in that both are incarnations of social power, including spatial and temporal dimensions (see Chapter 1). Like money, credit money asserts itself as a universal equivalent, which has the capacity to expand abstract wealth independently of exploitation (Clarke, 1994; Bonefeld, 1995). Credit money therefore also serves to destroy personal bonds of dependency and replace them with 'objective dependency relations' through which individuals relate to each other through things – most notably, market prices, e.g., interest rates, fees and late penalties as well as credit-rating scores. The free license given by states to capitalists to privately create money (credit) also facilitates the (re-)construction of the community of money (Marx, 2005).

The monetisation of social relationships (i.e., the relations between things), which underpins the community of money, is reproduced in consumer credit, too. The relationships between capitalists and workers, for instance, are converted, through the credit system, into relations between debtor and creditor. The latter relations are mediated by formalised abstractions (e.g., interest rates, late fees) as opposed to direct forms of domination between employer and employee. I pick up on this form of social power inherent to consumer credit below. For now, it is useful to identify three core differences between money and credit money.

The role of credit money in the processes of capital accumulation is distinct from money in at least three essential ways – all of which serve to heighten the tensions of capital accumulation as opposed to absorbing them. First, unlike other forms of money, such as cash, 'no matter how far afield a privately contracted bill of exchange may circulate, it must always return to its place of origin for redemption' (Harvey, 1999: 245–6). Second, unlike other forms of money, which are issued by the state, credit money is privately created money that can serve a social purpose when put into circulation. When the original debt is paid off, however, the credit money disappears from circulation. As such, credit money is continually being created and destroyed through the actions of private individuals (capitalists), as they seek to deal with the stresses in capital accumulation. Third, credit money entails what Marx refers to as fictitious value – an imaginary component – whereas 'real' money is tied directly to a money commodity, as discussed in Chapter 1 (Harvey, 1999: 267). The fictitious value in credit money also presents a potential source of crisis to capital accumulation, as it opens up a gap between itself and money, whose quality needs to be preserved at all costs.

Two types of credit money: fictitious capital and the money-form of revenue

It is vital here to distinguish between two broad types of credit money: fictitious capital and the money-form of revenue (Harvey, 1999). The latter type of money credit captures the forms of non-collateralised forms of consumer credit that we investigate in this book, e.g., payday loans, student loans, credit cards and so forth. It is also a type of consumer credit that Marx did not theorise, largely because consumer credit was not well developed in his day. In this sense, Leyshon and Thrift (1997) are correct that the Marxian understanding of money (or money credit, more specifically) requires updating. However, this does not mean that we need to reject the building blocks offered by Marx and theorists such as Harvey (1999). A Marxian theory of money and capital accumulation is an essential analytical foundation upon which to build our conceptual renovations.

In what follows, we should keep in mind that an important distinction between fictitious capital and the money-form of revenue (consumer credit) parallels the difference between money and capital. This becomes clearer as we proceed with our analysis. Suffice it to say here that, on Marx's insistence, Harvey urges us to avoid blurring money with capital, as there is a palpable difference between the circulation of money as capital (fictitious capital) and its circulation as mere money (the money-form of revenue). The distinction is also important in terms of consumer credit. The latter usually involves money circulating as money. It extracts interest and fees, not profit, which is extractable only in the realm of production. As such money circulating as credit involves different forms of exploitation (secondary forms) and relations of domination (creditor and debtor), but also engages and creates different tensions in the wider processes of capital accumulation.

Fictitious capital

The first of the two broad categories of credit money is fictitious capital. While both forms of credit money entail fictitious value, fictitious capital is implied whenever credit money is loaned out as capital, i.e., enters into the sphere of production. When credit money circulates as fictitious capital it is destined to enter the production process and create surplus value, or what becomes profit (e.g., $M\text{–}C\text{–}M^1$).

Fictitious in the context of Marxian theory does not mean that this form of credit money is not real. What Marx means is that this form of credit money does not entail value in itself. Instead, fictitious capital is a claim exercised by credit money over a share of future surplus value (profit), as opposed to existing commodities. Put another way, fictitious capital is implied whenever credit is extended in advance, in expectation of future labour as counter-value; that is, the extraction of surplus value through primary forms of exploitation (Harvey, 1999: 266). For Marx, government debt (e.g., government bonds) and land are the ultimate expressions of fictitious value. They have no inherent value, yet they can assume a price. These forms of fictitious capital are not yet real capital, as they have not extracted surplus value through the primary exploitation of labour (i.e., in the realm of production). They are, instead, debt claims. Our discussion of Mexican housing finance in Chapter 9 reveals the tensions inherent in lending fictitious capital to surplus workers. In particular, I examine how these contradictions have been resolved through expansionary policies in the credit system, such as the reliance on asset-backed securitisation schemes for low-income housing.

The creation of fictitious values prior to actual commodity production and realisation is always a risky venture (Harvey, 1999: 266). While fictitious capital plays a necessary role in absorbing tensions in capital accumulation, 'Marx is very clear that the credit system registers the "height of distortion" to the degree that the accumulation of future claims of labour as counter-value outruns real production' (Harvey, 1999: 269). When fictitious capital begins to dominate capital accumulation, as has been the case over the past several decades, links with the actual expansion of capital accumulation become strained, thereby threatening the quality of real money upon which credit money rests. The popular conception of capital as something with the properties of automatic self-expansion is strengthened and the accumulation of debts begins to appear erroneously as accumulation of capital (Harvey, 1999: 269). This also leads to the illusion that credit is somehow separated from the realm of production. Our theoretical lens prevents us from repeating this error. It also permits us to move beyond the power of this illusion by grasping credit money as part and parcel of the wider accumulation processes.

Money-form of revenue

A second type of credit money is what Marx refers to as the money-form of revenue that is not based on collateral. This includes credit cards, student loans and payday loans. This type of money credit reflects the majority of consumer credit explored in this book and will therefore be used synonymously with 'consumer credit' from this point onward (Marx, 1991, Ch. 28). Unlike fictitious capital, consumer credit is geared toward increasing the initial monetary outlay through interest payments and fees (e.g., late fees, administrative fees, etc.) as opposed to the creation of surplus value (Mandel, 1968; de Brunhoff, 1976; Bonefeld and Holloway, 1995). Instead of engaging in production and thus employing labour to produce surplus value (profit), consumer credit is circulated as money. In formulaic terms, this is represented as M . . . M^1 (where M is money and M^1 is interest). Because this latter circuit of the money-form of revenue bypasses labour and remains in the realm of exchange, many theorists, including Leyshon and Thrift (1997), have argued that the realm of production is not relevant to the study of consumer credit.

By contrast, in a Marxian understanding of capital accumulation the sphere of production and the sphere of exchange are not simply imbricated but inextricable. Credit does not emerge naturally from a harmoniously functioning (efficient and equilibrating) market; but instead represents social forms of power designed to resolve contradictions within the processes of capital accumulation. As such, the M . . . M^1 circuit of consumer credit is not based on magical, self-expansionary mechanisms; but instead are influenced, in part, through a complex assemblage of private and public governance strategies aimed at imposing market discipline on debtors to ensure that loans, or, at the very least, interest payments, are realised. That said, the proliferation of consumer credit to the poor and the relations of power therein, is also partly shaped by the tensions in the processes involved in capital accumulation and the tendency toward over-accumulation in particular. For example, in Chapter 6, I discuss how the student loan industry has expanded its reach to finance low-income students attending for-profit, private universities in the United States. Through asset-backed securitisation (ABS), for instance, these creditors offset the risks involved in lending to the poor (e.g., the high probability of defaults) by repackaging and reselling loans to other investors, such as pension funds, in the 'digitalised spaces' of global financial markets (Sassen, 2006, 2009). I discuss ABS as it relates to the poverty industry in more detail below.

For now, it is important to emphasise that in the M . . . M^1 circuit, which underpins the majority of the transactions in the poverty industry, the connection between consumer credit and the realm of production is not completely severed, as observed by Leyshon and Thrift (1997) in the introductory chapter of this book. The reason for this connection is that consumer credit entails secondary forms of exploitation whereby workers' real incomes can be modified (Harvey, 1999). Unlike primary forms of exploitation, which occur in the realm of production (see Chapter 1), secondary exploitation takes place in the sphere of exchange through the extraction of interest and fees from a loan. To repay the loan – or to make minimum payments on the principal amount, which is more often the case – workers must give up part of their income, savings, or even, as we will see in Chapter 7, their welfare cheques. While some workers are no longer in the realm of production (e.g., those in the low-wage service sector), consumer credit plays an important role in reproducing the labour supply, which is crucial for capital accumulation.

Because of the social power inherent in credit money and given that credit transactions occur within the realm of exchange, the interest and fees placed on consumer loans by creditors appear as a natural exchange of equivalents. Two parties enter a contractual agreement on a voluntary basis (see Chapter 1). Yet, credit money does not walk around with a natural price on its head. It must be constructed. As we will see in the following chapters, shifts in usury law by debtfare states have allowed the interest and fees applied to credit money to be framed as an equivalent exchange for a debtor's credit rating. This is based on alleged scientific and thus objective, calculations that determine the price of the loan (interest) based on perceived risk, e.g., losses to the creditor from non-repayment (Marron, 2007). Put another way, technologies and strategies such as risk-based pricing allows capitalists to charge poorer people more interest and administrative fees than materially better off workers (Wyly et al., 2009; Sassen, 2009).

Like real money, what consumer credit conceals are the exploitative relations of class-based power. In the wider community of money, for instance, the real (defetishised) relationships within the credit system become very difficult to distinguish, while the behaviour of economic agents as debtors is subject to different pressures compared with their behaviours as wage-earners (Harvey, 1999). Indeed, the designation of debtors with the seemingly apolitical and homogenous term 'consumer' seems to further obfuscate the real relationships upon which credit money is built, thereby making the unequal and exploitative relations difficult to discern. As we see below and throughout the book, the features of the community of money – democracy, freedom and equality – are mirrored in mainstream representations of the importance of extending credit money to the poor in the wider discourses of financial inclusion and the democratisation of credit.

While consumer credit does not flow directly into the production process, its ongoing expansion is as problematic as fictitious capital in that it resolves temporarily some paradoxes in capital accumulation while triggering more tensions. I discuss this further in the next section. Here it is useful to note that the temporary fix offered by credit money is due partly to the nature of credit money (i.e., it is privately created and must return to its origin for redemption) and partly to the fact that credit can only (temporarily) resolve the contradictions arising in the sphere of production from *within* the realm of exchange (Harvey, 1999).

The main point in this section is that credit money is both distinct from and similar to, its monetary base. The power of credit is derived, in part, from the processes of capital accumulation and, in part, from the ideological and regulatory backing of states. To elaborate on this point, we pick up on one of the key tensions in the processes of capital accumulation, namely, the continual production of a relative surplus population whose social reproduction is tenuous. In particular, we explore how and why capitalists have employed consumer credit as a means of solving this reproduction problem while creating new markets for interest- and fee-generating revenue. We will also begin to see how this solution serves to heighten rather than resolve this tension – an inquiry with which the rest of the book is concerned.

Credit and the surplus population: tensions, solutions and the poverty industry

The relative surplus population: meanings and problems for accumulation

> *The misery of being exploited by capitalists is nothing compared to the misery of not being exploited at all.*
>
> – Joan Robinson, 1962: 21

In his general law of capitalist accumulation in *Capital* (vol. 1), Marx discusses the social consequences of capital's drive for increased productivity of labour (and thus expansion of profit), namely: the production of a relative surplus population or reserve labour army, which is not only a key necessity and tension of capital accumulation, but also shaped by the contradictions in the processes of capital accumulation. As Marx (1990: 784) argues:

> But if a surplus population of workers is a necessary product of accumulation or the development of wealth on a capitalist basis, this surplus population also becomes, conversely, the lever of capital accumulation, indeed it becomes the condition for the existence of capitalist mode of production. It forms a disposable industrial reserve army, which belongs to capital just as absolutely as if the latter had bred it at its own costs. Independently of the limits of the actual increase of population, it creates a mass of human material always ready for exploitation by capital in the interests of capital's own changing valorization requirements.

The relative surplus population is an important analytical category in our analysis, not only because of its central role in credit-led accumulation in the poverty industry, but also because it allows us to grasp the sources from which marginalised workers emerge as debtors. For Marx (1990: 794), 'Every worker belongs to the relative surplus population during the time when [s]/he is only partially employed or wholly unemployed'. The relative surplus population is intrinsically connected to and defined by, the processes of capital accumulation. Moreover, this group of workers is a highly dynamic and heterogeneous group of workers that, for Marx, exist in several forms: the floating, the latent and the stagnant (Marx, 1990). As various authors have pointed out, these categories have varying degrees of importance for capitalists, depending on the historical and spatial context (Nun, 2000; Breman, 2003; Sanyal, 2007; Li, 2009). In the chapters that follow, I specifically define what I mean by surplus worker in relation to each case of the poverty industry under study. Notwithstanding my attempts to clarify the meaning of this labour category, it is important to underscore that the relative surplus population is a social relation that is based in, and created by, the wider dynamics of capital accumulation. The meaning of who is surplus is thus far from static or clear, as the lines separating surplus from non-surplus workers are, like all things in capitalism, perpetually in motion and often blurred.

In this book, I use the term relative surplus population interchangeably with surplus labour power, marginalised workers and low-income workers, as well as unemployed and underemployed workers. Regardless of the varied terms, the essence of Marx's definition of the relative surplus population remains. Aside from the treatment of this concept as a social category in the wider processes of capital accumulation, my understanding of the surplus population relates primarily to what Marx describes as workers in the 'floating' and 'latent' stratum, as these two categories reflect those 'embedded' in the industrial reserve army and thus are linked to the processes of capital accumulation. By floating Marx is referring to people who are already proletarianised, who have already been employed as wage-earners, who are temporarily unemployed and who, after a period of unemployment, are reabsorbed into the labour force as conditions for accumulation improve (Marx, 1976). As Harvey (2010a: 278) notes, the floating workers are roughly equivalent to the pool of unemployed, as recorded in the unemployment statistics, plus those classified as underemployed or as 'discouraged workers'.

Finally, according to Marx, the latent category of the relative surplus population describes peasant populations not yet absorbed into the wage-labour system. 'As soon as capitalist production takes possession of agriculture and in proportion to the extent to which it does so, the demand for a rural working population falls absolutely, while the accumulation of the capital employed in agricultural advances, without this repulsion being compensated for by a greater attraction of workers, as is the case in non-agricultural industries' (Marx, 1976: 795–6). The continual destruction of peasant or indigenous forms of subsistence farming and the proletarianisation of the rural world has pushed ever-growing numbers of peasants into wage-labour (Moyo and Yeros, 2005; Taylor, 2008; McMichael, 2009; Breman, 2012; White et al., 2012). This continues to be the case in neoliberal times and can be seen in a number of ways, such as the case of many members of the informal sector in Mexico, or (illegal) migrants from the global South to the United States, which we discuss in the case of the US credit card industry (see Chapter 5) as well as the Mexican case studies (see Chapters 8 and 9).

For Marx, the relative surplus population is 'the most powerful lever of accumulation' but also reveals why the 'accumulation of misery is a necessary condition, corresponding to the accumulation of wealth' (Marx, 1990: 772, 799). Capital accumulation both creates and is dependent upon the relative surplus population. As noted above, capital accumulation depends on a relative surplus population – not only because a ready supply of cheap workers is profitable for capitalists, but also because the reserve army places downward pressure on existing wage levels, threatens employed labourers with layoffs, discourages labour organisation and increases the intensity of labour for those employed. It is, therefore, in the capitalist classes' interests to manage the relative surplus population, through disciplinary tactics and ideological means, in such a way so as to perpetuate it (Marx,

1990; Denning, 2010; Harvey, 2010a). The relative surplus population must, there-fore, be able to socially reproduce itself by meeting basic subsistence needs.

Etching out survival at the margins of the expanded reproduction of capital is a difficult task for surplus labour at the best of times. It is downright grim during times when capital is facing the pressures of over-accumulation. These times have been marked by an ever-growing socio-economic gap between rich and poor, both within and between countries. As John Holloway (1994: 132) elaborates:

> Capital, in order to survive, needed to free itself from existing relations of exploitation, to spit out some of the workers currently being exploited, to restructure its relations with others, to go in search of new people to exploit. Capital takes flight from the inadequacy of its own basis: this flight is expressed in the conversion of capital into money and the movement of that money in search of profitable means of expansion.

If we continue with our attempts to defetishise what Marx refers to as the economic fiction that casts (capitalist) markets as natural phenomena, which – left largely to their own devices – magically reach equilibrium, we are faced with the question of how the silent compulsions that characterise capital accumulation have been continually reconstructed and legitimated with regard to the surplus population (Marx, 1990). How is dispossession, expropriation and dependence on the market imposed on the surplus population in such a manner that it appears as a natural and inevitable aspect of life, or the *ordinary run of things* (Marx, 1976; de Angelis, 2007)?

Unfortunately, we cannot turn to Marx for many answers, as he does not theorise the social reproduction of labour power, particularly the surplus population. For Harvey (1999: 163; see also, Lebowitz, 2003), since the quantity and quality of labour supply is an important feature to Marx's understanding of capital accumu-lation, 'this omission is, perhaps, one of the most serious of all the gaps in Marx's own theory and one that is proving extremely difficult to plug if only because the relations between accumulation and the social processes of reproduction of labour are hidden in such a maze of complexity that they seem to defy analysis. This is particularly true with regard to the gendered, racial and ethnic dimensions of social reproduction (cf. Katz, 2001; Rankin, 2001; Roberts, 2013). My analysis in the remaining part of this chapter as well as in the next chapter attempts to partially address this gap.

The (temporary) fix: credit-led accumulation and the poverty industry

The problem for capitalists faced with over-accumulated capital is two-fold. On the one hand, capitalists must overcome the barriers to capital accumulation by continually searching for more venues to extract revenue (interest and fees) through consumer credit (e.g., transactions based on M ... M^1). On the other hand, the burgeoning surplus population must be reintegrated into, or enclosed within, the community of money lest the myth that growth-driven capitalism benefits all be exposed. A key problem in the neoliberal era is how to enclose and depoliticise the spaces of marginality populated by the surplus population, while maintaining the (investment) integrity, stability and, above all, 'naturalness' of capitalism.

Capitalists, with assistance from the state and international organisations such as the International Monetary Fund, have historically relied on what Harvey refers to as a 'spatio-temporal fix' or 'displacement' to overcome the barriers to capital valorisation (Harvey, 1989, 2003; Sassen, 2010). This fix, which constitutes an important analytical tool, can be explained in the following manner: the surpluses of (real) money can be potentially transformed through temporal displacements, for instance, through investment in long-term capital projects or social expenditures in education and research (a temporal fix). Surpluses of (real) money can also be absorbed through spatial displacements such as the opening of new markets (a spatial fix). Temporal and spatial solutions to the strains in capital accumulation can also be combined to create spatio-temporal fixes. A good example of this is the creation of a housing market for low-income workers in Mexico with surplus money originating not only in Mexico but also from the United States and Europe (spatial displacement). Moreover, as we will see in Chapter 9, the interest extracted from these subprime mortgages has been temporally modified through asset-backed securitisation (ABS). The movement from a mortgage traditionally held by a bank for several decades to the dynamics of ABS may also be regarded as a type of spatial displacement from relatively more concrete moorings to virtual space, or what Saskia Sassen refers to as electronic mortgages operating in digital spaces (Sassen, 2009). I discuss mortgage securitisation in the context of Mexico in more detail in Chapter 9.

The point to keep in mind here is that given the tension-ridden processes inherent to the dynamics of capital accumulation, these fixes cannot be understood in isolation from each other; but instead must be seen as a continuum in which each fix builds on and in turn affects, the preceding solution.

Heightening tensions in spatio-temporal displacements

As we will see in Chapter 3, the expansive state policies promoting financial inclusion feed off of and, in turn, serve to discipline and recreate, advanced marginality. This is largely due to a shortage of work that prevents surplus labour from earning a living wage. The increasing role of consumer credit in the supplementation and in some cases replacement, of regular and living wages and adequately funded social programmes (e.g., old age pensions and care, health care, child care, education and welfare) has also meant a change in the form in which the social relations of power are articulated and fought out. These class-based relations of power are distorted in the realm of exchange, which is dominated by consumer credit and backed by the power of the state (see Chapter 3). It serves as a means to discipline, dispossess and (re-)impose silent compulsions and structural violence by (re-)integrating the surplus population into the capitalist system, even if only at the margins, as debtors. These disciplining and coercive features, in turn, allow workers to be ensnared in the invisible temporal and spatial constraints of consumer credit.

In this context, it is worth underscoring again that the sphere of production, not solely the realm of exchange, plays an immense role in shaping the effectiveness and stability of consumer credit for the poor. Indeed, as I have tried to suggest throughout this chapter, credit money is only a temporary solution to the tensions of capital accumulation. However, these stressors cannot be understood without taking into account both features of accumulation – the realms of exchange and production. The key tensions of consumer credit may be traced to the three distinctive characteristics discussed earlier, namely the existence of a reserve army, the ability of the capitalist to access credit and the creation of a market to absorb the increasing quantities of commodities produced. In what follows, I highlight some of the core tensions underpinning the poverty industry and its dispossessive strategies.

The social power of credit money and the continual dispossession leveraged through the poverty industry has facilitated an increase in the power of capitalists over the regulation and mediation of surplus workers. Capitalists not only create credit money, but also, through the monetisation of the creditor-debtor relationship, subjugate 'consumers' to the domination of abstractions such as interest rates and fee payments levied against future revenues, which appear external and independent to workers (debtors) (Harvey, 1989). A central tension in this form of credit-led accumulation concerns precisely where these revenues are to come from and when. If opportunities for work (in the formal or informal sectors) are forthcoming, then there is a potential that the fictitious nature of the value of consumer loan will not be called into question; that is, it will not result in default. If the debtor repays the loan, then consumer credit as a form of dispossession will have successfully extracted revenue for the capitalist, while also playing a role in reproducing insecurity and in disciplining workers, who either voluntarily submit to the structural violence of the workplace in order to pay off their debts, or, more often, simply make regular instalment payments on the interest. Nonetheless, consumer credit cannot escape the fact that it operates as fictitious value and thus continually threatens the stability of capital accumulation by gambling on the ability of debtors to repay their loans. If this gap widens too far it threatens the quality of real money, with the potential for a crisis to ensue. Since it is vital to protect the quality of (real) money to ensure its social power as the universal equivalent, capitalists created consumer credit to absorb these tensions.

Capitalists have devised temporal-spatial fixes to displace the above tension, in part through the increased use of asset-backed securitisation. ABS is a financial innovation that emerged in the early 1970s in the United States. Its use began to increase in the US during the late 1990s, before expanding to Europe and eventually the global South. Securitisation describes a process of packaging individual consumer loans (e.g., student loans, housing loans, credit card loans, etc.) with other debt instruments. This package is transformed into a security or securities, which enhances its credit status or rating to further its sale to third-party investors, such as mutual and pension funds (Elul, 2005; Sassen, 2008). Securitisation, also referred to as 'slice and dice' capitalism, essentially converts illiquid individuals loans into liquid, marketable securities to be bought and sold (Kothari, 2006). With this form of credit money based on future income streams, investors engaging in ABS anticipate that the borrower will be able to earn sufficient wages to continue making orderly payments on their loan.

While ABS can temporarily bridge the underlying gap between the fictitious value of the consumer loan and real money, it cannot resolve the fact that its success is dependent on a future gamble that the debtor can access enough funds to repay their loan. Herein lies another tension and defining characteristic of credit money: no matter how far afield consumer credit circulates, it must always return to its place of origin for recovery, namely, to the debtor. The debtor of consumer credit must pay the face value of the debt for credit money to close the circle of exchange. Given the precarious situation of the surplus population, however, the risk of default is a constant threat and poses a heightened tension in the use of credit money. The gamble with future of labour is intensified in consumer credit given its fictitious value. On the one hand, pressure is placed on the working poor to find employment of any kind at any price (wages) for the length of time necessary to make payments. On the other hand, in the current era of credit-led accumulation, employment offering living wages is hard to find.

Concluding remarks

Building on the conceptual base of the social power of money, this chapter explored the social power of credit. I argued that the structural violence and silent compulsions that mark capitalism cannot be adequately understood by beginning and/or remaining in the realm of exchange, which is, unfortunately, where much of the financialisation literature is fixated. Following a Marxian based understanding of money and credit, I suggested that a robust analysis must begin with an understanding of the monetary basis of credit within the wider, conflict-ridden processes of capital accumulation. I discussed the nature of credit by explaining how and why credit emerges. In short, it is employed by capitalists to overcome inevitable, yet unpredictable, stresses in the expansion of value, such as periodic events of over-accumulation. In addition, it facilitates the management of the relative surplus population. In the neoliberal era, this takes the form of credit-led accumulation. While this accumulation strategy serves capitalist interests, it has, as Marx suggests, heightened rather than resolved the paradoxes inherent to the processes of capital accumulation.

Because of these strains, credit and its monetary base necessitates an institution that is perceived as class neutral, i.e., existing beyond the realm of exchange and production, to help manage and depoliticise conflicts and tensions in the expansion of the poverty industry. In fact, although my analysis has kept the state analytically separate from money and credit thus far, I have done so only for the sake of clarity. Capital accumulation, as we will see in the next chapter, has always required capitalist states to secure its reproduction. Under neoliberalism, many states have accommodated the needs of capital and credit-led accumulation in particular. The next chapter explores the roles played by neoliberal states in facilitating the expansion and reproduction of the poverty industry through the social power of money.

Note

1   It is widely known that Marx never completed his analysis on money and credit. As Harvey observes, Marx's notes on credit were left in great confusion (Harvey, 1999). While it is true that Marxists continue to pay scant attention to money and credit, there have been several seminal works on the topic (Mandel, 1968; de Brunhoff, 1976; Amin, 1974; Clarke, 1988; Itoh and Lapavitsas, 1999). I draw on these authors but base my primary reading on Marx and Harvey. The latter (Harvey, 1989, 1999) provides, in my view, a more updated and complete reading of money and credit, as they relate to capital accumulation.

3

DEBTFARE STATES

As we saw in the previous chapter, the role of privately created money (credit) in the wider dynamics of capital accumulation is riddled with contradictions. A core tension that concerns us in this book is the need for the constant expansion of the poverty industry coupled with the reproduction of the surplus population. Because capitalism's claims to freedom of exchange and liberty of contract are a myth, the system requires a mediating social relation to facilitate the expansion and reproduction of capital accumulation that is at the heart of the poverty industry. In this chapter, I argue that neoliberal states have played a vital role in this process. In particular, I suggest that the debtfarist feature of neoliberal states provides vital institutional and ideological support to the growth of the poverty industry, not least by normalising and disciplining the dependency of the surplus population on credit.

Neoliberal states have played a vital role in legitimising, promoting and mediating the contradictions inherent to credit and the wider process of capital accumulation. I suggest that there are four core components of neoliberal states that have played vital roles in the expansion and reproduction of the poverty industry in both the United States and Mexico. These overlapping features are: monetarism, corporate welfarism, workfarism and what I refer to as debtfarism. Debtfarism plays a direct role in the ongoing reconstruction and normalisation of the poverty industry. As with monetarism, corporate welfarism and workfare, debtfarism seeks to achieve these goals by invoking the social power of money. This includes removing struggles from the realm of production and shifting them to the realm of exchange, where exploitation and class power is less visible.

Through a complex and tension-ridden web of regulative and rhetorical processes, debtfarism imposes market discipline while actively reconstructing and normalising the growing dependency of the surplus population on high-priced credit to subsidise their basic subsistence needs. Later in the chapter and throughout the book, I employ the term debtfare state. It is important to emphasise that by debtfare state I do not imply a standalone state. Instead, I use this term to capture the institutionalised rhetorical and regulatory practices of debtfarism, most notably usury and bankruptcy law, consumer protection legislation and dominant neoliberal tropes, such as financial inclusion and the democratisation of credit.

I develop this argument in five main sections. Section One elaborates on my understanding of a materialist conception of states. Section Two broadly the rhetorical and regulative manifestations of neoliberal state forms of intervention and some of their basic assumptions. Section Three discusses three core components of neoliberal states that undergird the poverty industry: monetarism, corporate welfarism and workfarism. Section Four explains the roles played by debtfare states in the expansion and social reproduction of the poverty industry. Section Five concludes by summarising the argument.

A Marxian understanding of capitalist states

Marxist, or materialist, state theories represent a diverse and contested terrain. My particular reading in this book draws on the work represented by the West German State Derivationist Debate[1] of the 1970s (Hirsch 1978, 1995; Altvater and Hoffmann, 1990) and various contributions from the Conference on Socialist Economists (CSE), which took place in the 1970s and 1980s (Holloway and Picciotto, 1978; Clarke, 1988). The many points of disagreement with regard to these various strands within broader materialist approach to the state have been well-documented.[2] For our purposes here, we focus broadly on the principal contribution of materialist state theories: capitalist states must be subjected to the same Marxian techniques of deconstruction (i.e., those based in historical materialism) that I employed in previous chapters to denaturalise money and credit. Just as Marx seeks to deconstruct seemingly neutral categories such as the commodity and money to reveal their inner social content, materialist state theories, which are based on historical accounts of Western liberal democracies, also attempt to deconstruct seemingly neutral categories, such as bourgeois law and parliamentary democracy to expose their inner social content. A materialist framing treats capitalist states as historical social relations that shape and in turn are shaped by, the dynamics of capital accumulation. It follows from this view that they are highly complex and contradictory fields of struggle that cannot be understood either as instruments of class rule or as autonomous political actors (Clarke, 1988).

A materialist view of capitalist states facilitates the deconstruction of states as autonomous political institutions along the same lines of analytical duality applied in the previous investigations into money and credit. On the one hand, we can study the fetishised articulations of capitalist states as democratic, pluralistic, egalitarian institutions that not only embody the common good in the judiciary, executive and political arenas, but also stand apart from the market (cf. Dahl, 1965; Evans et al. 1985). Much of the financialisation literature replicates this stance, relying on an institutionalised view of the state as removed from the dynamics of capital accumulation. Assuming the state occupies an extra-economic sphere, however, leads to an incomplete and overpoliticised explanation of the state (Strange, 1988; Helleiner, 1994; Germain, 1997; Leyshon and Thrift, 1997).[3]

It is worthwhile re-emphasising that designating state forms as fetishised does not imply they are illusions. Nothing could be further from the truth. These fetishised articulations of everyday social existence take differentiated but very real institutionalised forms. As Simon Clarke (1991: 10) argues, however, 'the central point is that these institutionalised forms only derive their content from the social relations which they express and so it is only on the basis of those social relations that they can be understood and their development explained'. Similar to the community of money, relations of power and class domination exist below the fetishised surfaces (forms) of bourgeois states and their apparently egalitarian institutions.[4]

Capitalist states assume separate and neutral forms to guarantee the expansion and social reproduction of capital accumulation because these functions cannot be fulfilled by individual capitalists and still maintain *economic fictions* aimed at representing capitalism as naturally evolving and harmonious in nature; that is, premised on freedom, democracy and equality (Hirsch, 1978; Holloway and Picciotto, 1978). Unlike the mainstream and post-structuralist accounts of states in the financialisation literature, materialist understandings of capitalist states do not see the emergence of the state as the result of the conscious activity of society in pursuit of its 'general will'; but instead, as the result of often contradictory and short-sighted class struggles and conflicts that frame, and are framed by, the dynamics of capital accumulation (Hirsch, 1978: 65). The nature of state intervention as a response to perceived threats to capital accumulation is complex, contradictory and dynamic. These interventions may best be designated as what Hirsch refers to as *reactive mediations*, by which he means that capitalist states are able to intervene into the processes of capital accumulation in an *ex post facto*, temporary and paradoxical manner only (Hirsch 1978; von Braunmühl *et al.*, 1973).

A materialist understanding of capitalist states allows us to see the class power, or *content*, inherent to all bourgeois state formations. States have institutional attributions, or concrete *forms*, that are spatially and historically differentiated. These take various expressions; for example, government departments or ministries that are populated by politicians, technocrats and bureaucrats that design, implement and articulate policies, regulations and laws. It cannot be stressed enough, however, that these institutionalised (concrete) state forms derive their content from the social relations of the capitalist mode of production and exchange and consequently reflect the tensions therein. To capture the institutional forms of capitalist states, such as debtfarism, I complement my materialist approach with theorists who employ different conceptual resources to analyse the class dynamics and power inherent in institutionalised articulations of state forms in contemporary capitalism, specifically neoliberalism (Peck and Tickell, 2002).

Neoliberalisation: meanings and assumptions

Rhetoric and regulation

The rhetorical landscape of neoliberalism in this study refers to the ideological and disciplinary features inherent to government policy, speeches from elected officials, bureaucrats and technocrats (e.g., legal and economic advisors), government-sponsored studies, special task force reports and so forth. I apply a materialist lens to these discursive state artefacts to understand how they naturalise and universalise neoliberal beliefs and values that are aimed at facilitating the expansion and reproduction of the poverty industry (Gramsci, 1971; Eagleton, 2007). In this sense, my understanding of rhetoric follows and builds on the work of Pierre Bourdieu (1991, 2009); Stephen Gill (1995); Loïc Wacquant (2009), Jamie Peck (2010) – all of whom, in different ways, stress the inseparability between institutional, material and discursive elements of neoliberalism and the power relations therein.

By regulative features of neoliberalisation, I am referring to the institutional expression of state powers in the form of laws issued and sanctioned by the state that pertain to the poverty industry, most notably usury and bankruptcy laws as well as consumer protection initiatives. The legal terrain explored in the case studies encompasses both informal (voluntary or soft law) and formal (mandatory or hard law) rules (Cutler, 2003; Leyshon and Thrift, 1997; Picciottio, 2011). The regulatory dimensions of neoliberal states are important for understanding the power relations of the poverty industry. This is because regulation aimed at not only depoliticising and managing (in an *ex post facto* manner) the tensions inherent to credit-led accumulation, but also imposing social discipline with regard to the surplus population. A Marxian lens allows us to pierce the fetishised appearance of the rule of law in all its various articulations (May, 2012, 2014) and grasp that inequality and class power are internal to law, despite its classical liberal claims of universal principles that strive to achieve equal rights and justice for all legal subjects (Mattei and Nader, 2008; Baars, 2011; Bruff, 2014). As will become clearer below, the appearance of neutrality in the law provides a cloak for extra-legal forms of state power (Picciotto, 2011) that act as scaffolding for the community of money.

Meanings of neoliberalism

Broadly speaking, neoliberal forms of state intervention first emerged in Chile in the mid- 1970s (Taylor, 2006) and then early 1980s in the Anglo-American countries (e.g., United States and United Kingdom) before spreading, albeit in a differentiated and uneven manner, throughout the world (Soederberg et al., 2005). Despite the variegated articulations of neoliberal state forms across regional, national and local scales of governance, there are several core features and fundamental assumptions shared and propagated, by all neoliberal states forms (Peck and Tickell, 2002; Brenner et al., 2010; van Apeldoorn et al., 2012).

First, neoliberal state forms emerged from the demise of previous state forms, such as Keynesian welfare states in the global North (Peck, 2010; Crouch, 2011) and their counterparts in the global South (Woo-Cumings, 1999; cf. Burkett and Hart-Landsberg, 2003; Soederberg, 2010c) to deal effectively with the underlying tensions and crises in capital over-accumulation and the subsequent social fallouts, such as labour unrests, civil rights movement, rampant unemployment, increasing levels of public debt, runaway inflation and low growth rates (Altvater, 1993; Bonefeld and Holloway, 1995; Harvey, 2005). Second, in response to these struggles and tensions, the rhetorical and regulatory features of neoliberal state forms include: a withdrawal or abstention by the state in economic matters; the shifting into the private sector (or, the contracting out) of public services and the commodification of public goods such as health, housing, safety, education and culture – e.g., radio and television – into commercial goods, turning the users of these services into clients; and a renunciation of the power to equalise opportunities and reduce inequality (Bourdieu, 2005: 11).

Neoliberalism is a complex, contested and contradictory set of rhetorical and regulatory processes that emerged from a theoretical perspective generally referred to as neoclassical economics, which is largely associated here with the highly influential Chicago School and its iconic scholar, Milton Friedman (1993, 2002; cf. von Mises, 2009; von Hayek, 2011). Neoclassical economics formed the intellectual basis for guiding state policy in the United States in the late 1970s because it was widely accepted by dominant classes at a particular point in history and not because it was analytically sounder than its theoretical rival, namely Keynesianism. In contrast, the Chicago School could best address the threats perceived by powerful classes to the expansion and reproduction of capital accumulation. As Robert Cox advises, 'theory is always for someone and for some purpose' (Cox, 1995: 85). In what follows, I identify some of the core assumptions of neoclassical theory not only because it deepens our understanding of neoliberal states, but also because these underlying premises require constant reproduction, if their universality is to be legitimately imposed and accepted.

According to Bourdieu, neoclassical economics rests on two pervasive postulates, which these theorists largely regard as proven. First, 'the economy is a separate domain governed by natural and universal laws with which governments must not interfere by inappropriate intervention'. Second, 'the market is the optimum means for organising production and trade efficiency and equitably in democratic societies' (Bourdieu, 2005: 11). Milton Friedman, for instance, suggests that the main goal of society should be to ensure political freedom to its citizens through the establishment of economic freedom, otherwise known as the free market (Friedman, 1993). Both freedoms, according to Friedman, are based on removing state interference into the operations of the market.

> Viewed as a means to the end of political freedom, economic arrangements are important because of their effect on the concentration or dispersion of power. The kind of economic organisation that provides economic freedom directly, namely, competitive capitalism, also promotes political freedom

because it separates economic power from political power and in this way enables the one to offset the other.

(Friedman, 2002: 9)

Because individuals are inherently rational, they will pursue their economic interests. The best way to ensure the collective good is to ensure that these individual pursuits occur without the interference of states through for instance, price and wage caps, social assistance programmes and so forth (Albo, 1994; Peck, 2001; Altvater, 2009). On this view, the market will thus reward and punish individuals if they possess the *correct* incentives to voluntarily and meaningfully participate in the market, i.e., surrender to the social discipline of the *abstract* forces of the market (World Bank, 2012d).[5]

The rule of individuals is a recurrent and central theme in neoliberal rhetoric supporting the poverty industry. In the words of a key promoter of neoliberalism as universal value, British Prime Minister Margaret Thatcher (1979–1990) stated that there is '"no such thing as society, only individual men and women" – and, she subsequently added, their families. All forms of social security were to be dissolved in favour of individualism, private property, personal responsibility and family values' (Harvey, 2007: 23; Wacquant, 2009). With this veneration of individualisation and responsibilisation, failure to achieve economic success is located not in inequities of capitalism; but instead, in individual failings such as laziness, lack of entrepreneurial skills, adequate levels of knowledge and so forth (Bourdieu, 2005).

The assumptions of neoclassical economics are what Pierre Bourdieu refers to as an *economic common sense* rooted in a system of beliefs and values, an ethos and a moral view of the world based on a particular case: the United States. Through various rhetorical and regulative processes, the neoliberal state form seeks to universalise these particular beliefs and values by spreading and embedding them throughout the world.[6] As many scholars have demonstrated, a crucial instrument for this attempt to universalise the ethos and moral views of neoclassical economics has been through the policies pursued by the World Bank and International Monetary Fund (e.g., privatisation, liberalisation and fiscal austerity) often referred to as the Washington Consensus (Fine 2006; Soederberg, 2004, 2006). Although there are multiple and competing meanings of the rule of law (Dworkin, 1985; Carothers, 1997), the Washington Consensus promotes a particular version formulated in universal terms (e.g., common values and norms) with great appeal to and concern for, protecting vulnerable populations largely by ensuring that governments maintain predictable and transparent investment environments (Mattei and Nader, 2008; May, 2014). This dominant view of the rule of law, which has been closely associated with good governance principles ranging from transparency to anti-corruption, is the aimed at creating social justice by promoting laws and regulatory institutions that promote economic growth by upholding private property rights, rights to appropriation and contractual obligations (Commission on Global Governance, 1995; Cooter, 1997).

As components of capitalist states, the rhetorical and regulative features of neoliberalism are neither natural nor neutral nor static. Following Jamie Peck and

Adam Tickell, we are better to think in terms of neoliberalisation: i.e. constantly evolving, contradictory, open-ended and adaptive processes (Peck and Tickell, 2002). As Jamie Peck explains (2010: 7), 'neoliberalism has never been about a once-and-for-all liberalisation, an evacuation of the state from the economy, but instead rolling programmes of market-oriented reform, a kind of permanent revolution of free-market liberation'. For Peck (2010) and others, a primary driver of continual experiments in market-based governance is the tension in the utopian nature of the assumptions underpinning neoliberalism, that is, the unrealisable goal of free markets (Altvater, 1993, 2009). Pierre Bourdieu (1998: 96), for instance, suggests that neoliberalism is based on a separation between economic and social realities and seeks to construct a reality in which an economic system corresponds to the (neoclassical) *economic fictions* of theory, a type of logical machine based on the assumption of rational actors, 'which presents itself as a chain of constraints impelling the economic agents'. While the continual attempt to reconstruct neoliberal state on these utopian premises of neoclassical economics leads to recurring paradoxes that must be resolved through rhetoric and regulations, or what Jamie Peck (2010) refers to as *fail forward* strategies, we must not lose sight of their connective tissue to the dynamics of credit-led accumulation, which includes the poverty industry and the power relations therein.

Having laid the conceptual floorboards of a materialist understanding of capitalist states, the remainder of this chapter turns to addressing two core questions: What roles have states played in facilitating the expansion and reproduction of credit-led accumulation and, by extension, the poverty industry? And, how have states sought to discipline and reimpose silent compulsions, while maintaining the illusions of the community of money and thereby masking the exploitative features of the poverty industry? To answer these queries, I identify several components of neoliberal states that have played central roles in facilitating these dispossessive strategies: monetarism, corporate welfarism, workfarism and debtfarism. Although each does so in different ways, all four neoliberal components actively draw on the social power of money and seek to shift the articulation of tensions away from the realm of production to the realm of exchange (e.g., the community of money). This serves to normalise and depoliticise struggles associated with the discipline and dispossession of surplus labour through the secondary forms of exploitation in the poverty industry.

The core components of neoliberal states

Monetarism and the social power of privately created money

Monetarism is central to our approach because it serves to frame the regulative and rhetorical landscape of neoliberalism and its interventions into credit-led accumulation. Monetarism describes a set of economic premises originally based in the neoclassical approach (Peck, 2010). According to monetarism, the key economic ills of the day were associated with inflation and the root cause of inflation is excess money. As such, to tackle high rates of inflation, or the general rise in prices – which grew rampant throughout many countries in the late 1970s and 1980s – central banks were urged to control the growth of money supply through the manipulation of interest rates (Cerny, 1997; Panitch and Gindin, 2012). Once the money supply is under control – and assuming governments do not engage in 'fine-tuning' the economy through redistributive policies characteristic of the proceeding Keynesian era – Friedman suggested that markets would equilibrate to create employment opportunities for those willing to work (Friedman, 2002). On this basis, monetarists were fundamentally against redistributive policies to alleviate unemployment and poverty.[7]

Monetarism reinforces credit-led accumulation in several important ways (Clarke, 1988). It assumes that when given the proper market-based regulative environment markets will miraculously reach an equilibrium from which most people will benefit. Monetarism moreover is based on the belief that unemployment is either voluntary (people prefer leisure to work) or due to barriers in the labour market, such as workers demanding higher wages and benefits, the existence of minimum wages, unemployment insurance and so forth (Albo, 1994; Drainville, 1995; Bourdieu, 1998, 2005). Largely due to its assumptions of the causes of unemployment, its hyper-individualised view of the world and its blind-faith in the market's natural ability to achieve full-employment equilibrium, monetarism justifies its focus on controlling inflation as opposed to reducing unemployment or addressing poverty issues.

To understand the class-based nature of this emphasis on inflation, it is useful to look briefly at who benefits the most from this policy focus in the era of credit-led accumulation.

Inflation is, of course, a persistent concern not only for states and capitalists, but also for ordinary people, particularly those on a fixed income, such as government assistance. However, powerful interests are also adversely affected by rising inflation levels. Financial institutions (e.g., banks, hedge funds, payday lenders, credit card companies, student loan providers, microfinance lenders and so forth), which are the key players in the poverty industry, dislike high inflation rates because it erodes the value of their (privately created) money. Jim Stanford (2008: 201–2) lucidly explains this position with the following example:

> If a bank charges 5 percent annual interest for a loan when overall prices are also growing at 5 percent, the bank's wealth doesn't change – because the loaned money, once repaid with interest, has no more purchasing power than it did when it was loaned out. If interest rates are *lower* than inflation, the real interest rate is *negative*: the borrower, not the lender, is better off at the end of the loan because the money they pay back is worth less than the money they borrowed.

As an integral feature of neoliberal state forms, monetarism is not a neutral and apolitical strategy; but instead a class-based project aimed at managing, absorbing and depoliticising struggles and tensions emerging from credit-led accumulation

(Clarke, 1988). Readers will recall from the previous chapter that unlike (physical) money, credit money is privately created money that emerges to deal with the strains placed on money as a store of value. However, due to its internal contradictions, credit can only provide temporary solutions to the strains in the processes of capital accumulation that it was intended to resolve. And, as discussed in Chapter 2, credit ends up heightening as opposed to absorbing these tensions. Credit money in the form of either fictitious capital or consumer credit is privately created and thus increases in volume in a disorderly (unregulated) manner to deal with the barriers to capital accumulation. As such, a core component of the social power of money is threatened. The ability of money to retain its social power – that is, its function as a trusted store of value – needs to be safeguarded.

Protecting the quality of money becomes difficult when privately created credit begins to dominate the accumulation processes. The tendency for credit to enter into swindling and gambling tendencies is always present, but is particularly acute in times when expanded value production is less lucrative than generating income through interest and fees (M ... M^1). Regardless of how far afield credit-led accumulation strategies move, however, they must ultimately return to their place of origin for redemption. If a substantial amount of debt along the complex chain of speculative transactions (as in the case of asset-backed securitisation) cannot be redeemed and/or if the gap between the fictitious value of credit and money becomes too wide, the quality of money is called into question, which threatens its social power. This situation has played itself out over and over again in the spate of crises over the past two decades, from the Mexican Peso Crisis in 1994–1995 (Soederberg, 2004) to the dot-com crisis in the early 2000s (Soederberg, 2010c and d) to the spectacular 2008 financial crisis, which was ignited by the US subprime mortgage debacle (Schwartz, 2009; Wyly et al., 2009; Konings, 2010).

The basic reason for this is that excess levels of privately created credit money (and their fictitious values) place downward pressure on the quality of money, which is devalued through inflationary pressures. Moreover, the tensions inherent to credit money inevitably result in crises of confidence in the value of money, in both its physical and credit forms. In contrast to Friedman and his followers, who assume that the only impact of money (viewed as a neutral object or thing) is to determine the absolute price level, our materialist understanding of money allows us to deconstruct its fetishised form to grasp that it is a social power without an intrinsic value. On this view, any policy designed to manipulate the supply of money (represented as a neutral *thing*) and its impact on the general price level is first and foremost a political act rooted in class-based power, not a technical exercise. It therefore comes as no surprise that such policies shift attention away from unemployment and poverty.

The ability to depoliticise neoliberal restructuring through monetarism has served as a formidable and effective way to mask the class nature of these policies as well as to subject people to the social power of money. A key state institution that bolsters this power is central banks. Central banks are the key places in neoliberal state forms that are in charge of fighting inflation and conducting monetarist policies. Central banks have the power to regulate everything from prices to job creation to incomes. Moreover, in many countries, central banks perform their duties without any direct accountability whatsoever to the broader population, or even to other segments of the state (Drainville, 1995; Stanford, 2008). Through a variety of regulative and rhetorical machinations, central banks are portrayed as independent and 'apolitical', that is, free from political interference or capitalist influence as well as free from democratic oversight, to insulate its inflation-controlling mandate from popular pressure (Stanford, 2008: 211).[8]

The illusion of neutrality of central banks and the class-content of monetarism aimed at subjecting the working poor to the exigencies of the self-equilibrating and rational market, while protecting the interests of capitalists benefiting from various forms of credit-led accumulation is vital to the general reproduction of capitalism. The representation and reproduction of the central bank as a nonaligned, technical and thus apolitical institution, is thus vastly important to managing paradoxes in credit-led accumulation, most notably ensuring the social power of money by guaranteeing its value. Seen from this angle, the shift to monetarism also represents regulative and rhetorical attempts by neoliberal state forms to depoliticise struggles.

Through monetarism and its institutional form of the central bank, neoliberal states have been able to protect and invoke the social power of money as a central disciplinary machination in credit-led accumulation. The basic expression of this power is its ability to veil and distort relations of exploitation, inequality and domination by shifting focus away from the sphere of production, which is a core source of the swelling surplus population. Rhetoric and regulative activities are instead transferred to the realm of exchange, which its formal emphasis on equality, democracy and freedom. As I discussed in Chapter 1, Marx refers to this illusion as the community of money.

The rhetorical and regulative features of monetarism support *economic fictions* suggesting that unfettered market freedom and competitive individualism can spur economic growth and break the rise of inflation. Given its ability to effectively reduce all social issues (poverty, unemployment, underemployment, etc.) to technical features of (objectified) money, monetarism acts to depoliticise overt class politics and has provided the ideological and institutional scaffoldings for credit-led accumulation to take hold and flourish. In doing so, it enables capitalists to make 'money out of money in a desperate attempt to accumulate as much as possible without getting dirty in the contested terrain of production' (Bonefeld, 1995: 55; see also, Clarke, 1988). The rise of the poverty industry in the 1990s is a case in point.

Corporate welfarism and the class power of privately created money

A second principal component of neoliberalism that has served to undergird the poverty industry may be captured by the term corporate welfarism. Although this term has been employed in different ways (Whitfield, 2001; Slivinski, 2006; 'The Corporate Welfare State: a cause to unite the tea party and the occupy Wall Street crowd', *The Wall Street Journal*, 8 November 2011), I view corporate welfarism as an integral feature of neoliberal state intervention that provides rhetorical and regulative forms of state protection for powerful capitalists. Complementing the broader neoliberal strategies of privatising state-owned enterprises as well as financial and trade liberalisation, corporate welfarism refers to a state strategy that seeks to meet the needs of capitalist interests and needs through government initiatives such as socialisation of investment risk and debt, subsidies, tax loopholes, loan guarantees and so forth (Soederberg, 2010b). Corporate welfarism plays a central role in the expansion financial corporations that dominate the poverty industry examined in this book, such as Sallie Mae in the student loan industry (Chapter 3), Advance America in the payday loan industry (Chapter 4), Grupo Elektra in microfinance industry in Mexico (Chapter 5) and so forth.

The legitimation underpinning corporate welfarism is based on the neoliberal belief in the power of markets to achieve economic growth and general prosperity for everyone. A key tenet therein is that states must facilitate powerful market actors, namely corporations, not through restrictive regulatory measures (e.g., interest rate caps); but rather by providing the most optimal investment environment in which corporations can flourish and, in turn, create jobs. Seen from a neoliberal perspective, states should strive to create a pro-competition and pro-business policy environment that will attract and retain corporations, or what Philip Cerny and others have described as competition states (Hirsch, 1995; Cerny, 1997; Soederberg *et al.*, 2005). Framed by the monetarist justification for lower policy prioritisation of unemployment and poverty, neoliberal states should neither strive to provide social protection for their most vulnerable citizens, nor aim toward redistribution of income through progressive forms of taxation, as was the goal of Keynesian welfare policies. According to the neoliberal paradigm, both of these goals are misplaced as they serve to distort price signals, dull the competitive nature of individuals and interfere with the inherent rationality of markets. As such, to ensure the social protection of the poor and, more generally, the creation of optimal conditions to foster employment equilibrium, states should strive to safeguard the economic well-being of corporations, as the latter are seen as playing an effective role in protecting the poor.

One way in which corporate welfare strategies have facilitated attempts to overcome the tensions of capital accumulation has been by channelling workers' old age savings (pensions) into corporate coffers (Minns, 2001; Soederberg, 2010a and b), As pension funds across the constituencies of the Organisation for Economic Cooperation and Development (OECD) have ramped up investment in corporate stocks and bonds, workers have become increasingly dependent on the economic performance of corporations for the value of their retirement savings. In 2008, in the wake of the Great Crash, pension funds still allocated about half of their assets, approximately $10 trillion, into corporate equity holdings. In the US alone, total assets in equity holdings amounted to $3.5 trillion, down from $5.6 trillion in 2007, but still higher than after the dot-com crisis at the start of the new millennium (OECD, 2009). Encouraged by the prescriptions of their creditors, particularly the World Bank (1994), the Mexican government, as with many countries in the global South, began privatising its old age pension system in 1997 (Madrid, 2002). This corporate welfare initiative was undertaken concurrent to reducing and closing many welfare programmes and institutions (Luccisano, 2006: 62; Marier, 2008).

Through corporate welfare initiatives neoliberal states have constructed a reality in which workers' savings in the form of pension funds feed off of both their own increased indebtedness and that of other workers, a condition driven largely by stagnant real wages, the absence of an adequate social safety net and high levels of structural unemployment and underemployment. As evidenced in the US, the dependence of pension funds on high-risk ventures leads to a situation in which investment strategies mutilate the value of pension savings with the advent of more frequent and intensified financial crises, wiping out gains made during a speculative run. Instead of serving to weaken credit-led accumulation, however, financial crises and subsequent forms of corporate welfarism, have had the effect of deepening neoliberalisation by allowing financial corporations that are tied to the poverty industry (and their shareholders, which include pension funds) to prey on dispossessed workers, who strive to maintain basic living standards through the credit system (Soederberg, 2010a). In the late 1990s, for instance, institutional investors such as mutual and pension funds began to seize hold of consumer debt (credit cards, student loans and so forth), transforming it into new and profitable investment opportunities. As discussed in Chapter 2, a key strategy used in generating interest income from consumer debt involves asset-backed securities. ABS involves bundling a stream of future repayments on, for example, student loans and credit cards, to provide the basis for the issue and payment of interest and principle on securities (e.g., dividends on corporate stock). I discuss this in more detail in Parts II and III of the book.

Despite their ability to invoke and protect the social power of money, as well as to guide policy formation for the other components of the neoliberal state (e.g., workfare and debtfare), monetarism and corporate welfarism do not directly manage the social reproduction of the surplus population. The neoliberal state feature that disciplines and normalises marginalisation through the social power of money is workfarism, to which I now turn my attention.

Workfarism and the social power of money

As I discussed in the previous chapter, the relative surplus population is inherent to the processes of capital accumulation, even if its articulations and constituency (in terms of race, gender and class identities) vary across space and time. The relative surplus population does not replicate itself automatically but has been socially reproduced historically by active forms of state intervention ranging from workhouses to welfare states (Shragge, 1997). Put another way, the coercive and ideological aspects of capitalist states have played a role in reproducing the basic imperative of surplus labour to earn a living based on dispossession, expropriation and dependence on the market as if it were a natural and inevitable feature of life (Denning, 2010). At a basic level, the motivation to socially reproduce the surplus population, which is a central feature of capital accumulation, is vital in order that capitalists have a ready and steady supply of eager and easily exploitable workers. Workfare states are the neoliberal variant of these state forms aimed at normalising and disciplining the relative surplus population.

Like monetarism, workfarism also relies on the social power of money (in the form of state benefits) to impose more direct discipline on the surplus population. Workfarism, which began to emerge in the early 1970s with the general decline of welfare states, refers to neoliberal strategies that have come to replace previous forms of disciplining labour, namely: welfare regimes (Piven and Cloward, 1993). Workfarism serves to regulate labour and discipline workers through the deterrence of claims for social assistance benefits (Jessop, 1993; Shragge, 1997; Collins and Mayer, 2010). In the wider parameters of neoliberalism – with its assumptions of hyper-individualism, its attempts to commodify all aspects of life and its demand for responsibility – workfare strives to socially reproduce the surplus population (cf. Wacquant, 2009). As Eric Shragge (1997: 29–30, quoted in Peck, 2001: 35) observes, 'The surplus population, though "excluded" from the labour market, is in other ways attached to it. Workfare policies tied the surplus population to the discipline of the labour market and workfare is the means of marshalling them towards it'. Workfare also serves to reinforce the dictates of neoliberalism and monetarism, regarding the common sense assumption that unemployment and, by extension, poverty is either voluntary or the result of labour market rigidities.

The rhetoric and regulative aspects of workfarism comprise an important feature of neoliberal state forms that are employed to individualise, demobilise and thereby strip away possibilities for collective action of marginalised workers, while subjecting them to class power in the impersonal form of the exigencies of the market. As Jamie Peck explains, workfare is aimed at getting the non-working poor (e.g., the unemployed) to work – a segment of the population that has been growing rapidly across the globe. The increased numbers of these workers is due, in part, to the nature of credit-led accumulation and its lack of investment in production in the United States; and, in part, to the draconian welfare reform in the United States in the mid-1990s, most notably the Clinton Administration's Personal Responsibility and Work Opportunity Reconciliation (or, PRWORA) of 1996. As discussed above, a key component of the workfare state is premised on the exchange of employment (e.g., cleaning public housing and the offices of the private agencies administering welfare programmes) for government assistance, with an eye on weaning people off the latter completely (Collins and Mayer, 2010). As Peck (2001: 10) explains:

> The essence of workfarism [in its variegated national forms] . . . involves the imposition of a range of compulsory programmes and mandatory require-ments for welfare recipients with a view to *enforcing work while residualizing*

welfare. This does not mean that welfare itself completely disappears, but it does mean that the logic, structure and dynamics of the system of poor relief are transformed so as to maximize work participation while minimizing 'dependency' on welfare.

Workfarism is a boundary feature of the neoliberal state in that it seeks to mediate the paradoxes in the labour market by socialising the surplus population, many of whom are single mothers, to the norms of the workforce (Peck, 2001; Wacquant, 2009). Workfare also creates and manages workers' expectations with regard to work and wages, employment continuity, promotion and security (Peck, 2001; Collins and Mayer, 2010).

While Peck's formulation of workfare was primarily in terms of Anglo-American capitalism, the normalising and disciplinary features of workfare are also evident, albeit in different forms, in Mexico. Despite neoliberal promises reflected in the Washington Consensus, wage stagnation, underemployment and inflation have served to erode the income level of some 31 million Mexicans and lead to ever-increasing socio-economic inequalities ('Mexico's Poverty Conundrum', *Financial Times*, 11 April 2013). For instance, real minimum wage has fallen in Mexico by 73 percent since 1976 to a historic low of 34 pesos per day (Barkin, 2009). According to Mexico's National Council on the Evaluation of Social Development Policy (or, CONEVAL), the number of Mexicans living in poverty in 2010 was 52.3 million, or 46.2 percent of the population (CONEVAL, 2012).[9] Yet, there is a growing and large part of Mexico's population that is not included in the counting of incomes and salaries. The National Institute of Statistics and Geography of Mexico (INEGI) says some 57 percent of Mexico's economically active population work in the informal sector ('Mexico's Poverty Conundrum', *Financial Times*, 11 April 2013).[10] The latter encompasses wide and varied forms of employment from street vendors to Mexico's expansive black market, i.e., counterfeit and stolen goods markets (cf. INEGI, 2012).

To deal with this growing mass of surplus labour, Mexico has turned to increasingly individualised and market-based strategies aimed at dealing with the growing surplus population. Since the mid-2000s, the government has cut broad-based social spending, opting instead to target programmes for those in extreme poverty, such as PROGRESA in 1997 and its replacement, Oportunidades founded in 2002 (Yanes, 2011; Soederberg, 2010c). In 2006, approximately one-quarter of Mexico's population participated in the conditional transfer payments that define Oportunidades (Moreno-Brid *et al.*, 2009).

Both PROGRESA and Oportunidades were specifically aimed at appeasing and depoliticising the increasing presence of resurgent popular movements, while acting as a bromide for the masses, so as to signal political stability and a well-disciplined and relatively cheap labour market [11] made possible by ongoing forms of the structural violence of labour, e.g., dereliction of labour laws and the dominance of precarious work (Wacquant, 2009). True to neoliberal assumptions and mirroring the US workfare state, Oportunidades strives to create a disciplined and productive labour force for the future by conferring greater responsibilities on the poor by drawing on the social power of money as a mechanism whereby the poor can begin to resolve *their* problems without relying on society (Barkin, 2009). Oportunidades draws on the social power of money to ensure that the poor, many of whom are mothers, embrace the spirit of responsibilisation and individualisation and become creditworthy consumers of welfare by, for example, working hard toward ensuring their children's human capital development (e.g., school attendance) (Luccisano, 2006). In this way, both Oportunidades and the Personal Responsibility and Work Opportunity Reconciliation Act (PRWORA) 1996 initiative in the US strive to create market citizens, but without the right to a living wage and thus the right to lay claim to basic subsistence needs.

As was the case with monetarism, workfarism emphasises the realm of exchange and its alleged freedoms (choice between working and not receiving welfare support), democracy and equality (equal exchange of work for welfare). The realm of production and neoliberal restructuring policies, which have served to throw these workers out of a living wage and social protections are not broached. The deleterious effects of neoliberal restructuring on the productive sectors in the US and Mexico are also avoided in the individualising and market-based rhetoric and regulative features of workfarism. This will become clearer in the following two parts of the book.

Debtfarism and the poverty industry

Debtfarism reinforces and encapsulates the three components of neoliberalism discussed above. The regulatory and rhetorical processes that mark debtfarism have directly facilitated the expansion and reproduction of the poverty industry since the 1990s by serving to naturalise the commodification of social reproduction. Paralleling the neoliberal insistence that there is no better alternative but for individuals to rely on the market, the rhetorical and regulative features of debtfare states serve to back widespread reliance on expensive consumer credit to augment and/or replace the social wage or a welfare cheque. In this sense, debtfarism supports workfare strategies by imposing market discipline on the working poor.

As with monetarism and workfarism, debtfarism calls on the social power of money to overcome the tensions that are heightened by the spatio-temporal fixes of dispossessive capitalism (see Chapter 2). By promoting the growing dependence of the poor on credit for basic subsistence, debtfarism draws on and, in turn, reinforces the *concrete abstractions* of money and the related monetisation of social relationships (i.e., relations between things), which underpin the community of money (Harvey, 1989). The secondary exploitative nature of consumer credit is concealed through the social power of money (realm of exchange) and its class nature is distorted through formalised abstractions (interest rates and late fees), as opposed to primary forms of exploitation between employer and employee.

Debtfarism embodies a complex, tension-ridden and differentiated set of rhetorical and regulatory processes aimed at facilitating and normalising the reliance on credit, while foregoing a material compromise with the working class (i.e., public support for the social wage). As we will see in the case studies that follow, this is accomplished in various ways, depending on the type of credit and the national context. However, there are three shared traits: selling the idea of financial inclusion and/or democratisation of credit; teaching people to fear market sanctions for transgressing the privilege of inclusion; and facilitating the further displacement of the underlying tensions of credit-led accumulation.

First, debtfare states seek, through regulative and rhetorical means, to (re-)create the community of money that reflects the constructed illusion of *one class, one society* (Gramsci, 1971). For example, the attempts by states at designating the poor as consumers or, as in the case as the United States, as middle class (Chapter 7), serves as a powerful trope to de-class, de-gender and de-racialise the working poor. In effect, this acts to depoliticise and naturalise debt relations among the poor. Put differently, debtfarism safeguards the illusions of market freedoms and equality to ensure that all *consumers* may benefit from standards of fairness, competition, transparency and accountability. These market freedoms backed by debtfarism are continually framed in the illusions of the community of money and bolstered by the seeming neutrality of the legal obligation of debt and consumer protection. It also bears repeating that as neoliberal forms of governance, debtfarism does not operate exclusively at the national level. Instead, it should be understood as multi-scalar in scope and meaning (Peck and Tickell, 2002; Brenner *et al.*, 2010; Macartney and Shields, 2011).

The above strategy of debtfarism is also evident in the democratisation of credit trope, which was the precursor to the financial inclusion agenda. In the the United States, a series of federal legislations during the 1970s, including the Equal Credit Opportunity Act of 1975 and the Community Reinvestment Act (or, CRA) of 1977, extended the provision of credit to hitherto excluded communities, effectively reducing credit-related discrimination (Federal Reserve Board, 2008). But these initiatives reinforced market individualism by attempting to shift democratic values (equality and freedom) from the political to the economic sphere in order to foster 'a broader sharing of the benefits of the society's economic endowments by a wider spectrum of consumers' (Austin, 2004: 1255). In doing so, the euphemism of democratisation of credit masked exploitative and unequal relations of power by locating, framing and solving struggles among poor 'consumers' within the (ostensibly) apolitical market.

Focusing on the realm of exchange allowed banks – rather than the cuts to public housing and social services that were driven by neoliberal restructuring policies – to be framed as the fundamental cause of the economic decline of inner cities (Minton, 2008). Within the parameters of the democratisation of credit, solving social problems rested on extending market citizenship to the poor based on credit scores that were allied to a false sense of respectability and security. As will become clear throughout the various case studies in this book, credit acceptance meant social inclusion into the community of money. Without a living wage, however, the price paid for this inclusion was particularly high for lower class Americans, especially for women, ethnic and racial minorities.

While debtfarism mediates the surplus population, it concurrently plays into the trajectories of capital accumulation at national and global levels. The democratisation of credit trope in the United States, for instance, emerged around the same time as usury laws regarding consumer lending were being dismantled in 1978. This was a key strategy to overcoming the inflationary barriers to capital accumulation. As I will demonstrate in Parts II and III of this book, financial inclusion as a core feature of the development agenda also coincides with a wave of financial liberalisation schemes and the rise of asset-backed securitisation (ABS).

Simultaneously, debtfarism has facilitated spatio-temporal fixes to credit-led accumulation strategies by allowing private creditors to supplement low-paying, low-benefit jobs. In doing so, debtfarism supports largely marketised forms of the social reproduction of segments of surplus labour (Collins and Mayer, 2010; Albeda, 2012). Second, debtfarism buoys consumption levels and thus creates markets for retailers (e.g., Grupo Elektra in Mexico as discussed in Chapter 8) and construction companies (e.g., CEMEX in Mexico as discussed in Chapter 9) by allowing the surplus population to continue to purchase durables (houses and cars) as well as non-durables (clothing, food, medicine and so forth). Such strategies are aimed at integrating members of the relative surplus population within capitalist society despite their exclusion from the capital relation in the most important sense, that is, without the ability to earn a social wage. Marx refers to this as the expanded reproduction of capital as opposed to interest-generating revenue (i.e., M . . . M^1, as discussed in Chapter 2).

A second, and related, feature of debtfarism serves to further expose the surplus population to market discipline by ensuring that debtors accept employment under any conditions to meet payment on their debts. The secondary forms of exploitation inherent to debt relations act to socialise and impose temporal discipline over the excluded masses in order to serve the prerogatives of capital. Citizens are taught to be respectful/fearful of the consequences of market discipline. These include the coercive tactics employed by collection agencies, such as the threat of court proceedings, prison and so forth; the less onerous imposition by creditors of expensive late fees and other pecuniary penalties; and the lowering of one's credit scores – all of which result in either lack of access to credit or higher risk premiums on the next issuance of credit.

As mentioned above, the disciplinary features of debtfarism intersect with other facets of neoliberal state forms, such as workfare. As we saw above, workfare also creates and manages workers' expectations with regard to work and wages, employment continuity, promotion and security (Peck, 2001; Collins and Mayer, 2010). Forced into low-wage employment, actual and former welfare recipients, many of whom are single mothers, turn to payday loans to subsidise subsistence needs (Karger, 2005). As we will see in Chapter 7, there appears to correlation between the boom in the payday lending industry in the mid-1990s and the introduction of workfare. One study has revealed a strong causality between welfare (workfare) recipients and payday borrowing (Stegman and Faris, 2005; see Chapter 6).

Debtfarism buttresses the disciplinary features of the workfare state by legally permitting payday lenders to target and exploit a specific segment of workers, thereby generating enormous amounts of income from uncapped interest rates and the continual extension of expensive forms of credit to the working poor. The expansion of payday lending to welfare recipients also subjects payday borrowers to the temporality of market discipline by compelling them to accept any form of work to meet the repayment criteria on their loans. Thus, aside from facilitating secondary forms of exploitation, consumer credit for the poor has become an effective neoliberal method for providing a social basis for dispossessive capitalism.

In keeping with the general tenets of neoliberalism, a central theme running through the concrete manifestation of debtfarism has been its ability to shift collective and rights-based worker protections toward individualised and marketised expressions of responsibilisation in which the state simply guarantees the formal equality of exchange. Through legal and regulatory means, for instance, the role of the debtfare state is to protect the ethos of freedom, equality and the hyper-individualised – as well as the de-racialised, de-classed and de-gendered – consumer by ensuring that payday lending companies act responsibly and rationally, upholding basic standards of fairness, transparency and accountability. This is evident in the consumer protection trope that runs through the case studies that follow.

Consumer protection is a key trope of debtfare, as it relocates social protection to the impersonal market and simultaneously redefines and normalises an individualised understanding of economic security in which the working poor are compelled to depend on themselves (e.g., to work harder, to work longer hours and to save more) and on the credit system, as opposed to relying on the protection of the state and/or employers. The dissemination of the idea that private consumption is more efficient than public consumption is central to neoliberalisation (Fine, 2002; Peck 2010).

Third and lastly, debtfarism serves to mediate the deepening tensions inherent to credit-led accumulation strategies. These include the persistent threat of defaults, weighing the fictitious value of credit against the need to guarantee money as a trusted store of value, managing the tendencies of credit to encourage swindling and gambling and so forth. As noted in Chapter 2, extending loans to the working poor entails a gamble with the future. For instance, debtors need to earn enough wages to sustain themselves (food, shelter and clothing) and meet the basic payment terms on their debt. The debtfare state mediates this tension by permitting creditors to rollover debts, as is the case of payday lending, facilitating coercive debt collection and management tactics through soft regulation, dismantling usury laws with regard to certain types of consumer credit and implementing increasingly harsh measures with regard to bankruptcy laws. As we will see in Part II, the continual revision of the US Bankruptcy Act is part and parcel of attempts to deal with the threat of defaults and thus reinforce the discipline and social power of credit money through the regulative processes of debtfarism.

Taken together, the above strategies of debtfarism bolster and reinforce the wider neoliberal state forms, such as monetarism, corporate welfarism and workfarism, to socially reproduce the growing numbers of surplus labourers while assisting in the continual expansion and intensification of credit-led accumulation. A common element running through all three strategies of debtfare is the continued attempts to reconstruct the fetishised appearance of the community of money and shifting the focus and root of struggle away from the realm of production to the realm of exchange. This, in turn, facilitates the normalisation of secondary forms of exploitation by guaranteeing appropriate and seemingly neutral structures of regulatory governance.

Debtfarism recreates the illusions of the community of money and upholds individualised market freedoms and responsibilisation, democracy and equality by actively representing consumer credit as a neutral and technical aspect of the market ruled by economics and law (bankruptcy laws, consumer protection legislation and usury laws). The implication is that this path is non-exploitative and class-neutral. The surplus population and capitalists thus confront each other as equal (i.e., voluntary agents as creditor and debtor), yet simultaneously unequal parties in the realm of exchange. However, neoliberal state forms are moving targets. The core components of neoliberal power, including debtfare and other intervention strategies, are constantly shifting and realigning to reactively mediate, depoliticise and absorb the unfolding tensions of credit-led accumulation.

To analytically capture the processes of debtfarism, I employ the term 'debtfare state' in the following six case studies. This term does not refer to a standalone state but rather to the institutionalised rhetorical and regulatory practices of debtfarism that have been embedded into the institutional forms of neoliberalism since the 1990s.

Concluding remarks

By providing a Marxian framing of state power in contemporary capitalism, I sought to complement our understanding of the social power of money and the paradoxes inherent to credit-led accumulation, with special reference to the poverty industry. I argued that a materialist understanding of capitalist states allows us to more fully grasp how neoliberal forms of domination have sought to mediate the poverty industry by invoking the social power of money to discipline and normalise the continual exploitation and marginalisation of the surplus population. In so doing, I explored the rhetorical and regulatory meanings of neoliberalism by identifying several of its significant – albeit not exclusive – components: monetarism, corporate welfarism and workfarism.

Moreover, I suggested that a particular component of neoliberal state intervention, namely debtfarism and its institutionalised expression – the debtfare state – plays a vital role in socially reproducing the expansion and intensification of secondary forms of exploitation of the working poor. Through its rhetorical and regulatory features, for instance, the debtfare state also draws on the social power of money to facilitate the general reproduction of surplus value in neoliberal times by ensuring that the dispossession and discipline of the surplus population appear as democratic, free and equal. Expressed differently, it is precisely because of the processes and structures discussed in the first three chapters of this book that the dominant illusion of freedom of exchange and liberty of contract continues to gull us all (Harvey, 1999, 2010a: 290). Framed in, and informed by, a historical materialist understanding of money, credit and states, the following six case studies strive to explain how and why the poverty industry and the surplus population have been reproduced and normalised.

Notes

1 In the 1970s and 1980s, the West German State Derivationist Debate emerged around questions regarding the (illusionary) separation between 'the economic' and 'the political' under capitalism (for an overview, see Carnoy 1980).
2 Contesting materialist accounts of state theory were widely and vigorously debated throughout the 1970s and early 1990s (Clarke, 1988; see also Carnoy 1984 for a good overview). Since this time, there have been few Marxian accounts of the nature of capitalist states with regard to money. This does not diminish the explanatory power of some of the general insights that can be gleaned from the general materialist approach to understanding capitalist states, however.
3 In Marxian terminology, this partial, institutionalised view of the state is referred to as the state *form*. On the other hand, however, we also see the capitalist content of the state's appearance by which we mean class-based forms of domination that are based in the processes of capital accumulation. Materialist state theorists refer to this side of the analytical equation as the state *content*. Unlike other approaches to states discussed earlier, a materialist perspective establishes and maintains the connective tissue between states and the processes of capital accumulation. This link is a vital method of materialism in permitting us to grasp the power and roles played by capitalist states in socially reproducing credit-led accumulation and the poverty industry in particular.
4 The question that emerges here is: 'What is it that gives rise to the constitution of the economic and the political as distinct moments of the same social relations?' (Holloway, 1994: 28). Or, as Marxist legal scholar Evgeny Pashukanis (1951: 185 quoted in Holloway and Picciottio, 1991: 113) queried in his famous quote:

> 'Why does the dominance of a class not continue to be that which it is – that is to say, the subordination in fact of one part of the population to another part? Why does it take on the form of official sate domination? Or, which is the same thing, why is not the mechanism of state constraint created as the private mechanism of the dominant class? Why is it disassociated from the dominant class – taking the form of an impersonal mechanism of public authority isolated from society'.

5 It will be recalled from our discussion in Chapter 1 that under capitalist social relations, individuals are compelled to surrender to the social discipline of abstract forces (e.g., Adam Smith's hidden hand of the market) that effectively govern their relations and choices (Harvey, 2010a: 42; see also, Wacquant, 2009; Peck, 2010).
6 The World Bank, for instance, actively encourages states to 'build institutions for markets'. The idea is that this will, in turn, foster competition within and between countries, firms, and individuals. The attraction and retention of foreign capital is expected to dramatically increase incomes and reduce poverty levels by modifying economic behaviour, i.e., by

introducing flexibility into markets, most notably labour markets (World Bank, 2002b). Labour flexibility, however, proved to be a euphemism for lifting social protection for workers, such as minimum wages, collective bargaining rights, social benefits, and so forth (Clarke, 1988; Taylor, 2008; Moody, 1997, 2007). Ultimately, labour market flexibilisiation eventually led to making workers more vulnerable to, and reliant on, the market for basic subsistence and social protection in both the global North and the global South.

7 In response to the inability of monetarist tools to achieve the natural full employment equilibrium, monetarism has been altered slightly. In an updated version of monetarism, it is also assumed that central banks should target the inflation rate to guide the economy to its full-employment equilibrium. Despite minor differences in its various incarnations, monetarism remains a central and extremely powerful component of neoliberal state forms (cf. Clarke, 1988; Peck, 2010).

8 The fetishised appearance of the neutrality of central banks is particularly poignant in the American case, as the Federal Reserve Bank is a complex mix of private and public governing agencies. Bourgeois law and the social power of money (expressed in terms of monetarism) underpin the ability of 'the Fed' to appear as class-neutral institution for the public benefit (see, for instance, Greider, 1989; 'Priceless: How The Federal Reserve Bought The Economics Profession', *Huffington Post*, 23 October 2009).

9 Another reading of these statistics sees a more positive trend, that is, extreme poverty down due to, among other things, the success of Oportunidades, For more information: www.wilsoncenter.org/article/mexico%E2%80%99s-latest-poverty-stats (accessed 17 January 2014).

10 The definition of informal workers is quite woolly and has been contested in the literature. For instance, the INEGI 2012 report, 'Mexico at a Glance', uses the concept of the informal *sector* to include informal commerce, which focuses data collection on housework, i.e., the 'percentage employed population that works in an economic unit operating with household resources' (INEGI, 2012: 16). The International Labour Organisation (ILO, 2003), however, prefers *informal economy*, which includes more categories of labour such as unemployed people who are interested in working but cannot find employment as well as auxiliary workers and relatives, without a contract or legal and/or social protection in formal and informal companies. The informal economy also includes workers employed in informal positions in formal and informal companies. The ILO's informal economy also includes categories of independent workers, and employers that own their own informal companies; as well as those who have formal positions in informal companies, and also members of cooperatives of informal producers (see, for example, ILO, 2012). Between 2006 and 2011, 65.8 percent of the new employment in Mexico was said to be created in the informal economy. For more information: www.idwn.info/news/mexico-658-informal-jobs-created-last-5-years (accessed 10 June 2013).

11 Wage stagnation in Mexico has closed the gap with their major competitor for foreign direct investment, China (see, for example, 'Mexican Labour: cheaper than China', *Financial Times*, 5 April 2013).

PART II

Debtfarism and the poverty industry in the United States

Preface to Part II

DEBTFARISM IN THE UNITED STATES AND THE MAKING OF THE POVERTY INDUSTRY

This second part of the book shifts the analysis to a concrete level of discussion of three significant features of the poverty industry in the United States: credit cards (Chapter 4), student loans (Chapter 5) and payday lending (Chapter 6). The US poverty industry entails a vast and multi-featured terrain, which includes automobile loans, pawnshops, subprime mortgage financing and so forth. As an integral feature of capital relations, the poverty industry is also highly dynamic and fluid in nature. This means, among other things, that the various components of poverty lending, such as the credit card industry, the student loan industry and the payday loan industry, do not exist in isolation from each other but are instead intertwined in at least three ways. The first is through the institutional, rhetorical and regulative pillars framing the credit system – all of which are linked to the state and, in particular, to its debtfarist modes of intervention. These pillars are anchored in, and also reflect, the power configurations in the wider dynamics of capital accumulation. Here I refer to both the realm of exchange and the sphere of production.

The second way in which the components of the poverty industry are intertwined is through their close alignment with mainstream banking, i.e., Wall Street; and the third is through the borrowing activities of debtors. A distressed debtor, for instance, may seek to pawn her wedding ring to help make a payment on her auto loan. A welfare-recipient who is strapped for cash after paying the minimum on her credit card may take out a payday loan to help buy school supplies for her children (Williams, 2004; Karger, 2005). A subprime homeowner may turn to his credit card to assist in meeting his monthly mortgage payment (Geisst, 2009). Although the following three case studies do not directly emphasise the linkages between different personal loans, the connection – implicitly made – is present in the everyday lives of the surplus population and increasingly in those of people with relatively more secure and well-paying jobs. The key difference between these two categories of labour power is that while surplus workers turn to expensive credit out of necessity, affluent workers use credit out of convenience.

In these chapters I examine the use of credit cards, student loans and payday loans. In current debates, these three nodes of the borrowing nexus remain undertheorised, especially with regard to the intersections of the social power of money, surplus workers and the state. The second reason I focus on these nodes is because they represent riskier forms credit. Credit cards, student loans and payday loans are non-collateralised debt, meaning they do not involve an asset or property that the debtor pledges to relinquish in case of default. The chancier gamble with the future entailed in non-collateralised debt to the poor facilitates the examination of the disciplinary features and paradoxes inherent to credit-led accumulation as it relates to the debtfarist roles of the state, the surplus population and the power of money.

The United States provides an important site to examine these cases for several reasons. First, as noted in the previous chapter, the United States represents the so-called heartland, or archetypal version, of neoliberalisation that the Global South has been urged to emulate (Soederberg, 2004). This occurs both through structural adjustment lending by the International Monetary Fund and World Bank and, less visibly, by credit rating agencies, institutional investors (e.g., pension and mutual funds) and private lenders (e.g., investment banks and equity firms) (Bourdieu, 1998; Soederberg, 2004, 2006; Wacquant, 2009; Peck, 2010). Part III of this book explores how similar features of the poverty industry in the United States are rapidly taking hold in Mexico under the ambit of financial inclusion. Understanding the poverty industry in the United States, therefore, is necessary to grasping the uneven nature of the expansion and intensification of credit-led accumulation on the global scale.

The second reason I draw on the United States is because, more than any other country, it allows us to study the tensions in neoliberalisation as they relate to the wider processes of credit-led accumulation. In contrast with the rhetoric of neoliberalism, the experience of market-led restructuring of capitalism in the United States has not operated to the benefit of all. Market-based neoliberal capitalism has resulted in the immense concentration of wealth at one pole and the increasing misery, degradation and toil of labour at the other. Socio-economic inequality, for instance, in the world's most powerful 'developed' country has widened dramatically over the past three decades (Bivens and Mishel, 2013). According to tax filings, 'The income gap between the richest 1 percent of Americans and the other 99 percent widened to a record margin in 2012. The top 1 percent of US earners collected 19.3 percent of household income, breaking a record previously set in 1927' ('US income inequality at record high', *BBC News*, 10 September 2013; Saez, 2013).

Since the 1980s, 'rent-seeking' (as opposed to wealth-creation activity) has been the primary means through which the top income earners extracted their wealth (Bivens and Mishel, 2013). One important example of this is the expansion of the poverty industry, which is marked by attempts to integrate the surplus population into secondary forms of exploitation through personal loans. In the absence of a living wage and state-sponsored social benefits and programmes, for instance, credit-led accumulation has benefited the top decile in the United States, while 90 percent of households saw a 4.2 percent *decline* in their market-based incomes from 2001 to 2005 (Sassen, 2010). Between 2000 and 2008, poverty in the suburbs of the largest urban areas – the former stronghold of middle-class America – increased by 25 percent. Poverty levels were exacerbated in the aftermath of the rent-seeking (credit-driven), US subprime mortgage debacle, which left 30 percent of the country's population below 200 percent of the federal poverty level (see Table 4.2 in Chapter 4 for more information). Suburbs in the United States became home to the largest share of the nation's poor (Brookings Institute, 2010; see also Table 6.4 in Chapter 6 for common reasons for payday borrowing).

A third and related reason that I concentrate on the US context is because of the exponential growth and expansion of credit-led accumulation aimed at extracting interests, commissions and fees from the working poor since the late 1990s. Two observations are worth raising here with regard to the meteoric rise of credit-led accumulation. First, this strategy, which has been carried out by capitalists and facilitated by the state, also involves ordinary workers through a phenomenon that may be referred to as cannibalistic capitalism. By this term I mean the processes by which workers' savings in the form of pension funds feed off of both their own increased indebtedness and that of other workers, a condition driven largely by stagnant real wages, absence of an adequate social safety net and high levels of structural unemployment and underemployment (Soederberg, 2010a). As evidenced in the United States, the dependence of pension funds on high-risk ventures leads to a situation in which investment strategies mutilate the value of pension savings with the advent of more frequent and intensified financial crises, wiping out gains made during a speculative run.

Instead of serving to weaken capitalism, however, financial crises have had the effect of deepening neoliberalisation by allowing financial corporations and their shareholders, which include pension funds, to prey on those dispossessed workers who strive to maintain basic living standards through the credit system (Soederberg, 2010b). This feature of credit-led accumulation has also meant that those benefiting from the poverty industry are not solely capitalists but also (non-surplus) ordinary workers, who unwittingly benefit from the secondary exploitation of the surplus population. Although this feature is not made explicit in the following three case studies, it is important to keep to keep in mind, as it not only reveals the complexities and tensions in the US poverty industry but also represents the culmination of past attempts by capitalists, with the assistance of the state, to deal with the tensions inherent to credit-led accumulation.

The second point I wish to make here is that the expansion and reconfiguration of credit-led accumulation in the United States has been facilitated by a key rhetorical and regulative feature of debtfarism: the democratisation of credit. As I discuss in the next chapter, this term has been associated with progressive struggles that emerged in the late 1960s and 1970s aimed at ensuring access to affordable credit for the poor (Austin, 2004). The democratisation of credit trope is powerful largely because the power of money allows for the illusions of freedom and equality to take hold. Seen through a Marxian lens, however, the democratisation of credit masks an underlying class-based strategy aimed at integrating excluded sectors of the working population – that is, the surplus population – into the mainstream credit system. Under conditions of stagnant real wages, the absence of an adequate social safety net and high levels of structural unemployment and underemployment, the poverty industry has become a site where the silent compulsions to earn a living based on dispossession, expropriation and market-dependence are constantly reproduced and reimposed in such a manner that it appears as a natural, voluntary and inevitable aspect of life, or *the ordinary run of things* (see Chapter 2).

The democratisation of credit is an integral feature in the social reproduction of the poverty industry. It represents the confluence of power and tension through the intersection of money, debtfarism and the surplus population. Owing to this, I provide here a historical account of the democratisation of credit and explain how lending to the poor in the United States shifted from illegal to legal framings due to changing material conditions and forms of state intervention. My aim is to problematise and deconstruct the illusions of the equality of exchange, and liberty of contract that is inherent to the democratisation of credit trope. In doing so, I reveal how the exploitative, disciplinary and unequal relations of power that constitute creditor–debtor relations are social constructions imbricated in the dynamics of capital accumulation and debtfarism.

To begin, it is important to note that the democratisation of credit is neither a new concept, nor one that is exclusive to neoliberalism. The idea 'that people of small means should be able to borrow small loans with dignity from banks in the same way as the wealthy, cutting out loan sharks' first emerged in the United States in 1914 (Burton, 1998: 92). Salary lending, the precursor to modern payday lenders, was a type of loansharking that emerged around the time of the so-called Gilded Age (i.e., 1870s) and reached its apex between 1900 and World War I (1914–1918).[1] Broadly, loansharking describes 'the lending of money at an illegal rate of interest and without holding a claim to some physical possession of the borrower as collateral' (Haller and Alviti, 1977: 126; Nugent, 1941). Loansharking emerged in a period that is characterised by the panics resulting from speculation and the tendency toward overaccumulation, particularly in 1873 and 1893. This, in turn, led to severe depressions accompanied by high unemployment and inflation rates (O'Rourke and Williamson, 1999).[2] The usury laws of most states in the late nineteenth century set the maximum interest rate so low (approximately 6 percent annually) that is was not profitable to operate a small loan company legally (Haller and Alviti, 1977; Woolston, 2010). Added to this, respectable opinion frowned upon consumer borrowing as a sign of moral weakness and lack of self-discipline, which was based in social disciplinary codes with regard to workers, e.g., employers often fired employees if it was revealed that the latter were in debt (Haller and Alviti, 1977: 127; Peterson 2003).

Salary lenders responded to this market. Salary lenders, unlike the later racketeer loansharks, did not resort to violence for debt collection. Instead, their effectiveness involved creating the illusion that the loan represented a legal obligation. As the next three chapters will demonstrate, the construction of the legal obligation is an important disciplinary feature of personal debt under capitalism. In the case of salary lending, legal obligation was achieved through various strategies. For instance, most lenders operated out of an office; a prospective borrower was investigated to determine whether he had a steady job; and the borrower signed complicated forms before receiving the loan. More importantly, to evade the illegality of their operations, salary lenders would treat the loan as a 'purchase' of the borrower's future salary. Until the early twentieth century, state sanctions against salary lenders were not rigorously imposed (Nugent, 1941; Austin, 2004).[3]

Access to credit offered by salary lenders was highly gendered. Borrowers were generally married men, who held steady jobs in large organisations: government civil servants, railroad workers, streetcar motormen and clerks in firms such as insurance companies (Haller and Alviti, 1977:128). Mirroring the motives of contemporary payday borrowers, the reasons why workers turned to salary lenders included unexpected illnesses in the family, the costs of moving, paying rent in advance and the need for funds for special occasions. The loans offered by salary lenders usually ranged from $5 to $50. It was not uncommon for interest rates to run at more than 1,000 percent when computed on an annual basis (Haller and Alviti, 1977: 132). The alleged reason for high interest rates was because administrative expenses (e.g., processing and collection) were the same for all loan amounts – large and small (Haller and Alviti, 1977).

In the early twentieth century, as demands for loans began to grow in the wake of further deteriorating economic conditions, public attention began to turn against salary lenders. The campaigns against loansharks sought to establish legal frameworks for small loans, so as to remove the dependency of workers on salary lenders. It is important to underscore that salary lenders framed the problem and the solution in the realm of exchange and its illusions of equality. The reason for usurious salary lending, for instance, was due to the existence of a market for small loans among underemployed workers (see Chapter 2). As in contemporary neoliberal times in the United States, the solution to this problem was not to impose requirements that employers pay workers a living wage and provide basic benefits to cover health, vacation pay, moving expenses and so forth. Instead, the solution was to establish a legal framework in which sources of small loans could be adequately regulated and set at interest rates that were considered *reasonable* for the borrower yet profitable for the lender.

Between 1910 and 1935, the modern era of consumer credit and the birth and expansion of instalment credit, alongside the strategy of democratising credit, began to emerge in the United States (Michelman, 1970; Calder, 1999). During this time, a variety of legalised small loan systems emerged in American states. In lieu of a living wage, for example, corporations and labour unions established credit unions for their employees and members. By the 1920s and 1930s, commercial bankers recognised the profitability and respectability of the small loans market and opened small loan departments. The suggested rate of 3.5 percent monthly was deemed necessary for a profitable small loan business. By 1933, 27 states had passed small loans acts (Haller and Alviti, 1977).

A key tension guaranteeing the quality of (physical) money and the price (fictitious value) of credit money emerged in the 1920s, leading up to the Great Crash of 1929. Notwithstanding the fact that lenders in many states were permitted to charge a profitable interest rate of 3.5 percent monthly, lenders faced declining profits, brought on by inflationary pressures and the increased risks of making loans for personal needs. During this period average loans were growing in the face of increasing unemployment and underemployment. Legal small loan operations thus left a gap, which was filled by a new type of illegal lender in the 1930s: the racketeer loanshark. Unlike salary lenders, the latter resorted to the threat of violence as the standard collection procedure (Haller and Alviti 1977).

In response to the global economic downturn and the devastating consequences of the Great Depression in the 1930s, the American state enacted a series of relief efforts to support the poor under the umbrella programme of The New Deal (1933–1936), including (old age) Social Security and unemployment and welfare provisions. In addition, the Fair Labor Standards Act was introduced to cover aspects such as minimum wages and maximum hours worked (Hilztik, 2011). After World War II (1939–1945), programmes geared toward the social protection of workers were further bolstered by Keynesian welfare policies, which, in turn, assisted in the expansion of mass production and consumption in the United States. As elaborated in Chapter 4, from the 1960s onward, the capitalist state undertook several regulative and rhetorical measures to encourage the democratisation of credit among those with steady employment. This included various consumer protection laws, such as the Truth in Lending Act (TILA) of 1968, the Marquette Decision of 1978, which allowed nationally chartered banks to export interest rates to states with stricter regulations and important revisions to the personal Bankruptcy Code (see Chapter 4 for a detailed account of these regulations).

As discussed above, the democratisation of credit refers to the removal of barriers that impede market access, particularly for the poor. In short, the poor are encouraged to participate in the realm of exchange by incurring debt. This, in turn, diverts our attention away from the class power and exploitation in the realm of exchange and obscures thus the root causes of poverty. Adhering to the neoclassical approach, high-cost, privately created money is expected to smooth the consumption needs of the poor such that they can lift themselves out of poverty. This is opposed to providing workers with living wages and the public provisioning of safety nets such as unemployment insurance, healthcare, old age pensions and so forth.

Another equality-based assumption underpinning the democratisation of credit is that all individuals – despite different resource endowments and different assets – can become good market citizens (cf. CGAP, 2010a; US Department of Commerce, 2010). The assumption here is that borrowers and lenders will interact in a mutually beneficial manner based on equal exchange. This level playing field also implies that the poor will be held accountable to meet their payment obligations in a timely manner with the same moral expectations applied to wealthy borrowers. In support of capitalist strategies to expand consumer credit, which we discuss below, the American state has heavily promoted the democratisation of credit and its underlying illusions of equality, freedom and democracy. Framing credit exclusively in the realm of exchange, attention is focused on questions of access, fairness and transparency, as opposed to creating a more level playing field by guaranteeing a living wage, social protection and the subsidisation of basic social services (Marx, 1990, 2005).

Grassroots campaigns waged in the 1970s by various organisations, such as the National Welfare Rights Organisation, sought to ensure that consumer credit was 'a right of American citizenship', particularly for poor and low-income people of colour (Austin, 2004: 1254). Drawing inspiration from the community of money, some supporters argued that democratic values (formal equality and individual freedom), which were believed to exist in the political arena, should be brought into the market in order to foster 'a broader sharing of the benefits of the society's economic endowments by a wider spectrum of consumers' (Austin, 2004: 1255). The American state responded to these claims and, in turn, nurtured the growth needs of the consumer credit industry, through several major pieces of legislation, including the Equal Credit Opportunity Act of 1975 and the Community Reinvestment Act (or, CRA)[4] of 1977 (Federal Reserve Board, 2008). In doing so, the state assisted in expanding the membership in the community of money and thereby imposing values based on market individualism and social discipline.

In what follows, I touch on the disciplinary strategies inherent to the democratisation of credit in the form of credit scoring. Before doing so, however, it is useful to highlight the term 'consumer', which is often used in the debates on this topic, as well as in the financialisation literature, but which is rarely problematised. The term 'consumer' (debtor) acts to mask the class-based power in the community of money. As discussed in Chapter 3, this is a powerful trope used in both regulatory and rhetorical framings to de-class, de-gender and de-racialise workers, who are homogenised, equalised and individualised as consumers. More importantly, the uncritical embrace and usage of the term 'consumer' ensures that the entire discussion of expanded access to credit remains within the realm of exchange, thereby obscuring the connections to inequality and exploitation rooted in processes of credit-led accumulation. As David Harvey notes, consumerism, along with individual libertarianism, were part and parcel of the neoliberal construction of a market-based popular culture (Harvey, 2005).

Mirroring the above sentiment that democratisation of credit creates equality in capitalism, Dawn Burton, a scholar of consumer society, suggests that providing appropriate access to credit will then ensure that poor consumers are active market participants in consumer society on an equal footing (Burton, 2008: 92). One way this equal footing has been achieved is through the application of risk-based pricing machinations to determine the interest that the poor need to pay to access credit.

FICO scores are the main mechanism for determining pricing for the poor in the United States. Although the credit card industry does not begin to entice surplus workers until the late 1980s, it is useful to explore briefly the meaning and nature of these credit scores, given their dominant role in disciplining debtors in the poverty industry.

The methods employed by FICO, which was established by the Fair Issac Corporation in 1965, are used by the three main credit reporting (and debt collection) agencies in the United States: Equifax, Experian and TransUnion. Through regulatory framings of debtfarism, FICO scores facilitated the expansion of the credit card industry, particularly to the surplus population, while justifying the stratification of the cost and amount of credit offered by banks.[5] The quantitative and mathematical nature of FICO scores not only facilitates the construction of 'ideal type' consumers but also allows for the application of market discipline. Furthermore, FICO scores serve to naturalise and normalise the power granted to banks to determine not only the value of credit money to be lent but also which workers are to receive the money. This in turn allows for the highly political, subjective and random setting of a 'price' for credit card loans based on class, racial and gendered differentiation (Dymski, 2009; Wyly et al., 2009; Roberts, 2013). Recall from our discussion in Chapter 2 that, like money itself, credit does not possess an intrinsic value, only a fictitious value. However, the latter requires validation and justification. Credit-rating agencies and techniques such as the FICO thus provide a valuable service to capitalists.

Based not on the subjectivity of the lender but on an individual's credit history, FICO scores are seen to determine objectively the amount and terms of a loan (e.g., length of time, interest rates, fees, etc.). Those with scores below 600 are categorised as *subprime*, or below the prime or benchmark. The stigma attached to the subprime category is associated with economic coercion in the form of higher interest rates and exorbitant fees (Montgomerie, 2010). Such devices also facilitate disciplinary measures regarding debtors' payment practices. If a borrower is late making a payment and is maxing out on lines of credit – issues that are prevalent among surplus labour – his/her credit rating is immediately affected, potentially making access to future credit more expensive (i.e., higher fees and interests). In the United States, where employers' credit checks are the norm, a poor credit rating may also result in the denial of paid employment, thereby reinforcing the multi-dimensionality and rewards of being a good market citizen. Ironically, poor credit scores in the United States are largely linked to unemployment, lack of health coverage and medical debt (Traub, 2013).

Determined by seemingly apolitical abstractions (i.e., interest rates, credit scores and so forth), FICO scores act not only as a formidable gate-keeper to the community of money, but also as a disciplinary mechanism for its existing and aspiring members (cf. Drysdale and Keest, 2000; Marron, 2007). As one legal scholar puts it: 'for middle and working class people, access to credit (and the denial of credit to others) [is] part of their sense of respectability' (Austin, 2004: 1254). The ability to transform the meanings of self-worth and citizenship in terms of the market has been a powerful disciplinary feature of the democratisation of credit. As the following three chapters demonstrate, this disciplinary power would not be possible, however, without the regulatory and rhetorical framings of the capitalist state and the social power inherent in money. It is only by unpacking these processes that we can understand how the social power of the state, capitalists and money work together, albeit in a highly paradoxical and tension-ridden manner, to expand and remake the poverty industry and reproduce the surplus population.

Notes

1   Salary lending arose in the post-Civil War period in the context of two legal small loan institutions: the pawnshop (the oldest and far more important in terms of the volume of business) and the chattel lender, who made small loans secured by a mortgage on personal property such as furniture, a sewing machine, or jewellery. By the 1880s, these lenders began offering loans without security (Nugent, 1941; Haller and Alviti, 1977).
2   As discussed in Chapter 3 with regard to the Marxian concept of relative surplus labour, unemployment rates act to decrease the level of the social wage. Absent from the capitalist scene at this time were welfare provisions and other forms of social protection such as unemployment insurance, minimum wage requirements, and so forth.
3   The law was sometimes unclear and penalties for usury were minimal, e.g., lenders were not subject to criminal penalties, and when this did occur, it was classified as a misdemeanour and no official had specific enforcement responsibility. Penalties ranged from forfeiture of the illegal interest to forfeiture of principal and interest. The penalty could only be imposed if the borrower undertook the expenses of a lawsuit (Haller and Alviti, 1977: 127).
4   The CRA was driven, in part, by the response of grassroots organisations and government officials to the lender-led practice of 'redlining' neighbourhoods in inner cities, i.e., drawing a red line, both literally and figuratively, around areas with perceived undesirable characteristics and systematically refusing credit to residents, regardless of individual creditworthiness (Austin, 2004).
5   The FICO scores are purported to give lenders 'the most accurate picture of credit risk possible using credit report data' (www.myfico.com). In 1958, two years after the FICO score was invented, Visa's precursor, the BankAmericard was issued by Bank of America (Geisst, 2009: 62).

4

DEBTFARISM AND THE CREDIT CARD INDUSTRY

In 1958, the BankAmericard was launched by Bank of America and subsequently renamed as Visa in 1976. BankAmericard introduced workers to an extended payment system in which individuals were permitted to pay their balances over time while being charged interest on the unpaid balance (Geisst, 2009). It wasn't until the late 1980s, however, that credit cards became a central feature of the burgeoning poverty industry in the United States.[1] From this time onward, the credit card industry rapidly expanded its lending activities to underemployed and unemployed workers, or the surplus population. In lieu of living wages, savings and adequate welfare provisions, credit cards have come to represent a privatised safety net for surplus workers to pay for essential services and subsistence needs (most notably health care), particularly when workers fall ill, divorce and/or lose their jobs (Warren and Tyagi, 2004; Bird, 1997; Stegman and Faris, 2005).

According to a 2012 study, 40 percent of households in the United States still rely on credit cards to pay for basic living because they did not have enough money in their chequing or savings account – a rate that that has remained constant since 2008. Among households with annual incomes of less than $50,000, this increases to 45 percent (Traub and Ruetchlin, 2012, see also Table 4.2). Behind apolitical economic terms such as 'consumption smoothing', credit card debt for the poor often involves a vicious debt cycle in which high fees and interest payments are paid monthly as opposed to paying off the balance. On the other side of the accounting ledger, it is clear that the increased reliance of the working poor on credit cards has come to represent one of the most lucrative sectors for the handful of Wall Street banks that dominate the industry.[2]

What remains less clear is why, and how, the dependence of the surplus population on privately created money (and the exploitative relations therein) has become normalised. This chapter seeks to shed critical light on these questions in two ways. The first goal is to denaturalise the emergence of the credit card industry and thereby reveal it as a socially constructed and capitalist phenomenon. The second and related goal is to deconstruct and explain the increased dependence of the surplus population on privately created money in the form of credit cards by identifying the rhetorical and regulative roles played by debtfarism.

The overarching argument in this chapter is that the US debtfare state has played a crucial role in both the expansion and the reproduction of the credit card industry. Debtfarism is central to the accumulation of fictitious value, a process that exposes ever-greater numbers of the surplus population to market discipline. A key way the debtfare state legitimises the increasingly coercive nature of privatising basic subsistence has been by framing and resolving tensions in the realm of exchange, where class power and exploitation are demystified by the fetishised virtues of equality, freedom and democracy given uptake by the community of money. The US debtfare state, for example, has facilitated an expansion of secondary forms of exploitation by permitting credit card issuers (banks) to generate enormous amounts of income from uncapped interest rates and fees by continually extending plastic money to the surplus population. This subjects surplus workers to the disciplinary requirements of the market across time, compelling them to find and accept any form of work in order to meet their monthly payment obligations. Thus, driven by economic distress, they behave as good market citizens.

This argument is developed in four main sections. Section One describes some of the key features of the credit card industry and its relationship to the US surplus population. Section Two explores historically the rise of the credit card industry in the United States by tracing three institutionalised regulative and rhetorical features: (1) consumer protection, (2) usury laws and (3) bankruptcy laws. Each of which strengthens and reproduces the illusions of the community of money. This section also maps the foundation of the US debtfare state, which will be vital not only to the present discussion, but also to our discussion of other cases of the US poverty industry, namely student loans (Chapter 5) and payday lending (Chapter 6). Section Three examines how the debtfare state has facilitated and mediated several spatio-temporal displacements in the credit card industry. Here I focus on credit card asset-backed securitisation (ABS), the wooing of undocumented workers, the Bankruptcy Abuse Prevention and Consumer Protection Act (BAPCPA) and the 2009 Credit Card Accountability, Responsibility and Disclosure Act (or, Credit Card Act). Each of these initiatives has had negative implications for the working poor, who have largely been ignored by the financialisation literature. Section Four concludes by summarising the argument.

The credit card industry and the US surplus population: an overview

Credit card industry

In contrast to the neoliberal rhetoric, the credit card industry is an oligopoly. Visa controls 50 percent of the market share, MasterCard controls an additional 25 percent, while American Express, Discover and other smaller companies share the remaining 25 percent (Karger, 2005). It is important to note that neither Visa nor MasterCard issues credit cards. Rather, these companies provide advertising, credit authorisation and payment services for their financial members, most of whom are large US banks (see Table 4.1).

Each bank sets its own credit card terms, interest rates, fees and penalties. The loose structure of Visa and MasterCard partly explains the vast range of credit card terms, fees and interest rates available (Manning, 2000). As we will see in the next section, the variability is also due, in part, to the regulatory environment. Visa and MasterCard, for instance, have long benefitted from having exclusive ties to banks, while the latter have benefitted from numerous loopholes available to corporations to circumvent anti-trust legislation, i.e., laws designed to promote free competition (Braithwaite and Drahos, 2000). In response to a US Supreme Court ruling regarding anti-trust violations, for instance, MasterCard and Visa filed initial public offerings (IPOs)[3] in 2006 and 2008, respectively, thereby transforming their structure from membership associations, jointly owned by banks, to public companies. Despite this reorganisation, the ownership of Visa and MasterCard remains largely in the hands of specific banks, whose concentrated power has been neither acknowledged nor addressed by the state agency responsible for regulating nationally chartered banks: the Office of the Comptroller of the Currency (OCC).

The largest banks still own half of MasterCard and Visa ('Chinese fund major investor in Visa IPO', *CBC News*, 25 March 2008). JP Morgan, for instance, is not only the largest shareholder of Visa, it is the company's largest customer, getting breaks on pricing not available to most other customers. The IPOs raised substantial amounts of money for the banks that own Visa and MasterCard. In the case of Visa, the IPO raised a record-breaking $17.9 billion for the banks – including JP Morgan Chase, Bank of America and Citigroup – which own it ('Visa's record IPO rings up 28 percent gain', *CNN.com*, 19 March 2008). The money raised in the IPO has also been used to pad the already considerable anti-litigation war chest of Visa and Mastercard. To get a sense of the size of this anti-litigation fund, MasterCard has $650 million at its disposal. The credit card industry remains an extremely effective cartel, represented by one of the country's most powerful lobby groups, American Bankers Association (ABA).

TABLE 4.1 Top four credit card issuers in the United States, 2009 (in billions $)

Rank†	Credit issued
1 Bank of America/MBNA	194.70
2 Chase	184.09
3 Citi	148.90
4 American Express	105.00

† The fifth-ranked bank was Capital One with $68.78 in credit issued.
Source: 'World's Top 10 Credit Card Issuers', CNBC.com; data compiled from CreditCards.com and Nilson Report, December 2009.

Two core sources of income for the credit card industry are fees (e.g., late penalties, administrative fees, annual fees, processing fees and so forth) and uncapped interest rates (see Table 4.7). Rates are set at the discretion of credit cards issuers. The type of debt that characterises credit cards is known as revolving credit, or unsecure debt, which describes open-ended loans with irregular balances that change on a monthly basis (Manning, 2000; Karger, 2005). So-called 'revolvers' are debtors who do not pay their credit card balance at the end of each month. Revolvers represent the most lucrative segment of credit card debtors, as card companies can extract interest payments for longer periods of time and collect higher fees, e.g., late penalties. Revolvers account for a substantial segment of credit card users in the United States and the total revolving debt is substantial. In 2009, for instance, 56 percent of card users had an unpaid credit card balance.[4] In 2011, the total amount of unpaid debt reached $796.1 billion.[5] Revolving debt levels have not only steadily increased since the 1980s, but also a disproportionate number of revolving debtors are non-white workers (African-American and Hispanic) from lower-income brackets (Bird *et al.*, 1997; Federal Reserve, 2001; Delpechitre and DeVaney, 2006). Recall from Chapter 2 that credit cards represent a form of credit money – that is, they are a money-form of revenue and thus contribute to the expansion of fictitious value. We pick up on this, again, below. For now, it is useful to briefly elaborate on the relationship between the surplus population and the US credit card industry.

The surplus population in the United States

In this chapter, I employ Marx's concept of 'surplus population'[6] to refer to 'poor' and 'low-income' individuals and households, following the definitions[7] of these terms used by the US government.[8] Specifically, low-income individuals and families have income below two-times the poverty threshold (or, below 200 percent of the poverty line), while poor individuals and families register incomes at or below 100 percent of the poverty line (see Table 4.2).[9]

TABLE 4.2 2013 federal poverty guidelines* (in $)

Household size	Below 100% of poverty	Below 200% of poverty
1	11,490	22,980
2	15,510	31,020
3	19,530	39,060
4	23,550	47,100

Source: FamiliesUSA: The Voice for Health Care Consumers (2013) '2013 Federal Poverty Guidelines', Washington, DC: FamiliesUSA. Available at: www.familiesusa.org/resources/tools-for-advocates/guides/federal-poverty-guidelines.html (accessed 13 June 2013).

* Calculations by FamiliesUSA based on data from the US Department of Health and Human Services (HSS). Based on poverty guidelines. See the HHS website at: http://aspe.hhs.gov/poverty/13poverty.cfm (accessed 13 June 2013). Data excludes Alaska and Hawaii.

Against the general backdrop of stagnant wages, rising costs of living and the steady withdrawal of publicly supported social services, the surplus population in the United States has grown steadily over the past several decades of neoliberalism (National Poverty Centre, 2012). While productivity has increased 80.4 percent from 1979 to 2011, the inflation-adjusted wages of the median worker grew just 6 percent and that growth occurred exclusively as a result of the strong economy of the late 1990s (Traub and McGhee, 2013). Over the past decade (2000–2011), earnings and income have taken a substantial hit, as the median family income in the US has declined 6 percent, from $66,259 to $62,301 (Federal Reserve Board, 2010a; Traub and McGhee, 2013). As Figure 4.1 reveals, the hardest hit have been the most vulnerable households. It should be noted that the wealthiest 20 percent of working families faired quite well during this time – taking home nearly half (48 percent) of all income, while the poorest 20 percent received less than 5 percent of all income (Roberts et al., 2013: 1).

As Table 4.3 demonstrates, the surplus population has been turning to credit cards.[10] While the change in credit card debt depicted in Table 4.3 has been celebrated as indicating both a rebound in the economy and a positive response to the implementation of the Credit Card Act of 2009, these numbers also reflect the loss of access to credit by many families during and after the 2007 subprime crisis, largely due to the debacles socio-economic fall out, e.g., job loss and/or loss of home (Traub and Ruetchlin, 2012). I discuss this point within the larger context of the Credit Card Act of 2009, which I discuss below.

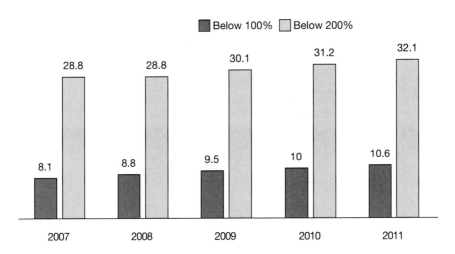

FIGURE 4.1 Working families by poverty status, 2007–2011 (in %)

Source: US Census Bureau, American Community Survey, cited in Roberts et al., (2013) Low-Income Working Families: The Growing Economic Gap. Washington, DC: The Working Poor Families Project, p. 2.

TABLE 4.3 Amount of credit card debt carried by surplus population, 2008 and 2012

	2008 (in $)	2012 (in $)	% change
All	9,887	7,145	-27.7
Age			
18–24	3,498	2,982	-14.7
25–34	10,407	5,156	-50.5
35–44	10,141	6,156	-39.3
45–54	10,154	8,408	-17.2
55–64	10,013	8,228	-17.8
65 and older	9,823	9,283	-5.5
Race/ethnicity			
African American	6,970	5,784	-17.0
Latino	9,049	6,066	-33.0
White, Non-Hispanic	10,358	7,315	-29.4
Income level			
Less than $35,000	7,763	5,405	-30.4
$50,000–$74,999	11,528	8,916	-22.7
$75,000 or more	11,896	9,235	-22.5

Source: Amy Traub and Catherine Ruetchlin (2012) *The Plastic Safety Net: findings from the 2012 National Survey on Credit Card Debt of Low- and Middle-Income Households*, New York, NY: Dēmos, p. 7.

The increasing economic insecurity of surplus labour lies not simply in the burden of the high-fee and high-interest debt cycle of credit cards; but also in the absence of living wages and stagnant labour market, as well as the decline of public support for basic subsistence needs – welfare, health, shelter and education (Katz, 2001; Wacquant, 2009). The vulnerability and profile of these debtors is clearly revealed in the demographics of personal bankruptcy filings (15 percent of all indebted households have declared personal bankruptcy and 20 percent have entered into a settlement agreement with a credit card company (Ausubel, 1997; Karger, 2005; Moore, 2009). There is also a tension in this particular form of credit-led accumulation, which relies on 'unsecured' (or, non-collateralised) forms of exploitation involving a gamble with the future, i.e., the ability of poor and low-income workers to make minimum interest payments on their debt (Bonefeld, 1995; Harvey, 1999). This is the core paradox of the credit card industry. As we will see, it demands continual intervention by the debtfare state.

The rise and oligopolistic power of the credit card industry did not emerge from the naturally evolving, competitive forces of the market. To provide an alternative to this dominant narrative, I turn my attention to a historical materialist explanation of the rise of credit cards and the integral role played by debtfarism.

Debtfarism and the making of the credit card industry

Consumer protection through disclosure

As the community of money expanded to include more and more surplus workers, so too would the state need to uphold the virtues of democracy, equality and freedom in the sphere of exchange by striving to protect consumers while normalising their exposure to secondary forms of exploitation through credit (see Chapter 2). Consumer protection was focused on ensuring that the loan contracts remained transparent, so that rational borrowers could make informed decisions about whether or not to enter voluntarily into debt with a credit card company. The protection thus offered by the state would guarantee transparency about the terms of the debt contract as opposed to the actual terms of payment and conditions therein. Consumer protection essentially forms the bedrock of the neoliberal move away from the collective and rights-based social and economic protection of workers toward monetised and individualised relations, as well as market-driven forms of citizenship whereby the state simply guarantees the formal equality of exchange.

A main regulatory feature of consumer protection in the United States is the Consumer Credit Protection Act of 1968 (hereafter: the 1968 Act). This Act is an umbrella consumer protection law that includes the Equal Credit Opportunity Act, the Fair Credit Billing Act, the Fair Credit Reporting Act and the Truth in Lending Act (or, TILA) that was originally part of the Consumer Credit Protection Act. It should be underlined that since the passing of the 1968 Act, there has been no comprehensive or overarching consumer protection legislation in the US. Instead, the emphasis has been on a series of separate laws that target specific business practices, industries and consumer products (Crane et al., 2011).

An important feature of the TILA is that it promotes a regulatory shift away from legally-binding contractual restrictions to relying on disclosure as a primary way of protecting consumers (Peterson, 2007: 1132). The TILA requires, for instance, that consumer creditors disclose all the specifics of a given loan in order to protect consumers (Drysdale and Keest, 2010).[11] The TILA also introduced minimum payments and standardised the calculation of interest with the creation of Annual Percentage Rates[12] (APR) (Peterson, 2003). With the exception of high-cost mortgage loans, the TILA does not regulate what charges may be imposed for consumer credit. Instead it requires standardised disclosure of the costs and charges imposed (Crane et al., 2011: 319).

Based on economic assumptions of rational individualism, TILA was not designed to protect borrowers in terms of the price of the loan (e.g., interest rates and fees), but instead to ensure that they were given a 'choice' (freedom) among lenders. Through its emphasis on consumer protection, the TILA also served to distort the arbitrary power of the state and credit card industry by rehearsing its commitment to formal equality and freedom for consumers as well as guaranteeing a level playing field through the act of disclosure (Peterson, 2003). The legalisation of revolving credit was also packaged as a convenience to the consumer, as opposed to a windfall for creditors.

In another effort to depoliticise its actions, the debtfare state sought to promote the informed use of consumer credit. Instead of implementing this through the OCC (the agency originally designed to deal with federal banking regulation), however, the state delegated responsibility to the central bank (Federal Reserve System). As one observer notes, TILA represented the only federal law ever passed dealing with interest rates, which makes the OCC conspicuous in its absence (Geisst, 2009). By ensconcing the TILA in the Federal Reserve, the social power of money could be invoked to impose market discipline and order on the emerging landscape of credit-led accumulation that was beginning to rise to the surface in the late 1960s (Peterson, 2003).

The TILA was far from neutral legislation. It was designed with an adequate number of loopholes for the banks to manoeuvre around the cap on interest rates, which was still in place at this time, by adding fees to card balances (Peterson, 2003). Moreover, by temporally extending card balances into the future under the guise of consumer protection, banks were able to generate more revenue. There remained a major obstacle to this strategy, however. The credit card industry was restricted to charging a limited amount of interest under existing usury laws. In 1978, the lifting of caps on interest rates through the revision of usury law marked a pivotal moment in the credit card industry and the wider poverty industry in the United States. The judicial decision served to legitimatise and naturalise, through the fetishised understanding of the neutrality of laws, the continual, albeit tension-ridden, expansion of fictitious value that drives the poverty industry.

Expanding fictitious value: lifting caps on usury laws and the landmark 1978 Marquette Decision

Despite the loopholes afforded to the credit card industry by the TILA, the primary barrier to making more money from expanding the money-form of revenue (credit) remained fixed interest rates, as usury laws were still in effect in most states. The McFadden Act of 1927, for instance, granted individual states the authority to govern bank branches located within state jurisdiction; prohibited interstate banking; and placed usury ceilings on lending institutions (Drysdale and Keest, 2000). Up to 1978, for instance, banks could charge no more than 2.5 to 3 percent higher than the cost incurred in making the loan.

One of the key tensions underpinning the credit system, namely, the gap between credit money and its monetary base opens up here (see Chapter 2). The main problem with legal caps on interest rates, for instance, was that they benefitted customers if rates rose, putting the risk and opportunity losses squarely on the banks that made the loans. Before the regulatory environment would facilitate asset-backed securitisation (ABS or securitisation), which I discuss below, banks had to leave the loans on their books and manage their own interest rate exposure accordingly. These *assets* (debt) were not sellable and could pose risks to the banks. Their lack of flexibility made them unmarketable to a third party (Geisst, 2009). The influential American Bankers Association repeatedly lobbied the government not only to lift the ceiling on interest rates but also to allow banks to charge these rates on revolving basis thereby creating a minimum balance. In effect, the banks were seeking to expand the base of the fictitious value tied to their consumer loans (see Chapter 2). Before turning to the loosening of usury laws in the United States in the late 1970s, it is useful to highlight the core legislative features of the credit card industry that acted as an impediment to lending to the poor and, subsequently to hedging the banks' gambles through ABS.

During the latter half of the 1970s, a tension emerged from the tight monetarist policies pursed by the Federal Reserve. High interest rates were serving to discipline labour to the power of money and protect the value of the dollar. But they also threatened to inflict a deathblow to large and highly indebted financial corporations such as Citibank. Under the new reign of monetarism, the high interest rates set up by the Federal Reserve to fight inflation were greater than the nominal interest rates banks were allowed to charge their borrowers. This was due to legal caps on interest rates (see Chapter 3). In other words, due to inflation large and powerful US banks were suffering from a gap between the legal limit of interest and the cost of money. In 1978, the US Supreme Court decision in *Marquette National Bank vs. First of Omaha Services Corporation* played a decisive role in repealing aspects of the McFadden Act of 1927, particularly with regard to lifting the caps on interest rates (Burgess and Ciolfi, 1986).

The freeing of privately created money in the form of credit cards occurred through the seemingly neutral and arbitrary arena of the legal system, as opposed to the more overtly political OCC. Reflecting Harvey's concept of a spatial fix, the Marquette decision effectively allowed lenders in a state with liberal usury rates to export those rates to workers residing in states with more restrictive usury ceilings thereby breaking through barriers to credit-led accumulation (Ellis, 1998). The decision sparked a race among states, particularly less affluent states like South Dakota, to attract banks by deregulating their usury caps on interest rates. The spatial barriers to accumulation were thus temporarily resolved through the Supreme Court. The removal of usury ceilings for national banks expanded access to consumer credit and higher level of personal bankruptcies (Ellis, 1998).

Bankruptcy laws and social discipline: the coercive side of the community of money

Around the same time as usury was legalised, another landmark decision took place, namely: the Reform of Bankruptcy Act of 1978, which represented the first comprehensive overhaul and replacement of the Bankruptcy Act of 1898. Among the various changes introduced by the Act, was the inclusion of new types of bankruptcy to the code, such as Chapter 13, or what is known as 'individual debt adjustment'. In contrast to Chapter 7 of the personal bankruptcy code (i.e., liquidation), Chapter 13 provides a longer and more onerous system of repayment for distressed debtors (Kirschner and Volpin, 2009). The Bankruptcy Reform Act of 1978 was, however, highly contested by the American Bankers Association, as it was believed that these new types of bankruptcies, despite their burdensome features, would result in more filings (Domowitz and Eovaldi, 1993). Put another way, creditors were averse to providing what they viewed as legal safe havens for delinquent debtors (i.e., market distortions). As we will see below, bankers continued to lobby the state to keep debtors out of bankruptcy protection, particularly Chapter 7.

This 1978 bankruptcy reform was a stark signal that the state was required to help mediate and legitimate continual marked-based forms of financial regulation and the spatial expansion of consumer credit. As long as the income extracted through fees and interest rates remained greater than losses of revenue through bankruptcy, credit card issuers were still ahead in terms of income-generation. Yet, this form dispossessive capitalism also depended on the constant discipline and social reproduction of the surplus population. One of the ultimate acts of disobedience (for borrowers) is the breach of the legal contract with their creditors. When this contravention occurs, the otherwise equal, voluntary and democratic nature of the credit system, asserts its class and coercive nature to protect and sanction the value of money and respect for the law. Personal bankruptcy laws are therefore an integral feature of the US debtfare state in its attempts at expanding and socially reproducing the credit card industry and the poverty industry, more generally.

Consumer credit was growing quickly among the lower socio-economic groups of society throughout the 1980s (see Table 4.4). From 1989 to 2001, for example, credit card debt among low-income families grew by an astonishing 184 percent (Dēmos, 2003). At the same time, however and despite the Bankruptcy Reform Act of 1978, personal bankruptcies continued to rise alongside poverty rates, unemployment rates and interest rates (Mishel and Bernstein, 1994; Dickerson, 2008). According to many legal scholars and industry observers, a key cause of these personal bankruptcies was workers becoming dependent on revolving credit card debt to help finance basic subsistence needs during hard economic times (Moore, 2009). The demographics of personal bankruptcies represent those groups and classes that were most vulnerable prior to entering into a contract with credit cards and other forms of consumer debt. African-American and Latino workers are 500 percent more likely than white homeowners to find themselves in bankruptcy. Other groups likely to file for bankruptcy are laid-off workers, whose numbers are rising; and older Americans, who are now the fastest-growing age group in bankruptcy (Rodriguez, 2007; Dymski, 2010; Traub and Ruetschlin, 2012; see Table 4.5).

The rise in personal bankruptcies over the 1980s also revealed that the limits of capital accumulation based on the money-form of revenue were re-emerging. As Marx reminds us, credit money is both 'the saviour of accumulation' and 'the fountainhead of all manner of insane forms' because credit 'suspends the barriers to the realisation of capital only by raising them to their most general form' (cited in Harvey, 1999: 270, 286). The expansion of the credit card industry to include the working poor thus accentuates the contradictions of capitalism by, for instance, increasing secondary forms of exploitation through the expansion of the money-form of revenue, which in turn depends on the *future* employment earnings of the surplus population (see Chapter 2). The ability of indebted surplus workers to meet minimum monthly payments on their credit cards depends, however, on their ability to earn wages in the realm of production – the sphere of capitalism where credit money is unable to resolve contradictions (Harvey, 1999).

Despite high earnings, the American Bankers' Association pressured the Clinton Administration (1993–2001) to impose tougher forms of market discipline to make bankruptcy less attractive to distressed debtors. The debtfare state responded by enacting the Bankruptcy Reform Act of 1994, which occurred a year prior to the draconian welfare reforms known as the Personal Responsibility and Work Opportunity Reconciliation (or, PRWORA), which launched the workfare state (Peck, 2001; Wacquant, 2009; see discussion in Chapter 3). Rising levels of impoverishment due to stagnant wages and rising costs of living were reflected in the rise of credit card debt among the poor a year after PRWORA was implemented. Studies show that 'in 1995, more than one in eight poor households had credit card debt greater than twice as large as monthly income. More than one in six had credit card debt as large as monthly income or larger' (Bird *et al.*, 1997: 11).

Among various changes made to the Bankruptcy Reform Act in 1994, consumers were encouraged to file under Chapter 13 (reorganisation of debts) rather than use Chapter 7 (discharge all debts), thereby aiding creditors in recovering claims against bankrupt estates (Ausubel, 1997). Making Chapter 7 a more difficult option for dispossessed debtors, these bankruptcy reforms were designed to benefit the banking cartel, while allowing creditors more time (as an expression of the social power of money) to impose market discipline and extract payments. As we will see below, the Bankruptcy Reform Act of 1994 would only deepen the tensions of credit-led accumulation. In the aftermath of the Act, for example, credit card delinquency rates exceeded 3.5 percent, the highest level since 1973, when statistics were first collected. Notwithstanding this development, the profit margins of major banks issuing credit cards continued to widen (Ausubel, 1997).

TABLE 4.4 Percent of families holding credit card balances, 1983 and 1989

Family income	(1989 dollars) 1983*	Level (percent) 1989**
Less than 10,000	11.9	15.0
10,000–19,999	26.3	27.3
20,000–29,999	45.5	48.9
30,000–49,999	53.0	55.0
50,000 and more	48.4	53.1

Sources: *Federal Reserve (1983) Panel Survey of Consumer Finances, Washington, DC: Federal Reserve.
**Federal Reserve (1989) Panel Survey of Consumer Finances, Washington, DC: Federal Reserve.

Taken together, these various pieces of legislation acted to expand the democratisation of credit, alongside the continual dismantling of the social welfare state and the lack of secure, high-wage jobs in the productive realm. This played an integral role in constructing a social reality that dragged poorer workers into a growing reliance on private provisioning (e.g., credit cards) to augment and/or replace not only their social wages but also essential services no longer provided by the welfare state (Stegman and Faris, 2005; Karger, 2005; see Table 4.5). More importantly, the expansion of the democratisation of credit also ensured that a larger segment of the surplus population would be contained, disciplined and socially reproduced. It is within this context that the US debtfare state begins to emerge and build upon the previous rhetorical and regulative landscape discussed above.

As discussed in Chapter 2, credit can resolve tensions in the realm of exchange only. Thus, for the credit card industry to ensure future income streams from a large number of debtors holding maxed out credit cards with high interest rates

TABLE 4.5 Credit cards in the income distribution, 1983–1995*

	1983	1989	1992	1995
Income below poverty line				
Percentage owning at least 1 card	18.4	22.5	36.6	38.9
Among them:				
Average number of cards	2.5	3.0	2.9	3.1
Percentage carrying a balance	58.7	54.1	71.7	68.1
Average balance	723	352	917	1,347
100–150% of poverty line				
Percentage owning at least 1 card	39.9	50.4	61.9	58.3
Among them:				
Average number of cards	3.2	3.7	3.8	3.9
Percentage carrying a balance	52.6	61.9	65.8	75.8
Average balance	449	948	1,100	2,070
150–200% of poverty line				
Percentage owning at least 1 card	52.7	60.8	73.6	71.3
Among them:				
Average number of cards	3.1	3.9	4.0	4.2
Percentage carrying a balance	56.7	62.0	69.9	63.2
Average balance	488	1,291	1,098	1,409

Source: Bird, *et al.* (1997) *Credit Cards and the Poor*, University of Wisconsin-Madison: Institute for Research on Poverty, Discussion Paper No. 1148–97, p. 10.

*All money figures are in real 1995 dollars. Data from Federal Reserve Board, Survey on Consumer Finances, 1995.

there must be a possibility for these workers to earn wages to service their debt. This situation cannot be directly mediated or controlled by either the credit card industry or the debtfare state. The tensions emerging from this can be mitigated by the debtfare state by facilitating ongoing forms of market-led discipline as well as the displacement of these contradictions through temporal deferral or geographical expansion, or what Harvey refers to as a spatio-temporal fix (Harvey, 2001).

Debtfarism and spatio-temporal fixes: expanding fictitious value and reproducing the credit card industry

Displacement of risk through time and (digitalised) spaces of expanding fictitious value: asset-backed securitisation

The key to making money from money in the credit card business does not involve collecting the original loan, but extracting the highest levels of interest and fees possible from the greatest number of people for the longest period of time. To remain viable, credit card issuers require a steady and rising number of workers who not only are willing (forced) to incur debt but who also may be charged the highest interest rate possible for the longest time possible, i.e., subprime borrowers. The limits involved in this form of accumulation, which is largely driven by credit money and its gamble with the future, requires hedging (mitigating risks). Breaking the barriers also entails devising ways to more rapidly extend credit to an increasing number of workers, particularly since credit card companies are not receiving the original amount lent out to the revolvers. The cash flow from interest and fee payments is also partly interrupted by the steady increase of personal bankruptcies.

The temporal fix devised by capitalists and facilitated by the debtfare state involves asset-backed securitisation (transforming illiquid assets into tradeable securities) and the creation of the swap markets (trading debt for something based on future cash flows) (Kothari, 2006; Elul, 2005). Reflecting the rise of credit card lending to the surplus population, the first case of credit card securitisation occurred in 1986, but it began to gain momentum in the late 1990s and took off in the 2000s. This was true of other forms of asset-backed securitisation of non-collateralised consumer debt, such as student loan securitisations (Chapter 5). The securitisation of credit cards helps to resolve the contradictions in the money-form of revenue through a temporal fix in which the originator of the credit card loans (banks) are able, with lightening speed, to transform this debt into a commodity (inclusive of fictitious value) and sell it (e.g., within a matter of hours or days) to various institutional investors (e.g., equity firms or pension and mutual funds) before the first minimum payment on the credit card falls due (e.g., 30 days). The particular form of credit money, coupled with information technology and algorithmic trading, allows for accelerated temporality in the buying and selling of credit card debt in what Saskia Sassen refers to as digitalised spaces of global finance (Harvey, 1989: 194; Sassen, 2006).

This temporal displacement also involves strategies and actors straddling the virtual-real geographic divide. The annihilation of space by time in the attempts to win the gamble with the future entails new actors, new strategies and the continual inversion of time and the expansion of virtual space to continue to fund claims on the fictitious value of credit. The temporal fix represented by credit card securitisation is represented by the over-the-counter credit derivative market (a largely deregulated market where investors purchase stocks and bonds from other investors as opposed to the issuing corporations). Most notably, these derivatives include collateralised debt obligations (CDOs) and credit default swaps (CDSs).[13] These instruments have taken securitisation to new levels of temporal displacement. Like credit card securitisations, they 'possess no market price or pricing mechanism – beyond the say-so of the rating agencies [fictitious value]' (Gowan, 2010: 60). According to the International Swaps and Derivatives Association, the CDS market exploded to more than $45 trillion in mid-2007. This represents roughly 'twice the size of the US stock market (which is valued at about $22 trillion and falling) and far exceeds the $7.1 trillion mortgage market and $4.4 trillion US treasuries market' ('Credit Default Swaps: the next crisis? *Time*, 17 March 2008). According to the Bank for International Settlements (BIS, 2013), notional amounts of CDS amounted to $25 trillion at the end of 2012. Regardless of these staggering numbers, it must be kept in mind that the real geographies underlying the digitised (virtual) spaces of asset-backed securitisation are constructed by people whose power derives from the regulatory structures ensuring finance is allowed to thrive, operate and reproduce (Sassen, 2006; Mitchell, 2008).

Banks engage in securitisation as a way to overcome the tensions involved in generating income from credit money. Securitisation facilitates temporal and spatial displacements that allow banks to shift loans off the balance sheet by selling them to outside institutional investors, such as pension and mutual funds. In this way, the problems involved in the future gamble with credit money are resolved by displacing them onto other people. The credit card issuers, for example, receive money from selling the loan (workers' debt) in order to be able to invest in more poor and low-income workers. On the demand side, institutional investors are eager to purchase credit card asset-backed securitises because they believe these will provide profitable revenue streams. It is useful to consider the reasons driving this belief, as they reveal not only the standards upon which the price of credit money (workers' commodified debt) is calculated, but also the unequal relations of power involved in credit card debt.

Credit card companies have at their disposal many coercive instruments to ensure that debtors make payments on a timely and regular basis. According to the Deutsche Bank, for instance, credit card issuers are able to increase yield on an existing portfolio by changing the financing rate charged and by altering late fees, over-limit fees and annual fees – all of which can be quite large. Credit card issuers (banks) can also reduce their risk by either closing accounts or pre-emptively lowering a cardholder's credit line. Moreover, as we saw in Table 4.1, the credit card industry is highly concentrated – larger players have economies of scale and

TABLE 4.6 Concentration of US top credit card issuers, 2000–2008

Year	Mergers and acquisitions
2000	Chase Manhattan Bank merges with JP Morgan & Co. to form JPMorgan Chase Bank
2004	Bank One Corporation merged with JP Morgan Chase and Company
2004	FleetBoston Financial Corp. merged with Bank of America
2005	Washington Mutual acquires Providian Financial, which is a major subprime credit card issuer
2006	MBNA Corporation acquired by Bank of America
2008	Discover purchases Diners Club
2008	JP Morgan Chase purchases Washington Mutual and thus owns former accounts of Providian

as part of larger banking networks also the advantage of scope (Kothari, 2006: 388). As Table 4.6 depicts, since 2000 the banking sector became increasingly centralised and concentrated, largely due to lax regulation by the debtfare state that consolidated power in the credit card industry.

Expanding the poverty industry: the undocumented and the newly bankrupted

Aside from its ability to invert time and to expand into more abstract (and thus less visible and depoliticised spaces) in order to offset risk and generate interest income, the credit card industry has also continually sought to expand its debtor base by tapping into the unbanked and underbanked sectors of the surplus population.

In an incessant search for income, credit card issuers began to enlist more debtors from the unbanked and underbanked categories, which still provide an untapped market. According to a Federal Deposit Insurance Corporation (FDIC) publication, *National Survey of Unbanked and Underbanked Households*, an estimated 9 million American households, in which 17 million adults reside, are considered unbanked. This refers to individuals who do not have accounts at banks or other mainstream (formal) financial institutions. According to the FDIC, 21 million individuals may be classified as underbanked, which describes a category of people who hold a chequing or savings account but are dependent on alternative financial services, such as payday loans, pawnshops, rent-to-own facilities and so forth (FDIC, 2009: 3; Rivlan, 2010). Predictably, both unbanked and underbanked workers are largely comprised of poor and low-income, ethnic and racial minorities as well as single-headed households (single mothers), which operate primarily, if not exclusively, with cash forms of money (FDIC, 2009).

Precisely because of their relative poverty, such households are identified as a sizeable market for the extension of formalised debt. According to a 2008 study conducted by the Centre for Financial Services Innovation (CFSI) and co-sponsored

TABLE 4.7 Percentage of families holding credit card balances, 1989–2009*

Percentile of income	Level (percent) 1989	1992	1995	1998	2001	2004	2007	2009†
Less than 20	15.3	23.4	26.0	24.5	30.3	28.8	25.7	28.4
20–39.9	27.6	41.9	43.2	40.9	44.5	42.9	39.4	38.2
40–59.9	48.9	51.9	52.9	50.1	52.8	55.1	54.9	50.7
60–79.9	57.3	55.6	60.0	57.4	52.6	56.1	62.1	56.9
80–89.9	58.3	53.6	61.0	53.1	50.3	57.6	55.8	51.9
90–100	40.5	37.9	47.3	42.1	33.1	38.5	40.6	32.4

Source: 2007 SCF Chartbook, p. 1157

* The *Survey of Consumer Finances* is published triennially. According to the Federal Reserve Board, the 2013 survey is expected to be conducted from April through December 2013. As such, data later than 2009 is not available at the time of writing.
† 2009 data comes from the 2009 *Panel Survey of Consumer Finances*, Washington, DC: Federal Reserve Bank.

by Citibank, Fidelity National Information Services, H&R Block and MasterCard, approximately 106 million individuals (40 million households) are unbanked and underbanked, representing billions of dollars of potential income. Among the individuals interviewed by CFSI, 41 percent were unemployed, 11 percent held part-time employment and 47 percent held full-time employment. Moreover, 25 percent of the respondents registered credit scores that were considered prime, while 42 percent had thin or no credit history (and thus could not be 'scored'), whereas 33 percent of the respondents were considered subprime (Centre for Financial Services Innovation, 2008).

As an example of this expansion of formal credit operations into informal spaces, the big banks that run the credit card industry have been targeting the approximately 10 to 20 million undocumented workers in the United States (Moore, 2009). Undocumented workers, like the surplus population in general, are not a homogeneous entity. Indeed, some illegal migrants earn enough money to place them squarely in the middle class.[14] Regardless of their income differentials, all undocumented workers usually live in a constant state of fear of deportation and police harassment, endure the stigma of being classified as an outsider/non-citizen and must cope with varying levels of economic insecurity. This susceptibility, combined with the burden of debt creates a well-disciplined labour force and a potentially lucrative clientele for credit card companies. According to a story in the *Wall Street Journal*, Bank of America has been offering credit cards to customers who don't have a Social Security number and who are usually undocumented immigrants. The credit cards are not cheap. They carry interest rates that typically hover at 21 percent and the fees attached to these cards are hefty. Observers estimate that card companies generate $4 billion to $5 billion annually through fees for financial services paid by the surplus population.[15]

This strategy of extending the democratisation of credit to undocumented workers allows the banks to break through barriers to capital accumulation while enticing 'non-citizens' to become part of the community of money, where they can experience (temporarily) formal equality and freedom. This also allows illegal workers to build a credit history so they can purchase cars, homes and other big-ticket items on credit ('Bank of America Casts Wider Net for Hispanics', 13 February 2007, *Wall Street Journal*). Again, the state plays a paradoxical role in terms of its support for the expansion of the community of money. On the one hand, it must be actively seen to clamp down on illegal immigrants and thereby to feed the social construction of protecting the interests of the American worker by demonising the 'other'. At the same time, the state's highly visible and coercive crackdowns on illegal workers serve to instil constant fear and, by extension, discipline among this segment of the surplus population ('Illegal-immigration crackdown on Chipotle restaurants could hurt workers, activist says', *LA Times*, 7 February 2011). On the other hand, the state has stepped in to ensure that undocumented workers pay taxes through the single taxpayer identification number (ITIN) issued by the Internal Revenue Service and have access to formal banking facilities, such as credit cards, mortgages and so forth in order to allow them to function at the bare minimum as market citizens ('Embracing Illegals: companies are getting hooked on the buying power of 11 million undocumented immigrants', *BusinessWeek*, 18 July 2005).

If this were not enough, the 2008 credit crisis in the United States presented opportunities to make money from another segment of the surplus population: the newly bankrupted. Workers facing foreclosures on their homes, including, as we will see below, the recently bankrupted, represent a potential source of income for credit card companies, particularly with regard to the fees and interests that can be earned through the issuance of secured credit cards. Secured credit cards require borrowers to guarantee the credit line in order to avoid default by supplying cash collateral through an escrowed savings account. These cards also come with extremely high interest rates and fees (Karger, 2005). Dispossessed workers turn to these sources of credit as they have no savings, no assets, no health insurance and for the most part do not earn a living wage. Although the default rate is high for secured cards, the combination of low lines of credit and extremely high interest rates and fees (e.g., origination fees, late fees, etc.) means that banks can still make a lot of money (Karger, 2005). It should be noted that the secured credit cards (or, subprime credit cards) are not an exclusive feature of the fringe economy. Some of the largest banks, such as Bank of America, Chase and Citigroup, have and continue to engage in the extremely lucrative and growing business of subprime credit card lending ('A big lenders credit card trap', *Bloomberg BusinessWeek*, 12 June 2006).

As an increasing number of subprime debtors started to default on their mortgages in 2007, credit card issuers increased their efforts to sign up such customers despite their tarnished financial histories. Direct mail credit card offers to subprime customers in the United States jumped 41 percent in the first half of 2007, compared with the first half of 2006, while direct mail offers targeted at customers with the best credit fell more than 13 percent. As home values decline and banks are turning away from issuing subprime mortgages, structurally dispossessed workers can no longer raise cash by tapping into their home equity. The only option left to these indebted workers can be credit cards. In an effort to distort and depoliticise the class nature of the subprime housing fiasco, the key lobby group for the credit card industry, the American Bankers Association (ABA), justifies direct mail offers in terms of market competition, saying they represent an attempt to lure customers who have credit cards away from competitors, which means better rates and terms for borrowers. According to an ABA senior economist, 'Consumers should be grateful that we have a very competitive market' ('Credit card companies woo struggling mortgage-holders', *The Boston Globe*, 4 September 2007).

It bears repeating that credit money temporarily resolves some of the paradoxes in capital accumulation while triggering more tensions. Among the core reasons for the inability of credit to permanently resolve the paradoxes of capital accumulation is the fact that privately created money must return to its origins for redemption. That is, despite the temporal and spatial fixes discussed above with regard to ABS and the expansion of the market to include more precarious workers, credit can resolve tensions only in the realm of exchange, not in the entire capital accumulation process. Because of this, the paradoxes that the US debtfare state will be required to mediate and depoliticise to guarantee the expansion and reproduction of the credit card industry, as well as the ongoing discipline of the surplus population, will also be aimed at the realm of exchange. Interestingly, both of the following cases of state interventions into the poverty industry are premised on invoking the trope of consumer protection, while more fully exposing workers to the discipline of the market expressed in terms of lower credit scores, higher interest rates, denial of credit, late fees and so forth.

State protection for banks and market discipline for distressed debtors: the Bankruptcy Abuse Prevention and Consumer Protection Act (BAPCPA)

The G. W. Bush Administration (2001–2009) enacted the draconian Bankruptcy Abuse Prevention and Consumer Protection Act (or, BAPCPA) in April 2005. The push for the BAPCPA was driven by the insistence of credit card issuers 'that the extraordinary increase in bankruptcy filings [over the past 30 years] is the consequences of declining stigma and "too-easy" protection of moral slackers, who refuse to pay their debts' (Sullivan *et al.*, 2006: 214). The BAPCPA, which made major changes to the 1994 Bankruptcy Reform Act, was seemingly created to protect creditors from bad market citizens, that is from consumer abuse and lack of financial responsibility (Mann, 2006). For its supporters, including the American Bankers Association and the US Chamber of Commerce, the statute would benefit both creditors and consumers equally. By making the option of personal bankruptcy less appealing for workers, its promoters argued that the BAPCPA would serve to reduce the losses by creditors and would therefore benefit consumers (workers) by lowering the cost of credit. The key point remains, however, that the record profits registered by credit card companies have never translated into lower costs to credit card debtors (Simkovic, 2009).

Aside from augmenting the income of credit card issuers (banks), the BAPCPA serves at least two purposes in terms of reproducing and legitimating credit-led accumulation by dispossession. On the one hand, the BAPCPA exposes dispossessed workers and their families to more pronounced and prolonged market discipline through debt management plans. On the other hand, as one legal scholar has astutely suggested, the statute 'facilitate[s] the credit card lending business model, by slowing the time of inevitable filings by the deeply distressed and allowing issuers to earn greater revenues from those individuals' (Mann, 2006: 375–6). Expressed differently, the BAPCPA allows credit card issuers a longer period of time to extract income from debt servicing revenues paid by distressed workers who are not yet in bankruptcy (Mann, 2006). The BAPCPA, for instance, not only increased the costs to file for bankruptcy, but also removed the right of debtors to choose between Chapter 7 bankruptcy (which discharges all debts) and Chapter 13 bankruptcy (requiring a repayment plan). If workers wish to file under Chapter 7, they must subject themselves to and pass, an intrusive and humiliating means test; if the debtor fails the means test, the bankruptcy must be filed under Chapter 13, if filed at all (Moore, 2009: 430). For that reason, it is viewed here as an integral expression of the debtfare state.

The BAPCPA reflects the power of money and its ability to impose market discipline by removing the right of self-determination by debtors to propose their own repayment plans. Under Chapter 13, for instance, debtfare determines how much a debtor must repay, based on their *disposable* income for five years, thereby also lengthening the repayment plan from three years. BAPCPA defines 'disposable income as the difference between debtors' average monthly family income during the six months prior to filing and a new income exemption'. The definition of disposable income is based on the determination by the Internal Revenue Services of an allowance for living expenses for each debtor (Moore, 2009: 430–1). The immediate effects of this particular definition of disposable income threatens the most vulnerable, namely, children and single mothers, as it allows more non-child-support debts to survive bankruptcy (e.g., credit card and auto loans) (Karger, 2005; Roberts, 2013).

The BAPCPA also permits creditors (banks) to threaten debtors with costly litigation. Debtors, many of whom cannot afford to defend themselves in court, will be coerced into giving up their legal rights (Karger, 2005: 192). Other examples of the imposition of market discipline, disempowerment and stigmatisation from the community of money enabled by the BAPCPA include making it easier for a residential landlord to evict a tenant who is in bankruptcy, even if the tenant has paid back rent (Karger, 2005: 193). In addition, under BAPCPA bankruptcy judges are not permitted to waive the means test even if the debtor has experienced a circumstance, such as a medical emergency (Karger, 2005: 192; Coco, 2012).

A final manner in which the social power of money by credit card issuers imposes discipline and thereby assists in socially reproducing credit-led accumulation is through the increased and legitimated role the BAPCPA granted to credit counseling agencies (or, CCAs) (Karger, 2005). Briefly, the CCA industry is financed through a mechanism called Fair Share. Under this policy, credit card issuers voluntarily return a percentage of each payment they receive through a debt management plan (or, DMP). If the DMP is accepted, the credit card companies may waive late and other fees and grant a lower interest rate. Although monthly payments are slightly reduced, the full balance is still owed and interest continues to accrue during the repayment period, which usually takes four to five years and has a high failure rate (only 26 percent of debtors complete DMPs) (Stehl, 1999; Karger, 2005: 177). However, in keeping with Mann's (2006) aforementioned observation, the DMPs, like the BAPCPA, allow for an extended period of time for credit card companies to receive payment on interest. Moreover, non-revolving debts, such as mortgages and auto loans, are rarely consolidated, which in turn has led to dangerous trade-offs whereby credit cards are given priority over homes and cars – two assets most workers require for shelter and work (Karger, 2005: 177).

The BAPCPA represented a huge win for credit card issuers. The banks were able to avert a number of legislative reforms demanded by various consumer advocacy groups that would have dampened the banks income-generating strategies, such as dramatically cutting fees and limiting abusive marketing tactics ('In victory for Bush, House approves Bankruptcy Bill', *New York Times*, 14 April 2005). Revolving debt per household showed its highest rate of increase in five years during the first year after BAPCPA. The reform, however, was not able to resolve the underlying tension of dispossessive capitalism, for while the bankruptcy rate decreased sharply after the law went into effect, it increased quickly thereafter: 'By the end of 2007, the US bankruptcy rate exceeded all levels recorded during the 1980s, approached the levels prevalent during the early 1990s and exceeded more than half of the level before the passage of the new law' (Weller *et al.* 2008: 1).

According to the 2010 year-end filings report of the National Bankruptcy Research Centre, for example, 'data show that filings for 2010 finished just above 1,500,000 [or, 1 in 150 people] about nine percent more than in 2009 and the highest since the two-million-plus filings in 2005' (National Bankruptcy Research Centre, 2011: 1). The 2005 bankruptcy legislation was also unable to mitigate the use of Chapter 7 (liquidation) and encourage the use of Chapter 13 (rescheduling), which further highlights the plight of dispossessed workers caught in the exploitative web of the high-debt, high-interest *modus operandi* of dispossessive capitalism. Indeed, there has been a continued decline in the use of Chapter 13 (only 28 percent of the filings in 2010) and ongoing prevalence of Chapter 7 (National Bankruptcy Research Centre, 2011: 2; Coco, 2012).

The Credit CARD Act of 2009: more consumer protection in the community of money

In the wake of the subprime debacle in 2007, increased foreclosures, rising levels of unemployment and general discontent over the massive corporate bailout by taxpayers, the credit card industry was thrust into the political spotlight again.

In May 2009, the Obama Administration implemented the Credit Card Accountability, Responsibility and Disclosure Act (or, Credit CARD Act).[16] The Credit CARD Act was described by the White House as sweeping reform aimed at protecting consumers by ensuring that credit card companies act responsibly, upholding basic standards of fairness, transparency and accountability (White House, 2009). Tellingly, the OCC – the key regulatory agency responsible for banks – once again faded into the background. Instead, the Credit CARD Act of 2009 involved an amendment to Regulation Z of the aforementioned Truth in Lending Act (TILA), which is to be carried out by Federal Reserve (Dickerson, 2008; 'Press release', Federal Reserve, 29 September 2009).[17]

On the surface, the Credit CARD Act appears to be a stronger version of previous attempts to mitigate certain practices of credit card issuers; for example in provisions for a 45-day notice if the terms of the card change and no interest rate increases in the first year. There are at least three reasons why we should be wary of the above positive spin given to the honeymoon phase of the Credit CARD Act.

First, in its attempts to protect consumers from predatory lenders, the Credit CARD Act only prevents issuers from raising rates retroactively. In other words, credit card issuers remain free to charge whatever rate they want at the start of the contract (Manning, 2000). While this has important ramifications for both secured and unsecured credit cards, workers, who only qualify for secured cards (e.g., illegal migrants, newly bankrupted, etc.), are particularly vulnerable to extremely high rates. In September 2010, Premier Bankcard of South Dakota mailed test offers of 79.9 and 59.9 annual percentage rates (APR) on credit cards with a $300 limit. The high APRs were justified by the risk-based pricing rationale. According to the CEO of Premier Bankcard, 'We need to price our product based on the risk associated with this market and allow the customer to make the decision whether they want the product or not' ('Credit CARD Act: one year later, how's it going?' *Daily Finance*, 3 June 2011; 'Issuer of 79.9 percent interest rate credit card defends its product', *CreditCards.com*, 12 February 2010). Premier Bankcard reported that the 79.9 percent APR was very popular with workers who have bad credit ratings. However, the card ultimately, and unsurprisingly, performed poorly. For example, 'A lot of the people ran up the card, defaulted and went directly to charge off.' Since then, nearly 700,000 people have signed up for the 59.9 percent card – and more than half of them carry a monthly balance' ('My card had a 79.9 percent APR', *CNN.money*, 14 February 2011). Again, it should be underlined here that in 2009 the Federal Reserve funds rate, or the interest rate at which the Federal Reserve lends money to commercial banks, stood at 0.16 percent.[18]

Second, while the Credit CARD Act has mitigated some of the predatory tendencies and excesses within the credit card industry, its most profitable feature, namely usurious interest ceilings, have remained untouched. Nor has the Credit CARD Act stopped banks from preying on the most vulnerable segments of society. On the contrary, the Credit CARD Act may have scaled back, minimally, predatory aspects of the credit card industry, such as placing a cap on fees. Its most salient feature, however, has been to legitimate the usurious practices of credit cards by providing a false sense of regulatory protection by the debtfare state. Various observers have suggested that the Credit CARD Act has made consumer credit 'safer and more transparent while interest rates and fees have stabilised since its passage in 2009' (Pew, 2011). Although interest rates stabilised in 2010, the spread between the prime rate set by the Federal Reserve (3.25 percent) and the average APR (on unsecured cards) at 14.06 percent was the widest in the past two decades ('A new landscape for credit cards', *Wall Street Journal*, 23 January 2011).

According to Pew's latest analysis, for example, the median advertised interest rates for bank credit cards ranged from 12.99 to 20.99 percent, depending on a consumer's credit history, remained unchanged from 2010 (Pew, 2011). In Table 4.7, I compare Pew data collected on APR and various fees issued by the 12 largest banks in the US, which account for about 90 percent of credit card outstandings (balance remaining on cards), prior to and after the enactment of the Credit CARD Act of 2009.

The Pew analysis is important as it serves to legitimate dispossessive practices by the credit card industry by naturalising and normalising usurious interest rates. It seems to buy into the regulatory hype of the debtfare state regarding consumer protection instead of grasping that the Credit CARD Act offers minor tweaking to the cannibalistic practices of the credit card industry's ongoing attempts to expand and intensify an exploitative form of credit-led accumulation (see Chapter 2). The Credit CARD Act allows credit card companies enough leeway to wiggle through the regulations.

As with its predecessor, the TILA, the Credit CARD Act ultimately reproduces fetishised sentiments of formal freedom and equality as well as individual

TABLE 4.8 Credit card annual interest rates (APRs) and fees, 2008–2009 and 2010–2011[a]

Median fee or charge	December 2008	July 2009	March 2010– January 2011
US prime rate[b]	3.25 percent	3.25 percent	3.25 percent
Purchase APR	9.99–15.99 percent	12.24–17.99 percent	12.99 percent
Cash advance APR	N/A	20.24–21.24 percent	20.99 percent
Penalty APR	27.99 percent	28.99 percent	24.24 percent
Late fee	$39	$39	$35
Over-limit fee	$39	$39	$35
Cash advance fee	N/A	3 percent	4 percent

a The Pew Health Group (2011) 'A New Equilibrium: After Passage of Landmark Credit Card Reform, Interest Rates and Fees have stabilized' (May). Available at: www.pewtrusts.org/ . . . /Reports/Credit_ Cards/Report_Equilibrium_web.pdf (accessed 26 May 2011).

b Wall Street Journal Prime Rate History. Available at: www.wsjprimerate.us (accessed 26 May 2011).

Source: The Pew Health Group (2009) 'Still Waiting: "Unfair or Deceptive" Credit Card Practices Continue as American Wait for New Reforms to Take Effect', *The Pew Charitable Trusts*, October. Available at: www.pewtrusts.org/our_work_detail.aspx?id=630 (accessed 26 May 2011).

responsibilisation (consumer beware!). That is, it looks for solutions in the realm of the market, as opposed to demanding rigorous state-led regulation that would put a cap on interest rates and ensure higher minimum wage laws, well-funded public housing, health, welfare and education programmes and so forth. The Credit CARD Act is thus designed to normalise the exploitative role (high-debt, high-interest) of credit cards in the everyday lives of workers, particularly the working poor and structurally dispossessed. It also presents credit card issuers as willing partners in empowering, as opposed to protecting, consumers. According to Kenneth J. Clayton, Senior Vice President and General Counsel for the American Bankers Association card policy, 'The bottom line is this: the credit card industry is changing and these new rules will help empower consumers to take control of their personal finances.'[19]

Third, for some observers, the Credit CARD Act has created some relief for distressed credit card debtors. As Table 4.3 shows, some families and individuals have indeed managed to pay down their balances through traditional means such as tax refunds, working extra hours and tapping into their savings (Traub and Ruetschlin, 2012). These figures must be understood in the wider context that approximately $193.3 billion of this credit card debt was charged off (i.e., a declaration by a credit card company that a specific amount of debt is unlikely to be collected) by issuers from 2009 through the third quarter of 2011, according to the most recent data available from CardHub.com. Banks, moreover, have written off billions in bad debt, which helps create a deceptively rosy-looking picture. According to Federal Reserve data, credit cards have the highest level of charge-offs compared to other forms of consumer debt and were particularly high from 2009 to 2011.[20] Dēmos cites Federal Reserve data showing that revolving credit dropped from $965.5 billion in 2009 to $798.6 billion in 2012 (Traub and Ruetschlin, 2012). With labour markets shedding jobs and credit markets tightening in the aftermath of the subprime housing fiasco, from 2009 to 2012, 39 percent of households, particularly low-income households ($25,000 to $50,000), which tend to suffer from higher levels of credit card debt, have either had credit lines cut or reduced, or been denied new credit, while 48 percent cut their spending as a result of increased economic pressure from the downturn. The surplus population would spend more to meet basic survival needs if they had access to more credit. Dēmos survey respondents, for example, have more debt in 2012 than they did in 2009 and fewer resources for paying it off (Traub and Ruetschlin, 2012).

To summarise this section: The Credit CARD Act may be seen as an attempt by the debtfare state to address the underlying tensions in credit-led accumulation, while at the same time guaranteeing the *illusion* of a naturally evolving, level, objective and individualised playing field in which consumers are protected from practices that run counter to freedom, democracy and equality. In reality, the Act traps people in the community of money. Furthermore, the Credit CARD Act, like BAPCPA, remains focused on and framed in, the sphere of exchange, where the social power of credit and the debtfare interventions that undergird them are aimed at socially disciplining surplus labour to the exigencies of the market as well as neutralising the class nature of secondary exploitation upon which the credit card industry is predicated.

Concluding remarks

As increasing numbers of poor and low-income workers rely on highly exploitative, corporate forms of social welfare and wage replacement/augmentation, so too have political modes of domination undergone a transformation, particularly in the face of growing levels of impoverishment and dispossession. In my attempts at denaturalising and politicising the credit card industry in the wider processes of credit-led accumulation, I have suggested that the rhetorical and regulative features of the US debtfare state play a strategic role in constructing, mediating the tensions within, and socially reproducing the credit card industry. By extension, these features also serve to discipline the surplus population to the exigencies of the market. The debtfare state has allowed the credit card industry to overcome the barriers inherent to forms of accumulation involving the expansion of the money-form of revenue by facilitating continual spatio-temporal fixes. These fixes, however, are not only temporary but also inherently paradoxical in nature, demanding further intervention by the debtfare state.

Credit cards are an important feature of the flourishing poverty industry in the United States. But they are neither the only sector, nor the largest segment of the poverty industry. In the next chapter, we turn to the role of the debtfare state in facilitating the meteoric rise of the student loan industry, gripping ever more members of the surplus population.

Notes

1 Credit cards have a long history in the US economy. In 1946, for example, the popular instalment credit plan (Manning, 2000) was replaced with the first credit card, the Charg-It plan. The Charg-It was followed by cards that were broader in scope in terms of uses, but were still casting a relatively small net of potential borrowers. These cards offered profitable but simple payment facilities: 'The balance had to be paid in full before credit was extended again' (Geisst, 2009: 62).

2 Banks specialising in credit cards have been much more profitable than banks in general. According to 2007 data from the Federal Deposit Insurance Corporation (FDIC), the return on equity was 15.1 percent for credit card banks, compared to 8.2 percent for all banks. Consumers Union (2009) 'Credit Card Facts and Stats', 21 May. Available at: http://consumersunion.org/wp-content/uploads/2013/03/credit-card-facts-stats.pdf (accessed 3 January 2012).

3 Initial Public Offerings refer to the 'first sale of stock by a private company to the public. IPOs are often issued by smaller, younger companies seeking the capital to expand, but can also be done by large privately owned companies looking to become publicly traded'. Available at: www.investopedia.com/terms/i/ipo.asp (accessed 3 May 2011).

4 About 56 percent of consumers carried an unpaid balance in the past 12 months. 'The Survey of Consumer Payment Choice', Federal Reserve Bank of Boston, January 2010. Read more at: www.creditcards.com/credit-card-news/credit-card-industry-facts-personal-debt-statistics-1276.php#ixzz1O8TUFoUJ (accessed 7 January 2014).

5 Ibid.

6 It will be recalled from our discussion in Chapter 2 that Marx's concept of the surplus population encompasses underemployed and unemployed. Counting both categories that comprise the surplus population has been fraught with many shortcomings. For instance, the government measures unemployment by the number of workers receiving unemployment benefits. This method, however, is misleading, since unemployment benefits expire. The US Bureau of Labour Statistics (BLS) is also based on a limited sample size of its monthly surveys on 60,000 households (out of approximately 115 million households in the country) (see US Department of Labour, 2009; US Bureau of the Census, 2012). The BLS surveys, like the federal government unemployment reports, fail to account for those no longer looking for a job, largely out of despair and/or other factors (child or elderly care, illness, and so forth).

7 Government definitions of poverty are also extremely problematic. According to its critics, the poverty line is simply too low, and does not adequately capture families and individuals who are unable to meet basic needs. As Jeannette Wicks-Lim points out, the official poverty line has been changed – augmented by the Supplemental Poverty Measure in 2011 – only *once* since it was established half a century ago ('Undercounting the Poor: The US's new, but only marginally improved, poverty measure', *Dollars & Sense*, May/June 2013). However, the categories of low-income and poor are consistent with the primary sources that measure credit card debt used in this study, including Dēmos and the Federal Reserve's triennial Survey of Consumer Finances (SCF). SCF is a household level survey that deals with a relatively small sample size, for instance anywhere from 3,143 household in 1989 to 6,492 households in 2010 (Federal Reserve, 1989, 2010). The SCF is also said to oversample wealthier households (Bird *et al.*, 1997). In contrast Dēmos conducts smaller surveys than the SCF (997 households in 2012), but concentrates on low-income and middle-class households (Traub and Ruetchlin, 2012).

8 There are minor differences in terms of the numbers collected by the US Census and the US Department of Health and Human Services. For further information on the two different ways the US government calculates poverty (e.g., poverty threshold versus poverty guidelines), see: www.irp.wisc.edu/faqs/faq1.htm (accessed 13 June 2013). The US Department of Commerce Bureau of the Census, for instance, draws on the poverty threshold definition, while the HSS employs the poverty guidelines measure. The differences between the two measures are slight, e.g., according to the US Census' preliminary estimate of weighted average poverty thresholds for 2012, one person with income of $11,722 or less is considered poor, whereas for a two-person household, the threshold is $14,960; for a three-person household, $18,287; and for a four-person household, $23,497. US Department of Commerce and Bureau of the Census (2013), *Preliminary Estimate of Weighted Average Poverty Thresholds for 2012*, Washington, DC: US Census. Available at: www.census.gov/hhes/www/poverty/data/threshld/index.html (accessed 10 June 2013).

9 For more information, see methods and definitions at the US Census website at: www.census.gov/hhes/www/poverty/methods/definitions.html (accessed 17 June 2013).

10 See also Table 6.4 in Chapter 6 for common reasons that working poor to turn to payday lending.

11 Most of the requirements imposed by the 1968 Truth in Lending Act are contained within a legal framework referred to as Regulation Z, although both TILA and Regulation Z are often used interchangeably (Drysdale and Keest, 2000). For more information on Regulation Z, see the Federal Deposit Insurance Corporation's website on this topic: www.fdic.gov/regulations/laws/rules/6500-1400.html (accessed 7 January 2014).

12 Annual Percentage Rates or APR refers to the yearly cost of the loan in terms of interest and fees. By law, credit card companies and loan issuers must demonstrate the APR of a particular agreement to facilitate transparency of the actual rates applied. Credit card companies are allowed to advertise interest rates on a monthly basis (e.g. 2 percent per month), but are also required to clearly state the APR to customers before any agreement is signed (e.g., 2 percent for 12 months reflects an APR of 24 percent).

13 Collateralised debt obligations (CDOs) represent various types of debt and credit risk. These different categories of debt are often referred to as 'tranches' or 'slices', e.g., junior and senior tranches. Each tranche has a different maturity and risk associated with it. The higher the risk, the more the CDO pays to investors. Investorpedia. Available at: www.investopedia.com/terms/c/cdo.asp (accessed 24 May 2011). Collateralised debt swaps (CDSs), on the other hand, describe unregulated 'insurance-like contracts that promise to cover losses on certain securities in the event of a default. They typically apply to municipal bonds, corporate debt and mortgage securities and are sold by banks, hedge funds and others. The buyer of the credit default insurance pays premiums over a period of time in return for peace of mind, knowing that losses will be covered if a default happens. It's supposed to work similarly to someone taking out home insurance to protect against losses from fire and theft'. Available at: www.time.com/time/business/article/0,8599,1723152,00.html (accessed 24 May 2011).

14 Conventionally based on median pre-tax income of $50,000 (US Department of Commerce, 2010).

15 'Prepaid, reloadable payment cards for immigrants roll out: The "no SSN" [Security Card Number] prepaid cards offer respite from high-cost fringe services', *CreditCards.com*, 19 September 2008. Available at: www.creditcards.com/credit-card-news/immigrants-prepaid-credit-cards-social-security-1282.php#ixzz1MixDgl3w (accessed 19 May 2011).

16 For more information, see 'The Credit Card Accountability Responsibility and Disclosure Act'. Available at: http://maloney.house.gov/documents/financial/creditcards/MAY22.CreditCardSummaryFinalPassage.pdf (accessed 4 April 2011). See also overview by the Federal Reserve Bank. Available at: www.federalreserve.gov/consumerinfo/wyntk_creditcardrules.htm (accessed 4 April 2011).

17 Some of the most significant features of the Credit CARD Act of 2009 included: 45-day notice if the terms of your card change; no rate increases in the first year; payment dates must be the same every month; statements must be delivered at least 21 days before the due date, and the statement must be explicit about late fees and other consequences of late payment; fees cannot exceed 25 percent of the initial credit limit on the card; over-limit fees are no longer permitted, and so forth ('Press Release', Federal Reserve, 29 September 2009).

18 Historical Data 'Federal Funds', Board of Governors of the Federal Reserve System. Available at: www.federalreserve.gov/releases/h15/data.htm (accessed 1 June 2013).

19 'Consumers Benefit from Fed's Sweeping New Credit Card Rules', News Release, American Bankers Association, 12 January 2010. Available at: www.aba.com/Press+Room/011210FedCreditCardRules.htm (accessed 1 June 2011).

20 See, for example, 'Charge-Off and Delinquency Rates on Loans and Leases at Commercial Banks'. Available at: www.federalreserve.gov/releases/chargeoff/chgallnsa.htm (accessed 24 June 2013).

5

DEBTFARISM AND THE STUDENT LOAN INDUSTRY

Registering $1trillion in April 2012, student loans in the United States exceeded the total amount of all other forms of unsecured consumer debt.[1] Educational loans remain the only form of consumer debt to markedly increase since the peak of household debt in late 2008 (Federal Reserve Bank of New York, 2012). The student loan industry is comprised not only of private lending institutions, such as Sallie Mae, Wells Fargo and JP Morgan Chase, but also the US state, which operates its own lending facility. This formidable component of the US poverty industry has become a highly lucrative venture for private lenders. In the wake of the 2008 financial crisis, however, policy pundits and economists have been very concerned about rapidly increasing levels of student loans because educational loans act as a drag on housing recovery, as highly indebted recent graduates cannot afford to purchase a home ('Student debt is stifling home sales', *Bloomberg* 23 February 2012).

Other groups, such as the National Association of Consumer Bankruptcy Attorneys, are concerned about what they call *the student loan debt bomb*, as they view current debt levels of recent graduates, parents who co-signed their loans, and older students returning to school for job training, as unsustainable. Defaults on student loans have steadily increased from 6.13 percent in the first quarter of 2003 to 8.69 percent in 2012, with delinquency rates higher than that of mortgages, auto loans and home equity lines of credit (Federal Reserve Bank of New York, 2012). The growing numbers of student debtors, who have been subjected to the devastating and humiliating social consequences of default, have also vented their anger and frustration with the nature and management of these loans through numerous acts of protest and active lobbying, most notably, the Occupy Student Debt Campaign[2] (Collinge, 2009).

The main objective of this chapter is to denaturalise a key feature upon which the student loan industry has been constructed: the continued expansion of a loan-based system of higher education. Drawing on the historical materialist analysis developed in Part I of the book, I offer the following three-pronged argument. First, I suggest that the student loan industry is an integral feature of the wider processes of credit-led accumulation. Seen from this angle, there is a central paradox inherent to the student loan industry: on the one hand, an incessant drive by capitalists to expand fictitious value tied to credit (i.e., private and federal student loans) and, on the other, the increasing inability of the surplus population (students) to meet payment obligations, leading to a greater number of defaults.

Second and related, I argue that the institutionalised debtfare strategies pursued by the state have played an integral, albeit contradictory, role in resolving various articulations of this core tension of the industry. In its capacity as both lender and *super-creditor*, for instance, the debtfare state ensures that tensions emerging from credit-led accumulation are resolved within the bounds of the neutral authority of the law, that is, by upholding the bourgeois construction of the legal obligation of debt repayment through constant revisions of the bankruptcy law. These state interventions are bolstered by and, in turn support, the (re-)construction of monetised and individualised relations between creditor and debtor that appear to be ruled by abstractions such as interest rates as opposed to a class-based relation of exploitation. The debtfare strategies pursued by the state also attempt to depoliticise and mediate paradoxes, while facilitating the expansion and reproduction of the student loan industry through what Harvey (1989) describes as spatio-temporal displacements.[3] These fixes are evident, for example, in the central role played by student loan asset-backed securitisations (hereafter: SLABS) and what I refer to as the commodification of debt.

Third and related, I suggest that the unfolding rhetorical and regulative intervention of the debtfare the state assists in constructing and normalising the growing dependency of the surplus population on credit to fund higher education through a loan-based system as opposed to grant-based aid. In doing so, the debtfare state validates and perpetuates what for many indebted students has proven to be an expensive myth: improving one's *skill sets* through higher education will result in a middle-class lifestyle at best (US Department of Commerce, 2012; Traub et al., 2012).[4]

I develop this argument in three main sections. Section One provides an overview of the student loan industry and discusses the meaning of students as surplus population therein. Section Two embarks on a historical materialist analysis of the role of the debtfare state in the expansion and reproduction of the student loan industry from the 1970s to 2010. Section Four provides concluding remarks by highlighting the key findings of a government report that identifies private student loans as the main problem of student loan debt in the US.

The student loan industry and students as surplus population: an overview

The student loan industry

As noted above, total educational loan indebtedness surpassed the shocking level of $1 trillion in 2012, up from $663 billion in 2003 (Federal Reserve Bank of New York, 2012). The majority of this debt is comprised of federal government loans, with about $150 billion stemming from private loans (Coco, 2013). As will become clearer below, the burgeoning student loan industry is part and parcel of the neoliberal shift away from public support for higher education to placing the burden of financing on the individual. This move is evident through, for instance, the steady shift away from grant-based aid to predominantly loan-based aid (Traub et al., 2012; Coco, 2013). The student loan industry has grown steadily over the past several decades in lockstep with rising student demand and rapidly rising tuition fees (US Department of Education, 2012). The industry is comprised of two main categories of loans and lenders: public student loans, which are issued by the federal government and represent the largest type of loan (85 percent) (Consumer Finance Protection Bureau, 2012) and private student loans, which are issued by banks such as JP Morgan Chase and Citibank. Private lenders, primarily banks, have played a critical role in the industry, supplying about 80 percent of the $55 billion to $60 billion in new federal loans made annually from 1998 to 2008 and $15 billion to $20 billion in the form of private loans (Ergungor and Hathaway, 2008).

The Guaranteed Student Loan Program was established in the Higher Education Act of 1965 and was later renamed the Federal Family Education Loan Program (FFELP). The FFELP guaranteed and subsidised student loans, which were originated and funded by private lenders, most notably banks. Key loans that constituted the FFELP program included: federal Stafford loans (the largest type of student loan), unsubsidised federal Stafford loans, Perkins loans, FFELP PLUS loans and FFEL consolidation loans (Eglin, 1993). FFELP loans can be applied to both public and private colleges. These guaranteed FFELP loans place the full faith and credit of the US government behind a private bank loan to each student. With the exception of the unsubsidised Stafford loans, the state pays interest on the loan during periods of grace (six-months after graduation) and deferment, in addition to paying the difference between a set low interest rate and the market rate after graduation (the so-called 'special allowance') (Corder and Hoffman, 2001). Aside from subsidising interest rates, the state guarantees a large portion (97 to 100 percent) of the FFELP loan if a parent (typical co-signer) or student defaults (Fried and Breheny, 2005).

To help raise capital and ensure liquidity to assist in guaranteeing federal student loans, the government set up a government-sponsored enterprise (GSE) – Student Loan Marketing Association (or, Sallie Mae) in 1972. As I discuss below, Sallie Mae raised funds through the issuance of student loan asset-backed securitisations (SLABS), which created an efficient way of generating money to help finance low interest rate loans to students by subsidising and guaranteeing repayment to their private lenders (Federal Reserve Bank of New York, 2012). Sallie Mae was privatised in 1996 (SLM Corporation) and eventually became the largest issuer of SLABS in both federal and private student loans, as well as the largest educational lender of private student loans in the US. The poverty industry has proven such fertile ground for generating revenue that the corporation has expanded into other areas of consumer finance (e.g., mortgages, credit cards, car loans) and created Laureate, an online loan delivery system.[5] The company has also moved into debt collection and guarantor servicing. Sallie Mae has been growing at such a rapid and highly profitable pace that in 2013 it announced it intended to split into two separate, publicly traded companies: 'an education loan management business and a consumer banking business' ('Sallie Mae to split loan and banking businesses into two separate companies', *The Guardian*, 29 May 2013).

The passage of the Health Care and Education Reconciliation Act in 2010 put an end to the FFELP programme, replacing it with the William D. Ford Direct Student Loan Program (or, DLP). Under this new law, public student loans originate directly from the US Department of Education, effectively ending the ability of private banks to originate – but not to profit from – student loans backed by the federal government. Like the FFEL loans (e.g., Stafford loans), DLP loans can be applied to both public and private colleges. I address the Stafford loans in more detail below.

Although federal student loans remain the largest category of educational lending, private student loans have been growing at a swift pace over the past decade (CFPB, 2013). Default rates on private student loans, which carry higher interest rates than federal student loans, are high and show no signs of abating. The percentage of borrowers who defaulted on federal loans within the first three years of payments rose to an average of 13.4 percent in 2011. This number was considerably higher, 22.7 percent, for students who attended for-profit colleges (US Department of Education, 2012). Students attending for-profit, private universities – also known as proprietary schools – tend to have higher levels of student debt, given the comparatively higher tuition fees and other costs (see Table 5.2) (Lynch *et al.*, 2010). For instance, while 62 percent of students graduating from public colleges held some kind of student debt, 72 percent of students attending private colleges, particularly for-profit, private colleges, many of whom are from a low-income bracket, held a student loan (Johnson *et al.*, 2012).

The precise debt load of recent graduates is difficult to ascertain given the variation in public and private debt as well as the nature of the higher education institution (e.g., public colleges, for-profit private colleges, non-profit private colleges) across state lines.[6] According to an oft-cited source, in 2011 two-thirds of all college students held an average of $26,500 in student loan debt upon leaving college.[7] One in ten borrowers now graduates with more than $54,000 in loans. The colour of student debt is also noteworthy:

> African-American and Latino students are especially saddled with student debt, with 81 percent of African-American students and 67 percent of Latino

students who earned bachelor's degrees leaving school with debt. This compares to 64 percent of white students who graduate with debt.

(Johnson *et al.*, 2012: 1)

Students as surplus labour

As discussed in Chapter 2, the relative surplus population is a highly dynamic and heterogeneous segment of the population that is comprised of underemployed and unemployed workers. Seen from the wider processes of the student loan industry, students may be regarded as surplus labour. They attempt – often in failure – to move beyond this category by obtaining a higher education. It is only after graduation that students will find out whether they are indeed surplus labour or not. In the meantime, they will have accumulated hefty debt loads, thereby amplifying the risks involved and feeding the coffers of the student loan industry.

Many students carrying an average debt load (and higher) do not earn a median income immediately after graduation. Aside from poor employment prospects,[8] 'more young graduates were considered underemployed. Among those who wanted to be working full time, as many as 19.1 percent were either working part time or had given up looking for work. Further, 37.8 percent of working young graduates had jobs that did not require a college degree, depressing their wages' (The Project on Student Debt, 2012: 2). Student debtors struggle not only with educational debt but also with the rising costs of health care and housing (US Department of Commerce, 2010). Coupled with poor job prospects, students have resorted to desperate measures by moving back home with their parents, defaulting, dropping out of college, working two jobs, putting off marriage and starting families and attempting to file bankruptcy to reduce overall debt loads (Traub *et al.*, 2012; Coco, 2013).[9]

Particularly hardest hit from the increasing shift from an aid-based to loan-based system of higher education have been low-income students. In this chapter, I define the latter category by drawing on the income limits employed by the US Department of Education to determine eligibility for Pell Grants. The latter, as I document below, are aid-based grants (i.e., money not requiring repayment) designed to supplement low-income students' higher education. In July 2012, the debtfare state revised the maximum adjusted gross income[10] from $30,000 per annum to to $23,000 per annum. This has made it more difficult for low-income students to access a Pell Grant. Moreover, based on the 2013 federal poverty guidelines laid out in Table 4.2 (see Chapter 4), this new income limit means that Pell grants are now geared primarily to those families living below 100 percent of the poverty line. The Pell Grant is also quite small in comparison with the rising cost of higher education. In 2012, for instance, while the maximum Pell Grant reached $5,500, the average amount of the grant dispersed was only $3,800.[11] In 2013, Pell Grants reached their highest level at $5,635. Yet even if this full amount were to be awarded to low-income students, it would cover only one-third of the average cost of college – the lowest since the start of the programme in 1972 (Reimherr *et al.*, 2013: 3).

A historical materialist account of the making of the student loan industry

Contextualising Sallie Mae

Sallie Mae was established in 1972 as a government-sponsored enterprise (GSE). It emerged from a specific political and material environment, which was marked, among other things, by Keynesian ideals of managed capitalism and the slowing of economic growth once fuelled by Fordist forms of domestic and international expansion of exports (Harvey, 2003). Under this configuration of state and material relations, the US saw an expansion of the middle class[12] in the 1950s and with it the belief that a college education leads to social and economic mobility. In the 1960s and 1970s, social and political pressure by the Civil Rights and Women's Rights Movements resulted in many policy changes, not the least in discriminatory practices regarding access to higher education and credit. These pressures coincided with increased demand for higher education and the sector experienced a period of unprecedented growth. The state infused money into higher education to fund academic research, expansion of colleges and federal loans (Gumport *et al.*, 1997). In this context, student loans played a secondary role to grant aid under the Higher Education Act (HEA) of 1965. In a reauthorisation of the HEA in 1972, for instance, Senator Claiborne Pell, sought to expand federal aid directly to low-income students rather than through the institutions. The Pell Grants would serve to reduce the need for low-income students to borrow money to pay for their higher education. As one legal scholar notes, the logic behind the 1972 Act was to shift the majority of the costs of attending college 'from low-income students and their families to the federal government' (Coco, 2013: 584).

Seen against the above backdrop, Sallie Mae was a state-led attempt to influence the flow of capital and credit to the student loan industry by absorbing the financial risks (defaults and bankruptcies) involved in lending to students (Corder and Hoffman, 2001). Like other GSEs, such as Freddie Mac and Fannie Mae, Sallie Mae was a special type of government-backed, shareholder-owned, for-profit corporation. Unlike other GSEs, however, Sallie Mae was legally permitted to purchase, service, sell, or otherwise deal in government-issued student loans, which were, in turn, fully guaranteed and directly subsidised by the state (Corder and Hoffman, 2001). The official justification for this state guarantee was due to the high-risk nature of student loans. Notwithstanding the subsidised interest rates, special allowances and other state guarantees, lenders (mostly large commercial banks) were unwilling to participate in the programme because student loans not only represented forms of unsecured debt (i.e., an absence of collateral), but they were also illiquid and long-term (Kothari, 2006). As we saw in the previous chapter, in the tumultuous environment of the 1970s, interest rates would at times fall below the rate of inflation, cancelling state subsidies to the banks.

To overcome this barrier, Sallie Mae raised funds in two ways. First, it sold debt securities (e.g., bonds) on secondary markets. Second, after the passage of the

Education Amendments in 1980, it was permitted to securitise its financial 'assets' (student loans) (Corder and Hoffman, 2001). This second and related method of subsidising lenders pursued by Sallie Mae coincides with what I refer to here as the commodification of debt and the rise of the neoliberal state, with its underlying neoclassical assumption that private consumption is superior to public consumption (see Chapter 3 and Fine, 2002; Peck and Tickell, 2002).

Before continuing with the historical materialist analysis, it is useful to expand upon and deconstruct student loan asset-backed securitisation (SLABS), as this strategy acts as a portal through which we can gain more insightful understanding of the tensions inherent to the student loan industry and the displacement of the social dimension of risk to the surplus population.

An interlude: deconstructing SLABS and the commodification of debt

A central, yet undertheorised, feature of the student loan industry is student loan asset-backed securitisation, or SLABS.[13] This refers to a technique in which illiquid assets such as student loans are transformed into tradable securities through a legally created tax-exempt entity called either a Special Purpose Vehicle (SPV) or a Special Purpose Entity (SPE) (Elul, 2005). Since the 1980s, SLABS has represented the backbone of the student loan industry, accounding for over 100 percent of student loans in 2006.[14] According to industry observers, SLABS act as the 'main artery through which funds are channelled from investors to students' (Ergungor and Hathaway, 2008: 2). SLABS is often presented as offering a highly efficient method of raising capital and mitigating or, as some claim, reducing risk for lenders, including the threats of default and bankruptcy (Gorton and Souleles, 2007; Fabozzi and Kothari, 2008). Government and private educational lenders represent SLABS as a neutral, financial instrument that afforded Sallie Mae an efficient way of raising money to help finance low interest rate loans to students by subsidising and guaranteeing repayment to private lenders (Federal Reserve Bank of New York, 2012).

It is important to move beyond this economistic understanding of SLABS as an apolitical, efficient, win-win financial instrument. This view suggests SLABS limit or reduce risk, creating more credit by transforming student *debt* into *assets* that can be bought and sold in the digitalised spaces of finance[15] (Sassen, 2006). I begin the analytical deconstruction by maintaining that SLABS is not a thing, but a social relation that embodies both temporal and spatial sources of social power that play themselves out in the concrete geography of the community of money (Harvey, 1989). SLABS, for instance, is a form of privately credit money, or more specifically and drawing on our discussion in Chapter 2, a money-form of revenue. It should be highlighted that credit entails the creation of fictitious value that is mediated by formalised abstractions (interest rates, risk-based pricing, fees and so forth) as opposed to direct forms of domination between employer and employee. SLABS represent a temporal displacement or what Harvey refers to as a *fix*, given that it aims to accelerate the transaction process. A necessary condition for this temporal power is the ability to create what Marx refers to as fictitious value (Harvey, 1989).

In Marxian terms, fictitious value draws our attention to the fact that credit in the form of student loans (interests and fees), including their extensions in the form of SLABS, do not possess an inherent value, yet they can assume a price (Harvey, 1999: 265ff). While the price used to value SLABS is believed to be objectively set through various complex metrics based on algorithms and sanctioned by credit-rating agencies, the construction of the price given to various SLABS ultimately rests on the trade in promises to pay. These promises are not solely based on the cultural features of the credit system, e.g. relationships of trust, subjectivities and performativities. Instead they depend on the political and legal relationships that command repayment from borrowers regardless of their ability to make such payments, or the social costs involved in doing so.[16] It is, therefore, fundamentally an issue of power.

The relations of power underpinning SLABS must contend with an inherent feature of credit money: 'no matter how far afield these various bills of exchange circulate, they must always return to their place of origin for redemption' (Harvey, 1999). Put another way, SLABS, as with student loans, ultimately relies on the viability of future labour (e.g., students' salary or wage earnings upon completion of college) as a counter-value, making it inherently risky for all parties involved – although, as we will see below, the risk is distributed unequally among creditors and debtors.

SLABS, therefore, not only wield temporal power over debtors, they are simultaneously able to accelerate the payment time of the student loan to suit capitalists' interests and needs. A freshman at UCLA who gets a four-year, $25,000 student loan from a private bank (e.g., post-1996, privatised Sallie Mae), for example, will end up paying, depending on the repayment schedule and an interest rate based on creditworthiness, anywhere from $50,545.95 (based on a 145-month repayment plan) to $70,259.07 (based on a 193-month repayment plan) or even $74,126.61 (based on a 144-month deferred repayment plan) to Sallie Mae.[17] On the other hand, shortly after making the transaction, the originator (Sallie Mae) sells this loan, as well as a bundle of other student loans, to an outside investor, thereby receiving a payment immediately, as opposed to receiving small monthly payments for 12 to 16 years from the student and taking the risk that the student may default on his/her loan during this time. The basic belief driving this transaction is that the student loan (debt) is an asset – a commodity that can be owned or controlled to produce value (e.g., interest, commission and fees).

I describe this process, which shifts financial risk to debtors and institutional investors, as the commodification of debt. Mitigating or even eliminating risk (e.g., default and bankruptcy) linked to lending to students is one benefit of SLABS. But there is another fee-generating perk: By receiving the funds today from selling the student loan to investors, the educational lender has the opportunity to profit further by originating even more loans and thereby earning origination fees (Elul, 2005).

The processes involved in the commodification of debt are not technical and apolitical, but are imbued with social relations of power that are asymmetrical and exploitative in nature. Following Marx, the latter term refers to secondary forms of exploitation that occur through dispossessive strategies pursued through the credit system, which are aimed at modifying workers' wages and salaries through interest, commission and fee payments (Harvey, 1999; Sassen 2009).

SLABS are class-based attempts to overcome the contradictions inherent in credit-led accumulation by reducing financial risk and increasing liquidity for educational lenders, so that they may continue to extend credit to primarily high-risk (subprime) borrowers (students, particularly low-income students). Yet, student debtors are afforded no protections in terms of dealing with the social consequences of risk, such as the inability to find employment, illness, inflation of health-care and housing costs, inability to complete an educational degree and so forth (Traub *et al.*, 2012; Johnson *et al.*, 2012). Student debt burdens must be understood alongside the unemployment rate for young college graduates, which has risen from 8.7 percent in 2009 to 9.1 percent in 2010, the highest annual rate on record (CFPB, 2012; Project on Student Debt, 2012). As a result of these conditions, student debtors are also carrying higher levels of credit card debt (Federal Reserve Bank of New York, 2012) – all of which serves to increase pressure on students' debt burdens. Indeed, almost three-quarters of students who default on their educational loans (many of whom are minority students from low-income backgrounds) have done so after withdrawing from school and failing to complete their studies (Lynch *et al.* 2010).

The unequal and exploitative relations of power involved in securitising student loans are concealed in the dominant representation and depoliticisation of risk in exclusively financial terms. As I discuss below, these relations are further masked by the legal obligation between creditor and debtor. Here, it is important to note that risk, as it is used in the financial industry, has at its roots in dominant neoclassical theory and its underlying assumptions of rationality, efficiency and individualism. For instance, risk understood exclusively in financial terms relates to uncertainty and/or potential financial loss for the lender (Luhmann, 2008). With regard to securitisation, this prevailing meaning of financialised risk includes probable harm only to 'key participants' in SLABS: *securitisers* (e.g., a government sponsored enterprise or a trust), originators of the assets (educational lenders) and investors (e.g., pension and mutual funds)[18] (Federal Reserve Bank of New York, 2012). Yet, if we understand SLABS and the wider credit system as relations of power imbued with the ability to wield command over time, risk also has social dimensions, notably in the form of defaults. The social dimension of risks for student debtors is thereby expunged from the sanitised, mathematical and technical understanding of neoclassical economics (Bourdieu, 2005). As this exemplifies, in the highly abstract world of neoclassical economics and its narrow view of individual rationality, there is a constant severance of the economic from the historical and social conditions in which risk is constructed, defined, governed and reproduced (Bourdieu, 1998).

Risk and its strategies of mitigation and measurement are profoundly social questions of power. This is particularly the case if we accept the premise that credit entails not only social power over time and space but also is, in effect, a gamble with the future lives of student debtors. Financial corporations (e.g., SLM Corporation) possess the power to sell (and transform) unsecured debt into *assets* in order to accelerate the temporal dimension of repayment on their initial outlay plus interest, fees and commission. They do so, however, by displacing the social dimensions of risk involved in this process onto student debtors. This is not a neutral, natural and inevitable feature of the market driven by competitive forces and technological innovation; instead, it represents a socially constructed reality that is both highly dynamic and paradoxical in nature. A central force in governing the social and financial dimensions of risk in the student loan industry is the debtfare state and its role in displacing and disciplining student debtors.

Debtfarism and the mediation of the social dimensions of risk

During the period of economic instability in the 1970s and much of the 1980s, many students graduating from colleges were unable to secure well-paying jobs to meet their loan obligations. Indeed, as one commentator notes many graduates at this time were either unemployed or employed in jobs that they could have secured without post-secondary education (Wiese, 1984: 459). Unsurprisingly, default rates on student loans rose, as did student loans discharged in bankruptcy. In 1975, there was a 59.9 percent increase over the number of claims filed in 1974. Toward the end of 1975, the federal government and guaranty agencies had reimbursed lenders for $20.9 million of guaranteed student loans discharged in bankruptcy (Birdwell, 1978: 593). Despite these trends, the debtfare state was busily creating more demand for federal loans and, by extension, private banks. In 1978, for instance, the government permitted most middle-class Americans to access federal loans without the requirement that students demonstrate financial need (Grant, 2011).

To deal with the social risks involved in rising default rates on student loans during this period, Congress enacted disciplinary policies to restrict access to bankruptcy relief for student debtors. For instance, student loans were dischargeable until Congress enacted the Higher Education Act of 1976 (§439A), which in effect made student loans non-dischargeable if the first payment came due within five years of bankruptcy, unless the debtor could prove undue hardship. The temporal dimension is important to note here, as it reveals the relations of power and their ability to dictate the time horizons of repayment. Moreover, these temporal dictates and the burden of undue hardship were further reinforced by the debtfare state with a revision to the Bankruptcy Act. As I discussed in the previous chapter, US Congress repealed the Bankruptcy Act of 1898 and replaced it with the Bankruptcy Reform Act of 1978. In terms of educational loans, the latter approved the Education Amendment provision to the original §523(a)(8): no discharge unless the first payment became due more than five years prior to the bankruptcy filing *or* the debtor could demonstrate undue hardship (Grant, 2011). It should be underlined that the undue hardship clause is an exception to education loans. In other words, debtors with other kinds of debt are not laden with the task of proving undue hardship. Some observers critical of §523(a)(8) have pointed out that undue hardship is 'unnecessarily harsh, denying debt relief to all but a few select debtors and usually only to those with dependents and medical conditions that prevent gainful employment' (Grant, 2011: 819).

Despite concerns of rising defaults on student loans, the debtfare state was actively promoting and subsidising through Sallie Mae, the growth of proprietary schools (for-profit, private universities) in higher education. During the 1980s, proprietary schools represented one-half of the increase in higher education enrolment (Beaver, 2012). The proprietary schools benefitted from federal student loans, but these loans were often accompanied by a private loan, given the high tuition fees charged by these schools (see Table 5.2). As with their federal student loan counterparts, private lenders securitised their private loans to students to offset the financial risks involved in repayment. The social risks were left to the debtfare state to mediate and depoliticise, largely through a revision of the Higher Education Act (HEA) of 1976 and the Bankruptcy Reform Act of 1978.

Set against the backdrop of a bleak economy, the dual growth in enrolment of proprietary schools and the higher levels of student indebtedness pushed up defaults on student loans. In 1985, 600 for-profit, private (or, proprietary) schools reported default rates of over 50 percent (Beaver, 2012: 3). Nonetheless, with the probusiness legislative environment of the Reagan Administration and government subsidisation (corporate welfare), it was business as usual for proprietary schools. Between 1983 and 1990 loan volume of private student loans increased by 83 percent, while defaults increased by 336 percent (Beaver, 2012). Indeed, while default rates were climbing across the higher-education system, proprietary schools were the worst offenders. 'While proprietary schools account for 33 percent of Stafford loans, they are responsible for 48 percent of defaulted student loans' (Eglin, 1993: 54).

Instead of mitigating the social dimensions of risks by, for instance, taxation for education, subsidising public universities to help suppress the steady rise of tuition fees, allowing for greater protection in bankruptcy proceedings and so forth, the debtfare state facilitated new venues of dispossessive capitalism by promoting proprietary (private, for-profit) schools and, by extension, private student loans, which, in turn, carried higher rates of interest and stricter repayment schedules (US Department of Education, 2012). At the same time, the Reagan administration (1981–1989) was eager to impose major cuts to the federal student grants programme, which, by 1985 surpassed total federal grant aid by over $3 billion (Coco, 2013). The Reagan administration used the reauthorisation of the HEA in 1986 to cut rather than expand aid to needy students, even with 60 percent tuition hikes at colleges across the country. Congress also assumed a similar approach by making it more difficult for low-income students to qualify for and obtain, Pell Grants. To fill the funding gap caused by cuts in government aid, Congress drafted a loan provision allowing lower and middle-income students to borrow more per year to fund their education (Altbach *et al.*, 2007; Coco, 2013).

The state as super-creditor and the displacement of financial risk

The early 1990s saw further changes to legislation governing student loan debt, which was aimed at creating more dependency of students on credit to pay for higher education. Before continuing, it is important to underline that the debt-fare state enjoys *super-creditor* status, meaning that it has limitless powers (to garnish wages, tax refunds and even Social Security payments) and unlimited time (no statute of limitation) to collect student loan debt (Coco, 2013: 589). The debtfare state thus wields enormous temporal power over debtors through the means of the seemingly neutral legal framework. The class nature of this power and social discipline is masked by the social power of money and the continual imposition of legal obligation between creditor and debtor. In turn, this serves to reproduce the monetisation, responsibilisation and hyper-individualisation of social relations. This allows the debtfare state to depoliticise the tension between the increasing expansion of the student loan industry, on the one hand and increasing default rates, on the other.

In 1990, for instance, two important revisions to the Bankruptcy Reform Act of 1978 were undertaken that had important ramifications for distressed student debtors. First, the debtfare state was able to lengthen the temporal period in which distressed student debtors had to wait before they were permitted to file a bankruptcy claim from five years to seven years. Second, the further narrowing placed on dischargeability of educational loans was revised with an amendment to §523(a)(8) in 1990. The section effectively exempts educational loans made, insured, or guaranteed by a governmental unit or non-profit body (Pashman, 2001). Supporters of the amendment to §523(a)(8) note that educational loans are not granted on the same basis as other loans. Lenders or guarantors who participate in educational loan programs typically extend credit to students who might not qualify for credit under traditional standards. In the desire of the state to promote access to educational opportunities (democratisation of credit), interest rates and repayment terms are made to be very favourable to the student borrower and no security (collateral) is usually required. Seen as a benevolent and public-spirited act, students failing to respect the terms of their student loan contract are, therefore, viewed as irresponsible market citizens who harm the good of the wider society by opting to default.

To absorb the social dimensions of risks rooted in the commodification of debt and articulated in the form of default on student loans and to introduce more disciplinary measures with regard to the collection of debt owed to the government, the debtfare state introduced the Higher Education Technical Amendments in 1991. These amendments effectively removed all statutes of limitation (previously it was six years) with regard to the collection of student loan repayments or grant overpayments under the Higher Education Act student assistance provisions. In effect, the 1991 Amendments protected the profits of debt collection agencies, particularly those that specialised in student debt, by allowing these companies to tack on hefty collection and commission fees of 25 and 28 percent, respectively, to what students already owed (Ferry, 1995).

A further HEA reauthorisation created the unsubsidised Stafford Loan programme in 1992. Stafford loans are federal student loans that are either subsidised or unsubsidised. The primary difference between these two categories is the amount of interest students are required to pay on their loan. In 2013, subsidised Stafford loans were geared toward low-income students and carried an interest rate of 3.4 percent, plus a one percent origination fee and a lifetime loan limit of $23,000, whereas unsubsidised Stafford loans carried an interest rate of 6.8 percent, plus a one percent origination fee and a lifetime limit of 34,500 for undergraduates.[19] These regulatory initiatives pursued by the US debtfare state facilitated increased borrowing by low- and middle-income students to fund their education. By the close of the 1990s, the debtfare state had managed to increase student loans 125 percent in comparison with a 55 percent increase in aid to low-income students (Coco, 2013: 586). As we will see below, the debtfare state also increased the interest rate on unsubsidised Stafford loans, which hit low-income students particularly hard.

At the same time student loans were expanding, further amendments to the Higher Education Act in 1994 (also known as the 1994 Regulations) assisted in decreasing the involuntary lender involvement in and need for, collection litigation by giving defaulting student loan debtors a new option of entering into 'affordable' repayment agreements that were aimed a rehabilitating their loans, thereby permitting them to be removed from default status (Ferry, 1995).

It should be flagged here that since lenders involved in FFELP loans are protected against the risk of non-payment, only educational lenders pursue collection on defaulted student loans to the point of litigation. Seen in this light, the 1994 Regulations may also be understood as an effort to mitigate the financial risks for educational lenders issuing private student loans. These measures, which aimed at making debt collection more efficient, also reflected the increasing levels of consumer indebtedness in the 1990s (US Department of Commerce, 2010; Draut, 2011). Indeed, in 1996, Congress enacted the Debt Collection Improvement Act, which, among other changes, permitted Social Security benefit payments to be used (garnished) to repay defaulted federal student loans (Pashman, 2001).

These legislative modifications pursued by the debtfare state reflected the sentiment that risk, understood exclusively in financial terms and thus concerning lenders, was given higher priority through the creation of SLABS. The social risks associated with educational loans were muted and usually represented by the media and Congress as individualised acts of irrationally, immorality and/or irresponsibility. It was, therefore, acceptable to garnish old age and disability benefits that fall under the Social Security program in the United States. In the context of the bankruptcy system, the burden of proof was placed on the debtor to provide adequate evidence, which could be reduced and tested mathematically, to satisfy the court's subjective understanding of 'undue hardship' (Pashman, 2001; Coco, 2013).

Despite the increases in student loan defaults in the 1990s, Sallie Mae was quite effective in managing financial risks for private lenders by operating with its implicit assumption of guarantee and by engaging in asset-backed securitisation of student loans in the early 1990s. While FFEL loans were guaranteed by the federal government, there was no such explicit government guarantee of GSE debt, i.e., loans purchased from private providers and resold in secondary markets. Yet, there remained a very strong market perception that GSE securities are very much like US Treasury issues. This implicit perception by investors, along with changes to Sallie Mae's charter, resulted in a rise in the amount of loans sold by Sallie Mae in secondary markets, increasing from less than 30 percent from 1981 to 1985 to about 60 percent from 1988 to 1990 (Lea, 2005; US Treasury, 2006).

Political questions concerning the social fallout of risk rose to the foreground in the mid-1990s, as attention began to turn to the privatisation of Sallie Mae (Lea, 2005). Adhering to neoliberal logic, it was argued that privatising Sallie Mae would benefit lenders and borrowers, increasing efficiency and competition through market exposure. For example, as a private market participant, Sallie Mae could redirect its focus from encouraging bank lenders to sell their student loans to encouraging colleges and lenders to become business partners and distributors for a Sallie Mae-branded set of student loan-related products and services (Lea, 2005: 5).[20]

The privatisation of Sallie Mae

In 1996, Sallie Mae became the first government-sponsored enterprise in the US to privatise. The former GSE was subsequently renamed the SLM Corporation, although it is still commonly known as Sallie Mae. Almost four years earlier than planned, its GSE activities were completely terminated in 2004. A key reason for this accelerated target date was due to its high volume of securitisation (commodification of debt), which, in effect, allowed it to raise capital through the selling of assets (student loans). One year prior to the termination of its GSE status in 2004, for instance, Sallie Mae issued $20.3 billion of non-GSE financing, which, combined with securitisation, equalled 2.4 times its student acquisitions. For those in favour of privatisation, this was suggestive of Sallie Mae's ability to finance itself in a post-GSE environment and signalled the viability of securitising student loans. From this period onward, Sallie Mae has continued to be the largest issuer of SLABS (see Table 5.1) and thus plays a central role in ensuring funds are channelled from institutional investors to students (Ergungor and Hathaway, 2008).

It is important to note that the student loan industry is highly concentrated. Prior to 2010, when major reforms were introduced, 91.5 percent of the new Stafford and PLUS loans and 99.8 percent of consolidated loans were originated by only 100 lenders, with Sallie Mae dominating the industry after its privatisation (Ergungor and Hathaway, 2008). Moreover, the intensifying depth and breadth of over-the-counter (OTC) derivative markets, in which SLABS and other asset-backed securities emerged through active state intervention, aimed at re-regulating financial markets to facilitate greater risk-taking activities. The idea was to design

TABLE 5.1 Ten top issuers of SLABS in federal student loans (in billions of $)

Issuer	2005	2006	2010
Sallie Mae	26,990	33,752	6,103
Nelnet Student Loan	6,540	5,313	1,183
SLC Student Loan Trust	4,350	4,912	920
Brazos Higher Education Authority Inc.	3,717	243	1,120
National Collegiate	3,487	4,724	N/A
College Loan Corporation Trust	2,700	1,700	N/A
Collegiate Funding Services Educational Trust	2,700	N/A	N/A
Access Group Inc.	2,074	1,007	464
Wachovia Student Loan Trust	1,800	1,611	N/A
GCO Education Loan Finding Trust	1,130	2,643	N/A

Sources: Data collected from *Asset Backed Alert* and Wachovia Capital Markets, LLC in E. Walsh (2008) 'Student Loans ABS' in B. P. Lancaster, G. M. Schultz and F. J. Fabozzi (eds) *Structured Products and Related Credit Derivatives: a comprehensive guide for investors*, Hoboken, NJ: John Wiley & Sons, p. 135; SLM Corporation (2011) 'ABS East Conference', October. Available at: https://www1.salliemae.com/NR/rdonlyres/50F355EE-8FA7–49FA-AABF-D4A4B507A89C/15130/ABSEastConference vFinal.pdf (accessed 1 October 2012).

instruments that insured investors against a potential default while allowing them to extract revenue from credit money, such as credit default swaps.

In 1998, for instance, the Chairperson of the Federal Reserve Board, Alan Greenspan, argued that there was no reason why derivatives markets 'should be encumbered with a regulatory structure devised for a wholly different type of market process, where supplies of underlying assets are driven by the vagaries of weather and seasons. Inappropriate regulation distorts the efficiency of our market system and as a consequence impedes growth and improvement in standards of living' (Federal Reserve Board, 1998, 2008). In the wider context of market-friendly re-regulations (e.g. the Gramm-Leach-Bliley Act of 1999, or GLB), educational lenders such as Sallie Mae thrived. Between 2000 and 2005, for example, Sallie Mae's fee income increased by 228 percent (from $280 million to $920 million), while its managed loan portfolio increased by only 82 percent (from $67 billion to $122 billion). Sallie Mae's stock increased by more than 1600 percent between 1995 and 2005, which represented an average annual rise of about 160 percent (Collinge, 2009: 5).

At the same time as the GLB Act was signed, SLM Corporation aggressively pursued several key acquisitions in the student loan industry, which gave the company more reach into various aspects of lending. In 1999, for instance, SLM Corporation purchased Nellie Mae, a non-profit student loan company, which was quickly followed by the acquisition of two of the country's largest non-profit student loan guarantors, the USA Group and Southwest Student Services. In the early to mid-2000s, Sallie Mae acquired two of the largest student loan collection companies in the United States – Pioneer Credit Recovery and General Revenue Corporation

– as well as Arrow Financial Services in 2004 and GRP Financial Services in 2005 (Collinge, 2009: 12–13; see also Table 5.1). Procuring some of the largest collection companies and numerous guaranty agencies (i.e., institutions that administer the FFEL program loans) Sallie Mae represents the largest private lender of student loans and collector on student loan debt. It also owns the largest guarantor companies, whose lifeblood is comprised of penalties and fees attached to defaulted loans. Sallie Mae, therefore, benefits greatly from all aspects of the lending transaction: securitising student loans, lending and debt collection ('Does Sallie Mae Want Students to Default?' *Forbes*, 6 June 2012). Thus, state strategies have facilitated the concentration and centralisation of capital to form oligopolistic financial companies with massive political influence and market power in the student loan industry.

Debtfarism, discipline and the depoliticisation of social risks in the 1990s

While private educational lenders were enjoying the highly lucrative environment fuelled by state-led subsidisation and market-friendly framings of SLABS, the social dimensions of risk linked to the commodification of debt have been playing themselves out on the ground. Despite the promise to students, particularly the low-income demographic, that a college degree would deliver higher paying jobs, the service sector was the fastest growing and largest employer from 1989 to 1990. According to the Bureau of Labour Statistics (BLS), private service providing industries accounted for 90 percent of the job growth in the 1990s (BLS, 2002). Within this category, low-wage retail and service sector jobs accounted for 70 percent of all new job growth between 1989 and 2000. The majority of these so-called *McJobs* were filled by by women (Collins and Mayer, 2010: 6). Moreover, the BLS reports that employment in the temporary help services industry, which predominately employs women, grew from 1.1 million to 2.3 million during the 1990–2008 period and thus represented a larger share of workers than before in higher skill occupations.

During the 1990s, the Clinton Administration (1993–2001) actively pursued sharp spending cuts to decrease the budget deficit by slashing financing in key social programmes such as welfare and higher education (US Department of Education, 2012). Low-income and middle-class Americans turned increasingly to consumer credit to deal with overall higher living costs, decreased welfare benefits and stagnant wages. At the same time, as the state's support for higher education and grant-based aid were rapidly dwindling, tuition and fees at public universities and colleges increased by 112.5 percent between 1990 and 2010. Moreover, the budgets of public universities and colleges have gone from a 23.2 percent dependency on tuition and fees in 1986 to 43.3 percent in 2011 (Coco, 2013: 589).

Seen within this wider context of the neoliberal restructuring of labour markets and public provisioning, defaults on student loans and increasing delinquent payments continue to mark the consumer debt landscape of the US. In an attempt to tackle the issue of defaulting student loans, the Clinton Administration signed into law the Higher Education Amendments of 1998, which removed the seven-year exception leaving only the undue hardship exception to non-dischargeablity regarding student loans (Pashman, 2001). In accordance with this change, Congress revamped the Bankruptcy Code, once again in 1998 with the Bankruptcy Review Act. As noted above, prior to 1998 student loan debts were non-dischargeable unless: (1) the loans first become due more than seven years before the debtor filed for bankruptcy, or (2) not allowing the student loans to be discharged would impose an undue hardship on the debtor and/or the debtor's dependents (Pashman, 2001: 605; Coco, 2013). Yet, Congress has refused to provide a definition of undue hardship, opting instead to transfer responsibility for interpretation and thus punishment, to the courts. This has created a situation in which 'there are as many tests for undue hardship as there are bankruptcy courts' (Pashman, 2001: 609). As one legal scholar observes, 'The rigidity of some of those "tests" (e.g., means testing) almost suggests that *the solution to human suffering lies in the application of algebraic equations*' (Pashman, 2001, my emphasis).

The increased use of abstract mathematical tools to deal with social problems is both rooted in, and reflected by, the dominant position of neoclassical economics in the policy formation of the debtfare state as well as the social power of private lenders (banks) in the student loan industry. This method of testing is also instrumental in depoliticising the disciplinary nature of bankruptcy and, by extension, those debtors considering or entering into default, by expunging social considerations and upholding the myth of impartial and expert interpretation inherent to the legal framing of undue hardship. Class power is thus effectively erased from the individualised and monetised relations between debtor and creditor. Seen from this angle, the dispossessed students who fail to meet their legal obligation are conveniently deemed not only as undeserving (morally weak and fiscally irresponsible) of empathy by the law, but also as abusing the bankruptcy system (Pashman, 2001).[21]

It should be noted that the amendment of the Bankruptcy Code to limit bankruptcy relief only on the grounds of undue hardship lacked any convincing empirical evidence to support the claim that students and graduates were trying to take advantage of the bankruptcy system, or that such bad actors actually posed a threat to the continued viability of student loan programs and the role of the benevolent state and taxpayers in their efforts to ensure educational access for all Americans (Pashman, 2001; Coco, 2013). Congress represented its actions as sending a message to abusive student debtors to protect the solvency of student loan programs. In particular, the state was concerned by reports of irresponsible students and recent graduates declaring bankruptcy as a way to avoid repayment of student loans on the eve of lucrative careers. §532(a)(8) of the Bankruptcy Code was a disciplinary tactic to remove the perceived temptation of recent graduates to use the bankruptcy system as a low cost method of unencumbering those future earnings. This representation continued despite the availability of evidence by the General Accounting Office that only a fraction of one percent of matured student loans had been discharged in bankruptcy, a rate, at the time, which compared favourably to the consumer credit card industry (Pashman, 2001; see also Chapter 4).

Preying on the dispossessed in the new millennium: capitalising on the unmet needs of the surplus population

In the first decade of the new millennium, under the leadership of the G.W. Bush Administration (2001–2009) and its explicit embrace of private consumption, federal funds flowed into proprietary schools (private, for-profit colleges), from $4.6 billion in 2000 to $25 billion in 2010 (Gorski, 2010). During this time, enrolment in proprietary schools increase 37 percent compared to the 11 percent average during the previous decade. Interestingly, the demographic of these students shifted. According to a study by the US Department of Education, the majority of students enrolling in the for-profit, private schools are more than 25 years of age. There also appears to be a gender and racial dimension to the student bodies, as slightly more women are returning to school (US Department of Education, 2012). Moreover, the majority of students attending proprietary schools are from low-income backgrounds and stem from minority groups (Lynch et al. 2010).

According to The Project on Student Debt, African-American undergraduates were the most likely to take out private loans, with the percentage quadrupling between 2003–2004 and 2007–2008, from 4 percent to 17 percent (Project on Student Debt, 2012). In 2003, without Congressional approval, the US Department of Education modified the financial aid formula governing student eligibility for federal grant-based aid (Coco, 2013: 587). This approach substantially reduced the debtfare state's contribution for federal grants to low-income students thereby cutting hundreds of millions of dollars in Pell Grants and increasing the dependency of these students on the loan-based system.

Private student loans are closely linked with the rapid rise in enrolment of for-profit, private universities over the past decade.[22] The for-profit higher education sector charges some of the highest tuition fees in the country, which means that low-income students usually turn to private educational lenders, such as Sallie Mae, to top up their federal student loans and grants. Once grant-aid is taken into consideration, the out-of-pocket cost – or unmet need[23] – for low-income students at proprietary schools is even higher than at private non-profit colleges, which draw on institutional grants to defray college costs (Lynch et al. 2010: 3; see Table 5.2). 'At four-year for-profits, low-income students must find a way to finance almost $25,000 each year, with only a 22 percent chance of graduating' (Lynch et al. 2010: 3). This means that low-income students in the for-profit, private schools are borrowing heavily, which results in an increasingly large debt burden. Moreover, given that the graduation rate at four-year, proprietary schools is 22 percent (compared with 55 percent at public and 65 percent at private, non-profit colleges and universities) the chances of income improvement to meet loan payments are low. Data collected from the US Department of Education's

Integrated Postsecondary Education Data System (IPEDS) reveals that the graduation rate at the nation's largest for-profit university – the University of Phoenix – is only 9 percent (Lynch *et al.* 2010).

A Harvard-based study on proprietary schools revealed that six years after graduation students – many of whom were from low-income families – who attending proprietary schools are more likely to be unemployed as well as to be unemployed for periods longer than three months. Moreover, if these students manage to find employment, students who attend for-profits make, on average, between $1,800 and $2,000 less annually than their peers who attended other institutions (Deming *et al.*, 2012). Despite these grim numbers, proprietary schools have expanded rapidly in the neoliberal era. They have become the fastest growing feature of the US higher education sector, with enrolment increasing from 0.2 percent to 9.1 percent of total enrolment in degree-granting schools from 1970 to 2009. Moreover, private, for-profit schools account for the majority of enrolments in non-degree granting post-secondary schools (Deming *et al.*, 2012). As noted above, the largest private, for-profit educational institution is the University of Phoenix with an enrolment of 450,000 students, which makes it the second largest university in the US (Beaver, 2012).

The financial risks associated with the issuance of federal student loans and private student loans for the rapidly rising proprietary sector of higher education were offset

TABLE 5.2 Unmet need among low-income students, 2007–2008

Type of institution	Cost of attendance	Expected family contribution[†]	All grant aid	Unmet need
Four-Year				
Private, for-profit★	$31,976	$ 3,518	$ 3,501	$24,957
Private, non-profit	$34,110	$ 3,911	$13,624	$16, 574
Public	$18,062	$ 3,798	$ 5,676	$ 8,588
Two-Year				
Private, for-profit★	$26,690	$ 1,882	$ 3,736	$21,072
Public	$11,660	$ 3,659	$ 2,523	$ 5,478

★ Proprietary schools, such as University of Phoenix, attract a large segment of low-income, minority students (Deming *et al.*, 2012; US Department of Education, 2012).

† The expected family contribution (EFC) is an index number that the debtfare state has set to determine how much financial aid a student should receive. It is a calculated according to a formula established by law and is based on a family's taxed and untaxed income, assets and benefits (e.g., unemployment or Social Security).[24]

Source: Education Trust analysis of NPSAS:08 using PowerStats; Full-time, full-year, one-institution dependent students in the bottom half of the income distribution are included in this analysis. Lynch, M., J. Engle and J. L. Cruz (2010) *Sub-prime Opportunity: The Unfulfilled Promise of For-Profit Colleges and Universities*, Washington, DC: The Education Trust, p. 3. Data from National Centre for Educational Statistics, 2011.[25]

by the issuance of SLABS in private student loans. Key SLABS issuers in the area of private student loans in 2008 included SLM Private Credit (which represented the largest issuers of private SLABS), First Marblehead, Access Group Inc. and Keycorp (Walsh, 2008; see also Table 5.1). The industry thrived off of the double-digit growth rates of private student loans in the late 1990s and early 2000s, reaching its peak in 2007–2008, with the advent of the subprime crisis. According to the Consumer Financial Protection Bureau (CFPB), private student lender under-writing standards loosened considerably during this time. Between 2005 and 2007, coinciding with its peak phase, private lenders, such as Sallie Mae, embarked on aggressive lending techniques in which an increased percentage (from 40 percent to over 70 percent) of loans were made to undergraduate students without school involvement or certification. Additionally, during this period, lenders were more likely to originate loans to borrowers with lower credit scores (CFPB, 2012: 3). Private lenders could offload their financial risks, of course, through the issuance of SLABS.

By the mid-2000s, the G. W. Bush Administration was forced to deal with the tension between supporting, on the one hand, proprietary schools and educational lenders and depoliticising the social risks inherent in the increasing levels of educational debt and the rise of defaults on private student loans, on the other. The debtfare state undertook at least two major moves in the attempts to resolve this tension. First, the government implemented the Higher Education Reconcilia-tion Act of 2005, which effectively cut $12.6 billion from student financial aid. This made it more expensive for students to pay for their education, forcing them to turn to private student loans to make up the difference (see Table 5.2). Second, the Bush Administration responded to the risks tied to increasing default rates by implementing draconian changes to the Bankruptcy Code in 2005 with the enactment of the Bankruptcy Abuse Prevention and Consumer Protection Act (or, BAPCPA).

There are at least two major features of this Act that are relevant to understanding the coercive features of the debtfare state and its attempts to manage social risks generated by the student loan industry. First, BAPCPA was designed to keep debtors out of bankruptcy. Of the two basic options of obtaining relief from creditors, namely Chapter 7 liquidation or Chapter 13 adjustment of debts for debtors who have adequate income to repay all or part of their debts through a repayment plan, the former was made extremely difficult to obtain. Under Chapter 13, if the student debtor is granted bankruptcy by convincing the courts of undue hardship, loan repayment plans revise the temporal span of indebtedness and usually assign some sort of debt management plan (see Chapter 4; Coco, 2012). This attempt to keep debtors out of bankruptcy has important consequences for distressed student debtors who may be seeking relief in other areas of indebtedness, such as credit card debt (New York Federal Reserve, 2012).

The second major feature of the BAPCPA with regard to the student loan industry was that it further reduced the minimal consumer protections under the Bankruptcy Code for student debtors. For instance, BAPCPA amended §523(a)(8) in order to broaden types of educational student loans that cannot be discharged absent proof of undue hardship. As Coco notes, according to §220 of BAPCPA, debtors are no longer able to discharge private educational loans, which have higher interest rates and less flexibility in repayment. Private lenders such as Sallie Mae now possess similar status and thus power and state protection, in bankruptcy under §523(a)(8). Through the continued categorisation of educational debtors as eligible for a conditional discharge only (Coco, 2013: 597), the US debtfare state draws on the temporal power of money and the (fetishised) neutrality of the law to impose market discipline on student debtors by ensuring they avoid seeking relief through bankruptcy.

In addition, under §220 of the BAPCPA, the protections afforded to the state and non-profit lenders have been extended to private student loan lenders. Sallie Mae, for example, now enjoy the same *super-creditor* status as the US debtfare state in the bankruptcy system because private loans are non-dischargeable pursuant to §532(a)(8) (Coco, 2013: 593). This extension of super-creditor status by the US debtfare state to Sallie Mae has important social implications in terms of the deepening of the hold of corporations over higher education financing, especially given the fact that one out of five students also carry more costly private loans, where unlike government loans, interest rates are in the double digits and fees add to the balance (Draut, 2011).

Given the inherent tensions in credit-led accumulation, most notably the imperative that credit money needs to return to its origins for redemption, the BAPCPA would only temporarily resolve the paradoxes and associated risks in the student loan industry. Despite the restrictions imposed by BAPCPA, for instance, a growing number of desperate former students have opted for bankruptcy in the hopes of gaining some relief in terms of repayment procedures in other areas of indebtedness such as credit card debt (CFPB, 2012). Two years after the BAPCPA was enacted, federal loans accounted for 70 percent of the educational funding provided to students (Coco, 2013). The debtfare state would, once again, intervene in order to ease the pressures of overburdened debtors, who could no longer turn to bankruptcy as an option. Hence, the debtfare state's reauthorisations of HEA in 2007 and 2008 were concerned with loan repayment plans, interest rates and limited loan forgiveness – all of which were compounded by the financial crash of 2007–2008 and the onset of the Great Recession (Coco, 2013).

Mediation of risks in the community of money: corporate welfare and debt management

The credit crunch that ensued in the wake of the 2007 crisis had an immediate impact on the student loan industry. To manage with the increased defaults of highly indebted, low-income students, the College Cost Reduction and Access Act was signed into law in 2007 (hereafter: Access Act). The Access Act created a system of income-based repayment plans for, among other constituencies, lower-income graduates with typically high debt loads. Under this income-based programme, the student debtor must pay 15 percent of his or her discretionary income for a period of 25 years after which the borrowers can apply for a cancellation of the remaining debt (Coco, 2013: 589–99). Again, this solution reflects attempts by the debtfare state to impose social discipline on the debtors by injecting just enough relief to ensure that the debtor can meet regular payment schedules, while shifting the problem into the future (e.g., 25 years).

Educational lenders had no one to sell their government guaranteed loans to in order to offset their financial risks. One of the first measures the federal government established to deal with asset-backed securities was the Term Asset-Backed Securities Loan Facility (or, TALF) in 2008. According to a 2010 Government Accounting Office (GAO) Report, in the post-crisis environment the TALF program spent $7.15 billion propping up asset-backed securitisations, including SLABS (GAO, 2010).[26]

Meanwhile, the social dimensions of risks tied to high student loan debt, especially, but not exclusively, with regard to private student loans, intensified due to the crisis. By 2009 the unemployment rate for private student loan borrowers who began their studies in the 2003–2004 academic year was 16 percent. Default rates began to spike considerably following the subprime housing crisis of 2007–2008 (CFPB, 2012).

To ensure that liquidity (trading activity) remained stable in education lending, the Bush Administration implemented the Ensuring Continued Access to Student Loans Act (or, ECASLA) in 2009. ECASLA authorised the US Department of Education to purchase FFELP loans outright if secondary demand dipped. In effect, the ECASLA represented a major, yet largely unnoticed, government bailout of the student loan industry. The ECASLA was originally to be a temporary program, to exist only until 28 February 2009 and was to use approximately $6.5 billion. According to the US Department of Education, 'the Department [of Education] will purchase loans [from the private sector, e.g., Sallie Mae, JP Morgan Chase, Wells Fargo, Discover Financial Services, Bank of America and so forth] at 97 percent of the principal interest coincidental with the standard guaranty rate for these loans'. The US Department of Education anticipated purchasing up to $500 million in loans *each* week up to an aggregate of $6.5 billion during the designated time-period (US Department of Education, 2011). As the banks demonstrated continued disinterest in lending to students in the immediate aftermath of the subprime crisis, the ECASLA was subsequently extended and augmented.

In 2010, the US Department of Education projected that it will eventually purchase $112 billion in FFELP loans from private lending corporations (US Department of Education, 2011). To manage rising and untenable levels of student debt, President Obama sought to address further income-based repayment in the 2010 Health Care Reform Act. The latter, for instance, reduced payment amounts and (temporal) length of payment for the income-based repayment plan or the Public Service Loan Forgiveness Program (PSLF) discussed above. Student debtors, for instance, who qualify for the PSLF programme, are now required to pay only 10 percent of their discretionary income over a ten-year period (Coco, 2013: 599).

In an effort to depoliticise growing anger over government bailouts of private student loan providers, the Obama Administration (2009–2017) reintroduced the controversial Federal Direct Loan Programme. According to the Congressional Budget Office (CBO), the direct loan programme could save the government $67 billion over the next decade (CBO, 2010). These savings presented an attractive cost-offset to the Health Care Reform Act for the Obama Administration. Included as a rider clause to that Act, as of 1 July 2010 the $60 billion-a-year FFELP was replaced with the Federal Direct Loan Program, making it the only government-backed loan programme in the US. From that time on, the direct lender of all federal student loans was the US Department of Education and not private banks. The Democrats touted the legislation, which was represented as a key feature of President Obama's education agenda, as a 'far-reaching overhaul of federal financial aid, providing a huge infusion of money to the Pell grant program and offering new help to lower-income graduates in getting out from under crushing student debt' ('Student loan overhaul approved by congress', *New York Times*, 25 March 2010).

Upon closer inspection, however, the Direct Loan Program did not introduce far-sweeping changes to the student loan industry. For one thing, as noted above, the family income threshold for a student to qualify for this grant has also been lowered from $30,000 to $23,000 further reducing the numbers of eligible students from low-income families and, in turn, making these excluded students more dependent on the loan-based system. Moreover, the maximum Pell grant award climbed from $5,550 for the 2010–2011 academic year to $5,900 in 2019–2020 (CBO, 2011). This is an insignificant amount given it covers only a third of the cost of attending a public university, compared to three-quarters when the program began in the 1970s. More importantly, as discussed above, the majority of low-income students are attending proprietary schools, whose tuition rates are several times the price of most public universities. As such, the major winners of the Direct Lending Program remain the financial markets, which continue to benefit from the low-risk SLABS that rest on the market perception of government guarantees to solidify the compulsion of debtors to repay.

Despite the fact that the 2010 Health Care Reform Act cut private lenders, out of the lucrative business of originating new federal student loans (the US debtfare state now originates student loans directly), private lenders and Sallie Mae in particular, have nonetheless benefited from the 2010 Health Care Reform Act ('Sallie Mae split marks bet on much-abused private student loans', *Bloomberg*, 31 May 2013). In addition to its role as the largest private student loan provider in the US, key student loan debt collector and the country's largest issuer of SLABS, Sallie Mae, along with four other corporations (i.e., FedLoan Servicing, Great Lakes Educational Loan Services, Inc., Nelnet and Direct Loan Servicing Centre) have been assigned the role of the federal loans servicers.[27] In this capacity, Sallie Mae continued to grow by acquiring in 2010 $28 billion of securitised federal student loans and related assets from the Student Loan Corporation, a subsidiary of Citibank (SLM Corporation, 2010). It also reported that it would begin loosening its restrictive lending practices in 2010 and that 'volumes should pick back up as the company did some "tweaking" to its standards' ('Sallie Mae cuts private-loan rates to maintain volume growth', *Wall Street* Journal, 16 May 2011). Relaxing its allegedly strict lending requirements meant enticing more low-income students to sign a private student loan and thereby expand its net to capture more subprime borrowers (CFPB, 2012).

Due to these changes, Sallie Mae provides service to 3.6 million loan customers on behalf of the US Department of Education and is prospering from its new status as service provider to the debtfare state. In 2011, the company earned $63 million in servicing revenue from its US Department of Education loan-servicing contract, compared to $44 million in 2010 (SLM Corporation, 2011). The combination of the government bailout and loosening lending restrictions has benefitted the country's largest private educational lender and issuer of SLABS. Sallie Mae reported a 19 percent increase in loan originations for 2011 and a 29 percent increase in loan originations in the third quarter of 2011 alone (SLM Corporation, 2011). In the fourth quarter of 2012, Sallie Mae reported a 22 percent increase in private education loan originations to $3.3 billion, decreased delinquency rates and core earnings of $237 million (Sallie Mae, 2013). Student loans proved to be very lucrative for the US government, too. From 2008 to 2013, the US Department of Education is believed to have generated $101.8 billion in revenue from student loans.[28] The government has been able to generate this revenue by exploiting a spread between the low interest rate the government pays to borrow from the Federal Reserve (e.g., 10-year Treasury bonds were at 2.52 percent as of 28 June 2013)[29] and what it charges to students (e.g., 6.8 percent for Stafford loans).[30]

Concluding remarks: mitigating social risk through consumer protection

In response to the rising concerns and contestation around mounting student debt, the Consumer Financial Protection Bureau (hereafter: CFPB) and the US Department of Education released a 2012 joint-report about the state of student loans in the United States (hereafter: Report), with a specific focus on private student loans.[31] The Report argues that risky lending practices tied to private student loans have not only increased more rapidly than public student loans over the past decade but also have come to share many similarities to the 2007 subprime mortgage crisis (CFPB, 2012). According to the Report, private lenders issued loans without considering the repayment ability of borrowers. The lenders (private banks) then securitised the loans to mitigate their losses when students default and resold the loans to investors. According to the Report, since the 2007 crisis, there were more than 850,000 cumulative defaults in private loans, which exceeded $8.1 billion (CFPB, 2012).

For the CFPB and the US Department of Education, private student loans represent a riskier form of credit for students than federal student loans because, interest rates tied to these loans are far higher than public loans. Moreover, unlike other consumer loans, repayment plans for private student loans are neither based on income nor can these loans be discharged through bankruptcy proceedings. The Report suggests two main reasons for the increase in private student loans and subsequent defaults. The first is the lack of proper financial education on the part of students and their families, as public student loans are far more economical (i.e., lower interest rates) and have better consumer protection clauses built into their loan products (CFPB, 2012). The second reason for the increases in defaults proffered by the Report is greed, fuelled by institutional investor appetite for SLABS. This, in turn, facilitated the growth of the private student loan market from less than $5 billion in 2001 to over $20 billion in 2008, before contracting to less than $6 billion in 2011 (CFPB, 2012: 3). The private educational lenders' aggressive lending practices, which lie at the heart of this growth, prompted the Secretary of Education to argue that subprime lending has moved from the housing market to colleges (CFPB, 2012).

The above reading of the student debt crisis is based on a somewhat misleading private loan–public loan dichotomy, which represents the student loan industry in largely ahistorical and apolitical terms and thereby glosses over, and even serves to distort, the significant role played by the state and its unfolding forms of debtfarism in the construction and normalisation of students' increased reliance on loans – both public and private – to fund their higher education. These tendencies toward debtfarism are evident in the following three solutions pursued by the state. The state left largely unaltered the 'main artery' of the student loan system, including the allegedly riskier private student loan sector: SLABS. The Dodd-Frank Wall Street Reform and Consumer Protection Act of 2010 (Dodd-Frank), for instance, did not impose legal limits to risk production on the part of financial markets and various sectors therein, nor did Dodd-Frank seek to cap interest rates and fees.[32] Second, federal student loans have become more expensive for low-income students. On 1 July 2013, the interest rate on new *subsidized Stafford loans* doubled to 6.8 percent from 3.4 percent. The increase will affect approximately 7 million student debtors by increasing the cost of their federal subsidised Stafford loans by an additional $1,000 per year ('Sallie Mae's profits soaring at the expense of our nation's students', *BillMoyers*.com, 12 June 2013).

Third and last, the only substantial regulation that the US Department of Education issued to deal with the social risk inherent to the student loan industry was the introduction of the 'gainful employment' clause in 2011 targeted at private, for-profit universities. Essentially, the gainful employment clause suggests that private colleges will lose eligibility to participate in the federal student loan program, if less than 35 percent of their graduates are repaying the principle on their loans and if loan repayments exceed 30 percent of a typical graduate's discretionary income and 12 percent of their total earnings. However, no penalties will be imposed on schools until 2015 (Beaver, 2012: 277). In 2012, the state also sought to deal with increasing default rates by, once again, redefining the temporal meaning of default, extending the length of days from 270 to 360 in the Direct Loan Program (under 34 CFR 668.183(c).[33] Thereby pushing a central feature of credit money into the future, i.e., the contracted bill of exchange (loan) must always return to its place of origin for redemption.

While the predatory nature of private student loans and their servicing tactics should be critiised, the distinction between private and public student loans is not as clear cut and unproblematic as presented by the Report and other scholarly treatments of private student loan debt (CFPB, 2012; Beaver, 2012). The literature concentrating on the abuses linked to private student loans and, by connection, the for-profit, private colleges and universities not only downplays the role played by the debtfare state, but also, by extension, public student loans, in subsidising capitalist interests through dispossessive practices. For-profit colleges, for instance, derive 66 percent of their revenues from federal student loans (Lynch *et al.*, 2010). Through its neoliberal restructuring strategies, the debtfare state has played a central role in promoting and permitting the private student loan market to thrive and feed off of low-income students and their families, i.e., constructing silent compulsions among the surplus population. The borrowing limits on public student loans have not kept pace with the rapidly increasing tuition fees in both private and public colleges over the past several decades thereby forcing students to turn to private loans, which have higher borrowing caps. As I have demonstrated in this chapter, the state, through its unfolding forms of debtfarism, has facilitated the rapid rise of for-profit, private universities by encouraging the expansion and reproduction of the student loan industry.

Notes

1 Only mortgages surpass educational-related loans (Federal Reserve Bank of New York, 2012).
2 For more information, see: www.occupystudentdebtcampaign.org/our-principles/ (accessed 1 June 2013).
3 Although I do not discuss this point explicitly, it is worth highlighting here that the student loan industry also serves as a spatio-temporal fix in terms of warehousing bodies in colleges before their release into the job market, where unemployment and/or underemployment awaits a vast majority of indebted student, particularly low-income students.
4 Indeed, the steady increase in student intake in higher education over the past several decades of neoliberalism attests to the strength of this rhetoric. For example, total enrolment in higher education institutions in the US grew from 12,096,895 in 1980 to 20,994,113 in 2011. National Centre for Educational Statistics (2012), 'Digest of Educational Statistic – Table 223, Total Fall Enrolment in Degree-Granting Institutions, by Control and Level of Institution: 1970 through 2011'. Available at: http://nces.ed.gov/programs/digest/d12/tables/dt12_223.asp (accessed 28 June 2013).
5 For more information, see: https://opennet.salliemae.com/ (accessed 1 June 2012).
6 '[S]tate averages for debt at graduation from four-year colleges ranged widely in 2011 from $17,250 to $32,450' (Project on Student Debt, 2012: 2).
7 The average student-loan debt of borrowers in the college class of 2011 rose to about $26,500, which represented a 5 percent increase from approximately $25,350 in 2010 ('Student-Loan Borrowers Average $26,500 in Debt', *New York Times*, 18 October 2012; see also Project on Student Debt, 2012).
8 According to a Georgetown University study, the overall unemployment rate for college graduates (ages 22 to 26) fell from 8.9 percent in 2012 to 7.9 percent in 2013. 29 May 2013. Washington, DC: Georgetown University. Available at: www.georgetown.edu/news/cew-report-college-graduates-unemployment.html (accessed 1 June 2013).

9 According to one study, 'In 2009, the average graduating college senior from a four-year institution was saddled with $24,000 in debt, a number that has been rising steadily. This works out to a monthly payment of $276, or 9.5 percent of the typical graduate's income'. Yet repaying student loans will be even more difficult for many graduates given that the unemployment rate for young degree-holders soared to 8.7 percent in 2009 (Traub et al., 2012: 2).

10 The gross income amount is based on Federal income tax returns of the students' parents.

11 Association of Community College Trustees (2012) 'Pell Grant Eligibility Changes'. Available at: www.acct.org/files/Advocacy/Factsheets%20and%20Summaries/pell%20grant%20eligibility%20changes%20website.pdf (accessed 1 May 2013).

12 Middle class has always been a slippery concept that has been notoriously difficult to define and measure. Meanings of the middle class in the US range from identities to incomes. The latter ranges anywhere from $32,900 and $64,000 a year (a Pew Charitable Trusts study), between $50,800 and $122,000 (a US Department of Commerce study), and between $20,600 and $102,000 (middle 60 percent of incomes according to the US Bureau of the Census'), see 'Middle class a matter of income, attitude', USA Today, 14 April 2013. The elusiveness of this term has no doubt part of its mystical appeal in the idea of the 'American Dream' and the reproduction of the status quo. I pick up on the significance of the middle-class trope in the wider debtfare policies in next chapter where I discuss payday loans. For now, suffice it to say that as a basic and rough guideline to grasping what the average debt level means in terms of middle-class students carrying an average debt load of $26,500, the median household income in the United States in 2011 was $50,054, 1.5 percent lower than 2010 (US Bureau of the Census, 2012).

13 Notwithstanding the significance of SLABS to the student loan industry, there has been little scholarly work on the topic outside of economistic analyses (cf. Ergungor and Hathaway, 2008; Fried and Breheny, 2005) and legal commentary (Simkovic, 2013).

14 Annual securitisations may exceed the yearly origination of new loans because new securitisations can include seasoned loans (i.e., a loan that has been out for a year) on the balance sheet (Ergungor and Hathaway, 2008).

15 A swap is designed to transfer the credit exposure of fixed income products between parties. A credit default swap is also referred to as a credit derivative contract, where the purchaser of the swap makes payments up until the maturity date of a contract. Payments are made to the seller of the swap. In return, the seller agrees to pay off a third party debt if this party defaults on the [student] loan. A CDS is considered insurance against non-payment. A buyer of a CDS might be speculating on the possibility that the third party will indeed default.
Available at: www.investopedia.com/terms/c/creditdefaultswap.asp (accessed 26 June 2013).

16 The cultural dimensions of trust, performativity, and belief systems play an important part in this story, as recounted by various excellent studies of how these promises are constructed and sold to various actors in the credit system (Leyshon and Thrift, 1997; de Goede, 2005; Mackenzie, 2006; and Langley, 2008). Yet, as detailed in Chapters 1 and 2, the analysis of power in consumer credit cannot begin and end with cultural analyses.

17 These totals were based on a high-end (i.e., higher risk debtor), fixed-interest rate with the following percent rates: The total amount of $50,545.95 is based on 11.88 percent interest, the total of $70,259.07 was calculated using 12.38 percent (fixed payment) interest, and the deferred payment plan amounting to $74,126.61 was based on a 12.88 percent interest rate. Available at: http://smartoption.salliemae.com/Entry.aspx (accessed 10 October 2012).

18 For a detailed discussion of the connection between workers' old age savings in the form of mutual and pension funds and the wider securitisation processes, see Susanne Soederberg (2010) *Corporate Power and Ownership in Contemporary Capitalism*, London: Routledge, and Susanne Soederberg (2010) Cannibalistic capitalism: the paradoxes of

neoliberal pension securitisation', Leo Panitch, Greg Albo, Vivek Chibber (eds) *Socialist Register 2011: the crisis this time*, vol. 47, London: Merlin Press, pp. 224-241.

19 For more information, see: www.staffordloan.com/stafford-loan-info/unsubsidised-student-loan.php (accessed 4 May 2013).

20 For more information about the changes made by the US Treasury Department to the interest rates on student loans, see: www2.ed.gov/students/college/repay/2006-changes.html (accessed 1 July 2013).

21 As I noted in the previous chapter, the discipline attached to this stigma carries on beyond the default. Rampant use of credit checks by employers in the United States (Traub, 2013) also reinforces the representation of debtors, who are unable to meet their payment obligations, as untrustworthy and irresponsible market citizens.

22 National Centre for Educational Statistics (2012), 'Digest of Educational Statistic – Table 223, Total fall enrolment in degree-granting institutions, by control and level of institution: 1970 through 2011'. Available at: http://nces.ed.gov/programs/digest/d12/tables/dt12_223.asp (accessed 28 June 2013).

23 The unmet need of these students refers to the difference between college costs and what students can afford to pay on their own and/or with aid that does not need to be repaid (Choitz and Reimherr, 2013). This need, which has widened enormously over the past several decades of neoliberalism, is not a natural phenomenon of the market; but instead, as the above discussion has revealed, has been created by the loan-based system of funding higher education and the general lack of public support for college. In the 2007-2008 academic year, for example, 'Over 98 percent of independent full-time community college students with incomes from the bottom three income quartiles (≤ $30,622) had unmet need' (Choitz and Reimherr, 20013: 1). This constructed reality has also provided a profitable opportunity for private lenders and proprietary schools ready to fill the gap.

24 For more information about the EFC see: http://studentaid.ed.gov/fafsa/next-steps/how-calculated#whats-the-expected-family-contribution (accessed 18 May 2013).

25 For updated tuition fees for the years 2009 to 2012, see the National Centre for Education Statistics (2012) 'Digest of Educational Statistic – Table 381, Average undergraduate tuition and fees and room and board rates charged for full-time students in degree-granting institutions, by level and control of institution: 1969-1970 through 2011-2012. Available at: http://nces.ed.gov/programs/digest/d12/tables/dt12_381.asp (accessed 28 June 2013).

26 See Federal Reserve System, 'Securities Loan Facility (TALF)'. Available at: www.federalreserve.gov/newsevents/reform_talf.htm (accessed 28 June 2013).

27 For more information, see: http://studentaid.ed.gov/repay-loans/understand/servicers (accessed 28 June 2013).

28 According to the Congressional Budget Office, the government is set to generate $106 billion in loans to college students in the fiscal year ending 30 September 2013. This amount will be returned to the government plus $39 billion when the loans are paid back with interest. In 2014, the revenue that the government will be able to generate from the student loan programmes is expected to be $34 billion ('Does the Government Profit from Student Loans?' *The Wall Street Journal*, 15 February 2013). For more information, see the US Congressional Budget Office's data on the federal student loans programme. Available at: www.cbo.gov/sites/default/files/cbofiles/attachments/43913_StudentLoans.pdf (accessed 12 June 2013b).

29 US Treasury, 'Daily Treasury Yield Curve Rates'. Available at: www.treasury.gov/resource-center/data-chart-center/interest-rates/Pages/TextView.aspx?data=yield (accessed 29 June 2013).

30 Federal Reserve (2013) 'Selected Interest Rates (Weekly) – H.15', Release Date: 24 June 2013. Available at: www.federalreserve.gov/releases/h15/current (accessed 27 June 2013). There has been a debate about whether or not the government has in fact generated revenue from federal student loans. For a good overview, see 'No, the government does not profit off student loans (in some years – see update)', *Washington Post*, 20 May 2013).

31 The Report was pursuant to the Dodd-Frank Wall Street Reform and Consumer Protection Act of 2010. For more information see 'Implementing the Dodd-Frank Wall

Street and Consumer Protection Act'. Available at: www.sec.gov/spotlight/dodd-frank.shtml (accessed 24 June 2013).

32 Indeed, in a report to Congress the Federal Reserve concluded that due to the 'considerable heterogeneity' between the asset classes, it was 'unlikely to achieve the stated objective of the [Dodd-Frank] Act – namely, to improve the asset-backed securitisation process and protect investors from losses associated with poorly underwritten loans' (Federal Reserve Board, 2010b). Put differently, it was unlikely that SLABS would be subject to any legally binding or state-led forms of regulation.

33 'Defaulting on Student Loans'. Available at: www.finaid.org/loans/default.phtml (accessed 3 January 2013).

6

DEBTFARISM AND THE
PAYDAY LOAN INDUSTRY

Payday lending is a highly lucrative and rapidly growing segment of the poverty industry that preys on the working poor. Payday loans, also known as 'deferred deposit services', are small, short-term, unsecured cash advances that are due on the customer's next payday (usually two weeks). The size of the loan permitted varies by state jurisdiction and ranges from $50 to $1,000, with $325 being typical (Peterson, 2007; Advance America, 2010). Several studies indicate that general average payday loan rates range anywhere from 364 percent to 550 percent Annual Percentage Rate (APR), not including common charges such as late fees and bounced cheques fees, which can cost nearly as much, or even more, as the loan itself (Graves and Peterson, 2005: 661; National People's Action, 2012).

In 2004, when Advance America – the country's largest payday lender – decided to go public (with Morgan Stanley leading the offering), the company posted profit margins of 23 percent. To put this in perspective, only the most successful technology companies at that time posted numbers in this range (Rivlin, 2010). The high profitability of payday companies rests on their ability to trap customers into spiralling debt cycles, or what is referred to in the industry as 'rollover' loans (Damar, 2009). Studies have revealed, for instance, that 75 percent of payday debtors are unable to repay their loan within two weeks and are forced to get a rollover loan at additional costs (Chin, 2004; Graves and Peterson, 2005; US Department of Defense, 2006; Consumer Financial Protection Bureau, 2013). If the borrower agrees to pay the rollover fee, by contrast, the loan is usually extended for another two weeks. 'Nearly 90 percent of payday lending revenues are based on fees stripped from borrowers who have flipped loans and are trapped in a cycle of debt. The typical payday borrower will have an outstanding payment for 30 weeks' (Jory, 2009: 319).

There appears to be a consensus among both the industry's supporters and its critics that many payday borrowers tend to fall into recurring debt patterns

(Peterson, 2007). The average payday borrower is said to receive eight to 13 loans per year, which represents the backbone of the industry (Chin, 2004). According to a non-profit consumer advocacy group, the Centre for Responsible Lending (CRL), the typical payday loan borrower ultimately has to pay $800 for a $300 loan (CRL, 2011). Unlike other forms of consumer credit, payday loans are relatively quick to obtain. They do not require a credit report and decisions on whether to issue a loan can be made on the spot using the borrower's paycheck or proof of a government benefit, such as a welfare cheque, as collateral (Graves and Peterson, 2005). The convenience and swiftness in obtaining cash linked to payday loans has been increasingly intensified with the aggressive expansion of Internet-based lending, which I discuss below (CFPB, 2013).

Predatory lending often emerges as a descriptor for the debates on payday loans.[1] There is, however, no clear legal meaning of predatory lending in the United States, which attests to the social power of the poverty industry. That said, various public agencies define predation in the credit system by relying on the principle of disclosure, which forms the basis of consumer credit protection laws in the US (see Chapter 4). For the US Department of Housing and Urban Development (2001), predatory lending refers to manipulation and/or providing incomplete information. It affords benefits to the lender while taking advantage of the borrower's lack of knowledge regarding the terms of the loan. Whereas the Federal Reserve defines subprime lending as an extension of credit to those with a significantly higher risk of default than other borrowers (Karger, 2005).

Scholars, who question the welfare-enhancing features of payday loans, highlight the exorbitant interest rates attached to these loans and the ensuing debt trap that occurs when many borrowers cannot make their payment and thus select to rollover their loan for longer periods of time, incurring more interest and fees. For these authors, the predatory nature of payday loans, which is marked by over-lending, over-charging, deception and targeting certain consumer segments, is inappropriate based on grounds of the moral predicate (Chin, 2004; Morgan, 2007). As a corrective, these observers champion the reform of usury laws, which they regard as a feature of consumer protection law that serves to 'protect the needy from the greedy' (Drysdale and Keest, 2000: 657). The lending system would thus become more moral through the enactment of laws that encourage more effective and fair ways of determining whether a loan is appropriate for a borrower on the basis of their capacity to make the required repayments (Austin, 2004; Woolston, 2010).

The above readings and resolutions to predatory lending fail to grapple with the inherent social structures and processes that lead to and, in turn, perpetuate payday lending. To fill this gap in the literature and thereby provide a more complete explanation of the power and paradoxes of the payday lending industry, this chapter questions and transcends two core assumptions upon which predatory lending is based: first, the uncritical liberal embrace of the market as a naturally evolving arena marked by individualised expressions of liberty, equality and freedoms (based on legal contract and private property); second, the assumption that credit is a thing (neutral object) that has evolved to become a core component of the social safety net for the working poor (Austin, 2004: 1227) as well as a primary mechanism to augment (non-living) wages.

The reliance of the surplus population on private provisioning for basic subsistence needs is not interrogated as a construction. Remaining exclusively in the realm and exchange, these discussions are devoid of considerations of class relations and state power in the wider processes of capital accumulation. As such, these discussions are unable to provide an adequate explanation as to why – despite public outcry and continual attempts at reform – payday lending not only continues to thrive, but also has proven to be wildly lucrative (Peterson, 2007; National People's Action, 2012).

This chapter addresses the above oversights by developing the following two-pronged argument. On the one hand, I suggest that payday loans are not characterised by market freedoms, but instead are socially constituted forms of silent compulsions inherent to the processes of credit-led accumulation. To deal with these paradoxes, the payday loan industry is compelled to continually undertake spatio-temporal displacements to overcome tensions in the credit system. A spatial fix might entail an expansion of the payday industry to a physical space (e.g., opening storefronts in locations of convenience near to the working poor's places of employment) or digitalised space (i.e., online lending), whereas a temporal fix could denote strategies that seek to lengthen the payment time as in the case of rollover loans. On the other hand, I suggest that the state and, in particular, its regulatory and rhetorical forms of debtfarism, play an integral role in the expansion and reproduction of the payday loan industry. Aside from facilitating and depoliticising, albeit in a contradictory manner, the above spatio-temporal displacements, the debtfare state acts to naturalise the commodification of social reproduction. One primary way this is achieved is by bolstering the fetishisations of the community of money, particularly in terms of consumer protection and the framing of debt as a legal obligation.

I develop this argument in three main sections. Section One provides an overview of the payday loan industry and describes the core features of its debtor base, namely: the surplus population. Section Two maps the rhetorical and regulative landscape of debtfarism with an eye to explaining how these processes have served to expand and reproduce the payday lending industry. Section Three provides concluding remarks.

The payday lending industry and the surplus population: an overview

The origins of contemporary payday lending may be traced to 1993, when *Check Into Cash, Inc.* of Tennessee opened the first payday loan store in the United States (Chin, 2004). During the late 1990s and early 2000s, the industry experienced significant growth (National People's Action, 2012). There are four main providers of payday lending in the US: local, privately owned, or what some refer to as 'mom-and-pop' providers; large national providers; national banks; and Internet providers[2]

(Mann and Hawkins, 2007). The 10,000 payday stores that were in operation in 2000 grew to over 21,000 by 2004 (Rivlin, 2010). By 2010, there were 22,000 lending companies, which are dominated by 17 major firms (National People's Action, 2010, 2012). The largest payday lenders, such as Advance America, dominate the industry and control a significant proportion of market share (see Table 6.1). According to the industry, this growth is explained as a response to the decreasing availability of short-term consumer credit alternatives from traditional banking institutions, as well as the relatively low-costs of entry and the regulatory safe harbour that many state statutes provide for cash advance services (Advance America, 2010: 5).

With the exception of national banks, usury laws in the United States fall under state jurisdiction, meaning payday lenders are subject to different (and highly variable) usury laws (Graves and Peterson, 2005: 673). States maintain primary, albeit not exclusive, jurisdiction over these non-bank lending institutions, particularly with regard to interest rates (Mann and Hawkins, 2007; Peterson, 2007).[3] Although the activities and product innovation of payday lenders are expanding and diversifying, they are very much shaped by the geographies in which they operate. Advance America, for example, offers instalment loans directly to customers in Illinois and Colorado and second mortgage loans in Ohio. Other products offered by Advance America include costly pre-paid Visa debt cards[4] and so forth (Advance America, 2010).

In 2000, the payday industry established two national organisations that spend millions of dollars in lobbying and public relations (Peterson, 2007). The Community Financial Services Association of America (CFSA) forms one group, which is 'dedicated to advancing financial empowerment for consumers through small-dollar, short-term loans'.[5] The second is the Financial Service Centres of America (FiSCA), which was established to keep pace with the 'expanding industry of financial services providers in local communities across the country'.[6] Both CFSA and FiSCA are formidable lobby groups and actively seek to counter legislation that its members perceive to be harmful to daily business operations, such as caps on interest rates and excessive fees and regulation regarding rollover or refinancing loans (Drysdale and Keest, 2000).

It should be emphasised that the payday industry is in no way peripheral to credit-led capitalism, i.e., Wall Street. Payday lenders are financed by and have strong ties to, mainstream financial institutions (see Table 6.1).[7] Wells Fargo, for example, is a key financier of payday lending – offering credit to one-third (32 percent) of the payday loan industry, based on store locations (National People's Action, 2010: 5). The close relations between Wall Street and the payday loan industry became apparent in 2004, with Advance America's first public offering, which was led by Morgan Stanley, one of the largest investment banks in the US (Karger, 2005). Moreover, the investment banking arms of Wells Fargo and Bank of America were among those lending their names and sales teams to the effort under the 'rent-a-bank' scheme, i.e., forging partnerships between payday lenders and national banks to evade state-imposed interest rate caps, which I cover later

TABLE 6.1 Payday lenders and financing profile, 2009

Payday company	Size	Sources of finance
Advance America, Cash Advance Centres, Inc.	Over 2,500 stores operating in 32 US states, as well as Canada and the United Kingdom, issued over $1.2 billion in payday loans in 2009 in US.	Wells Fargo, Bank of America, US Bank and Wachovia provided a $275–300 million line of credit.★
ACE Cash Express†	Over 1,800 stores.	Wells Fargo, JP Morgan Chase, US Bank and KeyBank National provided $300 million in financing in 2006.
Dollar Financial Group Inc.	Some 1,200 stores in the US and abroad. The company claims to have 'the largest financial service store network of its kind' in Canada (461 stores) and the United Kingdom (337 stores) and the second-largest network in the US (358 stores). In 2009, it originated 4.1 million single payment consumer loans.	Wells Fargo and Credit Suisse $475 million in 2006.
Cash America International	Approximately 670 payday lending stores. A major payday lender on the Internet, with 1.7 million online loans made in 2009.	Wells Fargo along with eight banking lending partners (including JP Morgan Chase, US Bank and KeyBank) provide $300 million line of credit.
First Cash Financial Services	546 locations in 12 US states and 16 states in Mexico.	Wells Fargo and JP Morgan Chase provide the company with $90 million.
EZ Corp, Inc.	Operates 479 stores nationwide.	Wells Fargo lead lender, providing $50 million of the total $120 million in credit.

Source: National People's Action (2010) 'American Profiteers: How the Mainstream Banks Finance the Payday Lending Industry'. Available at: www.npa-us.org (accessed 14 July 2013).

★ In 2009, Advance America was able to lend out in the form of payday loans over 4.4 times their credit limit.

† ACE Cash Express was formerly a publicly owned corporation, but turned to private hands in 2007.

in the chapter (Chin, 2004; Consumer Federation of America, 2004; Mann and Hawkins, 2007). According to the Securities and Exchange Commission (SEC), major banks provide a minimum of $1.5 billion in credit to payday lenders, who fund an estimated $15 billion in payday loans every year (National People's Action, 2010). Aside from financing payday lending, national banks have been swiftly moving into the lucrative payday business. I return to this topic in Section Three.

The segment of the surplus population that relies on payday lending does not involve the poorest of the poor – many of whom are considered 'unbanked' because they do not possess the requisite chequing account for payday loans. This segment functions in the cash economy, relying on alternative lending facilities such as pawnshops (Austin, 2004; Karger, 2005; Rivlin, 2010; National People's Action, 2012). Payday lenders target the segment of the surplus population with income sources and a chequing account and/or proof of a government subsidy, such as a welfare or Social Security, but whose daily lives are characterised by high levels of economic insecurity. This, for example, would include workers living from paycheck to paycheck, with no financial wiggle room for emergencies and/or illnesses. According to the website of the CFSA:

> Payday advance customers are the face of America: Men and women with families and jobs who sometimes have unbudgeted or unexpected expenses between paychecks and need small dollar, short-term credit to meet their obligations. In addition to steady sources of income, 100 percent of our customers have a chequing account at a bank or credit union.[8]

While exact numbers of payday borrowers are difficult to obtain, estimates range from 12 million to 30 million (cf., Logan and Weller, 2009; National People's Action, 2010). Data regarding the income profiles of payday borrowers range slightly from study to study. According to some scholars and consumer advocacy groups, for instance, half of payday loans are issued to people earning between $25,000 and $50,000 per year (Karger, 2005; Logan and Weller, 2009). National People's Action also cite this salary range, noting that 75 percent of borrowers had an annual household income of less than $50,000 and one-third had a household income below $25,000. Similarly, a 2013 study conducted by the Consumer Financial Protection Bureau (CFPB) observes that payday borrowers have income that is largely concentrated in income categories ranging from $10,000 to $40,000 on an annualised basis (CFPB, 2013: 17).

Despite the above differences in income levels, the data shares a commonality in that the income of payday borrowers remains with the range from low-income individuals and families have income below two-times the poverty threshold (or, below 200 percent of the poverty line), while poor individuals and families register incomes at or below 100 percent of the poverty line (see Table 4.2 in Chapter 4). Data also reveals that borrowers also tend to be disproportionately female, with single mothers making up a key segment of payday customers. African-American and Latino customers also comprise a disproportionate number of payday borrowers (National

People's Action, 2012: 6). Furthermore, over one-quarter of all bank payday borrowers are recipients of Social Security benefits (CFPB, 2013; CRL, 2013).

A historical materialist understanding of the payday loan industry

The emergence of legalised payday lending

With the rise of credit-led accumulation in the late 1970s, two trends have gone hand in glove. First, the era has been characterised by a rise in low-wage, unskilled labour, which constitutes the fastest-growing and largest segment of employment in the country. According to the Bureau of Labour Statistics (BLS), this pattern is expected to hold until 2020 (Moody, 2007; Bureau of Labour Statistics, 2012).[9] Low-wage retail and service sector jobs, for example, 'accounted for 70 percent of all new job growth between 1989 and 2000. And the majority of these jobs are filled by women' (Collins and Mayer, 2010: 6). Second, under neoliberalism, there has been a steady withdrawal of public and corporate support of the social wage (Katz, 2001). Both trends have resulted in a subsequent reliance on private credit to secure and sustain social reproduction. Taken together, the absence of a living wage coupled with the persistence of stagnant real wages, high levels of (long-term) unemployment and the ongoing structural violence of labour – e.g., dereliction of labour laws, the dominance of precarious, low-wage work that falls disproportionately along gendered and racial/ethnic lines (Peterson, 2003; Wacquant, 2009; LeBaron and Roberts, 2010; McNally, 2011) – has led to the creation of a lucrative market of surplus population upon which payday lenders prey.

Coinciding with the rise of the payday loan industry was the introduction of the draconian welfare reform in the United States in the mid-1990s and its turn to workfarism (Peck, 2001). As discussed in Chapter 3, the workfare state was premised on the exchange of employment for government assistance, with an eye on weaning people off the latter completely. As Randy Albeda (2012: 12) puts it, 'the new mandate for poor adults, especially single mothers [during this time], was to get a job – any job'. Seen from this angle, there may be a connection between the boom in the payday lending industry in the mid-1990s and the introduction of workfare. One study has revealed a strong connection between welfare (workfare) and payday borrowing: 10 percent of current Temporary Assistance for Needy Families (TANF) recipients and 15 percent of leavers used payday lenders, compared to nine percent of all low-income families (Stegman and Faris, 2005). We explore the profile of payday borrowers below.

Aside from payday lenders, clear beneficiaries of this turn to privatised and individualised forms of the provisioning of social reproduction through credit have been low-wage employers (e.g., Wal-Mart), who can hire cheap hourly workers without providing social benefits (Karger, 2005). By permitting and legitimating the commodification of basic subsistence among the surplus population, the state and, in particular, its debtfare forms of intervention, assists in facilitating credit-led accumulation in two ways: first, it allows for the social reproduction of a large segment of the American labour force (surplus population) by permitting private creditors to supplement low paying jobs that lack benefits; second, in doing so, it supports the largely marketised forms of the biological reproduction of this segment of the workforce (Collins and Mayer, 2010; Albeda, 2012).

Debtfarism and the remaking of the payday industry

One class, one society: the middle-class trope in the payday loan industry

> *I turned to Advance America not because I was frivolous or careless with money. I turned to them because at the time I didn't have the funds available. We are Americans who work hard and live right. Things happen. And when you have places like Advance America that can help everyday people, that's a good thing.*
> – Advance America Customer, Advance America, 2010: ii

In the consumer society, class boundaries have been blurred as opposed to clearly demarcated, due in large measure to an exclusive focus on the realm of exchange (see Chapter 3; Burton, 2008; cf. Fine, 2002). This distortion is reflected in dominant tropes used by the payday lending industry. To gloss over the vulnerability of the workers upon which it preys, the payday loan industry insists on portraying its customer base as *Mainstreet USA* or middle-income consumers (Advance America, 2010). The blurring of class differences based on income is also created by rhetoric employed by the state in its debtfare capacity. The middle-class ideology is an extremely powerful cultural trope in terms of depoliticising the socio-economic inequalities within and between states that have heightened under neoliberal rule (Harvey, 2005; cf. Wacquant, 2009). As we saw above, the payday loan industry has also described its consumer base as middle class. Before turning to a closer inspection of this trope in the context of the payday lending industry, it is helpful to grasp the meaning of the middle-class trope as it is employed by the US state, for example, in the form of G. W. Bush's 'Ownership Society' (Soederberg, 2010c), followed by US Vice-President Joseph Biden's 'Middle-Class Task Force' (MCTF).[10]

According to a study commissioned by the MCTF, simply aspiring to be middle class is as important an indicator of middle-class status as income levels (US Department of Commerce, 2010: 5). Although the report admits that 'it is harder to attain a middle-class lifestyle in 2008 than it was two decades ago, particularly since the real prices of the signifiers of middle class have increased in relation to average wages and salaries' (see Table 6.1), it is by no means impossible. Signifiers of this coveted status (homes, college education, health security and so forth) can be purchased through savings and hard work (US Department of Commerce, 2010: 5), although the MCTF study does admit that incomes below the poverty line 'cannot support a middle-class lifestyle', i.e., economic security (US Department of Commerce, 2010: 3; see Table 6.2).

TABLE 6.2 Price changes in key middle-class items, 1990–2008 (inflation adjusted)

	1990 prices in 2008 dollars	Actual 2008 prices (dollars)	Price change in inflated-adjusted terms (%)
Housing (Median Value)	126,600	197,600	56
Health Care (Premium and out-of-pocket expenses)	2,000	5,100	155
College Four-year public college (Tuition, fees and room and board)	8,400	13,400	60
Four-year private college (Tuition, fees and room and board)	21,200	30,400	43

Source: US Department of Commerce, Economics and Statistics and Administration (2010) *Middle Class in America*. January. Prepared for the Office of the Vice-President of the United States and the Middle-Class Task Force, Washington, DC: US Department of Commerce, p. 24.

In contrast to the portrayal of the middle class by the American state and the payday lending industry, the reality is that the United States has become increasingly polarised, not only through the pursuit of free market policies such as the commodification and privatisation of health and education, but also through the growing prevalence of low-wage and precarious jobs, the rise of workfare policies, regressive taxation practices, the ongoing subsidisation of capitalist enterprises and so forth. It is important to stress, once again, that the growing socio-economic divide has not only manifested itself along the lines of class, but also race (notably Latino and African-American) and gender (single-parent, predominantly female, households) (Peterson, 2003; Dymski, 2009; National People's Action, 2012; Roberts, 2013).

Data from the MCTF Report (see Table 6.3) reveal that female-headed, single-parent households fall into the average payday borrowers' income range, that is, $25,000 to $50,000. This, in turn, supports a payday industry study that reveals the typical payday customer is female with children living at home, is between 24 and 44 years of age, earns less than $40,000 a year and has little job security (Karger, 2005: 19). As noted in Table 6.3, the primary reasons for borrowing from payday lending reflect basic subsistence needs, as opposed to conspicuous consumption. According the 2010 Annual Report of Advance America, payday lending is a seasonal business. Demand is highest during the third and fourth quarters of each year, corresponding to the back-to-school and holiday seasons, which suggests that spending may be geared largely toward children's needs such as clothing, school supplies and presents (Advance America, 2010).

TABLE 6.3 Income levels for selected families, 2008 (in dollars)

	In the distribution of two-parent two-child families	In the distribution of one-parent two-child families
Lowest quartile cut-off *(25th percentile)*	50,800	13,200
Median *(50th percentile)*	80,600	25,200
Highest quartile cut-off *(75th percentile)*	122,800	44,000
Poverty Line	21,800	17,300

Source: US Department of Commerce, Economics and Statistics and Administration (2010) *Middle Class in America*. January. Prepared for the Office of the Vice-President of the United States and the Middle-Class Task Force, Washington, DC: US Department of Commerce, p. 2.

The class, racial and gendered lines of payday borrowers are also revealed in a study that investigates the differences between payday loan borrowers and non-borrowers using figures from the Federal Reserve's 2007, *Survey on Consumer Finances* (hereafter: SCF), which, for the first time, data on payday loans (Federal Reserve Board, 2007; Logan and Weller, 2009). Not unsurprisingly, this study found that families, who turned to payday lenders, earned considerably less than non-borrowers. Moreover, while CFSA-sponsored studies report that the majority of payday loan customers are married (Elliehausen and Lawrence, 2001), SCF data suggest that 40 percent of payday loan borrowers are a married couple, while 41 percent of families who borrow from a payday lender are headed by single women. With the decrease in family income and rise of poverty levels from 2007 to 2010, the reliance on payday lending has not only continued, but also increased (Federal Reserve Board, 2010a; National Poverty Centre, 2012). According to the SCF 2010 survey, for instance, 3.9 percent of families reported having taken out a payday loan in 2010, which represents an increase of 2.4 percent from 2007 (Federal Reserve Board, 2010a).[11]

In terms of race, 38 percent of those who have borrowed a payday loan within the last year were non-white, while just 22 percent of families who did not take out such a loan were non-white. Minority families are more likely to have borrowed from a payday lender than white families. Additionally, payday industry data indicate that African Americans make up a larger share of payday customers than of the general population (Logan and Weller, 2009). This finding has been reinforced by a study conducted by the Centre for Responsible Lending, which found that payday lending has a disparate impact on communities of colour (Li *et al.*, 2009).

Another finding interrupts the depictions of payday borrowers as middle-income consumers by revealing their precarious position relative to consumers who are not economically insecure: The 2007 SCF data reveal that families who borrowed from payday lenders had a mean net worth of $22,616. Families who did not rely on payday loans enjoyed a mean net worth more than 20 times that of payday loan users, i.e., $469,374. The median net worth of payday loan borrowers was, by comparison, $0. Families who did not take out a payday loan possessed a median net worth of $80,510. Another difference between payday borrowers and non-borrowers was reflected in the total value of their assets. In 2007, payday loan borrowers' mean asset value was $73,309, less than one-eighth of the mean value of non-payday loan borrowers' assets, which stood at $639,467. The median asset value of families who withdrew a payday loan was $4,550, while those who did not take out a payday loan had a median asset value more than 44 times as large – $201,000 (Logan and Weller, 2009: 8–9). The borrowing histories of families were also considerably different. The 2007 SCF data show that the share of payday loan borrowers who previously applied for but were denied any type of loan within the last five years was 33 percent, compared to 10 percent for non-payday loan users (Logan and Weller, 2009: 9).

Seen from the above angle, the middle-class trope promoted by the debtfare state serves an important role in constructing consent around the existence of, and reliance on, payday loans by erasing (depoliticising) class, racial and gendered differences through the portrayal of society as *one (middle-class) class*, evoking previous cultural tropes such as the Ownership Society (Soederberg 2010b). The cultural trope of debtfare also serves to promote the illusion in which rational and individualised consumers can seek economic protection and security by participating (consuming, borrowing) in a free, equal, democratic and competitive market. In what follows, we lift the veil off of this debtfare trope to expose the gendered and racial features of the middle-class consumers of payday loans.

Spatial and temporal constructions of 'convenience'

> *Just as many consumers prefer the convenience of specialty stores to large department stores, many consumers prefer the efficiency and convenience of financial service centers over banks. They prefer transacting at FiSCA member stores because of their neighborhood locations and longer hours of operation and the friendly service they receive.*
> – Financial Service Centres of America (FiSCA)[12]

As noted above, unlike other forms of consumer credit, payday loans are relatively quick to obtain, as they do not require a credit report and decisions on whether to issue a loan are made on the spot, using as collateral the borrower's paycheque or proof of a government benefit such as a welfare cheque (Graves and Peterson, 2005). Nor do payday lenders generally report the borrower's repayment history later on (Peterson, 2007). The convenience and speed associated with payday loans has been increasingly intensified with the rapid expansion of largely unregulated, online payday lending. While online payday lenders still comprise a minority of the total loan volume, some industry analysts believe it may eventually overtake storefront loan volume (CFPB, 2013). As I noted earlier, the social power of money expresses itself in terms of space and time (Harvey, 1989). The word 'convenience' figures prominently in the payday industry literature. Ease and accessibility to credit are indeed important elements of the wider trope of the democratisation of credit (Advance America, 2010). According to FiSCA and other reports, the ease of payday loans helps to 'bridge the unexpected need for short-term credit when other options are not available'.[13] The business strategy of payday lenders is based on the assumption that customers will be attracted to lenders based on proximity to their workplace. Some scholars have suggested that the only factors a payday borrower takes into consideration are convenience of location, ease of process and speed of approvals and not the interest rate (FDIC, 2009). The convenience factor also explains the growth in Internet-only payday lenders (UNC Centre for Community Capital, 2007; Francis, 2010: 619).

The centrality of convenience in payday lending is also confirmed in Table 6.4. Two points are relevant here. First, given the demographics of the payday borrowers, convenience cannot be considered in isolation from other reasons listed, particularly basic consumption needs, including food, gas, vehicle expenses, medical payments, utility costs, or rent (Federal Reserve Board, 2010a). Second and related, convenience is not only a social construction of space that is connected to the social power of money, but also to wider compulsions and structural violence in neoliberalism, such as workfare states, lack of social protection and living wages, the ability of banks to charge exorbitant fees and interest on bounced cheques and so forth. As the following discussion of the 2006 military ban – one significant ban of many – on payday lending demonstrates, the construction of convenience with regard to the geographies of storefronts is also sanctioned by debtfarism. Although the payday industry denies targeting people of colour, 'payday loan stores are highly

TABLE 6.4 Reasons for borrowing from payday lenders, 2007 and 2010

Reason	Share of borrowers, 2007* (%)	Share of borrowers, 2010† (%)
Convenience	34	21
Emergency	29	36
Basic consumption needs	21	20
Home	9	N/A
Only available option	8	N/A
Need to pay other bills and loans	N/A	11
Other needs, e.g., 'Christmas' and need to 'help family'	N/A	12

Source: A. Logan and C. E. Weller (2009) *Who Borrows from Payday Lenders? An Analysis of Newly Available Data.* Washington, DC: Center for American Progress, p. 11.

*Logan and Weller's calculation based on *2007 Survey of Consumer Finance Data*, Washington, DC: Federal Reserve Bank (i.e., totals 101% in original).

†Federal Reserve Board (2010a) *2010 Survey of Consumer Finance Data.* Washington, DC: Federal Reserve Board, A47. Percentages rounded by author.

concentrated in African-American and Latino neighbourhoods' (National People's Action, 2012: 6).

Various scholarly studies have concluded that payday lenders actively target spaces in urban areas with: more people on public assistance; fewer banks per capita than other spaces; relatively higher minority concentrations, including areas with more recent immigrants and others who are less likely to speak English; a higher percentage of people in the military; and people with less formal education (Burkey and Simkins, 2004; Graves and Peterson, 2005; US Department of Defense, 2006; Gallmeyer and Wade, 2009). As noted earlier, this targeted demographic is not the unbanked but the underbanked. The latter category, according to the Federal Deposit Insurance Corporation (FDIC), comprises 17.9 percent of the US households. Roughly 21 million people are underbanked (i.e., possess a chequing or savings account and rely on alternative financial services such as payday loans) (FDIC, 2010: 3).

One study reveals that payday lenders actively seek people who are already served by banks, suggesting that payday lenders are attempting take advantage of the increased debt levels among 'banked' households and/or the payday loans are becoming more mainstream, which in turn has prompted entry into these spaces (Damar, 2009). The social space of accessibility and ease of payday lending is also linked to the temporal violence associated with the loan in the form of the rollover phenomenon or, debt trap.

Unmasking 'predators who care' and best practices

Following the general neoliberal trend of corporate caring and good citizenship, or what I have elsewhere referred to as the 'marketisation of social justice' (Soederberg, 2010b), the payday industry has engaged in aggressive campaigning to rebrand itself as a respectable lending institution that is engaged in 'helping hardworking Americans meet their financial obligations' through the creation of programmes such as the 2010 *America Needs a Raise* campaign[14] in which the corporation does not recognise and award Americans for their 'extraordinary service' in their spaces of employment, but rather outside of the workplace (Advance America, 2010). Aside from the façade of the friendly neighbour to be reconstructed by the industry, the middle-class trope, as is the community of money in which it represented, is protected and reproduced. Our gaze is moved away from the wider dynamics of capital accumulation in which these workers earn wages or extract benefits to make payments on their loans.

The payday industry is also vested in signalling its good citizenship by adhering to consumer protection laws and meeting other requirements set by regulators. In the attempts to curtail meaningful regulation regarding its interest rates and fees, for instance, the payday lobby organisation CFSA has announced its strong support of the Consumer Financial Protection Bureau's (CFPB) recommendations for a principles-based reform approach to ensure fair treatment for all customers through the focus on disclosure (cf. Lamoreaux, 2010; CFPB, 2013). Advance America has stressed it will meet these requirements 'by promoting transparency on all aspects of lending practices, improving and streamlining disclosures to enable customers to easily compare borrowing options and ensuring that similar products are regulated in an equitable manner to support market competition' (Advance America, 2010: iii). To this end, FiSCA lists a 'Code of Conduct'[15] and the CFSA has devised a 'Customer Bill of Rights', including a list of coercive collection practices that they dissuade their members from considering or using as a threat toward a customer (US Department of Defense, 2006; cf., Picciotto, 2011).[16]

These absences of legally binding rules in consumer finance have resulted in not only higher priced credit for the poor, but also inferior legal protections (Drysdale and Keest, 2000). Legal obligation continues to act as a coercive and ideological frame governing the relations between debtors and creditors, while the latter are able to evade any meaningful legal obligation and, as we will see, are even permitted to distort the meaning of legal obligation in the same manner as the salary lenders. For instance, although the CFSA's list of 'best practices' prohibits the threat of prosecution as a collection tactic, many payday lenders use this approach to collect past due accounts. What is more, some lenders do not limit themselves to merely threatening debtors with criminal prosecution, but also moving forward with this threat in court. In one Dallas, Texas precinct in one year, payday lenders filed over 13,000 criminal charges with law enforcement officials against their consumers (Drysdale and Keest, 2000: 610).

What is not well known among payday loan borrowers – despite the financial education services that the payday lending industry allegedly offers – is that a post-dated cheque given to someone who knows that it will not clear, rarely supports criminal prosecution. As a federal district court in Tennessee noted, one should assume that the borrower does not have enough money in the bank to cover the cheque – otherwise they would not be in court: 'Certainly a lender's exaction of a fee to "defer" deposit signifies the requisite acceptance on his part necessary to remove the transaction from the realm of the criminal bad cheque statute' (Drysdale and Keest, 2000: 611). Notwithstanding the absence of criminal prosecution threats, however, payday debtors, who default on loans are subject to punitive charges in the form of delinquency and collection fees. Payday loans are the only type of consumer debt that can trigger treble damage penalties upon default[17] (Drysdale and Keest, 2000).

In keeping with voluntary-led regulation based on neoliberal assumptions of market freedoms, since the early 1990s many US corporations, including payday lending companies, have required borrowers to sign contracts to compel them to resolve any dispute between the payday company and the consumer in the form of mandatory arbitration. In contrast to litigation, mandatory arbitration, which is backed by the Supreme Court, is contentious due to its private and often non-consensual nature (Schwartz, 1997; Jory, 2009). Although it may only be flagged here, mandatory arbitration should be viewed as a political response to the ongoing tensions in dispossessive capitalism, which are evidenced by the growing number of defaults and debt collection lawsuits and the booming debt collection industry, which is the fastest growing industry in the United States, according to the Bureau of Labour Statistics. Mandatory arbitration should also be understood as part of wider debtfare strategies regarding bankruptcy law. The Bankruptcy Abuse Prevention and Consumer Protection Act of 2005[18] has been the most recent and coercive expression of the state's attempt to deal with the paradoxes inherent in secondary forms of exploitation of the working poor.

Debtfarism, rhetorical payday bans and salience distortion

A narrow definition of usury is the taking of more for the use of money than the law allows. Usury laws are believed to protect against the oppression of debtors through excessive rates of interest charged by lenders. Since there is no federal usury law, each state has its own percentage rate that is considered a de facto usury rate (Jory, 2009: 321). But, for the most part, usury laws have failed to regulate the payday lending industry (Peterson, 2007). Thirty-six percent (APR) is the limit set by the Federal Deposit Insurance Corporation's (FDIC) Responsible Small Dollar Lending Guidelines and is double the cap for federally chartered credit unions. A majority of states have statutes regulating what loan terms are permitted and prohibited.[19] The statutes also entail penalties for non-compliance. Many of these states even cap the interest or fees lenders can charge to consumers (Plunkett and Hurtado, 2011). Most of these states limit the number of loans that can be made or renewed with the aim of reducing predatory cycles of debt (Johnston, 2010).

Yet, debtfarism – in both its federal and state articulations – has facilitated the evasion of usury laws by payday lenders. After conducting a rigorous empirical study of 50 state usury laws, legal scholar Christopher L. Peterson, concludes that since 1965 usury law has become more lax, more polarised and more misleading. He refers to this trend as 'salience distortion' (Peterson, 2007: 5). Seen from our theoretical frame, Peterson's views reflect wider attempts by the debtfare state to assist payday lenders by depoliticising increasing public criticism and controversy regarding the industry's disregard for consumer protection laws and the creation of so-called debt traps (i.e., rollover loans). In what follows, I outline some examples of salience distortion exercised by debtfare practices with regard to usury laws.

When faced with usury caps or an outright ban of payday lending from state legislatures in the early 2000s (e.g., Georgia and North Carolina in 2004), payday lenders created 'rent-a-bank' partnerships with nationally chartered banks. This move was largely facilitated by previous debtfare interventions, such as the Marquette Decision of 1978 (*Marquette Nat. Bank of Minneapolis v. First of Omaha Service Corp.*), which allowed banks to circumvent state usury laws (Johnston, 2010; see Chapter 4). Briefly, the Marquette Decision represented an attempt by the US federal government to displace state regulation (Mann and Hawkins, 2007). The US Supreme Court ruled that lenders in a state with liberal usury laws (e.g., Delaware and South Dakota) could apply rates to workers residing in states with more restrictive usury ceilings (Peterson, 2007).

Significantly, the Marquette Decision served to undermine usury protection, which was a vital step in the growth of secondary forms of exploitation. The American state thus effectively legalised usury in 1978. From this time onward, any national bank was permitted 'to charge an interest rate as high as the maximum rate permitted by the laws of the state where the bank is located' (Mann and Hawkins, 2007: 871). And, while this pertained to national banks, it played a major role in normalising usury across the United States, allowing national banks to charge, among other things, over 4,000 percent (median) interest rates on overdraft cheques (i.e., in excess of 20 times that of payday loans), creating a ludicrous situation in which payday loans become a cost effective alternative (Fusaro, 2008).

Seen from the above perspective, the clear beneficiaries of interest rate caps on payday loans across several states[20] are not the working poor, but national banks. Around the time of the start of various payday bans in 2004, the bounced cheque rates in both Georgia and North Carolina increased. Eager to take advantage of this new opening, the federal government passed the Check Clearing for the 21st Century Act in 2003 (or, 'Check 21'), which came into effect in 2004 (Morgan and Strain, 2008). One of the features of this new law effectively enhances bank profitability with regard to bounced cheques. For instance, the Act allows depository institutions to debit payers' accounts more quickly (using electronic presentment) without crediting payees' accounts more promptly. Less 'float' for cheque writers means more bounced cheques revealing the social power of money through its temporal dimension (Morgan and Strain, 2008: 14).

To avoid regulation, some payday lenders shut down their physical offices in states with severe restrictions and began conducting payday lending via the Internet, where they charge higher rates and issue loans in greater amounts than their brick-and-mortar stores (Johnston, 2010). Since 2006, for example, the state of California's Department of Corporations has been trying to force these unlicensed, Internet-only businesses to adhere to the same rules that govern the state-licensed (brick-and-mortar) payday loan stores that offer short-term, unsecured loans of up to $300 and cap the annualised percentage rate at 459 percent for a maximum 31-day period. Internet payday lenders have been allowed to circumvent state law by claiming that they are associated with sovereign Aboriginal nations that operate outside of California and are thus immune from state regulation. Authorities estimate that these Aboriginal-based Internet-only lending companies involve thousands of websites that generate billions of dollars in revenue nationwide ('Internet payday lenders with ties to Indians dodge California regulators', *LA Times*, 13 April 2009).

Other online competitors are also attempting to reconfigure the spatio-temporal dimensions of short-term loans and, in doing so, may affect the dominant position of virtual payday lending. ZestCash, an online small-loans lending company established in 2009 by former Google executive Douglas Merrill, raised $73 million of funding in early 2012 to expand the company's operations ('Former Google CIO Raises $73 Million to Reform Payday Loans with Data-Driven Startup ZestCash', *TechCrunch*, 19 January 2012; zestcash.com). ZestCash offers loans of up to $800 but, unlike payday lenders, allows the loans to be repaid over a period of months, as opposed to weeks. According to its website, by using 'analytical techniques', ZestCash suggests that it is able to offer a fair, lower cost alternative to people 'who do not have access to traditional credit'. Yet, like payday borrowers, these lenders require a bank account and a source of income. Moreover, ZestCash still charges triple-digit interest rates, when computed in terms of APR. Although it markets its product as 50 percent cheaper (for those with relatively better credit ratings) than traditional payday lenders, ZestCash loans, according to the company's website, average 365 percent APR as opposed to 480 percent APR of payday loans.[21]

Two further examples of how payday lenders have circumvented state usury laws due to the existence (and maintenance) of loopholes are worth mentioning here (Woolston, 2010). The first is the case of Ohio. In 2008 and in response to increasing pressure from constituents and consumer advocates, the Ohio State Legislature passed and signed into law the Short-Term Loan Act to curb predatory payday lending. The Act essentially capped the maximum loan amount at $500, limited the APR on loans at 28 percent and made the maturity date a minimum of 30 days. Additionally, the Act banned lenders from issuing more than four loans per year to the same borrower. The statute also addresses a common circumvention technique of out-of-state lenders – issuing loans via the Internet or telephone – by banning out-of-state lenders from issuing loans to Ohio residents (Johnston, 2010). After mounting a $20 million campaign to overthrow the new law through a voter initiative on the November 2008 ballot, Ohio voters overwhelming defeated the industry's initiative.

The payday lenders, however, quickly found legal loopholes through salience distortion (Peterson, 2007; Johnston, 2010). While only 19 lenders, for instance, obtained a licence under the new law, the majority of lenders were licensed under either Ohio's Mortgage Loan Act, which does not require issuance of an actual mortgage and does not place limits on the interest rates that can be charged, or under Ohio's Small Loan Act, which permits payday lenders to charge 423 percent APR, even higher than the 391 percent allowed under the repealed payday lending statute (Johnston, 2010). In a 2009 study, *every* payday lender surveyed in Ohio charged triple-digit interest rates and required loans to be paid back within two weeks or less. Furthermore, the majority issued loans in amounts exceeding $500 (Johnston, 2010: 12–26). Yet, to date, neither the state of Ohio nor the federal government has enacted any meaningful laws or regulations that curtail this practice (Woolston, 2010).

Texas also provides a good example in which to gain insight into the loopholes involved when banning or mitigating payday lending in the name of consumer protection. To overcome the rent-a-bank prohibition, payday lenders in Texas have been exploiting a loophole in a broadly worded statute that allows them to operate as 'credit service organisations' (or, CSOs) (Mann and Hawkins, 2007). CSOs were originally established in the state to improve a customer's credit rating. In Texas, CSOs are legally required to pay a $100 registration fee to the Secretary of State, post a $10,000 bond for each store, disclose contract terms and costs to borrowers and permit borrowers three days to cancel a contract ('The perils of payday', *The Texas Observer*, 30 April 2009). Payday lenders use the CSO status to process loans from third parties and then collect fees – not interest – thereby evading usury laws (Johnston, 2010: 17). Targeting low-income neighbourhoods in the state, payday lenders grew from 1,513 storefronts in 2005 to more than 2,800 in 2009. Like the rest of the United States, the payday lending business was extremely lucrative in the wake of the 2008 recession ('The perils of payday', *The Texas Observer*, 30 April 2009).

Legal protection for some

When faced with pressure from specific segments of power within the state, the debtfare system is able to impose laws without legal loopholes. In the early 2000s, in the context of growing discontent and attacks on payday lenders, commanding officers at military bases in the United States began complaining about the active targeting of their personnel by payday companies (Graves and Peterson, 2005). According to the Centre for Responsible Lending, one in five military members had taken out a loan in 2004 versus one in sixteen civilian Americans (Logan and Weller, 2009; Rivlin, 2010). The demographics of the military reflect those of payday borrowers, i.e., there is a disproportionate representation of African-Americans and Latinos with limited educational backgrounds (Graves and Peterson, 2005: 676).

According to the Pentagon, payday borrowing does more harm than good for the military (Johnston, 2010). In a 2006 report issued by the US Department of Defense, 'service members need better enforcement from Congress and state credit regulators to prevent predatory lending abuses, which undermine military readiness and harm the morale of troops and their families (US Department of Defense, 2006: 9). Moreover, 'the President of the Navy Marine Corps Relief Society called payday lending 'the most serious single financial problem that we have encountered in [a] hundred years' (Centre for Responsible Lending, 2007, cited in Carrell and Zinman, 2008: 3).

The payday industry normally wields power in the Senate Financial Services Committee, but this battle was waged by the Pentagon's Armed Services Committee. In the summer of 2006, Senator Jim Talent (R-Missouri) and Senator Bill Nelson (D-Florida) added an amendment (also known as the Talent-Nelson amendment) to the annual defense authorisation bill that capped the payday loan rate for military families at 36 percent (Mann and Hawkins, 2007; Rivlin, 2010). The Pentagon successfully lobbied Congress for the implementation of the Military Lending Act of 2006, which was a binding federal cap on loans to military members and their families (36 percent APR) effective 1 October 2007 as part of the John Warner National Defense Authorization Act (Carrell and Zinman, 2008).

The military payday ruling was important for several reasons. First and foremost, it underscores the fact that usury law is a highly political affair, as opposed to a technical exercise to be left primarily to lawyers and corporate lobbyists. Indeed and in contrast to state legislatures, Congress has the power to cap interest rates for both banks and non-depository lenders alike (Peterson, 2007). Second, the 2006 ruling reveals the social configuration of power between various departmental units within the neoliberal state as well as the larger geo-political context of the time, namely: the Second Gulf War, fought in the name of freedom. And, third, this case also indicates shifting configurations of power in the payday lending industry; a key segment of which involves large national banks (see Table 6.1; Center for Responsible Lending, 2013).

Competition from national banks: good for consumers or a spatial fix?

As noted earlier, large, national banks play an integral role in financing payday lenders. The banks listed in Table 6.1, most of which received Troubled Asset Relief Programme (TARP)[22] bailout funds in 2008–2009, have benefited from other types of state subsidisation in the form of accessing capital at exceptionally low interest rates from the Federal Reserve (National People's Action, 2010; Centre for Responsible Lending, 2013; for various Federal Reserve lending rates, see Chapter 4). These banks loaned money to payday lenders at an average of 4.1 percent and 7.76 percent in 2007 and 2008, respectively. Payday lenders then used this credit to issue millions of loans to the working poor at average rates of 400 percent APR (National People's Action, 2010). Given these lucrative spreads, it should not come as a surprise that some banks, particularly those that acted as creditors to payday lenders (e.g., Wells Fargo) have been aggressively entering the payday lending industry since the mid-2000s.

Over the years, national banks, which do not have to abide by state usury laws, have been increasing their competition for a share of the lucrative $30 billion-a-year payday lending market and its estimated $7.3 billion generated by fees ('Bad Credit: how payday lenders evade regulation', *The Nation*, 25 April 2011). Since the 1980s, non-interest income (e.g., fees) has grown twice as fast as interest income and accounts for half of all bank revenues (Stegman, 2007). According to one industry estimate, 60 percent of service fee revenue comes from non-sufficient funds (NSF) fees (Fusaro, 2008).[23] Competition from payday lenders has driven banks to increase overdraft fees and reduce the availability of free chequing accounts (Meltzer and Morgan, 2009).

The national bank payday loans took off after the FDIC issued its Affordable Small-Dollar Loan Guidelines in 2006.[24] In the wake of the 2005 ban on rent-a-bank partnerships, these guidelines (read: not legally binding) were aimed at 'non-member banks to encourage them to offer small-dollar loan products that are affordable. FDIC-supervised institutions that offer these products in a responsible, safe and sound manner may receive favourable consideration under the Community Reinvestment Act' (CRA).[25] In terms of interest rates, the FDIC noted that:

Pricing may vary depending on the risk profile of the target group. For example, a number of institutions have developed affordable small-dollar credit programs with APRs that range between 12 percent and 32 percent with no or low fees. We encourage lenders to offer small-dollar credit with APRs of 36 percent or less.[26]

Despite these guidelines, national banks such as US Bancorp, Wells Fargo and Fifth Third Bancorp – all three recipients of taxpayer bailout funds (TARP) – have been creating their own payday loan products with triple-digit interest rates to serve their chequing account customers (National People's Action, 2010). Banks make payday loans by depositing money into a customer's chequing account. According to the Centre for Responsible Lending (CRL, 2011), 'The bank then automatically repays itself in full by deducting the loan amount, plus fees, from the account when the customer's next direct deposit paycheck or other benefits income comes into the account'. Depending how quickly the loan is repaid, APR can range from 120 to 365 percent on these 'chequing account advance' or 'direct deposit advance' accounts (CRL, 2010; 'Report blames big banks for payday loan growth', *Wall Street Journal*, 14 September 2010). Moreover, studies by the CRL of actual chequing account activity found that *bank payday borrowers are in debt for 175 days per year*, i.e., twice as long as the *maximum* length of time the FDIC has advised is appropriate (CRL, 2011).

Due the doctrine of federal preemption with regard to national banks – which falls under the purview of the Office of the Comptroller of the Currency (OCC), the Federal Reserve Board and the Federal Deposit Insurance Corporation – banks can continue making loans in states that permit payday lending as well as in states that prohibit or restrict the product from non-bank lenders. Bank payday loans have also undermined federal protections of the Military Lending Act of 2006 discussed above (CRL, 2013). National banks are able to evade this law by rejigging the structure and nomenclature of loans. For example, since the 2006 regulation covers 'closed-end' loans, banks refer to their loans as 'open-end' loans, despite the fact that the due date for the loan, like the closed-end loan, is fixed as the next deposit date or, at the latest, after 35 days (CRL, 2013: 7).

Aside from the sheer volume of capital they possess vis-à-vis payday lenders, banks are not only immune from state usury laws, but because overdraft protection is not legally recognised as a loan, banks are not required to comply with the Truth in Lending Act (TILA) or the disclosure of APRs (Fusaro, 2008: 251). Banks argue that unlike payday lenders, customers can't extend or rollover the loans because the amount owed is automatically repaid with the next direct deposit. According to the banks, this restriction mitigates the debt chain to which many payday borrowers have been exposed. The default risk for banks is also minimal, since borrowers who sign up for the loans agree to give the banks first dibs on their next direct deposit of $100 or more. In contrast, most payday companies still rely on customers showing up with a cheque (CRL, 2010). As one industry insider notes, the banks 'get to charge a 120 percent interest rate on what is essentially a risk-free loan ... It shouldn't be a mystery why banks are doing this' ('Biggest banks stepping in to payday arena', *Star Tribune* [Minneapolis-St. Paul] 6 September 2009). As of 1 March 2013, bank payday lenders received another perk. After this date, electronic distribution of government cheques became mandatory. Given that one-quarter of all bank payday borrowers are Social Security recipients, upon receipt of the electronic government benefit, banks are now able repay themselves the payday loan amount before any other expense or creditor (CRL, 2013; CFPB, 2013).

FiSCA and CFSA have fought back against competition from national banks by aggressively lobbying Congress on the grounds of market freedom, competition and transparency – all in the interest of consumer protection.[27] For example, the Urban Institute for the US Department of Treasury has said that: 'Narrowing the credit market could reduce price competition between lenders and raise prices', and warns that 'restricting supply can reduce consumer well-being, as consumers turn to inferior products or options to deal with inferior products or options to deal with credit needs' (Advance America, 2010: 4). In an ironic twist of events, the payday lending industry, known for circumventing state law (see above), has complained that banks like Fifth Third are ignoring interest rate caps imposed under state payday lending statutes (Johnston, 2010: 20). The fact remains, however, that national banks do not have to abide by state usury laws, as they are regulated by federal banking legislation (Johnston, 2010: 21). As other commentators have noted, while national depository institutions have no incentive to reveal the APR of their chequing advance products, payday lenders have aggressively publicised the results of a 2008 FDIC study on the costs and usage of overdraft credit (cf. Peterson, 2007; Melzer and Morgan, 2009; CFPB, 2013).

Debtfarism and regulatory remedies in the bounds of consumer protection

> *The CFPB [Consumer Financial Protection Bureau] has a statutory obligation to promote markets that are fair transparent and competitive.*
> – CFPB, 'Payday Loans and Deposit Advance Products: A White Paper of Initial Data Findings, 2013: 4

In the aftermath of the 2007 subprime crisis and in the renewed spirit of reforming the predatory practices of consumer finance, two legislative bills were introduced in 2009 to reform the payday lending industry: the Payday Loan Reform Act and the Protecting Consumers from Unreasonable Credit Rates Act. Notably, neither bill has been enacted at the time of writing. As we will see, each bill has a built in loophole that not only allows the payday lending industry to engage in business-as-usual behaviour; but also does little to radically alter the existing conditions and violent nature of payday lending practices in the United States. The proposed bills – informed by the central trope of consumer protection – do not challenge the disciplinary and exploitative nature of dispossessive capitalism, but rather aid in the remaking of the illusions of the community of money.

Introduced by US Representative Luis Gutiérrez (D-Illinois), head of the House Financial Services Subcommittee on Financial Institutions and Consumer Credit, the Payday Loan Reform Act of 2009[28] requires lenders to provide specific disclosures to payday loan customers and claims to extend protections of the Military Lending Act to all Americans (Johnston, 2010; Francis, 2010). There are very useful features of the proposed bill, particularly with regard to collection practices. Under the bill, for instance, payday lenders are not permitted to threaten or seek to have consumers prosecuted in criminal court to collect outstanding loans. In addition, the bill forbids lenders from taking a security interest in property to secure the loan (Johnston, 2010). For legal scholar Creola Johnson, however, the bill provides the following loophole: 'It shall be unlawful for a payday lender to require a consumer to pay interests and fees that, combined, total more than 15 cents for every dollar loaned in connection' (Johnston, 2010: 24). This provision will, in effect, grant Congressional approval to lenders that charge triple-digit interest rates for payday loans. Thus, the bill is 'an ersatz reform that would allow payday lenders to charge at what amounts to an APR of 390 percent' (Johnston, 2010: 24; '391 percent payday loan', *New York Times*, 12 April 2009).

The Protecting Consumers from Unreasonable Credit Rates Act of 2009 was introduced by Senator Richard J. Durbin (D-Illinois) to establish 'a national usury rate for consumer credit transactions'.[29] In contrast to the Gutiérrez bill, consumer protection proponents support Durbin's bill. Like the Military Lending Act, Durbin's bill would cap interest rates at 36 percent. While there are some strengths of the bill, it falls short in terms of providing needed consumer protection. A critical component of the bill, for instance, is section 141(b)(2) under the heading 'Tolerances'. This section provides that the definitions of 'fee' and 'interest rate' do not include 'credit obligations that are payable in at least three fully amortising installments over at least 90 days' (Johnston, 2010: 27). In addition, for loans of $300 or more, payday lenders are permitted to charge additional fees, which include: origination fees of no more than $30, as well as late fees of either $20, or a fee authorised by state law. As history has shown, lenders will draft loan contracts to circumvent the purpose of the legislation (Johnston, 2010).

The fact that neither bill has been enacted, despite their industry-friendly formulations, is telling. The payday lending industry is central not only to highly lucrative forms of secondary exploitation, but also to the commodification of social reproduction in the United States as a disciplinary device. Moreover, it is telling that the debates remain within the moral bounds of usury law, which, as many authors have noted, has been a historical source of conflict that predates capitalism (Peterson, 2007; Graeber, 2011).

What is omitted in these reforms are the relations of power that have a vested interest in constructing and reproducing a social reality in which the working poor are made dependent on private credit as a primary means of obtaining economic security. This position is mirrored in a 2013 study on the payday loan industry by the CFPB. The report begins by uncritically accepting the existence of payday loans. 'The CFPB recognises that demand exists for small dollar credit products. These types of credit products can be helpful for consumers if they are structured to facilitate successful repayment without the need to repeatedly borrow at a high cost' (CFPB, 2013). The report goes on to investigate and suggest various ways payday loans can be transformed into what they refer to as 'sustained use' (CFPB, 2013).

Issues that remain out of bounds in terms of discussing (let alone achieving) a *reasonable* interest rate, include living wages with mandatory social benefits by employers as well as adequate state provisioning of education, housing, health, old-age and child care and so forth. This is symptomatic of a major trend in advanced forms of neoliberalisation, namely: the neglect of poverty and how to address it. According to Randy Albelda (2012: 11), this has been not figured prominently on the national agenda since the 'welfare reform' debates in the 1980s and 1990s.

Concluding remarks

In this chapter, I have sought to denaturalise the payday loan industry and, in doing so, transcend the assumptions underpinning the economistic treatment of money and legalistic literature that dominates the subject. The payday loan industry provides an important example of how the state and capitalists have attempted to construct debtfarism, alongside the credit card industry and the student loan industry. Drawing on the theoretical framework established in Part I of this book, I argued that the payday loan industry cannot be understood simply within the realm of exchange, but instead must be seen as an integral part of the wider dynamics of capital accumulation and the tensions therein.

I also suggested that through processes of debtfarism, the state facilitates the expansion of credit-led accumulation by supporting ongoing spatio-temporal displacements in the interest of banks and the payday loan industry. Debtfarism has also served to smooth tensions arising from the commodification of social repro-duction, from which the payday lending industry extracts its revenue. The state, through its debtfare forms of intervention, strives to forge consent in the community of money through the protection of consumers (disclosure and fairness) and borrowers (legal obligations) as opposed to providing workers with social protection against market forces through, at a minimum, a living wage.

The legal and political framings of debtfarism have been successfully employed to bolster the payday loan industry and the underlying dynamics of capital accum-ulation. Since the 2007 subprime meltdown and subsequent recession, annual earnings for the country's (publicly-traded) payday corporations (e.g., Advance America, Cash America, Dollar Financial, EZ Corp, First Cash Financial, QC Holdings) have risen to their highest levels on record.

> Annual filings show that the nation's major payday lenders collectively earn more from their high-cost cash advances than before the financial crisis. From

2007 to 2010 their combined revenues from payday lending have increased
2.6 percent, or some $30 million in annual revenues.

(National People's Action, 2012: 10)

It should not come as a surprise that the rapid growth of payday lending is not
restricted to the US. The industry is also expanding rapidly into Canada, the United
Kingdom, New Zealand, South Africa and South Korea (Aitken, 2010; Bond, 2013).
Interest in payday lending is also emerging in the global South. In 2012, Grupo
Elektra, a retailer that specialises in expensive credit to the poor in Latin America
(or, what it refers to as 'underserved' consumers), acquired control of all outstanding
shares of the largest payday lender in the United States, Advanced America.[30]
I explore Grupo Elektra and its role in the Mexican poverty industry in Part III
of this book.

Notes

1 Given that the literature on payday lending has been dominated by legal (Mann and
Hawkins, 2007; Huckstep, 2007) and economic (Agarwal *et al.*, 2009; Edmiston, 2011)
scholars, it is not surprising that the debates about the societal benefits of payday lending
fall into one of two views – both of which remain within the realm of exchange (see
Chapters 1 and 2): that payday lending is welfare enhancing (Morgan and Strain, 2008),
or that it is welfare destroying (Carrell and Zinman, 2008). On the first view, it is believed
that payday loans can help distressed individuals to smooth liquidity shocks without
incurring the more expensive costs of overdraft fees and interests, bounced cheques, late
fees, and/or getting evicted or foreclosed upon (Meltzer and Morgan, 2009; Zinman,
2010). Here, payday loans fill an important void in the existing credit system, which is
evidenced by strong consumer demand for convenient, small amounts of short-term credit
at high rates of interest (Morse, 2009; Drysdale and Keest, 2000). On the 'welfare reducing
provision of credit' such as payday loans, critics point to the adverse economic effects of
over-lending, over-charging, deception, targeting certain consumer segments such as the
working poor (Morgan, 2007; cf. Austin, 2004).
2 Because local providers are not publicly traded, for instance, it is difficult to generalise
about their activities. However, it is clear that the much of the growth of the larger
providers is due to acquisitions of 'mom-and-pop' storefronts. Another interesting feature
about these local providers is that, given their size, they are exempt from usury limits in
the range of 20 to 30 percent (Mann and Hawkins, 2007). The most difficult sector of
the payday lending industry to study is online providers. Although I discuss Internet
providers later in the chapter, in this section, I concentrate on national providers and
banks, as information is readily available on these key industry players.
3 For an overview of different state regulations and interest rates, see: www.advance
america.net/apply-for-a-loan/fees (accessed 1 March 2012). Mann and Hawkins (2007)
identify three common patterns of usury regulation with regard to payday lenders. Some
states tolerate payday lenders with specific usury ceilings (e.g., Michigan), while other
states exercise an under-enforced prohibition. The latter normally implies a usury
ceiling that has no specific exception authorising payday lending transactions (Mann and
Hawkins, 2007). An example of this second category is Texas, which I discuss below.
The third category is true prohibition of payday lending, which usually involves a general
usury limit. New York, for instance, has a general usury ceiling of 6 percent (Mann and
Hawkins, 2007)
4 For more information about the fees tied to this card see the Advance America website:
https://www.advanceamerica.net/services/details/visa-prepaid-cards (accessed 3 July
2013).

5 For more information, see the CFSA website: http://cfsaa.com (accessed 4 July 2013).
6 For more information, see the FiSCA website: www.fisca.org (accessed 14 July 2013).
7 The National People's Action report notes that 'It is often difficult to determine the exact amount of financing provided by a given bank to a payday company because funding is often pooled from a variety of lenders and the specifics are not disclosed by the SEC [Securities Exchange Commission]' (National People's Action, 2010: 4).
8 CFSA, 'Customer Demographics'. Available at: http://cfsaa.com/about-the-payday-advance-industry/customer-demographics.aspx (accessed 1 May 2012).
9 For more information on the BLS projections, see 'BLS Forecasts Fastest-Growing Jobs', *The Wall Street Journal*, 2 February 2012.
10 See: www.whitehouse.gov/strongmiddleclass (accessed 16 May 2012).
11 The Federal Reserve will complete collecting data for the following SCF in December 2013, after the date of publication of this book. More information available at: www.federalreserve.gov/scf/ (accessed 12 July 2013).
12 'FiSCA History'. Available at: www.fisca.org/Content/NavigationMenu/AboutFISCA/FiSCAHistory/default.htm (accessed 20 April 2012).
13 FiSCA 'Consumer Fact Sheet'. Available at: www.fisca.org/Content/NavigationMenu/ConsumerCenter/ConsumerFactSheet/default.htm (accessed 24 April 2012).
14 See Advance America. Available at: www.americadeservesaraise.com/ (accessed 1 June 2013).
15 FiSCA 'Code of Conduct'. Available at: www.fisca.org/Content/NavigationMenu/AboutFISCA/CodesofConduct/default.htm (accessed 30 April 2012).
16 CFSA Customer Bill of Rights. Available at: http://cfsaa.com/cfsa-member-best-practices/cfsa-customer-bill-of-rights.aspx (accessed 20 April 2012).
17 These penalties are legally sanctioned by the civil bad cheque laws in several states. For examples of various state penalties for bad cheques, see: www.ckfraud.org/penalties.html#civil (accessed 1 June 2013).
18 I discuss this 2005 draconian revision to the Bankruptcy Code in more detail in Chapters 4 and 5.
19 Seven states (Arkansas, Connecticut, Maryland, New Jersey, New York, Pennsylvania, and Vermont) plus the federal district of Washington, DC protect consumers against abusive practices in small loan products (Plunkett and Hurtado, 2011: 37-38). Yet, five states set no usury caps for small loans, including Delaware, Idaho, South Dakota, Utah, and Wisconsin (Plunkett and Hurtado, 2011).
20 Since the subprime housing debacle of 2007, and the subsequent recessionary environment, several states have increased regulatory pressure on payday lending, including Arizona, Arkansas, Colorado, Montana, New Hampshire, Ohio, and Oregon – home to over 3,400 payday loan stores issuing over $3 billion in payday loans annually. These seven states have limited small-dollar loan interest rates between 17 percent and 45 percent APR, effectively ending or severely limiting payday lending (National People's Action, 2012; cf. Woolston, 2010).
21 For more information, see: www.zestcash.com/not-payday-loans/cheaper-than-payday-loans (accessed 14 May 2012).
22 For more information about TARP, see the Congressional Budget Office, 'Report on the Troubled Asset Relief Program – May 2013'. Available at: www.cbo.gov/publication/44256 (accessed 3 July 2013a).
23 As a paper issued by the Federal Reserve Bank of New York observes, 'For the median bank, NSF [non-sufficient funds] fee income accounted for 43 percent of non-interest income and 21 percent of net operating income ... Overdraft revenue accounted for 60.4 percent of credit union net operating income in 2005' (Melzer and Morgan 2009: 6).
24 FDIC 'Affordable Small-Dollar Loan Guidelines' (2006). Available at: www.fdic.gov/news/news/press/2006/pr06107a.html (accessed 4 May 2012).
25 Press release. Available at: www.fdic.gov/news/news/press/2006/pr06107.html (accessed 3 May 2012).

26 FDIC, 'Affordable Small-Dollar Loan Guidelines'.

27 On an industry's view of the state's decision to issue electronic transfers of government benefits, see 'Fisca criticises US Treasury for needlessly scaring seniors, vulnerable populations into electronic forms of government payments'. Press Release 9 January 2013. Available at: www.fisca.org/Content/NavigationMenu/GovernmentAffairs/Choice CampaignPublicPage/FiSCA_Critical_of_Treasury_Position_on_Electronic_Payments_ FINALwHEADER.pdf (accessed 14 July 2013).

28 For more information, see: www.opencongress.org/people/show/400163_Luis_Gutierrez (accessed 12 May 2012).

29 For full text of the bill, see: www.govtrack.us/congress/bills/111/s500/text (accessed 12 May 2012).

30 'Grupo Elektra to Acquire Advance America for $10.50 Per Share', 15 February 2012. For further information, see: www.advanceamerica.net/press/press-details/grupo-elektra-to-acquire-advance-america-for-10.50-per-share (accessed 12 May 2012).

PART III

Debtfarism and the poverty industry in Mexico

Preface to Part III

DEBTFARISM, DEVELOPMENT AND DISPOSESSION

In this third and final part of the book, I explore the poverty industry within the wider ambit of global development through the lens of the following three case studies: the attempts by the Group of Twenty (G20) at universalising financial inclusion (Chapter 7), Mexico's microfinancing industry (Chapter 8) and Mexico's housing finance industry (Chapter 9). Taken together, these three chapters look at the coercive and ideational processes involved in the expansion and reproduction of the poverty industry and the power relations therein.

As I have suggested throughout the book, debtfarist forms of state intervention have been integral to the expansion and reproduction of credit-led accumulation in the form of the poverty industry. Because of the fluidity and globality of capitalism, debtfarism does not take place exclusively within national spaces, but globally, too. In the context of this part of the book, the global spaces of debtfarism are represented by the regulations and rhetoric of core international development organisations such as the International Monetary Fund (IMF), World Bank, Inter-American Development Bank and G20, as well as prominent think-tanks, such as the Consultative Group to Assist the Poor (CGAP). As I demonstrate in my discussion of the G20's Principles for Innovative Financial Inclusion of 2010, the rhetorical and regulative features of global debtfarism serve to legitimise, normalise and universalise the poverty industry in both Bangladesh and Mexico.

The relationship between debtfarism at global and national (e.g., Mexican) scales should not be construed as a top-down, determinist relationship between domestic and international levels of governance. Instead, the multi-scalar articulations of debtfarism must be understood as involving messy, contradictory and dynamic interactions. These complex interactions reflect the power relations that play out across the spaces in which capitalists seek to rapidly increase the fictitious value of privately created money (credit) by lending it to the surplus population.

Seen from the above angle, Mexico provides an interesting context in which to study the intersections between global-national debtfarism, credit money and the surplus population. In part, this is because Mexico has long represented a showcase for the Washington Consensus (IMF, 1992, 2011). More than this, I have selected Mexico as a site for my case studies in Chapter 8 and Chapter 9 because of its economic position vis–à–vis the North American Free Trade Agreement (NAFTA) and because of its physical proximity to the heartland of neoliberalism, namely: the United States (Peck and Tickell, 2002)[1]. Due to its geo-political positioning as well as its historical configurations of capital accumulation, the contradictions of the neoliberal-led development project are easily legible in Mexico. In terms of the poverty industry, Mexico has a rapidly growing for-profit microfinance industry that includes some of the world's largest and most lucrative lending institutions for surplus workers (Chapter 8). The marketisation of mortgage financing aimed at the surplus population is also quite extensive in Mexico, as is the increasing integration of this financing in global financial markets (Chapter 9).

That said, each of the following three chapters shares the common goal of providing an interrogation into how various expressions of debtfarism have played a direct role in the construction and normalisation of the poverty industry. A central concern running through all three chapters is an analysis of the social powers and inherent tensions of privately created money (credit). I attempt not only to understand the role played by the revolutionary power of credit money in the wider dynamics of credit-led accumulation, particularly as this regards the surplus population, but also to reveal the ways in which the regulatory and rhetorical processes of the Mexican state strive to resolve the tensions in capital accumulation, including the expansion of the poverty industry.

The financial inclusion agenda, which has become the cornerstone of the neoliberal-led development project over the past decade, provides a useful portal into our investigation into the social power of money and its connection to debtfarism in the global South. Generally speaking, financial inclusion refers to increasing access to formal or semi-formal financial services (ranging from banking to micro-credit to housing loans) for approximately 2.5 billion poor adults (CGAP, 2009a).[2] According to the Centre for Financial Inclusion – a global initiative comprised of powerful private and public sponsors, such as the Citi Foundation, Credit Suisse, the World Bank's International Finance Corporation, the Inter-American Development Bank, Visa and MasterCard Worldwide – 'financial inclusion means that everyone who can use them has access to a range of quality financial services at affordable prices with convenience, respect and dignity, delivered by a range of providers in a stable, competitive market to financially capable clients'.[3] It should be noted that this understanding of financial inclusion stresses the importance of formal – that is, legally recognised – financial institutions, as opposed to informal institutions (e.g., local money lenders, family, friends and/or pawn-brokers), which are believed to be more expensive and less transparent (AFI, 2010; cf., Bateman, 2013). The widespread appeal of financial inclusion for development practitioners, governments and international organisations lies in its alleged benefits to promote economic growth, efficiency and increased welfare for the poor (CGAP, 2011).

Unlike many accounts that have sought to critique financial inclusion initiatives *within* the bounds of what Marx refers to as money fetishism, I neither assume that credit 'just is', nor that the political and legal structures and practices are either neutral or separate from the relations of power rooted in the processes of capital accumulation, including the role of the surplus population therein. Instead and armed with the historical materialist understanding of money and states outlined in Part I, I challenge a core and largely unquestioned, assumption in the financial inclusion agenda by asking, first, what is the capitalist nature of 'the financial?' And, second, how and why has 'the financial' been reproduced?

In posing the above questions, I challenge the financial inclusion agenda on two related counts. On the one hand, it is vital to interrupt the representation of the financial as a neutral legal contract into which the working poor enter, voluntarily and on equal terms and from which they are said to benefit through 'consumption smoothing', a euphemism for the ways in the surplus population has come to rely on credit for the provision of basic needs. According to the financial inclusion rhetoric, for instance, the benefits the poor allegedly receive upon entering a debt contract are both material, i.e., improved welfare and convenience, as well as immaterial, i.e., respect and dignity (CGAP, 2010a). On the other hand, the fetishised representations of the financial need to be deconstructed in order to reveal the underlying capitalist nature of the monetisation of the relations of power between creditors and debtors. Another feature that helps to frame, guarantee, mediate and normalise the coercive and exploitative nature of these monetised relations is the state – particularly its debtfarist interventions.

By undertaking a historical materialist interrogation of the financial inclusion agenda, we will gain deeper insight into the power and paradoxes upon which this project has been built. We will also be able to comprehend more fully the legal and political machinations involved in the reproduction of the poverty industry as a normal and essential feature of neoliberal-led development. It will become clear, for instance, that costly credit offered to the poor has not reduced poverty. The reason for this, of course, is that the lack of credit is not the cause of poverty and thus in many cases, high-priced credit serves to accentuate economic precariousness, not resolve it (Bateman, 2010; Roy, 2010; Taylor, 2011; Rankin, 2013).

The primary source of poverty for the surplus population in Mexico, as elsewhere, is the inability of these workers to secure a living wage. This point is, however, evaded in the mainstream treatments of financial inclusion. Remaining within the realm of exchange – itself a social construction that needs to be continually reproduced by debtfarism – the fundamental causes of poverty, as well as the material bases of inequality, disappear behind the mask of freedom, equality and democracy. In this context, the promotion of the benefits of financial inclusion can take place. The equality of exchange provides an enticing selling point, encouraging the poor to seek for-profit loans from formal lenders, especially when they are juxtaposed against informal lenders (e.g., relatives and pawnshops), which are represented as lacking not only transparency and, therefore, trust and account-ability, but also efficiency, particularly with regard to the pricing of credit (World Bank, 2006, 2007, 2014).

In contrast to the neoliberal promise that free markets can lead to material improvements for all, the vast majority of the working poor in the global South do not earn a living wage or benefit from any subsidised support (e.g., health care, old age provision, unemployment insurance and so forth) for social reproduc-tion (United Nations, 2012). In the case of Mexico, the underemployed and unemployed workers that comprise the country's large surplus population eke out a living in the informal sector, where wages tend to be lower than the formal sector and where workers lack social benefits and protections. According to a Report by the International Labour Organisation, 53.7 percent of Mexicans are employed informally (ILO, 2012).[4] Recent data from the National Council of Social Develop-ment Policy in Mexico (or, CONEVAL[5]) reveals that between 2006 and 2010 the people living in poverty (extreme and moderate) increased from 35 percent to 46 percent; this number rises to 53.8 percent among children (OECD, 2012). The socio-economic gap between rich and poor in Mexico remains very high. After Chile, which has often heralded by the IMF and other neoliberal ideologues as the poster child of successful market-led development, Mexico is the second most unequal middle-income country in the Organisation of Economic Co-operation and Development (OECD). According to OECD data, the bottom 10 percent of the distribution in Mexico receives around 1.3 percent of total disposable income, while the wealthiest 10 percent of Mexicans receive close to 36 percent (OECD, 2012: 8).

Consumer credit offered to the poor at high interest rates have led to growth and wealth creation, but not for the poor. The greatest beneficiaries of the poverty industry have been capitalists and institutional investors that comprise the lucrative poverty industry in Mexico. Ricardo Salinas Pliego, the majority shareholder of Mexico's Banco Azteca, which specialises in selling consumer credit to Mexico's working poor, is one of the wealthiest people in the world. Since 2005, Banco Azteca's highly lucrative business has expanded to other countries in Latin America, such as Panama, Honduras, Guatemala, Peru, Brazil and El Salvador. As I discuss in Chapter 8, the poverty industry in Mexico has also attracted and benefited other high-interest lenders, such as the microfinance behemoth, Compartamos, and Banco Walmart ('Mexican (Legit) Loan Shark Ricardo Salinas Is Making Billions the Old-Fashioned Way', *Forbes*, 18 April 2012; Euromonitor International, 2013). In Chapter 9, I analyse this concentration of wealth among poverty-industry capitalists within the context of low-income housing, where one of the world's largest building materials suppliers and cement producers, the Mexican-based CEMEX corporation, has been quickly moving into the housing financing business, too.

The financial inclusion agenda is a powerful rhetorical and regulatory feature of debtfarism that assists in reconstructing the moorings of neoliberal development through its ability to both identify problems and offer solutions exclusively in the realm of exchange, where exploitation and inequality are easily masked. This is reflected in the G20 Principles encompassing for instance, consumer protection, empowerment through financial education, and proportionality, particularly the latter's emphasis on risk reduction – all of which are supported by non-binding (voluntary) or 'soft' laws (Cutler, 2003; Picciotto, 2011). I discuss the G20 Principles in more detail in Chapter 7. Here, I want to stress that financial inclusion initiatives, executed at both global and national scales, are reinforced by the rhetorical and regulative framings of debtfarism and its continual efforts to translate and reposition struggles and solutions within realm of exchange. In this sphere of capital accumulation, the appearance of money as an abstract and universal measure of social wealth is heightened. The fetish of money (see Chapter 1) expresses itself as an external object capable of becoming the private property of *any* individual – wealthy or poor, man or woman. Marx refers to the generalisation of the money fetish as the community of money, which is marked by individualised meanings of equality, freedom and democracy (Marx, 1990, 2005). As a form of money, consumer credit masks the exploitative, disciplinary and unequal relations that underpin the community of money. Recreating and reimposing the illusions of the community of money are vital to the expansion and reproduction of the poverty industry.

The financial inclusion trope diverts our attention away from the powers and paradoxes in the realm of exchange, as well as from the root causes of poverty. Left unchallenged are the underlying reasons why people do not possess enough money to purchase basic necessities, much less lift themselves out of poverty through the entrepreneurial activities that financial inclusion is said to afford (cf. World Bank, 2014). The legal and political framing of financial inclusion masks the role of capitalist states in the construction and legitimation of debtfare. This, in effect, permits states to focus their attention on questions of access, fairness, education and transparency as opposed to the provision of a living wage and ensuring adequate social protection for the poor through public consumption.

When viewed through a historical materialist framework, financial inclusion represents a core feature of the neoliberal development project and shares many similarities with the core rhetorical and regulative feature of the US debtfare state: namely, the democratisation of credit (see Chapter 4). It will be recalled that the democratisation of credit is concerned with ensuring appropriate access to credit, which will, in turn, ensure that low-income individuals not only become active market participants, but also do so on an equal footing with other consumers. Both democratisation of credit and financial inclusion are similar in that they assume credit to be a neutral object devoid of the inherent social power of money. Both terms are also firmly entrenched in the realm of exchange, where the *illusions* of the community of money – i.e., democracy, freedom and equality (see Chapter 1) – prevail.

In addition to assisting the capitalist expansion of the poverty industry into the everyday lives of the surplus population, the portrayal of financial inclusion as a desirable and win-win strategy assists in the privatisation of the social reproduction of surplus population. Marx describes this social category in capitalism as 'the most powerful lever of accumulation' (Marx, 1976: 772). The commodification of basic subsistence for the surplus population, which is at the core of the financial inclusion agenda, serves to undergird the wider neoliberalisation processes, which champion the increased reliance on markets over states. The monetisation of the surplus population through processes of financial inclusion also acts to reproduce the basic imperative to earn a living based on dispossession, expropriation and dependence on the market in a manner that appears as a natural and inevitable aspect of life, or the *ordinary run of* things (Marx, 1990, 2005). The following three chapters attempt to peel away various layers of the fetishised understanding of money and states in order to reveal the silent compulsions and structural violence of capital accumulation that lies at the base of financial inclusion. Mirroring its US counterpart, the regulative and rhetorical features of debtfarism in Mexico aim to smooth the tensions associated with credit-led accumulation through, for example, the removal of interest rate ceilings and a the dominance of soft laws regarding the consumer credit. In so doing, the Mexican debtfare state has facilitated the expansion of credit money leaving, on the one hand, increasingly more members of the surplus population dependent on private provisioning to support their subsistence needs. And, on the other, paving the way for capitalists to accelerate and increase revenue by commodifying debt through means such as asset-backed securitisation (CGAP, 2010b).

As the lead chapter in this section, Chapter 7 takes us through the portal of financial inclusion such that we come face to face with the silent compulsions, paradoxes and relations of power involved in the expansion and reproduction of the poverty industry. To this end, the chapter has been structured to serve two purposes. First, its more generalised discussion reveals the broader rhetorical and regulative landscape represented by the G20 Principles regarding financial inclusion. This landscape both mirrors and supports ongoing debtfare strategies pursued by the Mexican state.[6] The analysis also demonstrates how restructurings of financial inclusion have facilitated spatio-temporal displacements of credit-led accumulation through, for example the securitisation of micro-finance institutions (MFIs). Second and related, the more generalised analysis of financial inclusion demonstrates that the expansion and reproduction of the poverty industry and the role of the state are not simply occurring in the United States and Mexico, but rather across many national spaces in global capitalism, albeit in a highly uneven and differentiated manner (von Braunmühl, 1973; Arrighi, 1994).

Notes

1   The uneven and tension-ridden nature of Mexican-United States relations is nicely summed up by the oft-cited quote by the Mexican President Porfirio Diaz (1830-1915): 'Poor Mexico, so far from God and so close to the United States!' 'Gently does it'. *The*

Economist 3 December 2009. Available at: www.economist.com/node/15019872 (accessed 23 September 2013).

2 CGAP (2009) *Financial Access: measuring access to financial services around the world*, Washington, DC: Consultative Group to Assist the Poor.

3 Available at: www.centerforfinancialinclusion.org/ (accessed 14 July 2013).

4 The International Labour Organisation (ILO) distinguishes between the informal sector, which describes informal businesses, on the one hand, and informal employment, which refers to informal jobs, on the other. Employment in the informal sector can be defined as the total of employment in the informal sector and informal employment found outside the informal sector. Available at: http://laborsta.ilo.org/applv8/data/INFORMAL_ECONOMY/2012-06-Statistical%20update%20-%20v2.pdf (accessed 25 July 2013).

5 The Spanish acronym CONEVAL stands for Consejo Nacional de Evaluación de la Política de Desarrollo Social. More information about poverty in Mexico is available (in Spanish) at: www.coneval.gob.mx/Medicion/Paginas/Medici%C3%B3n/Anexo-Estadistico-Pobreza-2010.aspx (accessed 25 July 2013).

6 CGAP, 'Mexico's National Council for Financial Inclusion', 16 February. Available at: www.cgap.org/blog/mexico%E2%80%99s-national-council-financial-inclusion (accessed 19 July 2013).

7

GLOBAL DEBTFARISM AND THE UNIVERSALISATION OF FINANCIAL INCLUSION

Financial inclusion has become the holy grail of poverty reduction and thus forms a core feature of the global development project (World Bank, 2014).[1] In the words of the Executive Director of the influential Alliance for Financial Inclusion (AFI), 'Financial inclusion is no longer a side issue in the global economic debate . . . It now has a permanent and important place in the global discussion on economic development and stability and its ability to reduce poverty'.[2] Financial inclusion describes a desired situation in which all working-age adults have access to credit, savings, payments and insurance from formal service providers, i.e., recognised legal status (CGAP, 2011).

In the wake of the 2008 financial crisis, which was, ironically, sparked by financial inclusion initiatives in the subprime mortgage sector,[3] the Group of Twenty (G20) leaders turned to financial inclusion as a core development strategy for overcoming poverty, the global recessionary environment and stabilising the global financial system. The G20 leaders emphasised, however, that these goals could not be achieved without a proper regulatory and supervisory framework (AFI, 2010). To enhance national financial inclusion initiatives, the G20 Financial Inclusion Experts Group forged the G20 Principles for Innovative Financial Inclusion in 2010 (hereafter: G20 Principles).[4]

What remains conspicuous in these discussions is the absence of any clear understanding of what 'the financial' means as well as how and why it has been socially reproduced.[5] The concept of the financial is arguably not problematised because it is widely assumed to entail a voluntary, yet legally binding, agreement between two equal parties: a lender and a borrower. However, the historical materialist framework (see Part I) reveals three fundamental reasons why the financial has not been critically investigated. First, privately created money (credit) has been assumed rather than explained. As such, questions of power involved in the creation and extension of privately created money to the poor have been bypassed.

Second, the rhetorical and regulative features of financial inclusion have remained firmly within the realm of exchange, disconnected from the wider dynamics of credit-led accumulation. This, in turn, facilitates the illusions of equality in exchange while masking the exploitative and disciplinary nature of the monetised relations inherent to financial inclusion. Third, insomuch as the G20 Principles represent non-binding legal framings (i.e., 'soft law'), they assume the appearance of neutrality while serving to reinforce underlying class-based power relations in the community of money. Soft law dominates the regulatory landscape of financial inclusion initiatives, as it is more easily circumvented to protect powerful creditors and impose market discipline on debtors.

I argue that when we acknowledge and transcend the above three social constructions, it becomes clear that the financial is neither a neutral nor a natural set of relations. The realm of financial inclusion does not refer to a place where borrowers and lenders enter voluntarily to engage in an equal, mutually beneficial exchange (i.e., wealth generation for creditors and welfare-enhancement for poor debtors). In contrast to this mainstream view, which has been propagated by the G20 Principles, I suggest that inclusion into the financial is constructed by neoliberal states and capitalists to ensure the (re-)imposition of monetised relations, including the disciplinary features therein, on the working poor. Like national articulations of debtfarism, the legal and rhetorical framings of the G20 Principles act to legitimate and reinforce the illusions of equality, freedom and democracy inherent in the financial. This, in turn, facilitates the expansion and reproduction of the poverty industry in the global South.

This chapter is organised in four main sections. In Section One, I discuss the meaning of soft law with regard to transnational regulatory strategies before turning to an outline of the G20 Principles. In Section Two, I examine the G20 Principle of Proportionality and its emphasis on risk reduction by surveying an important development in financial inclusion: the securitisation of micro-finance institutions (MFIs). In Section Three, I explore the G20 Principle of Protection and the Principle of Empowerment in the Mexican context. In Section Four, I conclude by reviewing the tensions and risks underpinning credit-led accumulation in the wake of the implementation of the G20 Principles.

Universalising financial inclusion: the G20 principles and soft law

Breaking the code of benevolence, freedom and equality

A good place to begin deconstructing the G20 Principles for Innovative Financial Inclusion is to look more critically at the word 'innovative'. This will allow us to decipher the power relations that the G20 seeks to legitimise, depoliticise and normalise (Bourdieu, 1991). Here the term innovation connotes rationality, modernisation, (self-)improvement, (self-) advancement and freedom in the form of independence (see Chapter 1). Innovation is understood and portrayed as part of an abstract vision of a market populated by rational and individualised actors interacting on a level playing field. It follows from this perspective that the failure to lift oneself out of poverty is explained away by blaming individuals for not taking the opportunity to join the financial, or lacking sufficient rational skills to engage in entrepreneurial activities. Thus, the historical dimensions of neoliberal development and the exploitative and uneven nature of capital accumulation are expunged as potential causes of poverty.

The historical materialist framework developed in Part I allows us to understand the term innovation as a social construction that leverages individualising forms of market discipline to mask secondary forms of exploitation involved in the monetisation of social relations (i.e., modifying incomes of the surplus population) (Harvey, 1989; Marx, 2005). Deciphered in this way, innovation is code for the expansion and intensification of credit-led accumulation. In the case of the microfinance industry, this extension, which began in the 1990s, includes the mainstreaming and commercialisation of microfinance institutions (MFIs) (Weber, 2002; Bateman, 2010; Roy, 2010; Harper, 2011; Rankin, 2013; Da Costa, 2013). A case in point here is the famous initial public offering of Latin America's largest and one of the world's most lucrative, MFIs, Compartamos Banco, in 2007 (see Chapter 8). Another oft-cited example of innovative financial inclusion has been the securitisation of MFIs, exemplified by the case of Bangladesh's BRAC in 2006 (Roy, 2010).

Reflecting back on the discussion in Part I of this book, it is important to keep in mind that 'the financial' is not neutral, nor does it emerge naturally from an apolitical market. The financial refers to privately created money. The inherent gap between money and the fictitious value of credit demands continual intervention on the part of capitalists and states and – by extension – international organisations such as the G20. I refer to the regulative and rhetorical forms of state intervention in the neoliberal era as debtfarism. Thus far, I have analysed the activities of debtfare at the national scale. Debtfarism, however, is present at other scales of neoliberalisation (Brenner et al., 2010). Because the G20 is not a standalone organisation but an institution that reflects the power configuration of global capitalism, it reinforces and legitimates, albeit in contradictory and contested ways, national debtfarist strategies (Gill, 1990; Petras and Veltmeyer, 2001; Harvey, 2003; Soederberg, 2004, 2006; Kiely, 2010; Panitch and Gindin, 2012). It does this against the backdrop of a world order dominated by the hegemonic role of market-led development symbolised by Anglo-American neoliberalisation (Soederberg, 2004, 2006). As I discuss in the next section, the construction of legality by the G20 advances dispossessive capitalism through the seemingly benevolent act of financial inclusion, wherein the G20 takes on the role of a 'provider of legitimacy' (Mattei and Nader, 2008).

Providing legitimacy for dispossession via 'the financial'

The G20 Principles were forged in the wake of the 2008 financial crisis to facilitate an enabling policy and regulatory environment for the expansion of dispossessive capitalism under the altruistic pairing of innovative financial inclusion and poverty reduction. Beneath the gloss, the target of this class-based project involved shifting the dependency of 2.5 billion surplus workers from informal lenders to formal (legally recognised) commercial lenders.[6] Like all social phenomena in capitalist society, the strategy of financial inclusion needs to be continually (re-)constructed and re-legitimised, particularly when its core prescriptions (e.g., market fundamentalism) are interrupted by the devastating consequences of financial crises, such as the US subprime lending crash in 2007 and the subsequent global recession. As mentioned above, the US-led crisis was itself driven by the principles of financial inclusion (Wyly et al., 2009; Sassen, 2009). Another relevant example that damaged the official portrayal of the credibility of the financial inclusion agenda was the wave of bad press associated with the commercialisation of large MFIs and their explicit links to Wall Street (Bateman, 2010).

To many supporters of financial inclusion, the case of Compartamos and its transformation into a publicly listed corporation in 2007 signalled a mission drift away from poverty reduction (see Chapter 8). In response, the microfinance industry and its supporters created various oversight bodies to reinforce the concept's ostensibly social mission. These included the Alliance for Fair Microfinance, established in 2007 and MicroFinance Transparency, founded in 2008 (Bateman, 2013). A code of conduct for the microfinance industry, known as the 2008 Pocantico Declaration, was also undertaken by the Deutsche Bank, the Boulder Institute on Microfinance, and the Consultative Group to Assist the Poor (CGAP) (Bateman, 2013).[7] These industry-based reforms were not based on mandatory, enforceable hard laws; but instead on the construction of soft laws.

Soft law has come to dominate most regulatory framings of financial inclusion in the neoliberal era. Soft law refers to publicly sanctioned codes, guidelines and laws that are neither mandatory nor legally binding, whereas hard law describes mandatory or legally binding law (May, 2014). While soft law marks the rhetorical and regulative landscape of financial inclusion, including the G20 Principles, it must be emphasised that it is accompanied and complemented by hard laws relating to the basic features of capitalist society: the protection of private property, rights to appropriation and freedom of contract (Harvey, 1989; cf., Brummer, 2012). Thus, laws that protect the interests of creditors are framed in hard law, that is, the coercive features of the capitalist state such as courts, police and prisons. As a World Bank publication argues, the creation and maintenance of a strong legal system to promote the proper functioning of markets (World Bank, 2004a, c).

Soft and hard laws are neither neutral nor natural evolutions of society (Cutler, 2003). Nor should laws be understood as some*thing* that stands either outside or above class relations in capitalist society (Holloway and Picciotto, 1991). Instead and drawing on the discussion from Chapter 3, laws should be seen as integral features of neoliberal (capitalist) states and by extension, international organisations. Seen in this way, laws are highly dynamic and contradictor institutionalised forms of state power that emerges from and is intrinsically tied to, the complex and dynamic configurations of class relations rooted in the wider processes of capital accumulation. Law as an extension of (capitalist) state powers thus performs a dual role of disciplining labour, while recreating, as discussed in Chapter 3, the illusion of a neutral state through the masking of extra-legal powers (Picciotto, 2011; Bruff, 2014).

Seen from the above perspective, soft laws facilitate the expansion and reproduction of the poverty industry in the global South in at least three ways. First, as a construct of capitalist interests, soft law creates a supportive structure for free-market values through its informal and discretionary application (Cutler, 2003). This legal shield of neutrality in soft law enables states to remove politically sensitive matters from public scrutiny. Such matters include: capping interest rates; limiting speculative attempts by microfinance industry insiders to overcome the barriers of credit-led accumulation through 'innovative' strategies such as an initial public offering (Compartamos), or asset-backed securitisation (as in the case of BRAC discussed below) (CGAP, 2010b).

Second, while soft law is less expensive and easier to implement than hard law, i.e., requiring less legislative hurdles to clear, it is also much easier to breach with impunity. Spatial expansion and temporal displacements pursued by capitalists to overcome barriers to accumulation are thus facilitated in soft law, as it gives rise, for example, to more opportunities for creative lawyering (e.g., identifying and exploiting legal loopholes) and the private shaping of legal regulation (Glasbeek, 2002; Cutler, 2003; Baars, 2011).

Third, soft law in the neoliberal era necessarily leads to the enhanced role of capitalists (individually as experts and collectively in epistemic communities) within public–private governance initiatives (Porter, 2007; Picciotto, 2011; Brummer, 2012). This expert knowledge is vital to the construction and legitimacy of the neoliberal regulation of dispossessive capitalism since, as Foucault notes, 'Knowledge linked to power not only assumes the authority of *the truth* but has the power to make itself true. All knowledge, once applied in the real world, has effects and in that sense at least, *becomes true*' (Foucault, 1980: 131).

An important knowledge-producing community driving the global financial inclusion initiative is the Alliance for Financial Inclusion (AFI).[8] The primary mission of the AFI is to promote the adoption of inclusive financial policies in the global South, so as to lift approximately 2.7 billion people out of poverty (AFI, 2011; CGAP, 2011). The AFI was established in 2008 as a Bill and Melinda Gates Foundation[9] project and was also supported by the Australian Government Overseas Aid Programme: AusAid[10] This private/public epistemic community is comprised of what is described as a 'knowledge network' of central banks and other financial regulatory bodies in developing countries. The AFI serves as one of the five implementing partners for the G20 Global Partnership for Financial Inclusion (GPFI), which includes the World Bank, the Organisation of Economic Cooperation and Development (OECD) and the Consultative Group to Assist the Poor (CGAP). In terms of forging soft law to enable the expansion of financial inclusion strategies, the AFI plays an important role in the Sub-Group on Financial Inclusion Data and Measurement[11] and the Sub-Group on the Principles and the Standard Setting Bodies (SSBs).[12] In addition, the AFI actively promotes the use of the G20 Principles among its members, documenting how countries have implemented the Principles and the challenges they have faced in doing so.[13]

Normalising innovative forms of financial inclusion: the G20 Principles

In response to the global financial crisis that began in 2008, G20 leaders at the Pittsburgh Summit in 2009 committed to improving access to financial services for poor people by supporting the spread of new forms of financial service delivery capable of reaching low-income adults (AFI, 2010). To achieve these aims, the G20 Principles were presented in 2010 at the G20 Leaders Summit in Seoul (see Table 7.1). The Access Through Innovation Sub-Group (ATISG) of the G20 Financial Inclusion Expert Group drafted the Principles.[14] The ATISG, which is an archetypal epistemic community empowered to produce expert knowledge, was comprised of three key partners – Alliance for Financial Inclusion, CGAP and the World Bank Group's private financing arm, the International Finance Corporation (IFC). From this heady mix of experts, the Principles for Innovative Financial Inclusion were drafted and later approved by G20 Leaders at the Summit in Seoul in 2010.[15]

The G20 is clear that the above Principles 'are not a rigid set of requirements but are designed to help guide policymakers in the decision making process' (AFI, 2010: 5). As such, the G20 Principles represent a regulatory framework based on voluntary guidelines, not legally binding rules.[16] The framing of financial inclusion in the realm of soft law serves to reinforce the illusions of the community of money while depoliticising spatio-temporal fixes inherent in dispossessive capitalism. In the remainder of this chapter, I examine how three of the G20 Principles have served to facilitate these displacements in the poverty industry. I do this by, first, deconstructing the Principle of Proportionality and its emphasis on risk reduction with regard to securitising microfinance institutions, with specific reference to BRAC in Bangladesh; and, second, exploring the G20 Principle of Protection and the G20 Principle of Empowerment in the Mexican context.

Deconstructing the G20 Principles of Proportionality and Risk Reduction: the case of securitising Micro-Finance Institutions (MFIs)

> Access to finance is widely recognised as a key to development. Being crucial to build assets, protect against risks, invest in income-generating projects and finance enterprise development, access to finance provides stability and opportunities to families and businesses and supports the economy as a whole. Families and business need affordable access to a safe, secure and reliable financial infrastructure . . .
>
> – Global Partnership for Financial Inclusion, *Report to the Leaders*, G20 Leaders Summit, Cannes, 5 November (CGAP, 2011: 4)

TABLE 7.1 G20 Principles for Innovative Financial Inclusion

Leadership:	Cultivate a broad-based government commitment to financial inclusion to help alleviate poverty.
Diversity:	Implement policy approaches that promote competition and provide market-based incentives for delivery of sustainable financial access and usage of a broad range of affordable services (savings, credit, payments and transfers, insurance) as well as a diversity of service providers.
Innovation:	Promote technological and institutional innovation as a means to expand financial system access and usage, including by addressing infrastructure weakness.
Protection:	Encourage a comprehensive approach to consumer protection that recognises the roles of government, providers and consumers.
Empowerment:	Develop financial literacy and financial capability.
Cooperation:	Create an institutional environment with clear lines of accountability and co-ordination within government; and also encourage partnerships and direct consultation across government, business and other stakeholders.
Knowledge:	Utilise improved data to make evidence-based policy, measure progress and consider an incremental 'test and learn' approach acceptable to both regulator and service provider.
Proportionality:	Build a policy and regulatory framework that is proportionate with the risks and benefits involved in such innovative products and services and is based on an understanding of the gaps and barriers in existing regulation.
Framework:	Consider the following in the regulatory framework, reflecting international standards, national circumstances and support for a competitive landscape: an appropriate, flexible, risk-based Anti-Money Laundering and Combating the Financing of Terrorism (AML/CFT) regime; conditions for the use of agents as a customer interface; a clear regulatory regime for electronically stored value; and market-based incentives to achieve the long-term goal of broad interoperability and interconnection.

Source: AFI (2010) 'Innovative financial inclusion: principles and report on innovative financial inclusion from the Access through Innovation Sub-Group of the G20 Financial Inclusion Experts Group', Alliance for Financial Inclusion (AFI), p. 5.

In this section, I explore the limits of the G20 Principle of Proportionality as it relates to the securitisation of micro-finance institutions (MFIs), with special reference to the securitisation of BRAC in 2006. The proportionality principle refers to 'the balancing of risks and benefits [of financial inclusion] against the cost of regulation and supervision' (CGAP, 2011: 12). Mirroring the mainstream debates about payday lending (see Chapter 6), the proportionality principle assumes and thus reinforces, a central *truth* in the financial inclusion initiative, namely: that financial inclusion results in 'economic growth, efficiency and increased welfare' – all of which offset and mitigate the risks of financial exclusion (CGAP, 2011: 2). More specifically, the assumptions of the Principle of Proportionality that risks are primarily economic in nature and that these risks can somehow be balanced by the benefits of innovative services and products such as the securitisation of providers of poverty credit are critically investigated.

The Principle of Proportionality and asset-backed securitisation: interrogating a win-win strategy

Securitisation is a financial innovation that emerged in the early 1970s in the United States. ABS began to increase in use in the US during the late 1990s before expanding to Europe and eventually the global South. Securitisation describes a process of packaging individual loans and other debt instruments (otherwise known as 'assets'), transforming this package into a security or securities and enhancing the credit status or rating to further its sale to third-party investors, such as mutual and pension funds (Elul, 2005). Securitisation, also disparagingly referred to as 'slice and dice' capitalism, essentially converts illiquid individuals loans, e.g., microloans, into liquid, marketable securities to be bought and sold (Kothari, 2006; Roy, 2010). Previously in the book, I have referred to these processes as the commodification of debt (see Chapter 5).

Proponents have represented ABS as an innovative way to create a win-win situation for both borrowers and lenders, particularly in the global South (IMF, 2001; Stieber, 2007). Since ABS separates the loans from the lender, the impacts from local economic slowdowns that affect repayment are, according to this view, buffered (Chen, 2007). Seen in this light, securitisation represents a significant advancement in financial markets because, among other things, it lowers risk exposure to creditors (Graffam, 2000). There are two questions that emerge here. Who benefits from ABS? And, who carries the risk? To adequately address these questions, we need to shift our analysis beyond the narrow confines of the technical and apolitical representations of risk and risk transfer. Accomplishing this task demands moving beyond the realm of exchange to the wider processes of capital accumulation and the role and power of credit money therein.

Depending on what type of debt is sold, ABS transactions involve either fictitious capital (in the case of mortgages; see Chapter 9) or the money-form of revenue (in the case of non-collateralised consumer loans such as microloans; see Chapter 8). Both forms of credit money, as discussed in Chapter 2, entail a basic tension: 'no matter how far afield a privately contracted bill of exchange may circulate, it must always return to its place of origin for redemption' (Harvey, 1999: 245–6). Moreover, both types of credit money operate with what Marx refers to as fictitious value (price). This is arrived at through the construction of truths obtained through expert knowledge (i.e., by those wielding social power over credit money, including credit rating agencies, large investment banks, powerful institutional investors, the G20, the AFI, etc.)

Regardless of the subjectively determined fictitious value attached to a bundle of consumer debt, the latter depends on the realisation of future labour as a counter-value, as it needs to return to the origins (i.e., the debtor) for redemption. Investors engaging in ABS anticipate that the borrower will be able to earn sufficient wages to continue making orderly payments on their microloan. ABS, like all forms of fictitious capital is based on a gamble. The seemingly technical and thus seemingly apolitical, transfer of risk, as represented in the ABS literature, does not imply that the gamble disappears (CGAP, 2010b). Instead, it is instead merely displaced through a temporal fix – at least for the lenders and investors involved in the securitisation transaction. For the borrowers, the element of gamble always remains. ABS is therefore not a technical and apolitical process; but instead is infused with social relations that wield temporal and spatial dimensions of power.

The word *gamble* is arguably a more accurate and politicised descriptor of ABS transactions than the preferred, technical and economistic term 'risk'. Risk, as I discuss below, generally imparts some sense of control, certainty, objectivity and predictability (i.e., statistical metrics); gamble, on the other hand, implies uncertainty, subjectivity, unpredictability and ultimately a lack of control over the future (Marron, 2007). Adhering to Stuart Corbridge's (1993) observation that 'naming is the first step to seeing', I draw the tensions between the rhetoric and reality of ABS into relation by using the concept of 'risk/gamble' in this section. My reasoning here is that risk/gamble helps us to see the politics and class power involved in the spatio-temporal fixes of credit money, which are at the heart of both ABS and the broader financial inclusion agenda embodied by the G20 Principles.

Generally speaking, there are two types of ABS: natural securities and synthetic securities. Natural securities describe debt instruments based on the direct payment of interest and principal by the obligor to the investor. The term 'natural' is curious and requires deconstruction, as it seems to represent a highly contrived, constructed and subjective financial instrument basically aimed at commodifying and profiting from consumer debt as a neutral transaction devoid of power. As we will see, this cannot be further from the truth.

To illustrate, a microfinance institution (MFI) – that is, the originator or issuer that owns the assets that will be securitised – offers a $100 microloan to a mother with an (average) interest rate (and fee) of 37 percent on a one-year loan ('Banks making big profits from tiny loans', *New York Times*, 13 April 2010). The MFI has the option of either holding this loan in its portfolio and receiving small monthly payments for the year, or moving the loan off its balance sheet by selling it to an outside investor. The increasingly credit-constrained, larger MFIs will more than likely opt for the latter, as they can receive funds immediately by selling the loan. This ensures the opportunity to profit further by originating even more loans and thus generating origination fees (Elul, 2005; CGAP, 2010b). By selling underlying 'assets' (in this case, microloans), they are moved off an MFI's balance sheet, which means, in accounting terms, that the securitised microcredit loan is neither an asset nor a liability for the MFI. Thus, the shift from on-balance sheet to off-balance sheet is an act of subterfuge that transfers the credit risk/gamble associated with the original loans (e.g., microloans) to investors and, indirectly, as I discuss below, debtors. This same sleight of hand holds true for the second type of ABS, to which I now turn my attention.

The second, and far more common, type of ABS is synthetic securities, which refers to derivatives. Derivatives are financial instruments that have existed for hundreds of years (Sassen, 2006), although their role in the form of ABS is rather recent. The mortgage-backed security was invented in 1977, although it was not widely used at that time (Sassen, 2008). The value of derivatives is dependent on, or derived from, one or more underlying assets. Derivatives are largely unregulated.[17] Synthetic securities (derivatives) recycle or divide either the cash flow or credit risk/gamble from natural securities to create multiple securities with revised bundles of rights and unique characteristics. To return to the MFI example, a securitised, one-year microcredit loan of $100 with 37 percent interest can be made more profitable through the creation of derivatives contracts that basically bet on whether the price of the natural security will go up or down by a specific date. Synthetic securitisation, which involves such 'innovative' products as credit default swaps[18] is global in reach and enormous in volume. According to the Bank for International Settlements (BIS, 2013: 44), in early 2011 the gross notional value of outstanding privately traded (i.e., over-the-counter and unregulated) credit derivatives in the global marketplace was $29 trillion. To put this number in perspective, the Gross World Product (GWP), which is a measure of the combined gross national product of all countries in the world, was around $71.83 trillion in nominal terms in 2012 (United Nations, 2012).

Reconstructing slice and dice development: temporally displacing the risk/gamble in digitalised spaces of global finance

The purported benefits of ABS have not been lost on official development institutions and practitioners. In the wake of the litany of financial crises in emerging market economies in the late 1990s and the subsequent scarcity of low-cost, long-term loans, the IMF (2001) was touting the virtues of securitisation as a way for private and public sector entities in the global South to raise funds, as well as to obtain credit ratings higher than those of their governments. The ability of an MFI, for instance, to turn to securitisation to raise capital means that more financially excluded people, who, in Western terms could be designated as subprime (high-risk/high-gamble) borrowers (i.e., those with little or poor credit history), are brought into the market by entering into a legal obligation of debt. ABS in the global South is quite small in comparison to US markets, but growing at a rapid pace.

According to the BIS (2011), of the estimated $4.5 trillion worth of securitised assets globally as of the end of June 2009, more than 85 percent were linked to US retail finance. Nonetheless, the use of securitisation in a wide variety of financial inclusion initiatives has been growing rapidly, albeit unevenly, since the late

1990s (Inter-American Development Bank, 2001). ABS products – ranging from microcredit loans derived from MFIs in Bangladesh to future tuition flows in private universities in Peru – have become an important instrument in raising capital to support the financial inclusion agenda. Mexico, for example, while small in comparison to its northern counterparts, now boasts the largest securitised mortgage market in Latin America (International Financial Corporation, 2009). I discuss this form of ABS in more detail in Chapter 9. It should be noted that in contrast to US securitisation, transactions in the global South often employ a structure known as 'future flows' ABS, describing a process in which the securities are backed by receivables that are not expected to be generated until *after* issuance (Graffam, 2000). This point becomes clearer later in this section, when I analyse the securitisation of MFIs with regard to BRAC.

Despite the opacity, increased risks/gambles and complexities involved in securitisation, particularly the synthetic variant, securitisation has been enthusiastically promoted by the IMF and World Bank as an innovative way of securing foreign capital flows and as a market-based approach to preventing the large-scale panic that may result when a country's foreign reserves suddenly dry up. In the early 2000s, around the same time that commericalised forms of the financial inclusion agenda began gaining in significance, ABS was increasing in popularity among investors (United Nations, 2003; World Bank, 2008). The International Finance Corporation (IFC), which represents the world's largest supplier of financial services to private sector entities in the global South and is part of the World Bank Group, has been a strong proponent and key player in the securitisation of financial inclusion.

According to a former IFC director, securitisation is attractive because it enables the IFC to expand its reach without expanding its risk/gamble (Graffam, 2000: 154; Stieber, 2007). On this view, ABS will do particularly well in markets where there is a shortage of funds and deficiencies in credit quality despite a growing capacity to service debt, such as developing countries. Securitisation thus provides an extremely important market-based intervention to solve the tension between the limited supply of capital for financial inclusion and the growing demand for financial products and services for the poor in the global South (World Bank, 2009a, 2014). Seen from a Marxian perspective, however, it is not so much the limited supply of credit money that is the issue, because investors are drawn to the high interest rate margins that the highly profitable poverty industry generates. The turn to securitising poverty credit is best explained as an attempt by creditors to accelerate the temporal span of the loan transaction, so as to harvest the interest more quickly, as well as to expand its lending operations to more surplus workers.

Financial inclusion as a spatial-fix: undermining proportionality through soft law

The neoliberal rhetorical and regulatory framework has enabled the rapid and widespread participation of private markets in financial inclusion. According to Deutsche Bank, private investors are drawn to the social mission, stable returns, low default rates and potential diversification of MFI-originated loans ('Nobel winner slams for-profit microfinance', *CNNmoney.com*, 28 July 2008). Another example of the growing trend of private market actors in financial inclusion has been the proliferation of Microfinance Investment Vehicles (MIVs) since the early 2000s. MIVs specialise in providing financing for MFIs, including ABS transactions (MicroRate, 2011). MIVs held an estimated total asset value of $7 billion in 2010, up from $1.2 billion in 2005, with a projected $8.3 billion for 2012 (MicroRate, 2011, 2012). This lucrative venue has caught the attention of large, US investment banks. In 2007, for instance, Morgan Stanley and the MIV BlueOrchard entered into a $108 million ABS transaction. The CEO of BlueOrchard noted that the deal would bring microfinance 'closer to the mainstream of the capital markets as a source of medium-term money at competitive rates' (Morgan Stanley, 'BlueOrchard in microfinance ABS', *Reuters*, 3 May 2007).

Mirroring other features of global financial markets, MIVs are not only highly concentrated (with the top 10 MIVs holding 65 percent of all investments) but also uneven in their investment reach. Preferring, for instance, to invest mostly in Eastern Europe and Latin America (Reddy, 2007). This growing trend toward the commercialisation of MFIs and deeper integration into global capital markets has also led to emerging and specialised forms of private governance, such as the creation of MicroRate in 2005 – the industry's first rating agency geared toward tracking and assessing MFIs (MicroRate, 2012).

The growing intensity of speculation involved in ABS transactions and the increased role of private, powerful and profit-oriented sources of capital to MFIs has important social consequences for vulnerable populations that have been made to depend on private credit markets to support basic subsistence. I now examine securitisation through the lens of the largest, non-governmental microfinance lending facility in the world, BRAC,[19] in order to reveal how securitisation further complicates actually existing power relations and deepens the exploitation inherent in the monetised relations that lie at the core of 'the financial'. In studying the BRAC, I am not attempting to draw generalisations from this case, as MFIs do not constitute a homogenous set of institutions within and across countries in the global South and Eastern Europe. What I am seeking to accomplish in the following section is to problematise the purported win-win benefits of securitisation and financial inclusion by emphasising the social consequences of further integration of the poor into credit-led accumulation – issues that are erased and depoliticised by the framing of the financial in the wider illusions of the community of money. These fetishisms are embodied, for example, in the G20 Principle of Proportionality, which assume an exchange of equivalence and the ability of markets to equilibrate risks and benefits in the wider processes of ABS.

Setting the scene of commercialising: Wall Street meets MFIs

A core function of MFIs is issuing of microloans. According to the Grameen Bank, microloans are small loans extended to very poor people for self-employment projects that generate income, allowing them to care for themselves and their families.[20] Following the premises of neoliberal-led development, many development pundits have insisted that microloans, particularly in their commercialised form, improve the welfare of the poor by reducing the variability of consumption and cushioning the impacts of income shocks (World Bank, 2009a).[21] It is widely assumed by the development community that commercialised MFIs carry out this service more efficiently than non-profit MFIs due to their overriding goal of profit maximisation and their greater reliance on private (rational) sources of funding, e.g., MIVs (Reddy, 2007; cf. Bateman, 2010).

Despite the spectacular growth in MIVs in the New Millennium, there continues to be a significant supply-demand gap for MFI services, particularly in countries outside of Latin America and Eastern Europe (MicroRate, 2012). In the early 2000s, for instance, while market demand for MFI services was estimated at more than $300 billion, market supply was just $4 billion (Grameen Foundation USA, 2004). In low-income countries that lie outside of the preferred investment sites of MIVs, such as Bangladesh, MFIs such as BRAC have sought not only to raise capital through securitisations but also have turned to ABS to reduce 'dependency on volatile donor financing' (BRAC, cited in Roy, 2010: 203). The question that emerges is: what social cost does the poor pay through the increased dependency of MFIs on volatile global capital markets? The case of BRAC helps to answer this question.

In 2006, the first of many securitisations of MFIs and other forms of financial inclusion occurred when Bangladesh-based BRAC, one of the world's largest national non-governmental organisations (NGOs) and microfinance providers, raised approximately $180 million in financing (Roy, 2010). BRAC's ABS involved two phases, each falling under the category of synthetic securities discussed above. In the first phase of securitisation, the Dutch Development Finance Company (FMO) and KfW Bankengruppe, a German development bank, purchased loans from BRAC for $8 million. In the second phase of securitisation, a finance company guaranteed the loans and sold two-thirds of the packaged guarantee and the microcredit loans to RSA Capital and Citibank Dhaka for $22 million. FMO held one-third of the loans. Citibank supplied the funding and management for their debt certificates. These two phases were repeated five times to generate a total of $180 million (Sengupta and Aubuchon, 2008). Through the use of (unregulated) derivatives and the framing of soft law that facilitates and legitimates these types of proprietary transactions, FMO's and KfW's original purchase price of $8 million has, through the 'slice and dice' processes that mark ABS, multiplied over 22 times.

Tellingly, the BRAC transaction has been represented in apolitical terms, despite being anchored in the power relations of debt. In the technical framework of securitisation, microfinance loans that are not yet repaid are not considered liabilities, but rather assets. Thus the ABS transactions undertaken by BRAC and its foreign financial investors are said to involve 'no debt relationship' (Chen, 2007). The ability of FMO and KfW to increase the value of their investment more than 22 times is, however, based on the assumption that the borrowers holding this debt will make their repayments in an orderly manner. More broadly, the shift in ownership over the 'assets' involves a reconfiguration of debt relationships in which the power and nature of social risk/gamble are inherent characteristics. In what follows, I highlight some ways that ABS has served to further intensify and complicate the relations of power and exploitation inherent to MFIs (Karim, 2011).

Mitigating proportionality through 'slice and dice' development?

The first social risk/gamble relates to both the structure of ABS and market pressure to increase loans to the poor. Securitisation of MFI loans is not an ongoing process, but occurs only once. Thus, the income generated from ABS is a one-off transaction. To receive more money, an MFI must make new loans. This may be a welcome incentive for promoters of increased financial inclusion. After its securitisation in 2006, BRAC, for instance, sought to expand its lending base to include 5 million new, low-income borrowers (Chen, 2007). As in the case of the US subprime mortgage crisis, MFIs desperate for cash infusions push new microloans on higher-risk/higher-gamble borrowers. Securitisation increases the amount of capital available so that more loans can be made to more people. Thus, the first social risk/gamble involved in the securitisation of financial inclusion strategies is that the process encourages a constantly expanding pool of debtors, which in turn pushes MFIs to more risky loans (Chen, 2007).

A second risk/gamble emerges from the reconfigured debt relationship between borrower and lender in securitisation. Under a standard ABS arrangement, loans ('assets' or receivables) are serviced by a third party; these 'assets' are then sold to institutional investors. To make these assets attractive to risk-adverse/gamble-adverse investors, the originator's institutional risks/gambles are separated from these assets. Moreover, the securitised loan, especially in its synthetic form, is not held by one investor as a single asset but rather is further divided between multiple private investors – all of whom demand particular procedures that the third-party servicer must follow. On the ground, these processes of ABS serve to reconfigure debt relations by, for instance, intensifying the already existing strict delinquency supervision and limiting the wiggle-room available for the servicer to change the terms of repayment on the microloans. This creates difficulties for poor debtors, who lack a safety net and are, therefore, vulnerable to a host of events outside of their control, including natural disasters and adverse weather, theft, or family illnesses that hamper their ability to repay (Bateman, 2010).

Another related social disadvantage caused by the reconfiguration of MFIs through ABS is the impersonal nature of the creditor-debtor relationship. There is no one with whom to discuss and possibly negotiate, changes in the terms of the loan to circumvent default (Chen, 2007). BRAC, for instance, relinquished its ability to change the terms of the loan when it entered the ABS transaction. The social risks/gambles for the borrower in this new relationship involve the increased likelihood of default, if there is no alternative (delayed) repayment. The social and economic consequences of default are significant, as borrowers who default will face difficulty in obtaining future loans. In a group loan setting, borrowers who default may also face tremendous social stigma, collective forms of discipline and even suicide (Karim, 2011). More fortunate clients, when faced with the prospect of default, may elect to sell off their assets (e.g., livestock, which is the most important household asset for the poor in the global South) to preserve their credit (World Bank, 2010b). Others may resort to applying for more loans and increasing their debt load – through formal or informal channels (Rankin and Shakya, 2008; Karim, 2011). In essence, new social risks/gambles and relations of power become shaped by the processes of securitising debt, which in turn may lead to creating more vulnerability for poor borrowers (Chen, 2007). This is particularly true in the advent of global financial crises such as the Great Crash of 2008.

In a joint paper, the Consultative Group to Assist the Poor (CGAP) and JP Morgan suggest that despite increased delinquency rates and dropping profitability levels, MFIs were doing well in 2009. Furthermore, equity valuations globally have been on the rise since 2007 and that sector has continued to attract a larger pool of capital with MIVs (e.g., BlueOrchard, MicroVest and Developing World Markets) establishing new MFI equity funds, while public investors (e.g., World Bank, USAID) significantly increased their financial commitments (CGAP and JP Morgan, 2010). The large, US-based investment bank Morgan Stanley has reported that worldwide loan portfolios of MFIs equal $17 billion and have the potential to grow as large as $300 billion over the next decade. As the global director of Citigroup's MFI division observes, 'They [the poor] have different risk sensitivities. They're often not part of any sudden boom, such as real estate. There are more resilient to some economic cycles' ('Citi sees microfinance growth even in downturn', *Reuters*, 21 December 2007). The poor are thus viewed as enduring and bankable even in the face of economic crises. The reason for this, according to Citigroup, one of the largest institutional players in MFIs, is that 'the poor have a lower threshold for risk as a class, which makes them more resilient to economic cycles and protects them from economic booms and depressions' (Diehl, 2009: 42). This statement by Citigroup reveals how the poor and their daily struggles to survive are glossed over in discussions of MFIs.

In 2009, and in contrast to the above-cited report it later published with JP Morgan, CGAP published a study that was based on a survey of over 400 MFI managers across the globe. The study concluded that sustained high food prices, severe economic contraction and massive job losses were hurting their borrowers. Moreover, MFI borrowers were prioritising food expenditures and experienced more difficulties in repaying their loans. MFIs also reported that it was more difficult for them to access funding. As in previous crises, the most vulnerable – particularly women and children – are likely to have been hit hardest (CGAP, 2009b). The World Bank also paints a darker picture of the post-2008 world, although it does place more emphasis on the MFIs than the poor. According to the World Bank, since MFI loans offer the only access to credit for basic subsistence for millions of low-income people, these borrowers will take their loans seriously and are very reliable payers (World Bank, 2009a). As such, the extent and depth to which the current crisis poses a risk/gamble for MFIs depends on the nature of external financing (Diehl, 2009). According to USAID, the increased reliance of MFIs on financial markets has meant that the contagion of the 2008 crisis has had a deeper reach than past crises, affecting financial markets, liquidity, trade flows, growth, employment, inflation and remittance flows because of fact that credit money is able to transfer across borders with greater ease than in the past (USAID, 2009).

As the 2008 crisis becomes a distant memory – at least for the small group of powerful people drawing their income from credit-led accumulation – there has been increasing pushback by capitalists against what had already been agreed to in the wake of the crisis (and bailouts!), as well as inadequate implementation of soft law responses to the crisis (IMF, 2012c). The Board of Governors of the US Federal Reserve System, for instance, has suggested that it will be difficult to comply with the recommendations of the Dodd-Frank Wall Street Reform and Consumer Protection Act (or, Act) regarding ABS (see Chapter 5). The reason for this, according to the Federal Reserve, is that due to 'considerable heterogeneity across asset classes in securitisation chains, deal structures and incentive alignment mechanisms [. . .] simple credit risk retention rules, applied uniformly across assets of all types, are unlikely to achieve the stated objective of the Act – namely, to improve the [ABS] process and protect investors from losses associated with poorly underwritten loans' (Federal Reserve Board, 2010b, 3; IMF, 2012a).

The above position by a key regulatory institution overseeing the largest ABS markets in the world contradicts the commitments of the Joint Forum of the Basel Committee on Banking Supervision regarding the re-establishment of sustainable securitisation markets as a high priority for G20 leaders, the Financial Stability Board and other international organisations and national governments since 2007 ('SIFMA: Uphold ABS exclusion in applying Volcker Rule', *Asset Securitisation Report*, 14 February 2012). In terms of the Principle of Proportionality and its focus on balancing risk involved in innovative finance with its benefits, it also signals that the wider regulatory context from which the G20 Principles emerged were aimed at recreating, in the first instance, an enabling framework for the expansion of the poverty industry as opposed to protecting the surplus population from market generated risk/gamble – much less attempting to lift these workers and their families out of poverty by introducing a living wage and guaranteed provisioning for basic subsistence.

Bringing the principles of protection and empowerment to life in Mexico's poverty industry

In this section, I explore the G20 Principles of Protection and Empowerment to demonstrate how these Principles not only mirror the illusions of the community of money, but also and by extension, support continual attempts by the Mexican state and capitalists to expand and reproduce financial inclusion strategies. It is important to emphasise that the G20 Principles do not determine the spatial displacements in credit-led accumulation in Mexico, but instead act to legitimate, depoliticise and normalise class-based strategies aimed at monetising the relations of the surplus population. Thus, the Principles contribute to imposing market discipline on workers, while exploiting them through high interest rates.

Alliance for Financial Inclusion Report 2011: an overview of the Mexican Case

In 2011, the Alliance for Financial Inclusion (AFI), in its capacity as the implementing partner of the G20's Global Partnership for Financial Inclusion (GPFI), released a report entitled: Bringing the Principles to Life (hereafter: AFI Report) in which it provided a description of how eleven countries in the global South have embraced the nine G20 Principles of Financial Inclusion (AFI, 2011). The AFI Report gave a brief but positive overview regarding the Mexican state's attempt to implement financial inclusion initiatives, although the text cautioned that it is too early to draw conclusions about the quality and extent of Mexico's adherence to the G20 Principles and suggested further observation and monitoring are necessary (AFI, 2011: 2). Reflecting the G20 Principles, the Mexican state defines financial inclusion as 'the access and use of a portfolio of financial products and services for the majority of the adult population with clear and concise information attending the growing demand under an appropriate regulatory framework' (AFI, 2011: 38). The so-called 'proper' regulatory framework in Mexico involves soft law for the poverty industry underpinned by hard law to protect the interests of capital, e.g., the protection of private property and the guarantee of legal contracts (World Bank, 2004c).

According to the AFI Report, the Mexican state has been promoting policies and legal reforms aimed at increasing the transparency of financial institutions, strengthening consumer protection and enhancing financial literacy since the mid-2000s (AFI, 2011). In 2007, for example, the Mexican state issued the Transparency and Financial Services Ordering Law (hereafter: Transparency Law).[22] The latter was to ensure, among other things, healthy banking and business practices and the use of non-jargon based language in order to facilitate the reading and understanding of contracts (Raccanello and Romero, 2011). Moreover, the AFI Report goes on to commend the expansion of the main financial regulator in Mexico, the National Banking and Securities Commission (hereafter: CNBV[23]) (AFI, 2011).

Under the Transparency Law, for instance, the CNBV's mission was broadened to include the promotion of a sound and inclusive banking system. In particular, the CNBV developed an Access to Finance Unit (AFU), which was set up to inform policy decisions on financial access issues, influence business models for providers and monitor progress, which in the context of the wider financial inclusion agenda, means conducting surveys and reports that analyse gaps between needs and supply. The CNBV has also sought to forge partnerships with other key government agencies devoted to consumer protection, most notably the National Commission for the Defense of Financial Services Users (hereafter: CONDUSEF).[24]

According to the AFI Report, the partnership between CNBV and CONDUSEF is significant in two ways. First, as the country's consumer protection agency, CONDUSEF is expected to work toward the reinforcement of the 2007 Law for Transparency by implementing transparency requirements regarding pricing, terms and conditions for products and services. CONDUSEF has also sought to ensure disclosure of information on periodic statements, contracts and promotions, grievances and redress mechanisms, sanctions and fines; and transparency and disclosure standards on fees charged by financial institutions, which is also part of the Law for Transparency (AFI, 2011: 39). For instance, the Transparency Law, which is a soft law, has sought to promote, albeit never clearly defining, *healthy* banking and business practices to help the poor understand the content of legally-binding debt contracts (Raccanello and Romero, 2011).

Second, CONDUSEF and the CNBV have partnered to conduct financial literacy focus groups (AFI, 2011: 38). Since 2008, CONDUSEF has held an Annual National Financial Literacy Week that focuses on family's budgets, savings, investments, credit and insurance. There are over 1,000 events across the country supported by government agencies, financial institutions, schools and universities. CONDUSEF also issued Guidelines for Financial Education for Elementary School. There are now six teachers' guides that provide simple and clear tools explaining basic economic and financial concepts for children. Since 2011, with the help of the Ministry of Education, these Guidelines have been distributed to Mexico's 98,575 elementary schools – reaching a total of 14.6 million students (AFI, 2011: 40). In 2011, the state launched the national financial education strategy to promote programmes, workshops and other initiatives related to financial education in order to reach as many low-income, financially excluded Mexicans as possible.

It should be noted here that the G20 is not the only international organisation that has reinforced the importance of financial education as a form of consumer protection. In 2013, for instance, the G20, World Bank and OECD hosted a conference on empowering consumers of financial products and services.[25] According to this view, through financial education financial consumers will gain more information about financial products and concepts thereby developing the necessary skills and confidence to function effectively in the market (OECD, 2009).

The AFI Report concludes its assessment by noting that Mexico's embrace of the above G20 Principles for Innovative Financial Inclusion, particularly the Principle of Protection and the Principle of Empowerment, has facilitated the expansion of financial inclusion. This is evidenced by the fact that formal lending institutions have almost doubled in number from 9,429 in 2009 to an estimated 20,000 by 2011 (AFI, 2011: 39). The trope of the Principle of Protection and the Principle of Empowerment serve to strengthen the illusions of the community of money, erasing questions of exploitation and power from the financial, as well as obscuring the structural violence inherent to neoliberal policies that have led to the dependency of the surplus population on privately created money for basic subsistence needs (cf. World Bank, 2014). As I have explained in previous chapters, the power of the community of money and its illusions of democracy, equality and freedom is based on its ability to conceal its connections to the realm of production and states. These assumptions are further rehearsed in the debates about the predatory nature of consumer credit for the poor in Mexico to which I now turn.

Debating protection and empowerment in the realm of exchange

As noted earlier, much of the regulative landscape of consumer credit in Mexico is framed in soft law. This provides considerable leeway for capitalists to continue to expand and intensify dispossessive strategies with regard to the unbanked population, comprised of large numbers of surplus labour. For instance, there are no legal limits on interest levels and little state oversight regarding formal lending institutions in Mexico, particularly those that comprise the poverty industry. CONDUSEF, for instance, does not publish the interest rates charged by banks for personal loans. Interest rates for consumer loans are high in Mexico for all income levels, but particularly for the poor. A credit card from BanCoppel has registered Annualized Percentage Rate (APR) interest rates as high as 88 percent, including added fees,[26] whereas a loan from an unregulated microfinance institution (MFI) in Mexico, which I examine in the next chapter, may reach as high as 229 percent APR (Bateman, 2013).[27]

Notwithstanding the 2007 Law of Transparency, the Mexican state has not required that interest rates on loans be reported to and subsequently published by, CONDUSEF. The justification for this position is that competition between financial providers and growing demand from consumers will ultimately create the optimal price level. The government should concentrate on fostering competition and refrain from interfering in this process so as to avoid distorting the rational and self-equilibrating forces of the market. This was the rationale behind the establishment of Multiple Purpose Financial Companies (or, as they are referred to by their Spanish acronym, SOFOMES[28]) in 2006. SOFOMES are not regulated.[29] In keeping with the ethos of market competition as a core way to achieve welfare for the poor, the Mexican Congress created SOFOMES to further deregulate the consumer credit industry and increase lending activities to the poor, such as providing payroll lending and microloans. According to data from CNBV and CONDUSEF there were approximately 3,400 unregulated SOFOMES operating in Mexico in 2011 (see Chapter 8; IMF, 2012e).

It is important to note that the debates about the high cost of lending in Mexico remain within the realm of exchange thereby reinforcing the associated illusions of the community of money. This can be readily seen in the solutions offered to the perceived problems in financial inclusion. To mitigate predatory lending, for instance, states should strengthen consumer protection through more disclosure and improving financial literacy, thereby empowering the poor. Commentators based in the economic paradigm, for instance, have suggested that the consumer protection laws in Mexico do not adequately protect the poor, who are the main target of financial inclusion strategies – many of which may be described as predatory lending. For these authors, predatory lending refers to credit practices that take advantage of the borrowers' lack of financial literacy and financial options in order to exploit customers through high-cost credit (Drury, 2009; Raccanello and Romero, 2011: 1). Increasing financial knowledge among the poor is viewed not only as combating predatory lending practices, but also as increasing savings and overall financial wellbeing, e.g., less reliance on the relatively higher-priced credit offered by pawnbrokers (Rutledge, 2010; CGAP, 2011).

The provision of adequate regulation regarding consumer protection is vital in avoiding predatory lending through the implementation of soft law. In contrast to the AFI's positive spin on consumer protection in Mexico and the 2012 creation of the Mexican National Council for Financial Inclusion,[30] critics suggest that the conciliatory and dispute resolution functions of CONDUSEF remain de facto ineffective (Raccanello and Romero, 2011). In 2007, the same year that the above-mentioned Law for Transparency was decreed, the consumer protection agency solved only 29 percent of conciliation reports. In this same year, however, only three cases came to arbitration. Aside from the usual lack of financial resources, an important reason for the lack of effectiveness of the consumer protection agencies is due to its design in soft law: financial institutions in Mexico are not legally obliged to abide by CONDUSEF'S recommendations (IMF, 2012d).

While the impotence of CONDUSEF – glossed over by the AFI Report – is problematic, the above critique of predatory lending in Mexico remains firmly entrenched in the depoliticising sphere of exchange. Thus, the source of the problem of predatory lending lies not in the exploitative and unequal relations of capital accumulation and, by extension, the absence of a living wage and social protections; but instead in the absence of a legal definition of predatory lending in Mexico. The solution to mitigating predatory lending practices in Mexico remains in the realm of exchange. The emphasis is on establishing a level playing field – and therewith rehearsing the illusion of an equivalence of exchange – through soft laws that emphasise empowerment and more effective forms of consumer protection, including strengthening the oversight powers of CONDUSEF. At the same time, by not grasping the wider dynamics of capital accumulation and the role of the Mexican state therein, these debates inadvertently support key economic fictions that serve to reproduce the relations of power in consumer credit, particularly as these relate to regulating interest rates. The Mexican state and CONDUSEF in particular, refuse to cap interest rates on lending because introducing interest rate ceilings would distort markets. Moreover, high interest rates for the poor are viewed as 'the natural result of market forces', since 'lower income levels often incur significantly higher APRs [Annual Percentage Rates]' (Euromonitor International, 2013: 13).

Despite the commendable progress made by the Mexican government in facilitating financial inclusion, the AFI Report identifies some challenges that remain unresolved, particularly the proportionality principle, as discussed above. The AFI, for instance, recommends that Mexican regulators strive to strike a balance between, on the one hand, the size of the loan to the poor and prudential requirements, i.e., the ability of the borrower to pay by identifying how best to balance obligations and the alleged soundness and solvency of the financial system, on the other (AFI, 2011). Remaining true to the neoclassical economic assumptions discussed in Chapter 3, the proportionality principle cannot be achieved through the implementation of legally binding (hard) laws that constrain the poverty industry and other forms of perceived government interference in the market. Instead, proportionality is achieved when *effective financial consumer protection* translates into *responsible market conduct* (CGAP, 2011: 5).

Viewing the challenges of financial inclusion in terms of a principle of proportionality does not address the high interest rates that characterise the poverty industry, which remains unregulated in Mexico. More importantly, this economistic framing also treats the relations between debtors and creditors as apolitical and thus devoid of questions of the power inherent in monetised relations. This view also reproduces two core assumptions of debtfarism: that exchanges between creditors and debtors are based on equivalence and that markets are capable of achieving equilibrating risks and benefits – that is, setting a *reasonable* price for credit (interest rates) while maintaining welfare benefits for the debtor.

Concluding remarks

In this chapter I tried to throw critical light on what is concealed by the G20 Principles and to explain why the G20's representation and promotion of financial inclusion is a social construct that entails the expansion and (re-)imposition of monetised social relations. Moreover, I sought to demonstrate that these relations are not, as the fetishism of the community of money attests, based on equality, freedom and democracy; but instead are exploitative, unequal and coercive. I argued that the G20 Principles play a supportive role in legitimating and normalising political and legal framings by states and capitalists in their ongoing attempts at expanding and reproducing the poverty industry through reconstructions of the illusion of the community of money.

By analysing three G20 Principles (the Principle of Proportionality, the Principle of Protection and the Principle of Empowerment) within the contexts of Mexico and global developments in financial inclusion in Bangladesh, I have shown that the G20 Principles should be understood as responses, constructions and consolidations of an underlying attempt to reproduce the neoliberal governance of dispossessive capitalism, including the regulatory preference for soft law to facilitate spatio-temporal fixes of credit money and the risk/gamble entrapment of the surplus population.

I have suggested that the G20 financial inclusion agenda is not a neutral project, but one that is aimed at constructing the dependence of the poor in the global South on privately created money (credit). Instead of leading to the neoliberal promise of growth through investments in production – and thus stable living wages and poverty reduction – the increased frequency and intensity of financial crises linked to credit-led accumulation has made developing countries and their populations more vulnerable. Notwithstanding the historical experience of neoliberalism since the 1980s, the solution to the latest crisis has been to include more poor people into a volatile, speculative and highly interconnected financial system, so that they may, in the words of the G20, 'manage their low, irregular and unreliable income' (AFI, 2010: 14).

In the next two chapters, I continue interrogating the capitalist nature of the financial. Specifically, I seek to show how the Mexican state and capitalists have constructed debtfarist policies to facilitate the expansion and reproduction of the poverty industry in Mexico. Through a historical materialist analysis, I deconstruct how debtfarism has served to reconstruct the financial and its illusions of the community of money, while concealing the underlying structural violence that silently compels the surplus population to enter into the disciplinary and exploitative realm of credit.

Notes

1 For a historical and critical analysis of the global development project, see: Philip McMichael, 2012: Vijay Pradash, 2013: and Sandra Halperin, 2013.
2 'Alliance for Financial Inclusion Reaches 100 Member Institutions', 20 March 2013. Available at: www.marketwire.com/press-release/alliance-for-financial-inclusion-reaches-100-member-institutions-1769906.htm (accessed 15 July 2013).
3 For more discussion of the US subprime crisis, see: Schwartz, 2009; Konings, 2010; Panitch and Gindin, 2012.
4 Consultative Group to Assist the Poor (CGAP) (2012b) 'Measuring Financial Exclusion: How Many People Are Unbanked?' Available at: www.cgap.org/blog/measuring-financial-exclusion-how-many-people-are-unbanked (accessed 24 July 2013).
5 To be clear, in drawing attention to this analytical blind spot, I am not suggesting that other scholars have not investigated questions of power with regard to financial inclusion strategies, only that these analyses do not follow the same line of questioning into 'the financial' as I do here (Rankin, 2001, 2013; Weber, 2002; Bateman, 2010; Roy, 2010; Taylor, 2011; Da Costa, 2013). What I am emphasising is that the capitalist nature of this power, especially its historical and social dimensions as regards credit money and its legal framings, has been ignored by the financial inclusion agenda as represented by the G20 Principles.
6 This is an estimated number of unbanked. It is important to emphasise that figures vary by source. Commonwealth Secretariat (2013) 'Financial Inclusion in the Commonwealth and Francophonie'. A Paper for the Commonwealth-Francophonie-G20 Development Working Group Meeting. 21 April 2013. Available at: www.thecommonwealth. org/files/254284/FileName/FinancialInclusionintheCommonwealthandFrancophonie-11April2013.pdf (accessed 22 July 2013).
7 The final draft of the Pocantico Declaration is available at: www.microfinance gateway.org/gm/document-1.9.24412/49313.pdf (accessed 16 January 2014).
8 More information about the AFI is available at: www.afi-global.org/ (accessed 15 July 2013).
9 More information about the role of the Bill and Melinda Gates Foundation and the AFI is available at: www.gatesfoundation.org/Media-Center/Press-Releases/2009/09/AFI-Develops-Financial-Services-for-the-Poor (accessed 15 July 2013).
10 More information about the role of AusAid in the financing of the AFI is available at: www.ausaid.gov.au/Publications/Pages/afi-funding-prop.aspx (accessed 15 July 2013).

11 For more information, see www.gpfi.org/about-gpfi/sub-groups-and-co-chairs/sub-group-financial-inclusion-data-and-measurement (accessed 15 July 2013).

12 For more information, see www.gpfi.org/about-gpfi/sub-groups-and-co-chairs/sub-group-principles-and-standard-setting-bodies (accessed 15 July 2013). Five SSBs – the Basel Committee on Banking Supervision, the Committee on Payment and Settlement Systems, the Financial Action Task Force, the International Association of Deposit Insurers, and the International Association of Insurance Supervisors – play an important role, albeit to varying degrees, in influencing 'how many poor households get access to what range and quality of formal financial services and at what cost' (CGAP, 2011: 1).

13 For instance, the Bill and Melinda Gates Foundation funded the Global Financial Inclusion Database (or, Global Findex), which has been endorsed by the World Bank. The Global Findex, which promotes the G20 Principles on its website, tracks the effects 'of financial inclusion policies globally and develop[s] a deeper and more nuanced understanding of how people around the world save, borrow, make payments, and manage risk'. World Bank (2012) 'Findex Notes'. Available at: http://siteresources.worldbank.org/EXTGLOBALFIN/Resources/8519638-1332259343991/N2savingsENG.pdf (accessed 15 July 2013).

14 For an overview of the various expert groupings involved in the G20 Principles of Financial Inclusion, see Global Partnership for Financial Inclusion. Available at: www.gpfi.org/get-to-know-gpfi (accessed 12 July 2013).

15 Global Partnership on Financial Inclusion (2011), *Report to the Leaders*. G20 Summit, Cannes, France, 5 November. Available at: www.gpfi.org/sites/default/files/documents/GPFI%20report%20to%20G-20.pdf (accessed 15 July 2013).

16 The Maya Declaration was signed in 2011 to complement the G20 Principles of strengthening and expanding financial inclusion. Around 80 countries, which represent over 75 percent of the world's unbanked population, are said to support the Maya Declaration. Similar to the G20 Principles, the Maya Declaration is based on, and thus serves to reinforce, voluntary guidelines ('soft law') as opposed to mandatory regulations of financial inclusion strategies. The membership base of the Maya Declaration was expanded in 2012 with the signing of the Cape Town Commitments, which is also aligned with the G20 Principles and underlying geopolitical and capitalist powers therein.

The Mayan and Cape Town Commitments played an important symbolic role in signalling the voluntary and 'grassroots' acceptance of the global financial inclusion initiative as a key priority goal in the development project. In this sense, the Mayan and Cape Town Commitments act as another layer of legitimating the expert truths, including their underlying neoliberal assumptions, of the global financial initiative by ensuring that the global South has a stronger voice and presence in the reconstructions of financial inclusion. For more information about the Maya Declaration see AFI, 'Strategy Development – Organizing for Financial Inclusion Supporting Strategic Approaches in the AFI Network'. Available at: www.afi-global.org/sites/default/files/publications/AFI_Strategy%20development_AW_low%20res.pdf (accessed 20 July 2013).

17 While US financial markets are less stringent in terms of regulating over-the-counter derivatives trading (e.g., credit default swaps), the European Union introduced more regulatory measures after the 2008 crisis. See, for instance, the European Market Infrastructure Regulation, www.esma.europa.eu/page/European-Market-Infrastructure-Regulation-EMIR (accessed 15 January 2014).

18 Credit default swaps (CDSs) are the most widely traded form of credit derivative. CDSs are contracts that are sold as protection against default on loans. CDS are private gambles in the sense that they are neither transparent nor regulated by the US government. Ellen Brown (2008) 'Credit Default Swaps: evolving financial meltdown and derivative disaster du jour', *Global Research*, 11 April. Available at: www.webofdebt.com/articles/derivative-disaster.php (accessed 19 July 2013).

19 The lending organisation was originally named the Bangladesh Rehabilitation Assistance Committee (BRAC) when it was formed in 1972 at the end of Bangladesh's War of

Liberation. BRAC maintains offices in 14 countries globally, including BRAC USA and BRAC UK. More information is available at: www.brac.net (accessed 15 July 2013).

20 Grameen Bank (2011) 'What is Microcredit?' Available at: www.grameen-info.org/index.php?option=com_content&task=view&id=28&Itemid=108 (accessed 15 July 2013).

21 World Bank, 'Microfinance tradeoffs'.

22 In Spanish the Transparency Law is known as *Ley para la Transparencia y Ordenamiento de los Servicios Financieros or LTOSF*). More information about the Transparency Law is available (in Spanish) at: www.banxico.org.mx/disposiciones/circulares/leyes/%7B24EF3EEB-A8A3-D421-2F2D-9FA43FA9850E%7D.pdf (accessed 15 July 2013).

23 The Spanish name for the National Banking and Securities Commission is the *Comisión Nacional Bancaria y de Valores or CNBV*. More information is available at: www.cnbv.gob.mx/en/Paginas/default.aspx (accessed 15 July 2013).

24 The Spanish name of CONDUSEF is the *Comisión Nacional para la Defensa de los Usuarios de Servicios Financieros*. More information about Condesuf (in English) is available at: www.condusef.gob.mx/index.php/english (accessed 24 July 2013).

25 Information about this conference is available at: www.oecd.org/daf/fin/financial-education/russiag20presidency-worldbank-oecdconferenceconsumerprotection.htm (accessed 15 July 2013).

26 'Mexican (legit) loan shark Ricardo Salinas is making billions the old-fashioned way', *Forbes*, 18 April 2012.

27 Calculating the APR of financial institutions lending to the surplus population in Mexico is difficult. I explore this issue in Chapter 8. In terms of the case of Compartamos' interest rates, see, C. Waterford (2008), 'Explanation of Compartamos Interest Rates'. Available at: www.microfinancetransparency.com/evidence/PDF/5.6%20Explanation%20of%20Compartamos%20Interest%20Rates.pdf (accessed 17 July 2013).

28 The Spanish name for these lending institutions is *Sociedad Financiera de Objeto Mutiple*.

29 The only exception occurs when national banks, which are regulated, own 20 percent or more stock ownership of a particular SOFOMS. In this case, the SOFOMES would be subject to regulation (BCP Securities, 2010). More information (in Spanish) available at: www.condusef.gob.mx/index.php/instituciones-financieras/sociedades-financieras-de-objeto-multiple (accessed 25 July 2013).

30 This initiative conveniently coincided with 2012 G20 Leadership Meeting that was held in Los Cabos, Mexico. For more information about Mexico's National Council for Financial Inclusion, see 'Mexico's National Council for Financial Inclusion', 16 February 2012. Available at: www.cgap.org/blog/mexico%E2%80%99s-national-council-financial-inclusion (accessed 19 July 2013).

8

DEBTFARISM AND THE
MICROFINANCE INDUSTRY

In 2007, Mexican-based Compartamos Banco (hereafter: Compartamos) became the world's first microfinance institution (MFI) to complete an initial public offering (IPO). By selling 30 percent of its company, Compartamos was able to raise $467 million, which it claimed was necessary to continue its goal of serving the financially excluded. The story of Compartamos, which began life as a non-profit, grassroots lending organisation in the 1990s before becoming the most lucrative, commercialised (for-profit) MFI in the world, is neither unique nor novel. Since the 1990s, international donors encouraged the shift away from informal (not legally recognised) and/or non-profit lending (Bateman, 2010). However, it was not until the mid-2000s that the phenomenon of commercialised microfinance lending began to grow – both in pace and breadth – in Mexico. Some of the key players in Mexico's for-profit microfinance industry, which I investigate in this chapter, include retail-based banks such as Banco Walmart and Multiple Purpose Financial Companies – or, SOFOMES.[1]

According to the National Banking and Securities Commission of Mexico (CNBV), the average size of MFI loans in Mexico falls within the range of $390 to $1,950, but the interest rates are high (CNBV, 2010). Compartamos, which caters exclusively to group loans (primarily to women) for micro-enterprises, has grabbed international headlines for its rates, which range from 110 Annual Percentage Rate (APR) to 195 APR (Roodman, 2011; Bateman, 2013). In 2012, retail banks, such as Banco Walmart, have been offering credit cards with interest rates posted at 94.30 percent APR.[2] And, SOFOMES such as CrediConfia charge clients as much as 229 APR.[3] Despite these high rates and a brief setback in the wake of the 2008 crisis, personal lending in Mexico – across all income ranges – has been expanding rapidly, with gross lending and returns on investment in the microfinance industry showing double-digit increases (EuroMonitor International, 2013; Bateman, 2013).

Guided by the financial inclusion initiative that has become deeply embedded in the neoliberal fabric of global development project, commercialised and formalised MFIs are widely seen by states, international organisations (e.g., World Bank, G20) and epistemic communities (e.g., CGAP) as a viable and effective solution to poverty, largely because they are able to offer a more expansive outreach and deliver more diverse financial products to the financially excluded than their non-profit and informal counterparts (Otero, 2005; Antón-Díaz, 2013).

Debates on the alleged link between the commercialisation of MFIs and their ability to reduce poverty are well documented (World Bank, 2001; Inter-American Development Bank, 2006; Lewis, 2008; Bateman, 2010, 2013; Roodman, 2011). Over the past two decades of commercialising the microfinance industry, many scholars have demonstrated that the connection between for-profit microfinance lending and poverty reduction is tenuous and, at the very least, problematic (Rankin, 2001, 2013; Elyachar, 2002, 2005; Roy, 2010; Weber, 2002; Taylor, 2011). One study, even suggests that Compartamos's high interest rates have not impacted the welfare-enhancing features of access to credit, such as smoothing liquidity shocks, although the study does cede that these loans have not facilitated wealth-generation among the poor (Angelucci *et al.*, 2013). In light of this, some major MFIs have cautiously begun to describe their activities not in terms of poverty alleviation; but instead as creating opportunities for the poor by granting them access to financial services. In words of the co-CEOs of Compartamos, 'we believe that microfinance is finance and has to be sustainable [read: profitable] . . . that the main contribution of microfinance is the expansion of the market' (Danel and Labarthe, 2008: 1).[4] According to its 2012 Annual Report, Compartamos is concentrating on eradicating financial exclusion as opposed to poverty (Grupos Compartamos, 2012).

Notwithstanding this more guarded position, the core *modus operandi* of commercial MFIs remains predicated on achieving a balance between social values and private objectives, which entail extracting high levels of interest (often higher than 60 percent APR) to make up for the costs of issuing and maintaining small loans ('Mexico's Banco Compartamos is seeking to buy micro-finance lender abroad', *Bloomberg*, 15 April 2010). Regardless of whether the social values have been met, it is unequivocal that the private objectives of commercialised MFIs have been reached. Compartamos's return on average equity was 31.22 percent in 2012, while its net earnings increased by 9.8 percent to 500 million pesos ($3.7 million) (Compartamos, 2012; 'Banco Compartamos to invest in $31.8 million in opening 75 new branches', *BN Americas*, 18 June 2012).[5]

This chapter will not re-enter the well-rehearsed debates about the connection between poverty reduction and for-profit, microfinance lending. Instead, it seeks to complement these discussions by examining the coercive and ideological machinations involved in the expansion and reproduction of Mexico's rapidly expanding commercial microfinance industry. To accomplish this task, it is necessary to contextualise the poverty industry within the wider dynamics of capital accumulation, which include *both* the realms of production and exchange.

This perspective allows for a more comprehensive understanding of the material basis of class and state power as well as the paradoxes driving social change and reproduction. Put another way, the complex and ongoing constructions and reconstructions of the microfinance industry are neither natural nor neutral; but instead, emerge from, and thrive off of, paradoxes inherent to the processes of capital accumulation.

Seen from the above angle, and in contrast with neoclassical renditions of self-regulating market, capitalists can neither proceed with the expansion of microfinance lending, nor can the surplus population be effectively reproduced without ideological and coercive state intervention. The rhetorical and regulative framings of the Mexican debtfare state, as with global debtfarism articulated by key global development institutions and organisations discussed in Chapter 7, act to mediate, legitimate and depoliticise these tensions. In doing so, debtfare strategies, facilitate the continued expansion of the microfinance industry on behalf of capitalists' interests, while employing a market-based solution to the reproduction of surplus labour power. One important, albeit powerful, rhetorical device used by global development institutions and neoliberal states, such as Mexico, to advance the need for financial inclusion as a key solution to poverty is to continually naturalise and individualise the causes of poverty. It is to an elaboration of this political act vis-à-vis Mexico's surplus population that I now turn my attention.

Denaturalising poverty and Mexico's surplus population

Within the ambit of market-led development and its neoclassical economistic underpinnings, poverty is largely seen as the result of individual choices (e.g., lack of entrepreneurial skills, financial illiteracy) and/or poor governance mechanisms (e.g., lack of transparency, accountability, rule of law, consumer protection and so forth), which lead to the failure of states to capitalise on the ability of markets to achieve economic growth for the benefit of all (World Bank, 2000/2001, 2002a; cf. Chang and Grabel, 2004).[6] Seen from this view, the corrective to poverty is to include the poor in 'the financial' by, first, offering them credit and, second, ensuring that 'the financial' is properly governed, for instance, through the application of the G20 Principles for Innovative Financial Inclusion, which I analysed in Chapter 7.

In contrast to the above perspective, a Marxian understanding locates the primary causes of poverty in the nature of capital accumulation. In particular, it draws attention to the inability of workers to earn a living wage and the unwillingness of states to compensate these wages with publicly funded social programmes and benefits. This category of labour is deemed the 'relative surplus population' as it is superfluous to the valorisation of capital, which I demonstrate below (Marx, 1990). The surplus population is important to our analysis, as is represents the target of the microfinance industry. In the financial inclusion agenda, which masks any trace of exploitation and power, the surplus population is depoliticised, dehistoricised and homogenised. This occurs through the labelling of members of the surplus population as the 'unbanked', the 'financially excluded', the 'base of the pyramid', and so forth (cf. Dogra, 2012). I explore this in more detail later in the chapter.

For now, it is important to reconnect the unbanked to the surplus population. Readers will recall from Chapter 2 that surplus labour power is vital to the expansion of capital accumulation, as the presence of surplus workers serves as a powerful, class-based disciplinary strategy to justify the lowering of wages and benefits, threatening layoffs and increasing the intensity of work without compensation (Marx, 1990; Harvey, 1999; Bieler and Lindberg, 2010; Morton, 2011). For the purpose of our analysis, it is useful to give the surplus population in neoliberal Mexico (1982-present) some defining characteristics. To this end, I draw on the income bracket that the state deems too low for workers to afford a home in the formal (legal) market, namely: zero to four times the minimum wage, which I discuss in the context of housing finance in Chapter 7 (Herbert et al., 2012). In 2013, for instance, the Mexican state increased the minimum wage by 3.9 percent to 65 pesos ($5.10) per day ('Mexico raises minimum wage by 3.9 percent for 2013', Wall Street Journal, 20 August 2013).[7] This benchmark also reflects the microfinance industry's target population. A 2012 report commissioned by the Consultative Group to Assist the Poor (CGAP), for instance, designated the poor and underserved customers (surplus workers) as belonging to mid- to low-income households with earnings below 18,300 pesos ($1,450) per month, which amounted to 22 million households or roughly 85 percent of the population (CGAP, 2012b: 1).

The informal economy encompasses the space in which the majority of Mexico's surplus population is situated. The informal economy includes workers 'who are not officially listed as operating registered businesses, or employees not listed in the official accounting of the labour force as determined by social security or similar entities and working without officially sanctioned labour contracts' (Cypher and Delgado Wise, 2010: 26; see also Tokman, 2007). Based on the above income cut-off, some surplus workers are also found in the formal economy and can earn less than workers in the informal economy. The difference is that formalised workers have access to more social protections and benefits (World Bank, 2013b). However, it is the surplus population in the informal economy that has been the target of the for-profit microfinance industry, as well as Mexican and global debtfare policies since the 1990s (World Bank, 2001; CGAP, 2012b; Grupo Compartamos, 2012).

The making of poverty in neoliberal-led development

In the wake of the 1982 debt crisis, the Mexican state shifted from Import Substitution Industrialization (ISI)[8] to an Export Oriented Industrialization (EOI) accumulation strategy (Soederberg, 2004). This took place under the tutelage and pressures of powerful capitalists, who aligned themselves with the neoliberal dictates of the Washington Consensus and the wider neoliberal-led development agenda, With proper regulation and good fundamentals, market-based restructuring was expected to produce a situation in which everyone would be materially better off (IMF, 1992; von Waeyenberg, 2006). As I discussed in Chapter 3, neoliberal restructuring also involved imposing market discipline on Mexico's poor by cutting and redesigning social programmes. As in the case of the US workfare state, this was intended to reduce the dependency of the poor on state subsidisation (Peck, 2001; Yanes, 2011).

Mexican history has revealed this stance to be an economic fiction perpetrated by those who benefit materially from this understanding of development (Chang, 2002; Reinert, 2008). In contrast to the promises of the advocates of market-led growth, EOI has 'been marked by stagnation, astonishingly high levels of emigration and an exploding "informal" economy where perhaps a majority of the economic population ekes out a precarious hand-to-mouth existence' (Cypher and Delgado Wise, 2010: 9). Mexico has registered lower growth levels in the post-1980 neoliberal era than during the 1960 to 1980 period. Moreover, it has experienced a continued lack of international competitiveness in terms of export and capital markets, persistent current account deficits, problematic levels of public debt and increasing levels of socio-economic inequality (US Congressional Research Services, 2010; Puyana, 2010; see also Table 8.1).[9]

Mexico's comparative advantage continues to rest on its great quantity of cheap and unskilled labour – that is, the surplus population. As many authors have suggested, the North American Free Trade Agreement (NAFTA) has been characterised by a tendency toward deindustrialisation (Cypher, 2001; Soederberg, 2004). As Kathryn Kopinak (1994) notes, the new industries in the *maquiladora* sector offer fewer jobs than the number lost from Mexican-owned industry and agriculture.[10] As *maquiladoras* expanded, manufacturing as a share of GDP stagnated and the manufacturing share of the labour force diminished (Jonakin, 2006). Moreover, jobs in the *maquiladoras* are comparatively unskilled and poorly paid, which results in a reduction in purchasing power and, in turn, an increase in economic inequality and inability to meet basic subsistence needs (Kopinak, 1994; Soederberg, 2004).

While EOI and trade liberalisation were to bring about economic growth in Mexico, the service sector (e.g., commerce, restaurants and hotels, communal

TABLE 8.1 Current account balance, 1990–2011 (US $ millions)

	1990	1995	2000	2005	2007	2009	2011
Exports of goods, services, and income	54,570	96,707	192,425	257,418	323,429	251,216	374,702
Imports of goods and services	63,504	98,571	211,531	262,252	332,110	277,768	406,633
Current Account Balance	–7,451	–1,576	–18,684	–4,386	–8,335	–5,021	–9,030

Sources: World Bank (2010a) *Global Development Bank – Debt*, Washington, DC: World Bank, p. 192; World Bank (2013a) *International Debt Statistics 2013*, Washington, DC: World Bank, p. 202.

services and construction) generated more jobs than manufacturing over the 1988 to 2008 period (Dussel Peters 2000; Puyana, 2010). From 1993 to 2008 and in contrast to neoliberal assumptions, growth rates in the relatively better paying jobs in manufacturing fell below lower paying employment in the service sector. Indeed, growth rates in Mexico remain below those registered under the Import Substitution Industrialization accumulation strategy, which spanned from the 1940s to late 1970s (United Nations, 2010; Morton, 2011).

The informal economy (e.g., street vendors, domestic labour, agricultural workers and so forth) increased prior to and after the signing of NAFTA, from 61 percent in 1991 to 64 percent in 2009. According to employment surveys, the percentage of the labour force that does not receive any income, or receives only twice the minimum wage, accounted for 66 percent and 65 percent of the work force in the years 1991 and 2009, respectively (Puyana, 2010: 15). Due to the absence of unemployment insurance in Mexico, the unemployed have to find work mainly in the informal economy. Employment with no contracts and no social security has meant that for many – and informal workers in particular – the embrace of market-led reforms imbued in the EOI have not translated into wage gains.

According to the Economic Policy Institute (2001: 12), 'underemployment and work in low-pay, low-productivity jobs (e.g., unpaid work in family enterprises) actually has grown rapidly' since the signing of NAFTA in 1994. In their attempts to earn subsistence wages, many Mexicans risk life and limb to gain employment that will yield a living wage, largely as illegal migrant labourers in the informal economy in the United States (LeBaron, 2014). Indeed, cheap, unskilled and often illegal, labour to the US has become an important Mexican export (Cypher and Delgado Wise, 2010). As I discussed in Chapter 4, Mexican migrant workers have also fuelled the expansion of the poverty industry in the United States.

Mexico's abundant less-skilled and underemployed workforce has also been experiencing worsening conditions of employment due to the nature of EOI accumulation and structural violence through the weakening of union power and overall labour flexibilisiation policies imposed by the neoliberal state. This has been exacerbated by increasing competition, most notably from China. From 1996 to 2002, Mexican workers' wages deteriorated by 50 percent in terms of their purchasing power and 73 percent of the population could no longer afford the shopping basket of 40 basic items (Charnock 2005: 6; Jonakin, 2006). According to a study conducted by Bank of America Merrill Lynch, Mexico's hourly wages are about a fifth lower than China's, its largest competitor – a huge turnaround from just ten years ago, when they were nearly three times higher ('Mexican labour: cheaper than China', *Financial Times*, 5 April 2013). This drop in wages was, however, not a natural reaction to the competitive forces of an apolitical, self-regulating market. Instead, it was an attempt to depress earnings, which were far from providing an adequate living wage, through coercive capitalist tactics, such as threatening to layoff or fire workers. Such tactics are only feasible due to the presence of a vast surplus labour force. By the mid-2000s, for instance, the EOI strategy was accompanied by one of the highest rates of unemployment.

To legitimate the alleged validity of market-led restructuring in the face of growing unemployment and underemployment, the Mexican state considers anyone who works for one hour of one day per week to be employed (Álvarez Béjar, 2006).

Credit-led accumulation emerged from the lack of profitable outlets in Mexico's EOI-led accumulation strategy. By the mid-1990s, for instance, private capital flows to Mexico began to overshadow public funds from bilateral and multilateral organisations, including aid (World Bank, 2012c). The high interest rates needed to keep inflation low as well as to draw in and retain much-needed foreign capital flows, for instance, have tended to attract short-term, speculative capital, much to the detriment of Mexico's productive structure (Zapata, 2006). While foreign direct investment in production facilities increased by 57.6 percent from 1989 to 1993, more mobile portfolio investment rose by more than 8,000 percent, or 86.8 percent of total foreign investment (Pastor 1999). The rise of credit-led accumulation does not imply a separation from the realm of production, however. The importance of a disciplined labour force is as important as signaling high interest rates and guaranteeing the value of money when luring private capital. As the Banco de México states, one of the reasons that foreign investment flows are attracted to Mexico is because of 'temporary contracts, low hourly wages and a reduction in wage compensation after labour disputes' (Banco de México, 2013: 10).

To encourage inflows of credit money from abroad, the Mexican state has pursued soft regulatory framings for the financial system, while actively pursuing monetarist policies in an attempt to control inflation through the reduction of money supply (Correa, 2006; Banco de México, 2013). The monetarist ideology is fuelled by the belief that unemployment, regarded as largely voluntary, will be resolved when markets achieve an equilibrium, thus bestowing benefits on all members of society (see Chapter 3). Closely tied to the dominance of monetarism in Mexico was the insistence of pursuing tight fiscality (austerity programmes), which was also aimed at limiting inflation (Soederberg, 2010c; Marois, 2012, 2014). Many socio-economic and political consequences of monetarism in Mexico impact the microfinance industry. Two specific consequences stand out for the analysis here. One is that this neoliberal policy direction served to weaken already frail social programmes, thereby shifting the reliance of Mexico's surplus population from state subsidies to private lenders. The second is that it ushered in speculative credit money primarily, although not exclusively, from the United States (Soederberg, 2004).

Overall, credit-led accumulation has proven to be detrimental to the Mexican economy.[11] The 1994–1995 peso crash and the 2008 financial crisis, speculative inflows render the economy vulnerable when investors (both Mexican and foreign) suddenly exited the country (Grabel, 1999; Williams, 2001; Hart-Landsberg, 2002; Soederberg, 2004; Marois, 2014). For approximately half of Mexico's population, the peso crash resulted in swelling rates of poverty and unemployment levels (United Nations, 2011). As with the 2008 financial crash, the aftermath of the speculative-led feeding frenzy of 1994–1995 peso debacle left the surplus population to contend with more costly prices on basic subsistence items such as food and rent as well as higher levels of unemployment (Puyana, 2010; Cypher and Delgado Wise,

2010). What is more, to defend the peso against speculators, the Mexican state, as with other countries in the global South, built up a substantial war chest of foreign exchange reserves to the detriment of state spending on infrastructure projects and social programmes (Ocampo *et al.*, 2007; Soederberg, 2010d; World Bank, 2013a).

The surplus population in Mexico has not benefitted from credit-led accumulation, in terms of either job creation or access to formal and affordable banking services. Nonetheless, policies pursued in the late 1990s were aimed at further liberalising the financial sector, which has led to the expansion and concentration of foreign ownership of banks, particularly from the United States, Canada and Spain, whose ownership levels topped 85 percent of all banks in Mexico in 2005 (Marois, 2012). Throughout the 2000s, the large, commercial banks catered to consumption lending (credit cards, personal loans and durable goods loans) for middle-class and wealthy Mexicans. Consumption lending proved to be a lucrative business and grew rapidly throughout the new millennium. Credit cards alone represented 51 percent of consumer banking loans in the early 2000s (World Bank, 2005a).

To sum up: In contrast to neoliberal postulates that market-led growth delivers universal benefits, capital accumulation in Mexico has yielded profits and interest-generating income for powerful capitalists, both inside and outside of the country, to the detriment of over half the population, who are surplus labour toiling in the economically precarious and insecure spaces of informality. Aside from revealing the roots of impoverishment of the so-called 'base of the pyramid', the above analysis has sought to shift our gaze away from the narrow and depoliticising boundaries of the realm of exchange, where the naturalisation of poverty and much of the analyses of the microfinance industry takes place, to the wider dynamics of capital accumulation.

The above framing helps us see that the reliance of the surplus population on privately created money (i.e., microfinance credit) is neither a natural feature of the market nor the result of voluntary inclusion (market freedom); but instead, a constructed act in which debtfarism plays a central role. As I demonstrate below, the decision of a surplus worker to choose to enter into a debt relationship with a microfinance institution is, in actuality, driven and shaped by the constructed silent compulsions and structural violence of neoliberal-led capitalism, including the role of the debtfare state, which regularises, individualises and depoliticises the microfinance industry.

Debtfarism and the commercialisation of the microfinance industry

In this section, I explore debtfarism in two ways. First, I examine some of the state's rhetorical interventions aimed at depoliticising the surplus population by recreating the assumption that poverty is something natural and voluntary to be resolved within the realm of exchange. Second, I analyse the regulative and rhetorical roles played by the Mexican debtfare state, as well as global debtfarism (see Chapter 7), in facilitating the expansion of formalised microfinance institutions

(MFIs) to support capitalist interests while providing a market-led solution to the social reproduction of the surplus population.

Relocating surplus labour in the realm of exchange: the politics of rebranding the poor as unbanked/financially excluded

In the 1990s, MFIs, many of which were reliant on some form of external aid, were strongly encouraged to become fully commercialised and privatised by their multilateral (e.g., IMF, World Bank) and bilateral (e.g., USAID) donors (Roy, 2010; Bateman, 2010). To meet these new objectives, many MFIs began re-orienting the social mission that purportedly drove their lending practices to the dictates of profit-maximisation by introducing market-based interest rates, cutting subsidies and encouraging savings (World Bank, 2001, 2009a; Harper, 2011). The commercialisation of MFIs was not a natural phenomenon, however. The shift to for-profit lending to the surplus population had to be legitimately constructed and normalised.

Debtfarist attempts at regularising for-profit MFIs as a solution to poverty involved multiple strategies (see Chapter 7). Here, I identify two important postulates in the Mexican context. First, commercialised MFIs are more efficient and effective in reducing poverty than their non-profit counterparts. Second, the poor are economic actors, who operate on a level playing field (i.e., devoid of power, history and politics) and who possess, or can be made to possess, the same rational skills and utility-maximising calculus as all 'successful' (read: 'non-poor') economic actors (Rankin, 2001). The primary rhetorical means to legitimate and actualise these neoliberal assumptions was to confine the surplus population to the realm of exchange and to leverage the social power of money to provide illusions of democracy, equality and freedom. The poor are thereby rebranded as the unbanked, the financially excluded, or the base of the pyramid (BOP). The realm of exchange effectively becomes 'the financial' into which the poor are included to alleviate the conditions of poverty.[12]

To deconstruct the rhetorical processes of debtfarism at work here, it is useful to centre our investigation on two basic questions: Who are the unbanked and financially excluded? And, why have they been drawn into commercial microlending? According to CGAP, a leading member of the epistemic community committed to financial inclusion, Mexico, like many developing countries, is still predominantly an informal, cash-based economy. Only 15 to 25 percent of urban households and as few as 6 percent of rural households have accounts with formal financial institutions and payment systems (CGAP, 2006). On this view, there is room for formalised banking systems, such as mobile banking and retail banking, to expand their operations under the rubric of financial inclusion and, by extension, to contribute to Mexico's 'growth potential' through 'innovative' poverty reduction (World Bank, 2006; Banco de México, 2011).[13]

The implication here is that the unbanked demographic continues to rely on largely inefficient and unregulated informal lending institutions, including *Cajas de ahorros populares*, moneylenders, friends and relatives and pawnshops, such as the longstanding, non-profit institute Monte de Piedad (World Bank, 2005a; Francois, 2006). Two points are worth mentioning with regard to the efficiency of the formal lending sector. First, while some moneylenders and pawnshops may charge interest rates up to 300 percent (APR), *Cajas de ahorros* charge, on average, lower rates than the commercialised microfinance lenders discussed below. Second, although informal lenders remain unregulated in Mexico, the formalised microfinance industry is predominately regulated by soft laws and some SOFOMES were designed by the state to be free from any regulatory restriction. Given the lax regulations in place governing the microfinance industry in Mexico (e.g., the absence of interest rate ceilings, weak consumer protection laws), the further leeway granted to SOFOMES is a strategy undertaken by debtfarism to entice capitalists, both inside and outside Mexico, to lend to the surplus population.

To construct legitimate social spaces for commercialised microfinance institutions (MFIs), it is necessary for the debtfare state to delegitimise informal lending. According to the official development rhetoric, while informal lending organisations provide a valuable service to the poor, their lack of accountability and transparency make them an inefficient means of moving Mexicans out of poverty and helping the unbanked strengthen and expand what the World Bank refers to as the poor's 'asset bases' (World Bank, 2005a). Following this line of reasoning, commercialised MFIs play an essential role in ending poverty insomuch as they encourage responsible and rational behaviour among the poor. That is, MFIs put everyone on the same page in terms of profit maximisation. The bottom line for the poor is that accessing credit from a commercial MFI is a win–win situation. According to the World Bank's study, 'banked households borrow far more than the unbanked and are also more likely to report consumption smoothing in the face of negative income shocks, suggesting that the opening of bank accounts does not just reallocate financial transactions to the formal sector but also has real welfare impacts' (World Bank, 2008). Consumption smoothing refers to the ability to draw on savings or borrow in times of uncertainty caused by, for example, job loss, death or illness, or to purchase basic survival items and services (World Bank, 2001, 2009b).

The neoliberal assumption driving the financial inclusion agenda is that the extension of commercialised credit to poorer segments of the population will create 'responsible', individualised and rational market citizens. The poor will learn to save and make regular and timely repayments on their debt. Fostering this entrepreneurial spirit among the unbanked allows profitable banking markets to thrive alongside growing consumption in durable and non-durable goods. This, in turn, helps to stimulate the economy and lead to growth from which everyone will benefit – at least in theory (World Bank, 2009).[14] It follows from this position that providing inclusive financial access is a logical, market-based strategy for ensuring the poor can lift themselves out of poverty (World Bank, 2004a, 2007a). The point also remains that by labelling the poor 'unbanked' debtfarism relegates the surplus population, and the causes of poverty, to the realm of exchange (Alliance for Financial Inclusion, 2013). Seen from this angle, the rhetoric of debtfarism and its emphasis on the realm of exchange, serves to facilitate the expansion of commercialised MFIs by erasing the links between the root causes of poverty and the power relations in capital accumulation.

The debtfarist rhetoric of financial inclusion also serves to homogenise and dehumanise the surplus population. According to a World Bank (2008) study entitled *Who Are the Unbanked?*, 60 percent of the unbanked in Mexico belong to a 'marginalised' group, since they work in the informal sector. However, the source of this marginalisation is erased by relocating the poor to the realm of exchange; that is, as the 'unbanked' or the 'financially excluded',[15] which masks the historical forms of structural violence with which workers have to contend under neoliberal-led accumulation (Hellman, 1988; Francois, 2006; Cypher and Delgado Wise, 2010; Morton, 2011; Marois, 2012). The surplus population is represented as a static group of poor people, who lack either proper financial education and/or an entrepreneurial spirit to overcome impoverishment. This point can best be illustrated by the manner in which financial inclusion represents gender.

According to the World Bank (2006), 80.9 percent of females in Mexico remain unbanked and three-quarters of these unbanked households have children or economic dependents. The underlying causes of their destitution cannot be explained away by lack of access to expensive forms of privately created money. Worse still is the fact that women are objectified and dehumanised in the financial inclusion rhetoric. In the microfinance industry, women are represented as relatively less risky investment choices because of innate gendered characteristics, such as the responsibility to nurture and work harder (Grupo Compartamos, 2012). By emphasising and thus reproducing, these constructed biological and social attributes of gender, the historical context of structural violence and the relations of power inherent to capital accumulation in Mexico – the factors that compel women to turn to high-priced credit to attempt to nourish, clothe, house and educate their families – are erased from the analysis (cf. Mohanty, 1995; Dogra, 2012). Another invisible feature of the monetised, as opposed to personalised, relations between women of the surplus population and creditors are the coercive tactics employed by MFIs (e.g., group pressure, forced savings) designed to ensure that women meet their loan payments (Rankin, 2001; Roberts and Soederberg, 2012; Kumar, 2013). I pick this theme up again later in the chapter.

For now, it is important to stress that by masking the connection between the surplus population and the processes of capital accumulation, the fundamental causes of the making and remaking of marginalisation in Mexico are expunged from the dominant financial inclusion rhetoric. Aside from naturalising poverty, the rebranding of the surplus population into the unbanked population in the realm of exchange also facilitates the proposed solution: financial inclusion. This strategy, as discussed in the previous chapters, implies that the removal of barriers to the realm of exchange ensures not only that all individuals are active market participants (savers and consumers), but also that these individuals, regardless of considerations of place, race, class and gender, are on equal footing (level playing field) (World Bank, 2005a). This neoliberal representation of the surplus population as economic actors devoid of context with respect to the material basis of power, history and inequality is starkly evident in Table 8.2.[16]

The typology of the poor prevalent in microfinance lending erases any trace of class-based power, inequality and exploitation from the representation of the realm of exchange that the poor are beckoned to join. The fact that the historically unfolding social structures of neoliberal-led capitalism have been removed from

TABLE 8.2 Rebranding surplus labour as unbanked: an illustration of a typology of poverty in Mexico (in US $)

Type of livelihood	Formal salaried	Informal salaried	Entrepreneurs	Seasonal/ agricultural
Average household income	$12/day	$15/day	$10/day	$4–10/day
Income structure	Fixed income at fixed periods of time –Fortnight or weekly	Variable amount at fixed periods of time –Weekly income perceived consistently but amount paid varies depending on hours worked or sales	Variable amount-daily –Income depends mostly on daily transactions, which vary day-to-day	Variable amount at irregular periods of time –Income from farming (agriculture and animal farming) is low and uncertain
Example of livelihood	–Store clerk –Plant employee –Janitor	–Cook at informal food stand –Wage worker –Construction worker	–Taxi driver –Merchant –Street vendor	–Smallholder farmer –Dairy products –Animal farming
Attitude/ behaviour	Prefer certainty; actively set and manage goals; focused in planning ahead; weary of credit Natural savers	Accustomed to uncertainty. Constant worry of meeting basic needs. Less rational choices	Business minded; seek opportunities to make money; risk taker; multiple financial relationships open at a time	Low-skilled, limited abilities to build financial assets; focused on getting by
Financial management strategy	Saving and Planning to fulfil aspirations	Managing cash to meet expenses	Actively managing financial assets	Managing costs with limited options

Source: CGAP (2012a) 'A Structured Approach to Understanding the Financial Service Needs of the Poor in Mexico'. Washington, DC: Consultative Group to Assist the Poor (CGAP), p. 3.

any discussion of poverty and its alleviation in the wider financial inclusion rhetoric has meant that the working poor in Mexico are often given no choice but to rely on private forms of money to meet basic subsistence needs. This is never problematised. As such, the inability or unwillingness of the marginalised (surplus population) to join the financial in order to overcome poverty is viewed as an individual weakness.

Opening and legitimising spaces of dispossession in the informal economy

In 2001, the Mexican state introduced a series of banking and financial sector reforms aimed at improving transparency to attract more investors. These included the Securities Market Law and the Mutual Funds Law (World Bank, 2005a). Against this backdrop, the state implemented the Popular Savings and Credit Act in 2001 (hereafter: 2001 Law) (World Bank, 2004a). The 2001 Law provides for the continuing integration of all non-bank savings and credit institutions into a new legal and regulatory agenda that aims 'to massively scale-up access to financial services for poor and marginalised people' (World Bank, 2004a: 6). At the time, this amounted to half of the Mexican population.

Two points are worth highlighting with regard to the 2001 Law. First, one of its main aims was to protect the interests of the public (World Bank, 2005a). The protection offered by the debtfare state was in the form of consumer protection, which, as we discussed in Chapter 7, is couched in soft law. Second, the 2001 Law did not include commercialised MFIs. A 2010 report issued by the National Banking and Securities Commission notes that 'In Mexico there are no accounting records to identify and separate microcredit portfolio from commercial use; the definition of microcredit was recently established in regulation of savings and loans in January 2008' (CNBV, 2010: 3). The regulatory institution goes on to suggest that outstanding issues that remain in the for-profit microfinance industry are, for instance, the need for transparency and credit bureaus and developing best practices for giving 'proper credit' (CNBV, 2010: 9).

To undergird the capitalist expansion of credit-led accumulation into the spaces of informality, as well as to strengthen the rhetoric of financial inclusion through for-profit MFIs, the Mexican debtfare state passed various legal reforms for financial services consumers under the rubric of consumer protection. In 1992, for instance, the state issued the Law for the Protection and Defence of Financial Services Users (hereafter: 1992 Law), which was the precursor to the 2007 Transparency Law discussed in Chapter 7. To support the 1992 Law, the Mexican state created a de-centralised body with a legal personality: the National Commission for the Defense of Financial Services Users, or CONDUSEF. [17] As noted in Chapter 7, CONDUSEF was mandated with promoting, advising, protecting and defending the rights of individuals who use financial products or buy financial services.

The 1992 Law was considered by many observers to be a significant advance for financial services consumer protection in Mexico, as it established that the rights granted by the act are itself are inalienable (IMF, 2012b). However and keeping with the soft law framings for market actors, financial institutions operating in Mexico are not obliged to abide by CONDUSEF's recommendations (Diaz, 2009). As such and despite the significance accorded to the 1992 Law and CONDUSEF, the commission only began functioning seven years later in 1999. Since that time, both the conciliatory and dispute resolution functions are still de facto ineffective. In the same year the 2007 Transparency Act was decreed, the commission solved 29 percent of the conciliation reports. During this same year, only three cases were brought to arbitration (CNBV, 2010). As with the case of the United States, consumer protection in Mexico is premised on the state's unwillingness to limit predatory lending, that is, the impose a ceiling on interest rates (Raccanello and Romero, 2011).

In addition to the above weaknesses regarding consumer protection, there are at least two further regulative gaps pertaining to bankruptcy protection and debt collection – both of which reveal the class-based power of the microfinance industry. Mexico's insolvency system for debtors is still governed by a legal framework forged in the nineteenth century, which is based on liquidation-without-discharge and fundamentally provides no incentive for distressed debtors to seek a safe haven in the bankruptcy courts (World Bank, 2012b). An update to the insolvency law in 2000 (*Ley de Concursos Mercantiles*) was applied to a total of just 305 insolvency cases out of 906 insolvency filings over a two-year period. The law was found to be 'so inadequate that in the vast majority of instances, debtors and creditors strive to avoid having to involve themselves with it and settle out of court instead' ('Mexican Law Firm Calls for Creditor Protection', *World Finance*, 1 November 2013).

The absence of a 'fresh start' mechanism in Mexico's bankruptcy system parallels the draconian revisions of the 2005 Bankruptcy Abuse and Consumer Protection Act (BAPCPA) (see Chapter 4; Coco, 2012). Mirroring the BAPCPA, the Mexican bankruptcy system also encourages debtors to stay out of bankruptcy, thereby leaving them exposed to the disciplinary features of the market and, in the case of group lending, the debtor's (monetised) community (Rankin, 2001; Taylor, 2011). Notwithstanding the Mexican Consumer Protection Law and CONDUSEF, the Mexican state has also failed to implement any comprehensive regulation with regard to debt collectors. According to a report issued by the Association of Credit and Collection Professionals, while debt collection costs can be charged to debtors in Mexico, there is no limit placed on these costs, although payment of the collection costs are enforced by the state (ACA International, 2010). More importantly, the absence of legal oversight of debt collection implies no protection from coercive tactics pursued by creditors to collect monies owed. The power of creditors (capitalists) over debtors (surplus labour) is clearly visible in these gaps in the consumer protection laws.

One year after the abovementioned 1992 Law was enacted, the Mexican state pursued a two-fold strategy. In the wider context of NAFTA negotiations and the need for American and Canadian financial institutions to expand into lending activities in Mexico, the state reformed the Law of Credit Institutions to create Limited Purpose Financial Companies, or SOFOLS, in 1993.[18] On the other hand, the creation of SOFOLS was seen by the Mexican state as a way to create financing for more low-income workers, who were neglected by mainstream commercial banks (World Bank, 2006). SOFOLS, which mostly finance the purchase of consumer durables, especially automobiles, may only provide credit services to one sector of the economy, such as personal loans, home mortgages, construction financing, corporate financing and loans for small and medium sized enterprises (World Bank, 2007b). As I discuss in following chapter, SOFOLS played a key role in the securitisation of housing finance in the 2000s. Compartamos and Financiera Independencia both began the ascent to Wall Street by transforming a non-profit organisation into a SOFOL in 2000 (CGAP, 2007a).

In addition to these regulations, the Mexican debtfare state has also sought to expand and 'modernise' (read: marketise) what is referred to as the 'social financial sector', that is, co-operatives and credit unions (World Bank, 2006). In 2008, for example, the Mexican government passed a Credit Union Law that would expand activities of credit unions and bring them in line with international governance standards. Some of the revisions pertinent to our discussion include the removal of restrictions on foreign investment, limiting the membership of credit unions to parties engaged in business and allowing credit unions to acquire shares in companies (with the commission's prior authorisation) (International Law Office, 2008). Aside from rhetorical insistence on good corporate governance practices and transparency, there remains a lack of effective consumer protection schemes.

This section has demonstrated that the rhetorical and regulative roles of Mexican debtfarism served to normalise the commercialisation MFIs as a poverty alleviation strategy for the surplus population, as well as facilitate the expansion of for-profit micro-financing lending in Mexico. The next section examines how this framing has facilitated the expansion and concentration of power and wealth in the microfinance industry as well as how this phenomenon has assisted in the social reproduction of Mexico's surplus population.

The microfinance industry: the expansion of monetised power and the social reproduction of surplus workers

Compartamos

Since 2000, for-profit MFIs in Mexico have experienced strong growth, as millions of (primarily) Mexican women who live in spaces of informality have attempted to gain more economic security for themselves and their families by becoming small-scale entrepreneurs (Bateman, 2010; Harper, 2011). A key player in this area of lending for the purpose of establishing micro-enterprises has been Compartamos Banco (translated as, Let's Share Bank), currently one of the most lucrative MFIs in the world and the largest micro-finance lender in Latin America. Operating in Mexico, Guatemala and Peru, Compartamos Banco has been registering annualised returns of around 43 percent since its transformation into a publicly listed corporation in 2007 (Rodriguez and Huerga, 2012). Compartamos began in 1982 as a youth organisation (Gente Nueva) aimed at improving the quality of life of marginalised peoples. Since this time, Compartamos expanded its operations throughout Mexico while maintaining its lucrative status. Against the backdrop of the push for commercialising MFIs in the 1990s, Compartamos transformed itself into a SOFOL to ensure a pool of loans from commercial investors so as to expand more rapidly (CGAP, 2007a).[19]

As I noted at the start of this chapter, Compartamos completed a landmark initial public offering (IPO) of its stock in 2007, thereby becoming the first MFI to transform itself into a publicly held corporation. The IPO has been a huge success and has generated high returns for shareholders. Compartamos has been dubbed 'one of Mexico's most financially successful banks, providing investors with an average annual return on equity of 53 percent from 2000 to 2007' ('Compartamos: from nonprofit to profit', *Businessweek*, 13 December 2007; Rodriguez and Huerga, 2012). In contrast with the mainstream narratives that the IPO was a natural phenomenon of the self-regulating market, Compartamos's IPO would not have been possible were it not for the lax regulatory and rhetorical framings provided by debtfarism.[20] The IPO was further enabled and legitimated by corporate welfarist strategies of global development agencies. The IPO would have not been possible, for instance, if key development agencies such as Accion International and the World Bank's International Finance Corporation, did not provide the financial and reputational backing for this move.[21]

A key reason for this financial success has been the extremely high interests charged by Compartamos. According to its website, the Bank's effective interest rate was 105 percent in 2007; the 2011 rate is estimated, depending on how one computes the interest, to be around 195 percent (Roodman, 2011). To put this interest rate in perspective, in Andhra Pradesh, the Indian state that has recently experienced a crisis of farmer suicides that have been linked, among other things, to high rates of indebtedness, the rate of interest was around 30 APR. The interest rates offered by Compartamos are well above this rate, e.g., 100 percent (CGAP, 2007a; Roodman, 2011; Taylor, 2011). Owing to the dominance of Compartamos, interest rates in the microfinance industry are believed to average 81 APR in Mexico (Bateman, 2010). To put these APRs into an even wider comparative context, the US payday lending industry has registered APRs ranging from 364 percent to 550 percent (see Chapter 6). In raising this observation, I am not suggesting that the high APRs in Mexico are insignificant. Instead, I wish to draw attention to the fact that even-higher interest rates on small consumer loans are realisable and normalised in a 'developed' country such as the United States. This does not bode well, given that payday lending is becoming a major growth phenomenon in the microfinance industry in Mexico (Euromonitor International, 2013).

As with most MFIs, Compartamos ensures repayment primarily through peer pressure mechanisms, ensuring that the bank is repaid, even if the small groups of mostly women clients have to make up the difference when a member is unable to meet her payment (Bateman, 2010; Taylor, 2011). Behind the dehistoricised and depoliticised claims that its clients 'are agents of change who are building a better country and world', Compartamos engages in secondary forms of exploitation that have made handsome dividends for shareholders (Roodman, 2011). There is a less visible and more coercive side to the community of money to which Compartamos belongs than that which it wishes to present to potential investors, borrowers and critics. Take, for example, Crédito Mujer ('Women's Credit'). This women's borrowing collective is not, as the rhetoric of Compartamos suggests, a cohesive group of agents of change. Under the pressures of debtfarism, surplus female workers must meet payments on a timely basis while desperately trying to cover basic subsistence needs. Women who fail to meet regular payments (so-called 'dropouts') are punished by the group and pushed further to the margins of their communities (Harper, 2011; Rankin, 2001, 2013).

Credit cards for surplus labour in the new millennium

Historically, major commercial banks in Mexico have not been interested in servicing the consumption needs of the surplus population through consumer credit loans. This began to change in the 2000s when a wave of for-profit banks began to arrive on the lending scene. As was the case with Compartamos and MFIs more generally, the debtfare state played a key role in facilitating the growth and high levels of income-generation in the retail-banking sector. This is readily observable with the case of credit cards in Mexico.

Although credit cards have been the fastest growing component of the financial system since 2000, representing 51 percent of consumer banking loans (World Bank, 2005a), the average per capita of credit cards circulating in Mexico in 2009 (0.6 cards per person) was nearly three times lower than the Latin American average (1.5 cards per person) (Franco, 2010). Visa-branded cards, which represent about 75 percent of total credit, dominate both the credit card market and ATM (debit) card market in Mexico (World Bank, 2005a). One consequence of this market domination is that Visa and MasterCard have effectively restricted entry into the credit card market. Assisted by the Mexican debtfare state, these card companies have influenced certain regulations such as ensuring that non-banks, such as retailers, cannot issue credit cards (World Bank, 2005a). An immediate result of this market control is that the annual interest rates of bank-based credit cards are high. In 2002, for example, the average rate was 39 APR, whereas at the start of 2011 the average rate was 30.1 APR in Mexico ('Mexico, interest rate record holder', *Mexican Business Web*, 8 September 2011).

Mexican banks have begun issuing credit cards, traditionally issued only to the most solvent consumers, to a much wider segment of the population, including surplus workers. According to a World Bank report, in the early to mid-2000s, card companies were aiming to serve Mexicans earning $180 to $550 per month (World Bank, 2005a). Given the power structures of the credit card industry in Mexico, credit cards for the poor are offered through different channels. Instead of the traditional commercial bank lender, retail lenders, such as Banco Walmart are now issuing a wide-range of credit cards to less solvent customers. I discuss the case of Banco Walmart below. For now, it is useful to explore briefly the growing integration between so-called fringe banking (commercial MFIs) and mainstream banking in Mexico – a phenomenon that is also evident in the poverty industry of the United States, as discussed in Part II of this book.

Banamex, Mexico's second-largest bank and a wholly owned unit of Citigroup, also forayed into the poverty industry by acquiring the MFI *Crédito Familiar* (Family Credit) in 2007. *Crédito Familiar* was established in 1996 to service working-class families. As of 2012, it includes 246 branches and serves 145,000 customers with an average loan size of just over $1,500 ('Scotiabank closes acquisitions of Credito Familiar', *Canada Newswire* 3 December 2012). According to data provided by the National Banking and Securities Commission (CNBV), Banamex's strategy of targeting what it estimates to be 112 million unbanked Mexicans (or about 55 to 65 percent of the country's population) has seen its outstanding loans increase by 22 percent over the 2011–2012 period ('Citigroup's Banamex sees outstanding loan growth in 2012', *Bloomberg*, 23 March 2013). In 2012, Banamex's *Crédito Familiar* program was acquired by a Canadian bank, Scotiabank. In its efforts to expand to the lucrative microfinance industry, not only in Mexico but also throughout Latin America (particularly Peru, Chile, Colombia, Jamaica, Uruguay and the Dominican Republic), Scotiabank stated that it could 'easily see a 15 to 20 percent compounded annual growth rate in the [base of the pyramid] segment', which it views as 'a source of future retail customers for us and a profitable business' ('Scotiabank to increase Small Loans in Mexico', *Bloomberg*, 18 January 2013).

The potential for reaping high-yielding interest from the surplus population has not been lost on retailers operating in Mexico. To overcome restrictions regarding the ability of non-bank entities to issue credit cards, retailers (e.g. Walmart) simply created banks. I discuss this more fully in the next section. Suffice it to say here that department stores such as Grupo Elektra and Walmart account for the largest source of credit for unbanked Mexicans (48.6 percent), which is considerable when compared to other sources of credit, such as friends (8.6 percent), credit unions (1.4 percent) and non-governmental organisations (1.4 percent) (World Bank, 2006). With the assistance of debtfarist interventions, large retailers have been able to transform and extend their credit operations by establishing themselves as banks and charging interest rates that far exceed the high levels of their chartered counterparts. In what follows, we explore the cases of Banco Azteca (a subsidiary of Grupo Elektra) and Banco Walmart.

Retail banking for the poor: the cases of Banco Azteca and Banco Walmart

In 2002, Banco Azteca opened over 800 locations focusing on low-income clients. Banco Azteca, like its parent, Grupo Elektra, Latin America's largest electronics and home appliance chain, enjoys the same ubiquitous presence and thus scale, that Walmart enjoys in Mexico. Similar to Walmart, Banco Azteca targets lower-income Mexicans, who account for around over 70 percent of total households earning between $5,100 and $33,600 per year and who form part of the informal economy. This group also includes small, informal businesses that lack the documentation necessary for obtaining bank loans (World Bank, 2009a). Drawing on Grupo Elektra's experience in making small instalment loans for its merchandise as well as its information and collection technologies, Banco Azteca charges annual percentage rates (APRs) ranging from 86 percent to over 100 percent. The bank operates on the same ethos of high-pressure employee quotas and incentives as its parent company, Grupo Elektra, particularly when it comes to convincing customers to spread payments over the longest possible period, i.e., 104 weeks. In 2012, Grupo Elektra's billionaire owner, Ricardo Salinas Pliego, acquired the largest payday lender in the United States, Advance America, which, as we saw in Chapter 6, charges the US surplus population much higher APRs than Banco Azteca ('Mexican billionaire buys advance America, largest payday lender in US', *Forbes*, 23 April 2012). This move not only reveals the continual trend toward the concentration of wealth in the poverty industry, but also the global dimensions of debtfarism and credit-led accumulation.

Banco Azteca has proven to be a lucrative venture, evident in its 22.3 percent return on shareholder equity ('The ugly side of micro-lending', *BusinessWeek*, 13 December 2007). In the absence of any meaningful regulation of debt collection by creditors, the well-organised and highly coercive features of Azteca's operations, including 3,000 loan officers and collection agents (*jefes de crédito y cobranza*) has proven highly effective in recouping delinquent payments. The World Bank, which has supported the initiatives of Azteca and similar organisations, has suggested that 'access to credit and savings of low income households has a significant impact on the labour market and income levels' in Mexico. At the same time, the World Bank also finds that while income levels for men and women increased, they did not improve enough to raise them completely out of poverty (World Bank, 2009a: 2). It is not too difficult to grasp that the surplus population, who, for the most part, neither earn living wages nor are entitled to social benefits (e.g., old age pensions, health care and so forth), have little expendable income after paying for basic subsistence needs to save.[22]

In the absence of effective consumer protection laws, particularly with regard to personal bankruptcy and collection agencies, the Mexican debtfare state has facilitated both the coercive and disciplinary techniques used by financial institutions like Azteca. With the assistance of its *jefes de crédito y cobranza* customers who fail to meet a payment are dispossessed of their basic and often shared familial, possessions in order to cover their debt. Due to its coercive debt-collection practices and its equally unregulated accounting practices, Banco Azteca claims a default rate on consumer loans of just one percent compared with banks serving more affluent clients, which average a 5.3 percent default rate ('The ugly side of micro-lending', *Businessweek*, 13 December 2007). In its efforts to ensure that as many unbanked Mexicans as possible are integrated into the web of credit relations, the debtfare state has also facilitated Azteca's ongoing dispossession strategies by granting the company exception status with regard to disclosure laws, which require banks to inform their customers of the total financing costs being charged. When Banco Azteca's average lending rate is translated into an Annual Percentage Rate (APR), used in countries like the United States, it amounts to 110 APR, double Azteca's claim of 55 APR. The primary reason for this is that Azteca charges interest on the entire amount borrowed throughout the life of the loan, not on the declining balance, as is common practice in the US ('Mexico toughens consumer credit rules for banks', *Reuters*, 9 December 2008; CNBV, 2010).

In November 2006, the Mexican debtfare state approved Walmart's Mexican subsidiary to operate a bank. Tellingly, Walmart failed to secure banking privileges in the United States, where banking and retail are still separated (Gelpern, 2007). The rhetorical justification behind the Mexican state's approval of the creation of Banco Walmart was to increase competition in the concentrated banking sector, to help reach the three-quarters of the surplus population and eventually to aid in lowering the cost of consumer borrowing. Walmart is Mexico's largest retail chain with over 997 locations, which include super centres, food and clothing stores and restaurants. Lowering the costs of credit is not, however, something Banco Walmart has been striving to achieve, with its credit cards hovering around 94.3 APR.

Banco Walmart is taking full advantage of a market where annual interest rates often exceed 100 percent. For example, a low-income Mexican worker can obtain a $1,100 Whirlpool refrigerator for 104 weekly payments of $23, which more than doubles the cost to $2,392. Banco Walmart is a highly profitable venture, which offers customers their first-ever savings accounts, credit cards (*Super Crédito* credit card) and microfinancing (supplier development through its *Credimpulsa* programme) ('Walmart banks on the "unbanked"', *Bloomberg BusinessWeek*, 13 December 2007). In 2011, Banco Walmart celebrated opening its 1 millionth account and announced its plans to open 62 new branches, which represents an increase of 24 percent over 2010. The primary aim of Walmart, aside from generating revenue through its high interest rate policy, is to eventually become a key source of credit for low-income Mexicans, so that they can buy Walmart products ('Walmart's Mexico bank aims at first-time savers', *Reuters*, 18 June 2010). The Mexican debtfare state reinforced these efforts by altering banking regulations to allow authorised retailers to use their cash registers as virtual bank branches, so that customers can make deposits and withdrawals from their accounts (Mas and Almazán, 2011).

Sofomes

The last example of for-profit actors in the microfinance industry that we will attend to in this chapter is the Multiple Purpose Financial Companies (*Sociedad Financiera de Objeto Mutiple*, or SOFOMES). SOFOMES are completely unregulated (CNBV, 2010). They were created by the debtfare state in 2006 in order to facilitate the expansion of SOFOLS and increase lending to the surplus population. In contrast to SOFOLS, SOFOMES are permitted to provide financing – for example, direct loans, financial leasing, or factoring – to more than one economic sector, e.g., mortgages and car loans (World Bank, 2012c). The Mexican debtfare state ensured that SOFOMES would be free from virtually all governmental regulation and oversight, unless a minimum of 20 percent of their stock is owned by a regulated, commercial bank.[23] As an added perk, SOFOMES have no limitations on foreign ownership. While SOFOMES may not accept deposits or provide saving services, they can receive funds through capital market transactions, government funds, self-financing (e.g., asset-backed securitisation) and lines of credit from development or private banks.

It is little wonder that since the mid-2000s, major financial institutions have been attracted to the high interest on MFIs. Hedge funds, venture capital firms and other big players such as pension funds are jostling to get in on the action. According to Scott Budde, a managing director at the US pension colossus, TIAA-CREF, which aims to invest $100 million in micro-financing, MFIs are 'not a charitable activity [. . .] We're looking to produce competitive returns' ('Micro-finance draws mega players', *Businessweek*, 9 July 2007). As of 2011, the number of unregulated SOFOMES officially registered with the CONDUSEF was 2,843, compared with 1,622 in 2010 (Banco de México, 2011).

In what follows, I briefly examine two unregulated SOFOMES: Financiera Independencia[24] and Crédito Real.[25] Both institutions lend to the low-income segment of the population, targeting primarily individuals in the adult working population who earn a household monthly income between $230 and $1,000). According to a US-based institutional investor, this represents 66.2 percent of the approximately 21.9 million Mexican households (BCP Securities, 2010). Founded as a SOFOL in 1993, Financiera Independencia provided loans to surplus workers in Mexico, drawing its financing primarily from state funds and international donors. It expanded rapidly in the 2000s. The banking behemoth, HSBC, acquired 20 percent of Financiera's shares only to resell 18.68 percent for $145 million to JP Morgan in 2008 ('HSBC sells 18.68 percent stake in Financiera Independencia for $145 million', *Wall Street Journal*, 19 September 2008). As with Compartamos, Financiera Independencia sold 20 percent of its shares in an initial public offering (IPO) in 2007. Since its IPO, Financiera Independencia has been one of the most lucrative and largest MFIs in Latin America (Multilateral Investment Fund, 2012). In February 2010, Financiera Independencia acquired the second-largest microfinance institution in Mexico after Compartamos, Financiera Finsol, thereby further concentrating power in the for-profit microfinance industry (BCP Securities, 2010).

Crédito Real is a privately held SOFOM, which is owned by Nexxus Capital and three powerful Mexican families, who also control Mabe, a Mexican-based conglomerate that designs, produces and distributes appliances.[26] Crédito Real is a leading payroll lending (the Mexican version of payday lending[27]), durable goods financing and micro-credit finance company, targeting the low- and middle-income segments of the population. The company offers various forms of direct and indirect financing in amounts ranging from $250 to $2,500. Payroll lending accounts for 79 percent of Crédito Real's total loan portfolio. Originated by independent distributors, these loans are not made to the poorest segments of the surplus population, but rather to low-income workers in the formal economy (BCP Securities, 2010). The rapid rise of payroll loans – a type of payday loan – has alarmed the Mexican state and investors alike, as loans are believed to be growing at a faster rate than the number of borrowers, which signals an increasing rate of indebtedness and a corresponding rise in the likelihood of delinquencies and defaults (EuroMonitor International, 2013: 1). In the wake of the 2008 financial crisis, a worrying and unusual trend identified by the Banco de México is compounding this issue: private capital inflows have been increasing since 2010 in the area of non-bank lending, that is, financial institutions not considered full-scale banks, which are authorised to engage in other lending services, such as the above discussed MFIs (Banco de México, 2013).

These concerns have prompted discussions and debates about the need to regulate the SOFOMES, given that these entities raise funds in the capital markets and, therefore, present systemic risk (Castañeda *et al.*, 2011). In 2013, the Mexican debtfare state sought to bring the unregulated SOFOMES within the wider regulatory regime of other SOFOMES, if they have economic ties with popular savings and credit cooperatives as well as savings and loans entities. According to the International Financial Law Review (IFLR), the reforms would also benefit commercial banks, as it will reduce competition from 3,000 unregulated SOFOMES ('Exclusive: Mexico's imminent financial overhaul dissected', *IFLR*, 8 May 2013). Regardless of these proposed reforms regarding the SOFOMES, it must be kept in mind that in the neoliberal era, these new regulations continue to be characterised largely by soft law and voluntary regulation. It should come as no surprise that SOFOMES have continued to increase in number and lending capacity up until the time of this writing ('Número de sofomes crece en el 2013', *El Economista*, 29 May 2013).

Concluding remarks

This chapter had two primary aims. The first objective was to draw connections between, on the one hand, the global debtfarism pursued by international development institutions such as the World Bank and G20 (Chapter 7) in the name of financial inclusion and the historical specifics of debtfarism in Mexico, on the other. To this end, I discussed ways in which this form of state intervention has facilitated the expansions and deepening of the micro-finance industry vis-à-vis the surplus population. The second and related objective of this chapter was to deconstruct key features of the Mexican microfinance industry and reveal its inherent relations of power and paradoxes. To accomplish this second goal, I contextualised historically the microfinance industry within the wider dynamics of capital accumulation. This analytical step allowed me to reveal and explain how and why the silent compulsions and structural violence inherent to the dynamics of credit-led accumulation have led to the dependency of the surplus population on privately created money as it relates to microfinance in Mexico. In doing so, I suggested that the constructed reliance on and relations of power involved in, high-priced microfinance loans – from which the key commericialised MFIs such as Banco Walmart, Banco Azteca, Compartamos and SOFOMES greatly benefit – is masked by the seemingly apolitical and democratic appeal of financial inclusion.

Aside from the legal and extra-legal powers of the Mexican debtfare state, the power of this appeal to deflect criticism lies in financial inclusion lies in the revolutionary power of money itself: the masking of the exploitative and unequal relations in the wider illusions of a community of money. Another source of this power lies in the ability of debtfare states to continually frame financial inclusion in the realm of exchange. Drawing on a historical materialist approach that allowed us to move beyond the realm of exchange and thus grasp the social power of money as well as the rhetorical and regulative roles of the Mexican debtfare state, this chapter sought to interrupt and deconstruct the economic fictions that the microfinance industry alleviates poverty exemplifies how states and capitalists work hand-in-glove to dehistoricise, individualise, depoliticise and normalise the site where poverty alleviation is believed to occur, namely: the market (Bourdieu, 2005; cf. World Bank, 2013b).

In the next and final chapter, I explore how capitalists and the Mexican debtfare state have drawn on the social power of money to promote the expansion and reproduction of another key facet of the poverty industry: financing for low-income housing.

Notes

1 In Spanish, SOFOM stands for Sociedad Financiera de Objeto Múltiple.
2 'Bank Credit Cards Walmart'. Available at:www.tudecide.com/Productos/Tarjetas_Credito/Banco_Wal-Mart/130/35 (accessed 5 August 2013).
3 'Nuevas alianzas en microfinanzas: CrediConfia-Acción Internacional', *El Economista*, 22 November 2012. Available at: http://eleconomista.com.mx/columnas/columna-invitada-valores/2012/11/22/nuevas-alianzas-microfinanzas-crediconfia-accion-intern (accessed 4 September 2013).
4 Carlos Danel and Carlos Labarthe (2008) 'A Letter to our Peers', 17 June. Available at: www.compartamos.com/wps/wcm/connect/?MOD=PDMProxy&TYPE=personalization&ID=NONE&KEY=NONE&LIBRARY=%2FcontentRoot%2Ficm%3Alibraries&FOLDER=%2FAcerca+de+Compartamos%2FDocumentos+es%2F&DOC_NAME=%2FcontentRoot%2Ficm%3Alibraries%2FAcerca+de+Compartamos%2FDocumentos+es%2FAlettertoourpeers.pdf&VERSION (accessed 3 September 2013).
5 The exchange rate calculations are based on 0.74 rate of conversion from Mexican pesos to US dollars on 5 August 2013 as per the website: www.x-rates.com.
6 This sentiment rings clear in the World Bank's 2000-2001 World Development Report, Attacking Poverty, which states that

> To achieve reductions in poverty, the report recommends a more comprehensive approach that directly addressed the needs of poor people in three complementary areas: promoting economic opportunities for poor people through equitable growth, better access to markets, and expanded assets; facilitating empowerment by making

state institutions more responsive to poor people and removing social barriers that excluded women, ethnic and racial groups, and the socially disadvantaged; and enhancing security by preventing and managing economy wide shocks and providing mechanisms to reduce the sources of vulnerability that poor people faced.

Available at: http://web.worldbank.org/WBSITE/EXTERNAL/EXTDEC/EXT RESEARCH/EXTWDRS/0,,contentMDK:20313941~menuPK:607028~pagePK:4780 93~piPK:477627~theSitePK:477624,00.html#2002_Building_Institutions_for_Markets (accessed 20 August 2013).

7 This wage rate is paid in the highest-paid Zone A, which includes the capital and major cities, and is thus lower outside these areas, such as in rural spaces of informality. It should also be kept in mind that for most labourers in Mexico the work week entails six days.

8 Import Substitution Industrialization (or, ISI) was based on capital-intensive forms of production, high tariffs on imports, an ever-growing surplus population, a meagre income distribution system, low levels of taxation, and heavily state-owned enterprises in key resource areas such as oil (Morton, 2011).

9 The market-led policies and regulations pursued by the neoliberal Mexican state have been chronicled in detail elsewhere (Petras and Veltmeyer, 1999; Soederberg, 2010c; Marois, 2012).

10 A *maquila* refers to a free trade zone that involves the import of material and equipment on a tax-free, tariff-free basis. The *maquilas* then assemble these intermediate imports, with little value-added, for re-sale in the export market (Cypher and Delgado Wise, 2010).

11 Major reforms passed in 2001, for example, – the Securities Market Law, The Popular Credit and Savings Law, and the Mutual Funds Law – was aimed at expanding the consumer credit market by allegedly improving transparency and increasing liquidity in the system by opening it to more investors (World Bank, 2005a).

12 It should be highlighted that the while the focus on the surplus population with regard to commercialised financial inclusion is also part and parcel of a wider initiative pursued by international development institutions such as World Bank aimed at normalising the informal economy (World Bank, 2013b).

13 In 2011, for instance, the Inter-American Development Bank launched its first forum entitled BASE. This forum brings together corporate executives, development professionals, entrepreneurs, government officials, 'impact' investors (so-called social investment funds), and other interested parties who are involved in the new and exciting work of creating innovative 'BOP business models' by connecting private sector resources and ingenuity with the untapped potential at the base of the socioeconomic pyramid. For more information, see http://events.iadb.org/calendar/eventDetail.aspx?lang=en&id=2884 (accessed 1 August 2013).

14 According to the World Bank, several studies have found a positive correlation, but not conclusive evidence, between access to finance and firm creation, economic growth, and poverty alleviation at the country level (World Bank, 2009a). This aggregate-based data, however, seems to overlook the increased socio-economic divide in the country, and recent reports of increased, not decreased, poverty rates in Mexico.

15 The 'marginalised' are overrepresented by indigenous peoples. According to another World Bank report, in rural areas, 61 percent of the indigenous population lives in extreme poverty compared with only 19 percent of non-indigenous Mexicans (World Bank, 2007a).

16 The data comprising Table 8.2 has been taken from a 2012 CGAP-funded study. According to this study, financial institutions are increasingly interested in serving the base of the pyramid, but few lenders have a textured understanding of how low-income people use money and financial products, and what sorts of borrowing strategies they may need to adopt to climb out of the depths of poverty and economic insecurity (CGAP, 2012a).

17 The Spanish name of Condusef is the *Comisión Nacional para la Defensa de los Usuarios de Servicios Financieros*. More information about Condesuf (in English) is available at: www.condusef.gob.mx/index.php/english (accessed 24 July 2013).

18 SOFOL is an acronym of their Spanish name, *Sociedad Financiera de Objeto Limitado*.

19 For more information, see: www.accion.org/our-impact/compartamos (accessed 13 August 2013).

20 For more information of the mainstream account of Compartamos's IPO, see: www.accion.org/our-impact/compartamos (accessed 6 September 2013).

21 Accion International is a major investor in Compartamos and is a private arm of the Inter-American Development Bank. Accion was established in 1961. Accion, which is a major promoter and facilitator of the global expansion of for-profit microfinance industries, also receives funds from USAID. More information is available at: www.accion.org/what-we-do/microfinance-services (accessed 6 September 2013).

22 Compartamos, for instance, engages in what is referred to as 'forced savings' by their clients. This requires debtors to have savings equal to 10 percent of the starting loan balance, as a kind of collateral or emergency fund for weeks in which repayment is difficult (Roodman, 2011).

23 Unregulated SOFOMES are still subject to annual and quarterly filings with the Mexican National Registry of Foreign Investment and Money Laundering (BCP Securities, 2010).

24 Information about Financiera Independencia is available at: www.independencia.com.mx/index.aspx (accessed 16 July 2013).

25 Information about Crédito Real is available at: www.creditoreal.com.mx (accessed 16 July 2013).

26 More information about Mabe is available at: www.mabe.com.mx (accessed 16 July 2013).

27 'Latin America's new credit frontier', *Wall Street Journal*, 6 January 2013.

9

DEBTFARISM AND THE HOUSING INDUSTRY

The right to adequate housing and shelter has long been recognised by states through the Universal Declaration of Human Rights and many national constitutions, including Mexico.[1] Despite these protections under the rule of law, adequate housing continues to be out of reach for about 1 billion people in the global South (UN-HABITAT, 2010b). According to the dictates of neoliberalism, which has guided global development since the early 1980s, the *only* effective way to deal with the housing shortfall is by providing the poor with efficient (private) housing finance, or what I refer to as the marketisation of housing rights (World Bank, 2009b; CIDOC, 2011; Herbert *et al.*, 2012; Charnock *et al.*, 2014). As a UN-HABITAT study notes, when properly implemented and executed, market-driven housing finance can play an important role in developing lower-cost housing through investment in social and affordable housing construction and investment in microfinance housing programmes that support progressive, self-help construction (UN-HABITAT, 2006, 2010: 2b; cf. Gruffydd Jones, 2012).

In its efforts to reduce the housing deficit of about 6 million units, the Mexican government has turned to mortgage securitisation (Standard and Poor's, 2006). Mortgage securitisation has become a significant feature of housing finance in global development as it is seen as a market-based solution to raise new funds for housing, while decreasing the risk/gamble for investors (Barry *et al.*, 1994; Jordan, 2008; World Bank, 2009c; Sanchez, 2010). Mortgage securitisation – which was also employed in the United States to bring subprime borrowers into the housing market – describes a type of asset-backed security that transforms illiquid assets, such as residential mortgages, into tradeable securities, which are then sold to investors (Elul, 2005). Since its first issuance in 2003, mortgage securitisation has been growing rapidly in Mexico and represents, at the time of writing, the largest market in Latin America (Inter-American Development Bank, 2011). Despite its significance to the wider debates on global development, mortgage securitisation in Mexico remains understudied.[2] Mortgage securitisation provides a useful window through which we can glimpse the capitalist nature of housing finance and, by extension, the wider processes of the marketisation of housing rights and the role of the Mexican debtfare state therein.

This final chapter has two overlapping objectives. First, it critically evaluates the claims that market-led solutions can provide adequate and affordable homes for the poor in Mexico. In so doing, it must be kept in mind that market-based solutions are not the *only* solutions to deal with the housing shortfall for the poor. Alternative options might include, for example, public housing and co-operative dwellings. The point is that we should strive to politicise and problematise the marketisation of housing by grasping it as a preferred 'fix' that benefits certain powerful interests over other less powerful interests. The neoliberal assertions underpinning the marketisation of housing rights, however, cannot be fully assessed and deconstructed by remaining within the realm of exchange, where both the housing problem and its solution have been formulated. This brings us to the second objective of this chapter, which is to historically contextualise and analyse mortgage securitisation in the processes of capital accumulation in Mexico and the class relations therein.

There are two analytical advantages in taking the above perspective. On the one hand, stepping outside the realm of exchange reveals another noteworthy reason for the lack of adequate housing: the absence of a living wage for a large majority of Mexico's population (Cypher and Delgado Wise, 2010). On the other hand, we can begin to deconstruct a commonly held assumption and one championed by the financial inclusion paradigm, that credit is a neutral object that is used by rational market actors to efficiently deliver a basic social need. Seen from a Marxian understanding, this representation of credit is an illusion that is continually constructed by the state and capitalists. Housing finance, including mortgage securitisation, are not 'things' but privately created (credit) money. As I have argued in this book, credit money is not an innocuous and neutral object on which actors bestow cultural meanings and infuse with power externally. Instead, credit money, which lies at the heart of mortgage securitisation, is a social relation of power that is employed by capitalists and facilitated by states, to overcome (spatial and temporal) barriers to capital accumulation. This is not a one-off solution, however, as the credit system is a product of capital's own endeavours to deal with the internal contradictions of capitalism and thus solutions pursued by capitalists end up compounding rather than reducing the paradoxes (Harvey, 1999).

As I attempt to meet the above two goals, I argue that mortgage securitisation is a capitalist strategy that has been supported by the rhetorical and regulative roles of the Mexican debtfare state. Debtfarism, for instance, plays a central role in housing finance by continually naturalising securitisation and facilitating its expansion. Mortgage securitisation is an attempt by the debtfare state to resolve, albeit in a reactive and contradictory manner, a particular tension inherent to capital accumulation, namely: providing a social basis for the reproduction of the surplus population, on the one hand and facilitating the expansion of the poverty industry that has been dominated by the housing finance and construction sectors, on the other.

Mortgage securitisation and the principle of proportionality: benefits and risks/gambles for whom?

As with the other forms of securitisation discussed in the book, residential mortgage securitisation has often been represented as a win-win strategy that allows the seller of debt to rapidly recover working capital and then recycle it to issue new loans to borrowers. 'This is how institutions that are not normally interested in the little guy' are making more credit available, generating liquidity through the purchasing of securitised mortgages (Emmond, 2005: 36). Mortgage securitisation, as noted earlier, has been widely viewed by economic pundits, policymakers and development practitioners as highly beneficial for developing countries, where extreme housing shortages continue to exist (World Bank, 2004b).

As with all asset-backed securities this involves the construction of a pool or portfolio of loans used to support the issuance of one or more types of securities in secondary mortgage markets (Kothari, 2006). In the case of mortgages, a government-sponsored enterprise such as the Mexican Federal Mortgage Company (SHF[3]), places these mortgages in a trust (also known as a special-purpose vehicle) and then insures the pool against default. This state-backed guarantee is known as a form of credit enhancement in that it makes the securitisation more attractive to potential investors, given that the state is backing up the transaction 100 percent (Elul, 2005; SHF, 2014). The sale of these securities to institutional investors such as pension and equity funds generates cash flow back to the originator of the pool, which can then use the funds to create additional loans.

I problematise this technical understanding of mortgage-backed securitisation promoted by the global and Mexican debtfarist rhetoric later in this section. For now, it is helpful to highlight at least two alleged benefits of mortgage securitisation. First, it is believed to reduce the risk to lenders while increasing the flow of funds into the mortgage finance sector. By reducing transaction costs it increases the scope of lending to the poor (Pickering, 2000; World Bank, 2009b). This was particularly important in terms of attracting foreign capital inflows to Mexico, especially in the wake of the 1994–1995 currency crisis (Barry et al., 1994; Pickering, 2000; Soederberg, 2004; Jordan, 2008; Marois, 2012). This position mirrors the Proportionality Principle, which readers will recall represents one of the G20 Principles on Innovative Financial Inclusion discussed in Chapter 7. To recap, the Proportionality Principle assumes and thus reinforces, a central *truth* in the financial inclusion initiative, namely that financial inclusion results in benefits: 'economic growth, efficiency and increased welfare' – all of which offset and mitigate the risks of financial exclusion (CGAP, 2011: 2).

Second, a well-constructed mortgage securitisation market can offer profitability to market participants and allow the low-income population access to formal credit to purchase a home and thus avoid further financial marginalisation (World Bank, 2004c; Arrieta, 2005). Securitisation provides a significant, market-based innovation in the resolution between the high cost of housing supply, on the one hand and the limited purchasing capacity of the near majority of the population, on the other

(Graffam, 2000; World Bank, 2002b). The Financial Stability Board (FSB), which is an international organisation that works alongside the G20 to coordinate national financial authorities and international standard-setting bodies, has championed the development of mortgage securitisation as a 'fundamental step towards further developing housing finance in Mexico and encouraging private sector entry into the market' (Bank for International Settlements, 2010: 29).

An underlying paradox of the marketisation of housing rights

The social reality in Mexico clashes with the conventional wisdom about mortgage securitisation. Despite the promises that all market participants are believed to benefit from the marketisation of housing rights, the following paradox continues to underpin the housing sector ensuing the issuance of the first mortgage securitisation in 2003. On the one hand, the construction industry and housing finance sectors continue to flourish with heavy state support (corporate welfare) that prioritises new homes over repairing existing stock and permits private companies to build on speculation and finance through mortgages guaranteed by the state (CIDOC, 2008, 2012; Monkonnen, 2011a).

On the other hand and despite the state's rhetorical commitment to housing rights for all, a substantial and growing number of low-income Mexicans continue to be excluded from accessing formal financing channels in order to obtain adequate and affordable housing (UN-HABITAT, 2011). For example, the least expensive homes in the urban Mexico market cost $13,000. The ability of lower income families to purchase homes on credit barely covers half of those families currently in need (UN-HABITAT, 2011: 4). In 2011, for example, 503,000 new homes were constructed but only 51 percent of the population was eligible to apply for a mortgage (SHF, 2011). On some estimates only 32 percent of Mexicans are 'mortgage-eligible' (UN-HABITAT, 2011). Despite the fact that the number of households receiving financing through state efforts has increased from 50,000 in 2000 to nearly 400,000 in 2010, low-income households have been systematically excluded from these opportunities (Herbert *et al.*, 2012: 9). According to the Mexican state, the greatest demand for housing in 2012 came from families, who earned 3.4 times the minimum wage representing 59.7 percent total demand (CIDOC, 2012).

While other income groups in Mexico have also been bypassed by the efficiencies of the market-based housing system, the low-income bracket, which is the focus of my investigation here, represents the largest segment of population without adequate housing.[4] According to a Harvard study, 'Among the nation's 28.5 million occupied housing units in 2010, 17.3 million, or roughly 60 percent, were owned without the use of financing' (Herbert *et al.*, 2012: 10). While some of these houses were purchased through savings, the vast majority are informal, self-built homes ranging from make-shift housing to homes that families spend, on average, up to 10 years constructing (GlobalLens, 2012). Many of these informal dwellings are also situated on 'irregular' land, e.g., communally owned ejidal land

(Herbert *et al.*, 2012; van Gelder, 2013). I touch on the issue of irregular land below. It is worth noting here that the upfront costs of acquiring informal housing are five to eight times lower than formal housing (SEDESOL, 2009). The Harvard study goes on to note that 'A slight majority of these households without a housing loan (9.2 million) earned less than four times the minimum monthly wage' (Herbert *et al.*, 2012: 10).

There appears to be another paradox inherent to the broader tensions described above that helps shed further light on why the construction and housing finance sectors have disproportionately benefited from debtfarist policies. Despite the fact that 20 million households face a housing shortage, construction of new housing has taken precedent over repairing existing homes (CIDOC, 2008, 2011). Over the past decade, there has been an increase in unoccupied and temporary-use dwellings, which stood at 5 million units in 2010 (CIDOC, 2011). The primary reason for abandoning these dwellings is due to the distances of these homes from places of employment, schools and family (UN-HABITAT, 2011). Many of the new homes have been constructed on urban fringes where land is relatively less expensive and can support new housing development for modest-income workers and on non-communally owned ejidal land, which is less costly to acquire (Herbert *et al.*, 2012).

Before turning to the central analysis of this chapter, two caveats are in order. First, the exclusion of the surplus population from access to formal and affordable housing finance is not an exclusively neoliberal phenomenon. What is different in the neoliberal era is the turn to market-based solutions, such as mortgage securitisation backed heavily by state funding. That said, the dual housing sector, along informal and formal lines, is a construct that was reproduced in Mexican capitalism well before the advent of neoliberalism in the early 1980s (Ball and Connolly, 1987; UN-HABITAT, 2011; cf., Breman, 2012).

Second, in the context of this chapter, the surplus population refers to those families earning zero to four times the minimum wage (MMW), that is, families that have been in most need of decent and affordable dwellings, although, as we will see, other income brackets have had problems accessing housing finance, too (UN-HABITAT, 2011). The zero to four times MMW is generally taken as the cut-off for the level of income below which it is difficult to afford a home in the formal market (Herbert *et al.*, 2012). The UN-HABITAT, the Mexican state and the Inter-American Development Bank use a lower income cut-off for this category of workers (i.e., zero to three MMW). It is important to draw attention to several aspects of this measure. The minimum wage in Mexico, as discussed in the previous chapter, is not only far from a living wage, but also is not adjusted to the rate of inflation, which for a country like Mexico, can substantially impact purchasing power for the poor. Moreover, families earning within this range are primarily based in the informal economy, where they may lack legal and social protections (e.g., pension coverage) and are often in precarious positions not only in terms of health and safety conditions but also in terms of job certainty (ILO, 2003). This means that an illness or unexpected external shock to the family household could entail a dramatic decline in the ability to save for a home or to meet regular mortgage payments.

Having said that, the above paradox upon which mortgage securitisation pivots compels us to ask not only what the sources of change are regarding the emergence of mortgage securitisation but also to investigate the machinations involved in socially reproducing large margins of exclusion vis-à-vis formal access to affordable housing finance. Specific questions that concern us here are not only *why* housing deficiencies have *continued* to affect a substantial and growing number of poor households in Mexico more than a decade after the first mortgage securitisation in 2003, but also *who* benefits from the social reproduction of relatively high-cost housing and the limited purchasing capacity of a large segment of the population?

Transcending the realm of exchange: situating mortgage securitisation in the processes of capital accumulation

The right to housing serves two fundamental purposes for the expansion and reproduction of capital accumulation. First, as has been well documented by economists, housing finance and construction represents a crucial driver of national economic growth, given its role, for instance, in spurring job creation and consumer spending (World Bank, 1993, 2004; UN-HABITAT, 2010b; cf., Bourdieu, 2005).[5] Second, housing provides a social basis for the reproduction of labour power. Like other forms of social expenditures and investments geared toward the same goal, e.g., education and health spending, providing workers with housing and shelter is not motivated by altruism but rather is directed at co-opting, integrating and repressing workers through ideological and coercive means (Harvey, 1989: 65–6).

Capitalist states often need to make such investments in order to create an adequate social basis for further accumulation (Hirsch, 1978; Harvey, 1989). The type and amount of money that the state will dedicate to these social expenditures are strongly affected by the historical nature of struggle and configuration of power within the wider dynamics of capital accumulation (Harvey, 1989: 66). As discussed later in the chapter, the Mexican state has historically favoured formal workers over informal workers with regard to housing policy. This is because the formal workers are relatively more powerful than their informal counterparts. As such, the state's first priority with regard to the development of mortgage securitisation was to target lower-income, formal workers through its Housing Provident Funds (HPFs). Private mortgage companies, such as SOFOLS, were introduced in the early 1990s to deal with the informal surplus population through market-based mechanisms. As I demonstrate below, the particular historical formation of power in Mexican capitalism has meant that the state has favoured formal, unionised workers and has also forged a close and dependent relationship with the construction and housing finance sectors.

Mortgage securitisation is a form of fictitious capital. As discussed in Chapter 2, fictitious capital refers to a flow of money not backed by any commodity transaction (Harvey, 1999: 265ff). It is central to the credit system and thus to a deeper understanding of the power relations involved in the construction and reconstruction of mortgage securitisation. Fictitious capital is implied whenever credit is extended in advance, in anticipation of future labour as a counter-value, e.g., government bonds and mortgage securitisation. As a synthetic form of money based on future income streams, mortgage securitisation anticipates that the worker will be able to earn wages to continue making orderly payments on their mortgage. Mortgage securitisation, like all forms of fictitious capital, is thus based on a future gamble.

To interrupt the economistic and rationalised representation of risk securitisation in Chapter 7, I problematised the one-dimensional, technical understanding of risk by referring to it as a 'risk/gamble'. Mortgage securitisation is distinct from traditional lending in that it uses only financial assets (e.g., mortgages) as collateral (Elul, 2005). Mortgage securitisation is thus not based on tangible property; but rather on the income stream this property is projected to produce in the future. As with the US experience with housing finance, the Mexican state plays a central role in backing these promises (e.g., offering 'credit enhancement') in secondary mortgage markets (Gotham, 2009; Schwartz, 2009).

As discussed in Chapter 2, the creation of fictitious values ahead of actual commodity production and realisation is a risky business. The credit system becomes *both* the cutting edge of accumulation and a key feature in dealing with the overaccumulation of capital and excess labour, with all the associated dangers of such exposure (Harvey, 1999). This becomes evident in our narrative, as fictitious capital play a central role in mediating the manifestation of capitalist crises in Mexico from the 1970s to the global financial meltdown of 2008. The credit system is thus a product of capital's own endeavours to deal with the internal contradictions of capitalism. What Marx shows us is how capitalism's solution ends up heightening rather than diminishing the contradictions (Harvey, 1999: 237).

Mexican debtfarism plays an integral role in smoothing, absorbing and depoliticising the contradictions emerging from the credit system and struggles therein. The state undertakes this task in a partially contradictory and *ex post facto* manner (see Chapter 7). As a historical social relation rooted in, albeit not determined by, the processes of capital accumulation and the power therein, the Mexican debtfare state also internalises and is, at times, also constrained by, these tensions. A fundamental reason why the state is limited by the above tensions lies in the nature of the marketisation of housing rights and its emphasis on solving problems in the realm of exchange. Paradoxically, this tends to heighten, as opposed to diminish, contradictions.

Framing the concrete discussion within this abstract lens allows us to see that mortgage securitisation has its roots in a wide *crisis-restructuring continuum* that has shaped and been shaped by, the collective nerve centre (i.e., the credit system) and the capitalist state, which governs and mediates the tensions therein (Chapter 3). This continuum may be understood as an interconnected and ongoing series of reconstructions and representations that constitute the contradictory and class-led evolution of neoliberal practice, which pivots on the inability of the credit system to reduce the underlying contradictions of capital accumulation (Harvey, 1999).

Historical materialist understanding of low-income housing finance: managing the right to housing in the Mexican 'Miracle'

As discussed in Chapter 8, capital accumulation in Mexico has continued to be marked by a large relative surplus population. As we will see below, the historical integration of the Mexican economy into the world market and the United States in particular, has continually relied heavily on the abundance of cheap and well-disciplined labour as a core feature in luring and maintaining foreign capital flows into the country. Reproducing this great mass of underemployed and unemployed workers required social expenditures that would co-opt, integrate and repress various segments of labour power. With regard to housing, these efforts can be traced to Mexico's Constitution, which states that all private enterprises are obliged to provide comfortable and hygienic housing for workers.[6] These legal measures were designed to protect workers, primarily powerful, unionised workers, in the formal sector. Public housing agencies for social housing, which began to emerge in 1925 with the rise of industrialisation in Mexico and thus rising levels of urbanisation, also reflected the state of class struggle in the country. For instance, the Housing Assistance Bank[7], which was created in 1943, catered primarily to salaried workers employed by the government and therefore did not represent a national housing policy (UN-HABITAT, 2011).

An important facet of the rapid industrialisation and urbanisation that marked the so-called Mexican 'Miracle' (1940–1970) was the construction industry. Ball and Connolly's study demonstrates that the construction sector, which represented one of the largest employers in Mexico during this time, was facilitated by active state expenditure on necessary physical structures, such as housing (Ball and Connolly, 1987). This employment of fictitious capital by the state also facilitated a financial dependence between state funds and the construction industry, which has continued to the time of writing. According to Ball and Connolly (1987: 156),

> Public agencies forward substantial advance payments [fictitious capital], which virtually cover the entire production costs, before work commences. Contractors are thus able to operate with a minimum of capital on their own, while dispensing with the need for credit from financial institutions except for short-term bridging loans.

The state's investment in construction also permitted the social reproduction of formal and informal labour, as discussed above. Aside from the role of the state in shaping and facilitating the construction industry through its various housing policies, two points elaborated on in Ball and Connolly's study are important for our discussion as they not only mark the housing landscape in Mexico to this day, but also relate directly to the above paradox underpinning mortgage securitisation.

First, the construction industry's continued reliance on a cheap, passive and almost endless pool of construction labour, largely based in the informal sector (Connolly, 2007). Second and related, housing in Mexico has and continues to be characterised by self-construction, or what Mexicans refer to as *auto-construcción* (the so-called do-it-yourself home building business) (Ball and Connolly, 1987).

Self-construction continues to make up 40 percent of all housing construction in Mexico and while some middle-class families engage in this activity, most are from the low-income bracket (GlobalLens, 2012; CIDOC, 2012). Self-construction dominates both Mexico's rural areas, where farming no longer yields subsistence incomes and *ad hoc* neighbourhoods around the fringes of Mexico's cities (*colonias populares*) (Sandoval, 2005; UN-HABITAT, 2011). Owing to its prominence in the housing landscape for the poor, it is important to consider the historical roots of self-construction, so that we can grasp how and why debtfare state has continued to facilitate this practice in the neoliberal era, i.e., within the marketisation of housing rights paradigm.

First and foremost, we need to begin our discussion by recognising that self-construction has been shaped and facilitated by a particular legal environment in Mexico regarding residential housing among the poor. This, in turn, is rooted in the particular mode of accumulation and the configuration of power in Mexico (Haenn, 2006). Briefly and broadly, Mexico has three basic schemes of land ownership: private property, which accounts for 37 percent of the land and social property, which accounts for 53 percent of the land. The remaining 10 percent falls into the category of federal land[8] (Inter-American Development Bank, 2011). Prior to 1992, Mexicans had the right to use social property, largely for subsistence farming, but did not have full ownership and could thus not sell the land (Inter-American Development Bank, 2011).

The large tracts of social property, much of which are near sprawling urban centres, facilitate a common practice among would-be homebuyers in the low-income brackets: the 'pay and build as you can' plan (Monkonnen, 2011a). As Barry *et al.* note, 'In the informal sector, individuals may merely "invade" a site, occupying it illegally and constructing a home on it. A person who occupies a site long enough is ultimately granted the right to stay' (Barry *et al.*, 1994: 187).[9] This explains, in part, both the high levels of self-construction projects in Mexico and the high level of homeownership, which some estimate to be around 80 percent (Inter-American Development Bank, 2011: 9). Although these homeownership levels are the highest in Latin America, the quality of these informal homes is considered below the living standards set by the Mexican government (UN-HABITAT, 2011). These houses, however shoddily built, are still a form of shelter and in some way help to provide the social basis for the reproduction of the surplus population. Thus, the Mexican landownership system and its legal framing permitted informal housing for the majority of its informal workforce, largely through legal negligence.

In 1963, the state sought to facilitate the industrialisation process, which also involved the rapid urbanisation of the rural population, by creating a second-tier development bank, the Fund for Housing Operation and Finance (FOVI). FOVI, which would later be replaced by the Mexican Federal Mortgage Company, was designed to provide low-interest mortgage financing to low-income and middle-income households, i.e., between three and six times the monthly minimum wage (Barry *et al.*, 1994). FOVI, with the financial assistance of the central bank (Banco de Mexico) and the World Bank, attempted to entice banks to lend to this income bracket by providing funds to the commercial banks. FOVI also engaged in risk sharing in case of default. Workers did not apply directly to FOVI for funds. Instead, builders and developers bid for FOVI funds through an auction process. One effect of this plan has been to favour new housing finance, which still shapes the housing sector today. FOVI largely failed to encourage commercial banks to lend to the poor. Mortgage finance in Mexico continues to be concentrated among a few large, foreign-owned, commercial banks that lend primarily to the upper-income brackets (World Bank, 2009b; CIDOC, 2011; Herbert *et al.*, 2012).

In response to the economic turmoil in the late 1960s, the Mexican state established two Housing Provident Funds (hereafter: HPFs or Housing Funds) in the housing sector in 1972: the Institute of the National Housing Fund for Workers (hereafter: INFONAVIT) and the Housing Fund of the Social Security and Services Institute for State Workers (hereafter: FOVISSSTE). According to labour law, private sector employers must make deposits to their workers' account at INFONAVIT equal to 5 percent of the workers' wages or salaries (Inter-American Development Bank, 2011). INFONAVIT holds this payroll deduction as a pension fund and uses it to create subsidies for housing loans at below-market interest rates for its members. FOVISSSTE operates in a similar manner to INFONAVIT, but targets public service workers (World Bank, 2009b).

The immediate effect of the creation of the HPFs was that government-sponsored affordable housing excluded informal sector workers from receiving any type of assistance (World Bank, 2002b). The HPFs play a major role in residential housing markets, ranging from 70 percent market share at the end of 2005 to more than 80 percent at end of 2009 – most of which has involved moderate-income households (Inter-American Development Bank, 2011). Given their central role in the industry, HPFs also facilitated the expansion of the housing market through active management of housing development and the issuing of mortgages and continued financing of the powerful construction industry (Inter-American Development Bank, 2011).

The rise of debtfarism and marketised housing solutions

Moving toward a market-oriented economy after the 1982 debt crisis, the Mexican state tried to walk the fine line between appealing to international investors while practising brokerage politics at home by expanding domestic debt through government-issued, peso-denominated bonds, or CETES (Mexican Federal Treasury Certificates).[10] Credit money in the form of fictitious capital allowed the state to continue to finance popular and politically necessary, yet debt-financed, programmes, such as INFONAVIT. Prior to 2000, for instance, both HPFs recorded default rates on mortgage loans in the excessive range of 20 to 40 percent.

INFONAVIT paid negative real rates of return on savings during much of the 1980s and 1990s (World Bank, 2009). This policy may have temporarily appeased some groups, such as powerful unions and the construction industry, but it came at the cost of increased inflation and high interest rates to attract investment.[11]

To placate the social dislocations brought about by the debt crisis and subsequent neoliberal restructuring and in an attempt to protect the value of the peso, the state nationalised the banking system in 1982 (Marois, 2014). This move allowed the state to use, in part, commercial banks as part of their strategy to provide a social basis for reproducing labour power with regard to low-income housing policy. Commercial banks, for instance, were required to preserve a fixed percentage, ranging from 3 to 6 percent, of their outstanding mortgage portfolio in so-called 'social interest loans'. These loans, which were partly funded by FOVI, served as a second-tier bank, channeling government funding to commercial banks for low-income housing finance (Pickering, 2000). The Mexican state continued with its brokerage politics regarding housing policy. With the social interest fund in place, the government modified, in 1983, Article 4 of the Mexican Constitution so that it read that *all* families have the right to a respectful and dignified home. In 1984, the country's first Federal Housing Law was established to secure this constitutional mandate. Given that these housing policies were highly influenced by the pressures that were brought about by large unions (formal workers), however, the reforms excluded workers in the informal sector (UN-HABITAT, 2011: 14).

In 1993, the World Bank released an influential report, *Housing: Enabling Markets to Work*, which would have important ramifications for the housing market in Mexico. In the report, the bank suggested that states should play a facilitating – as opposed to leading – role in housing finance. As the World Bank emphasises (1993:3) 'Policies which constrain market efficiency and the responsiveness of the housing supply system result in reduced investment, housing which is less affordable and of lower quality and a lower-quality residential environment'. Coinciding with the World Bank report and forged under the ambit of the NAFTA negotiations in December 1993, the Mexican state sought to deal with heightening contradictions in its housing policy by forging a new financial intermediary to focus on the mortgage market targeting middle- and low-income workers in the informal sector. These private, non-bank mortgage finance companies are known by their Spanish acronym as SOFOLS (*Sociedades Financieras de Objeto Limitado*). Ten years after their creation, the SOFOLS would issue Mexico's first securitisation in 2003. It is therefore important to look more closely at this market-based mechanism to deal with the housing shortfall for informal workers.

A SOFOLS is a limited-purpose financial organisation or 'niche lender'. SOFOLS differ from commercial banks because they can acquire assets through deposits and can grant loans only for the housing sector (World Bank, 2009b).[12] SOFOLS were established to serve workers who did not qualify for loans from the HPFs, i.e., 'unaffiliated' (informal) waged labour, such as migrant workers, taxi drivers, waiters, domestic workers and so forth. SOFOLS serve the middle and lower market with more than 50 percent of clients having incomes between three to eight monthly minimum wages (MMW) (World Bank, 2009b; Herbert et al., 2012). According to Mexico's Federal Mortgage Company, SOFOLS have strengthened their financial conditions, either through capital injections or through mergers and acquisitions with large commercial banks (Pickering, 2000). The Mexican government, development institutions and other industry insiders, are expected to play a more significant role in funding affordable housing production and mortgages by channeling credit into mortgage lending for low-income, unaffiliated workers and development financing for home builders (SHF, 2011: 9; Business Monitor International, 2011; Herbert et al., 2012).

In creating SOFOLS, the Mexican state was also hoping to spur greater competition and specialisation in the financial sector to assist in funding the built environment for the swelling numbers of informal workers (SHF, 2011). The privately owned SOFOLS, which were heavily funded at a reduced rate of interest by the World Bank's International Finance Corporation (IFC), the Inter-American Development Bank and the Mexican government (FOVI), were to fill the lending gap left by the social interest loans by providing a new means for originating and servicing FOVI-financed loans. During the early 1990s, Mexico's HPFs also underwent major reforms (IDB, 2011). One important change was the shift away from constructing homes to financing mortgages, which affected FOVISSSTE in 1991 and INFONAVIT in 1993 (UN-HABITAT, 2011). However, as one urban scholar suggests, the relatively low-cost housing involved was not geared to lower-income Mexicans but instead to middle- and upper-middle-class households, i.e., those beyond the four times MMW (Monkkonen, 2011b).

In the wake of the devastating peso crisis of 1994–1995, the state, through its debtfarist roles, sought to jump-start private housing finance by moving funds from FOVI to finance the SOFOLS. In the late 1990s, for instance, 14 SOFOLS were licensed to lend with FOVI funds (Pickering, 2000). The target borrowers of these SOFOLS were workers in the informal sector who did not have access to bank and government funding, e.g., the HPFs. Given that SOFOLS were the first lending institution permitted to issue securitised mortgages, it is useful to understand how this funding worked.

FOVI distributes its mortgage funds to the SOFOLS through auctions by housing developers. If the developer wins the bid, the developer is then obliged to cover the promised amount for each mortgage that is issued at the time the final buyer receives their mortgage from the SOFOL and takes possession of the home (Pickering, 2000: 8; Herbert et al., 2012). This dependent relationship between the state and the housing sector echoes the earlier description by Ball and Connolly, but with at least two key differences. First, the state is no longer directly involved in the construction of housing. Second, the dependent relationship involves SOFOLS and construction companies, with the state (FOVI) assuming an indirect though essential role as the guarantor of fictitious capital. As a result some developers have started SOFOLS in order to obtain financing from FOVI, or have merely established a working affiliation with one. Once a developer has won the right to attain mortgage funds from FOVI, for instance, the company is also able to apply for FOVI construction financing. FOVI will finance construction loans for up to 65 percent of the finished home sale value. SOFOLS originate and service these loans as well (Pickering, 2000: 8–9).

This transformation in lending relations has affected the way in which low-income housing is constructed and acquired. As an urban scholar notes, 'a majority of houses are now built by private companies on speculation and purchased with mortgages, rather than through the incremental process that previously governed urban development' (Monkkonen, 2011b: 406). This change is, however, neither a natural evolution of the market nor an efficient alternative in which everyone is better off. Instead, I suggest that it must be understood as part and parcel of a tension-ridden, class-based strategy. As the next section will clarify, debtfarism plays a central role in mediating these tensions, particularly in the form of the Mexican Federal Mortgage Company and the securitisation of the SOFOLS and HPFs.

Debtfarism and the construction of mortgage securitisation

Aside from the passage of several key reforms, including the Amendments to the General Law on Securities and Credit in 2000 and the Law on Guaranteed Credit in 2002, several state-led changes in the housing sector occurred during the early 2000s that helped facilitate the first mortgage-backed securitisation in 2003. In 2000, GMAC *Financiera* (hereafter: GMAC) was established in Mexico (IFC, 2005; Standard & Poor's, 2006). GMAC, which would be involved in the first mortgage securitisation in the country, is a wholly owned subsidiary of US-based Ally Financial, which is one of the world's largest financial services companies. Since its arrival in Mexico, GMAC has become an important source of funding for the SOFOLS. In 2001, INFONAVIT underwent comprehensive changes, which were aimed, among other things, at preparing it to move toward the mortgage securitisation issuance programme (IMF, 2008). INFONAVIT was also under pressure domestically and globally to increase its lending to lower-income Mexicans, thereby addressing a past trend of granting loans to higher-income affiliates (World Bank, 2002b).

Since the early 2000s, both HPFs have greatly expanded their lending volumes with particular emphasis on workers making between two and four times MMW. However, given the limits of resolving the housing problem in the realm of exchange without addressing structural issues, such as the absence of a living wage, there remain many 'affiliated' workers, who cannot afford homes in the formal sector (CIDOC, 2011; FOVISSSTE, 2012; Herbert *et al.*, 2012). Formal (affiliated) workers in the public sector are covered by the Institute for Social Security and Services for State Workers, or, in Spanish, *Instituto de Seguridad y Servicios Sociales de los Trabajadores del Estado*, or ISSSTE. Formal (affiliated) workers in the private sector are covered by the Mexican Social Security Institute, or, in Spanish, *Instituto Mexicano del Seguro Social* (IMSS).

With recommendations and funding from major international development organisations (including World Bank, Inter-American Development Bank, China Development Bank and the Financial Stability Board), the Mexican debtfare state established the Federal Mortgage Company (SHF) in 2001. The SHF, which replaced FOVI, was mandated to promote mortgage securitisation and increase private funding for the housing sector. SHF was created with the main objective of fostering a secondary mortgage market through its role as guarantor and liquidity provider. The main functions of the SHF are to provide long-term financing to SOFOLS and to act as collateral in securitisation issuances of SOFOLS. The SHF was initially established with an expiration date in 2009 but, as we will see below, this was subsequently repealed and extended to 2013 due to ongoing issues resulting from the paradoxes of capital accumulation in Mexico (IMF, 2008: 11).

The credit enhancement by the debtfare state through the Federal Mortgage Company for the securitisations of both the SOFOLS and the HPFs is fairly high, as investors view this as a risky investment. One of the risk-reduction strategies put in place by the SOFOLS involves the creation of investment units (UDIs), which are not denominated in pesos but US dollars, thereby offering shelter from inflation fluctuations (IMF, 2008).[13] Thus, the Mexican Federal Mortgage Company puts the 'full faith and credit' of the Mexican state (and fictitious capital) behind the mortgages (SHF, 2008). As in the case of FOVI, the SHF does not lend directly to those in need of a home, but instead guarantees the timely payment of mortgages. Thus, if a mortgage payment is six months behind, the 'SHF pays to the lender between 25 and 75 percent of the outstanding balance of the mortgage loan, plus interest, as well as insurance fees and any unpaid services' (Jordan, 2008). As I noted earlier, the SHF's credit enhancement is believed to generate extra money for lending institutions, which will, in turn, encourage them to issue more mortgages, preferably to lower-income workers in the informal sector.

With the legal, regulatory and ideological moorings in place, the first mortgage securitisation took place in 2003 and involved GMAC and two large SOFOLS – *Hipotecaria Nacional* and *Hipotecaria Su Casita* (Standard & Poor's, 2006; IFC, 2009). IFC was said to have played a major role in securing the deal by giving it credibility as well as 'bringing discipline to the table' in order to win over the scepticism of investors, particularly in the recessionary fallout of the dot-com crisis in the United States (IMF, 2008). The International Finance Corporation (IFC), for example, assisted the establishment and growth of residential mortgage backed securities (RMBS) in Mexico by offering the same 'risk/gamble' management techniques, funding instruments and ratings strategies that contributed to the US subprime debacle. In 2004, IFC shifted $718 million to support the issuance of more than $4 billion in mortgage securities, the majority of which included backed loans to middle-income households seeking new housing and excluding those in dire need of adequate housing, namely, those in the zero to three times MMW category (see Table 9.1; IFC, 2005). The IFC thus facilitated the expansion of subprime mortgages (i.e., making loans to risky, low-income workers). Mexico would thus follow the 'troublesome development path' in which securitised mortgages act as another mechanism of extracting value from low-income individuals and aid in the overall financial deepening (Sassen, 2008: 188).

With the introduction of RMBS, the Mexican state continued to introduce reforms to encourage more private sector participation in housing finance by, for example, allowing members of the HPFs to simultaneously originate the purchase of a house with a credit from an HPF and from a private lender (SOFOLS). The state also loosened the regulatory nets by allowing HPF members to use their savings as a down payment for a loan originated by another lender (World Bank, 2009b). In April 2005, the second largest SOFOL in Mexico, *Hipotecaria Su Casita and* INFONAVIT, closed a $100 million variable funding note program *(Hipotecaria Su Casita Construction Loan Trust)* (Jobst, 2006). To help generate funds, the Mexican state also initiated a securitisation programme for both of the housing funds (World Bank, 2009b).

Notwithstanding mortgage securitisation and its alleged win-win benefits for the poor, the paradox underpinning housing in Mexico would only be temporarily resolved through the credit system. Despite these financial innovations and low interest rates, the lower-income population, in both the formal and informal sectors, remained lightly served by SOFOLS and HPFs (World Bank, 2009b; Inter-American Development Bank, 2011). The housing market, however, experienced a boom from 2000 to 2008, which was led, in part, by a significant expansion of INFONAVIT'S mortgage issuance and, in part, by commercial banks and SOFOLS increasing their mortgage lending as well. In fact, the number of mortgages issued by commercial banks, which were aggressively re-entering the mortgage lending market and SOFOLS during 2007 almost doubled the previous 1992 peak (Inter-American Development Bank, 2011: 16). Total issues of mortgage securities reached over $6 billion in 2006 – tripling in volume since 2004 and making Mexico the largest RMBS market in Latin America (World Bank, 2009b).

Enticed by the profitability and ability of SOFOLS to target workers in the informal economy, as well as their growth rates, which led these non-bank entities to manage billions of dollars in home loans, Mexico's largest commercial bank, BBVA Bancomer, acquired Mexico's largest SOFOL, *Hipotecaria Nacional*, in 2004 (IMF, 2006). Unlike commercial banks, SOFOLS offer more flexibility in terms of minimum amounts required for applying for a bank mortgage, are able to provide loans in dollars and offer more flexibility in terms of repayment than banks (Knoweldge@Wharton, 2006; IMF, 2010).

In 2005, the construction sector was the most profitable in Mexico, with construction firms enjoying a 44 percent increase over previous annual returns (Jordan, 2008). Underpinning this growth in the housing sector is the fact that there has been a substantial reliance on new housing as the most appropriate way to satisfy demand in Mexico, as opposed to repairing the large number of existing homes (IDB, 2011). As such, in 2005, housing stock had more than tripled relative to the 1970s. To put this into perspective, in 2007, the housing stock replacement cost is estimated to have been 86 percent of GDP (UN-HABITAT, 2011).

Interestingly, 70 percent of existing housing stock is estimated to be affordable housing, or in the 'economic' category, i.e., coinciding with five to 10 times MMW, whereas, as we saw earlier, the greatest demand is needed in basic homes (zero to three times MMW) and social homes (three to five times MMW) (UN-HABITAT, 2011; Inter-American Development Bank, 2011: 9). While there are around 2,600 construction companies operating in Mexico, the sector is dominated by six large companies, the first four of which are publicly traded: Geo, Homex, Urbi, Ara, Sare and Consorcio Hogar (CIDOC, 2011; Inter-American Development Bank, 2011). Geo and Homex, Mexico's two largest construction companies by market value, both specialise in affordable housing. Yet, as we will see below, the definition of affordable housing does not coincide with the purchasing capacity of the majority of lower-income families, e.g., three to four times MMW (CIDOC, 2012).

In 2006, mortgage securitisation became the largest structured asset class, representing over 25 percent of total local structured issues. In this same year, housing construction represented almost 3 percent of the country's GDP, which is nearly on a par with Mexico's manufacturing leader, namely: the auto industry (IDB, 2011). In this same year, the debtfare state introduced regulatory changes to the insurance sector to facilitate greater competition in the housing financial market, thereby allowing the entrance of private sector financial guarantee providers for mortgage securities, such as the International Financial Corporation (IMF, 2008). This move had significant effects on the housing industry. As of October 2007, there were over $6.4 billion in outstanding mortgage securities issuances in the Mexican bond market by seven different SOFOLS, INFONAVIT and two commercial banks (Inter-American Development Bank, 2011). Alongside the spread of mortgage securitisation in both SOFOLS and HPFs, the construction industry, continued to grow, registering 6.8 percent of GDP in 2008 (CIDOC, 2008). Several years after the global financial crisis, construction continues to play a major role in the Mexican economy, although it has fallen to 6 percent of Mexico's GDP (BBVA Bancomer, 2013).

Despite the construction and financing boom in the housing market, low-income workers remained locked out of affordable homes. To address this tension, the Mexican state created the New Housing Law in 2006 (UN-HABITAT, 2011). Unlike the previous Housing Law of 1983, the New Housing Law recognised, at least in rhetoric, the central role of self-construction in providing shelter for the vast majority of Mexicans: the surplus population (GlobalLens, 2012).[14] In 2006, coinciding with the introduction of the Housing Law, the Mexican state set an all-time-high annual target of granting 750,000 new residential mortgage loans (Standard & Poor's, 2006). Although the 2006 Housing Law did not alter the direction of market-led forms of housing rights in Mexico, it did contain a revealing insight into the highly unequal nature of housing in light of the growing shortage of decent dwellings for the poor. The 2006 Housing Law, for instance, stated that housing is not only a basic human right but it is also a crucial factor in creating social order.

As such, it reflected an attempt by the state to create a social basis for further accumulation, as well as to appease the growing mass of unaffiliated workers.

Debtfarism and the marketisation of housing rights in the wake of 2008 crisis

The 2007–2008 sub-prime housing crisis in the US and its global recessionary fallout had a significant impact on Mexico, as it did on other countries. Hit particularly hard were those workers without savings and job security to cushion the blow of higher food and fuel costs, who were, once again, offered no social protection from financial speculation (Marois, 2014). With the advent of the 2008 global recession, Mexican real minimum wages (i.e., adjusted for inflation) fell below 1994 levels (Puyana, 2010: 14). This placed a strain on the demand for new housing from low-income workers, especially from the informal sector. Indeed, many SOFOLS began to encounter financial problems, as workers were unable to meet mortgage payments. By 2008, some mortgage SOFOLS were experiencing high delinquency rates (Knowledge@Wharton, 2011) and their overall market share dropped considerably from 2008 to 2009 (see Table 9.1). According to the International Monetary Fund (IMF), SOFOLS' non-performing loans have more than tripled since the 2008 crisis, which is rather worrying owing to the fact that the SOFOLS have become integrated into the rest of the financial system over the past several years (IMF, 2010). The strains of the recession would prove too much for the SOFOLS and these institutions, which were created as a market-based solution to the housing problem for low- and middle-income, unaffiliated workers, began 'to rely exclusively on the public sector for financial support, greatly diminishing their role in the market, leaving a significant void in lending to unaffiliated workers and homebuilders' (Herbert *et al.*, 2012: 4).

At the same time, government officials and industry insiders were lamenting the fact that the low-income population, in both the formal and informal housing sectors, was still underserved (World Bank, 2009b). According to the Mexican Federal

TABLE 9.1 Share in new housing mortgage loans★

Lending institution	2008 (%)	2009 (%)
INFONAVIT	56.90	59.30
FOVISSSTE	11.10	22.70
SOFOLS	10.30	2.7
Commercial banks	21.70	15.3

Source: BBVA Bancomer, October 2009 in Inter-American Development Bank (2011) *Housing Finance in Mexico: Current State and Future Sustainability*, Washington, DC: Inter-American Development Bank, p. 16.

★ Figures corrected for co-financed loans, i.e., granted by more than one institution, for instance by INFONAVIT and a commercial bank.

Mortgage Company, 'The financing schemes focus on the acquisition of new housing, which represents a costly and hardly accessible solution for the population with lower incomes, or salaries below or equivalent to four [monthly] minimum wages' (CIDOC, 2008: 37, 2012; SHF, 2011). Despite these tensions, the proffered solution remained framed ahistorically in the realm of exchange, as opposed to understanding the roots of impoverishment in past policy decisions and in the processes of capital accumulation.

This fail forward neoliberal strategy was to remain faithful to the solution of mortgage securitisation, thereby seeking to lock in the marketisation of housing rights in the post-2008 recessionary environment and subsequent restructuring phase of Mexican capitalism. According to its mandate in the post-2008 crisis environment, the SHF still 'considers the securitisation of mortgages as the *most efficient mechanism* of housing financing (SHF, 2014, my emphasis). With the proper market-friendly regulatory reforms[15], including the privatisation of the Housing Provident Funds, many economic pundits believed that the housing markets would be able to take advantage of what has become the new growth area in the post-2008 environment: affordable housing (BBVA Bancomer, 2011; Business Monitor International, 2011). According to industry observers, low-cost housing construction represents a thriving market that is expected to outperform the overall sector (Business Monitor International, 2011).

Efforts were undertaken to expand, accelerate and improve the efficiency of mortgage securitisation in Mexico, ostensibly in order to reach the poorest segment of the population (IMF, 2010). If we look more closely at some of these policies, however, it becomes clear that the construction and financial sectors benefitted greatly from state-led reforms to marketise housing rights. The Mexican state for its part has been actively seeking to depoliticise and activate the housing sector in the aftermath of the US subprime crisis by reinforcing the 2006 Housing Law. In addition, the state has maintained an emphasis on social order through such rhetorical devices as the *Housing Sector Program 2007–2012: Toward a sustainable housing development*, issued by Mexico's National Housing Commission (UN-HABITAT, 2011). The main thrust of this policy was to '[i]ncrease the amount of housing financing available to citizens, particularly low-income families' (UN-HABITAT, 2011). As I demonstrate below, the preference for building new houses over improving existing housing units benefits the construction and finance corporations. To put this demand for repairing existing homes in perspective around 9 million housing units were in need for improvement in 2012 (CIDOC, 2012).

To assist the Mexican government in creating a more efficient and independent mortgage securities market, in 2008, the World Bank provided a substantial loan of $1.01 billion to the SHF to help refinance its short-term debt. The idea behind this loan was to allow the SHF to support mortgage growth through the SOFOLS. The World Bank, however, made clear that the SHF and SOFOLS should expand its housing finance from its middle-income base include low-income households (those that make less than six times the MMW) (World Bank, 2008). According to the Financial Stability Board, 'This decision . . . proved crucial for maintaining liquidity to SOFOLS, which [have] relied on domestic wholesale financing [from the SHF] and experienced several liquidity pressures during the crisis' (Financial Stability Board, 2010: 29).

To regain investor confidence, the Mexican state issued new regulations requiring SOFOLS to meet similar accounting and transparency standards as banks, raise more capital and comply with new loan-loss provisioning rules (Inter-American Development Bank, 2011). These reforms would, in turn, assist the SOFOLS in diversifying their lending as well as help them partner with other lending institutions, such as commercial banks. The SHF has been working closely with SOFOLS to create new lending products geared toward the lower-income and informal sectors (Knowledge@Wharton, 2011; Herbert *et al.*, 2012).

At the time of writing, the technical and financial support from the SHF seems to be taking effect, as several SOFOLS have been creating new lending products for lower-income families. Some SOFOLS, for example, have created innovative products for street vendors and taxi drivers, who work in the huge informal economy and do not possess either documented salaries or credit histories (Knowledge@Wharton, 2011). Various SOFOLS are examining spending habits to establish applicant income and offering trial payment periods to prove borrowers can afford payments on entry-level homes that range from $17,000 to $37,000, i.e., within the scope of basic and social homes, respectively (UN-HABITAT, 2011; GlobalLens, 2012). It is worth repeating that these homes cost more than what many of the lower-income households are believed to be able to afford, e.g., $13,000 (UN-HABITAT, 2011). SOFOLS have continued to target the estimated 11 million Mexicans working largely as undocumented, migrant labour in the US with 'cross-border' mortgages to pay off homes in Mexico, giving them more control over the earnings they send relatives and cutting the time they need to work in the US to build a future in Mexico (Knowledge@Wharton, 2011).

It bears repeating here that despite and in contrast to, the neoliberal rhetorical about market-based solutions to housing finance, all these programmes are backed by the Mexican state, e.g., the Federal Mortgage Company. These reforms, coupled with the persistent economic downturn in the rest of the world, have made Mexico's thriving affordable housing market an attractive investment for a number of private equity funds keen to capitalise on the long-term growth potential and stable returns associated with the affordable housing sector (Business Monitor International, 2011).

Market-based 'affordable' housing: an efficient and effective solution for the poor?

The class-led advancement of neoliberalisation in the housing market has resulted in several characteristics that not only stand out after several years of mortgage securitisation but also will act as the starting point for renewed paradoxes to be resolved, once again, by the credit system – with the assistance of the Mexican debtfare state. According to the Mexican Federal Mortgage Company (SHF), the attempts to expand the mortgage securities market reveal comparatively higher levels of securitisation with regard to the Housing Funds than private issuances through *Hipotecaria Total* (or, HiTO), which is funded by – among other actors – the SHF, Soros Foundation and Netherlands Development Finance Company (FMO) (CIDOC, 2008; 'A Danish Model in Aztec Dress', *The Economist*, 4 January 2007).

As Figure 9.1 shows, the largest issuer of mortgage securitisation continues to be INFONAVIT, with 35 percent of the market (IDB, 2011). This implies that, contrary to the rhetoric of market-led efficiency, the state is not only playing a key role in the marketisation of housing finance, but also that the highest concentration of money raised for alleged redistribution to the surplus population will remain within the formal sector as opposed to the informal sector workers, who require decent and affordable housing. As of 2009, for instance, INFONAVIT and FOVISSSTE held 82 percent of the market for new mortgages, whereas SOFOLS held 2.7 percent (down from 7.6 percent in 2008) and commercial banks weighed in at 15.3 percent (down from 6.4 percent in 2008) (Inter-American Development Bank, 2011: 16).

The tight and dependent relationship between the Mexican state, construction firms and private housing finance companies such as SOFOLS, has not only continued to consolidate, but also has yielded a concentration of market power as opposed to increased competition as espoused by neoclassical economics. In 2008, four SOFOLS dominated 68 percent of the market share in construction bridge loans (Inter-American Development Bank, 2011: 24). In 2009, 60 percent of new house mortgages issued by INFONAVIT were built by 25 construction companies (IDB, 2011: 14–15; CIDOC, 2011). In 2010, 88 percent of mortgage financing

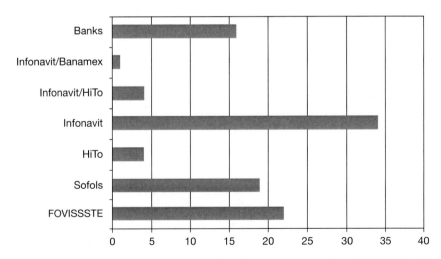

FIGURE 9.1 Primary issues of Mexican residential mortgage securities, 2003–2012 (in %)

Source: Infonavit cited in CIDOC (2012) *The Current State of Housing in Mexico 2012*, Mexico City, Mexico: CIDOC, p.35.

by INFONAVIT was built by Mexico's largest construction company, Homex (Business Monitor International, 2011).

The largest construction companies in Mexico continue to rely heavily on the debtfare state (e.g., Federal Mortgage Company and Housing Funds) to provide mortgage financing to low-income groups in the private and public (formal or affiliated) sectors (CONAVI, 2009; Business Monitor International, 2011). The close relationships between the Mexican state and major construction companies were also made evident, for example, in 2011 when delays in the '2×1' subsidy program, whereby the Mexican government offers one peso in subsidies for every two pesos that local governments pledge to help low-income families become homeowners, had an immediate and detrimental impact on six major construction companies, including Homex ('Mexico Builders Fall to Lowest Since 2009 on Subsidy Delays', *Bloomberg*, 1 November 2011).

Despite these synergies between state and capital, however, the tensions in the housing market continue to sharpen. In 2012, the year-over-year home repossessions more than doubled to a record 43,853 (Inter-American Development Bank, 2011; SHF, 2011). This, in turn, has also affected Mexico's large construction companies. Urbi and Geo both defaulted on bond payments in 2013 and are considering restructuring debt, including filing for bankruptcy ('In Mexico, Troubling Times', *Wall Street Journal*, 15 May 2013). Homex has sold its stakes in two prisons in an attempt to avoid following its peers into default. The company's currency reserves plummeted 86 percent to 322.7 million pesos as of 31 March from the end of 2012 ('Mexico's Record Foreclosures Impeding Home Ownership: Mortgages', *Bloomberg*, 1 May 2013).

Despite the renewed focus on providing affordable housing to the poor, the customer base of the SOFOLS did not expand to include the low-income segment of the population (UN-HABITAT, 2011). It is estimated that at least 40 percent of all existing homes have been constructed directly by the homeowners without either public or private help. Most of these homes belong to individuals in the low-income, informal sector (UN-HABITAT, 2011: 14; GlobalLens, 2012). Interestingly, the number of self-constructed, informal homes remains similar to the period prior to the introduction of mortgage securitisation in 2003, reflecting the importance of self-constructed homes in the built environment prior to the introduction of the marketisation of housing rights in Mexico (Ball and Connolly, 1987; GlobalLens, 2012).

The global corporate behemoth CEMEX, a Mexican-based building materials supplier and cement producer, has long-exploited this large and persistent market of self-constructed, informal dwellings through its micro-credit programme, *Patrimonio Hoy*, which roughly translates into 'Personal Property Today'. *Patrimonio Hoy* was created in 1998 in the wake of the recessionary environment of the post-peso crisis. CEMEX used this micro-finance strategy to boost sales in the face of rising unemployment and a drastically devalued Mexican peso to target its largest customer segment: the self-construction market (Sandoval, 2005; GlobalLens, 2006). Similar to the retail financing discussed in Chapter 8, the CEMEX lending programme is aimed at providing those shut out of the housing finance system with credit to purchase goods and services from CEMEX (CEMEX, 2010). Surplus workers, who earn less than four times the MMW, pay about $14 on a weekly basis for 70 weeks to CEMEX. This in turn purchases consultations and inspections by CEMEX staff and scheduled deliveries of materials divided into building phases spanning more than a year (CEMEX, 2010). For workers based in the informal economy, this commitment is steep. In the best-case scenario, the weekly payment of $14 translates into slightly less than three days of a worker's wages (e.g., the minimum wage, which it bears repeating is far from a living wage, was set at 65 pesos ($5.10) per day in 2013) (see Chapter 8). This assumes the worker is able both to earn the minimum wage and to find steady employment for the week.

Patrimonio Hoy is highly lucrative. In 2011, for instance, it generated a profit of $3.5 million from $45 million in revenues (GlobalLens, 2012). The micro-credit programme is championed as one of Latin America's most successful 'social enterprises' and has been expanded to several Latin American countries, including Colombia, Costa Rica, Nicaragua and the Dominican Republic.[16] In 2011 and mirroring the global debtfarist strategies covered in Chapter 7, the Inter-American Development Bank facilitated the further expansion of *Patrimonio Hoy* by providing the corporation with a partial credit guarantee of up to $10 million (GlobalLens, 2012). Reflecting the market-based ethos of housing for low-income Mexicans, it is interesting to note that Cemex, through its lending programme, *Patrimonio Hoy*, continues to benefit from the inability of the marketisation of housing rights to reach the poor. Despite Cemex's success, however, mortgage securitisation and its enabling debtfarist framings and interventions have not resulted in easing the housing deficit for low-income Mexicans. Instead, it has developed into a significant subsidy to the housing financial sector and construction industry, which stands in contrast to the rhetoric that it has been undertaken in the name of the poor.

Conclusion

Building on the insights from Chapter 7 and Chapter 8, this chapter sought to meet two objectives. First, through the example of mortgage securitisation, it evaluated the neoliberal claims that marketisation of housing rights is an efficient and effective solution to providing adequate housing for the surplus population in Mexico. Second, it sought to historicise and politicise mortgage securitisation by situating this class strategy in the wider dynamics of capital accumulation.

My research has demonstrated that the democratised access to credit money (fictitious capital) and the win-win narratives of mortgage securitisation that underpin the marketisation of housing rights remain mythical features of neoliberal narratives of market efficiency (see also Sassen, 2008; Wyly et al., 2009). In this chapter, I have revealed that the primary beneficiaries of mortgage securitisation in Mexico have not been the poor, whom securitisation is allegedly designed to serve, but instead large construction companies and the housing finance market comprised of state-subsidised Housing Funds and SOFOLS. This also includes the increasing number of foreign-owned commercial banks and institutional investors (e.g., equity funds, pension funds) that have been entering the field, particularly since the US sub-prime housing crisis of 2007–2008. Seen through a historical materialist approach, I have shown that mortgage securitisation is neither a natural evolutionary feature of the market nor has it produced a win-win scenario. Indeed, with the assistance of debtfarist intervention, primarily through the Federal Mortgage Company (SHF), the main beneficiaries of mortgage securitisation in Mexico continue to be middle-income workers in the formal sector earning more than six times the minimum monthly wage, the construction industry and the housing financial sector.

In closing, the historical materialist framework applied in this book has allowed us to move outside the realm of exchange – where both the housing problem (deficit for the poor) and its solution (mortgage securitisation) have been formulated by debtfarism. In this way, it has allowed us to trace the emergence and meaning of mortgage securitisation to the dominant neoliberal development paradigm, which emphasises the importance of financial inclusion as a central means to deal with the basic subsistence needs of the surplus population (e.g., housing and, by extension, the reliance on private and formal lenders to deal with housing needs). What emerges is a picture of the disconnect between neoliberal promises of financial inclusion and the harsh social realities for the working poor in Mexico.

Mortgage securitisation is not a neutral financial instrument that has emerged from a naturally evolving market, but rather a social phenomenon that has been heavily subsidised and normalised by the Mexican state and its debtfarist forms of intervention. If, when and at what social cost the ongoing processes of neo-liberalisation will result in housing gains for low-income families in Mexico remains an open question. What is certain is that the answer will be marked as much by the past contingencies and struggles inherent to credit-led accumulation as the ones that lie ahead.

Notes

1 Adequate shelter as defined by the UN-HABITAT refers to

> more than a roof over one's head. It also means adequate privacy; adequate space; physical accessibility; adequate security; security of tenure; structural stability and durability; adequate lighting, heating and ventilation; adequate basic infrastructure, such as water-supply, sanitation and waste-management facilities; suitable environmental quality and health related factors; and adequate and accessible location with regard to work and basic facilities: all of which should be available at an affordable cost. Adequacy should be determined together with the people concerned, bearing in mind the prospect for gradual development.
>
> (UN-HABITAT, 2010b: 6)

2 The scholarly literature on mortgage securitisation in Mexico has been sparse, particularly with regard to inquiries about questions of power. Where discussion has taken place, it has been dominated by economistic (Barry et al., 1994; Sanchez, 2010) and legal (Haddad, 1999; Poindexter and Vargas-Cartaya, 2003) analyses that were largely written

prior to the introduction of mortgage securitisation, meaning they tend to be devoid of historical and social context. These debates have yielded empirically rich and informative discussions about the legal and regulatory considerations involved in the shifting terrain of the housing finance system and its impact on mitigating risk with regard to the low-income segments of the population. However, due to the treatment of mortgage securitisation as a technical and ahistorical instrument, debates that have touched upon mortgage securitisation in Mexico have failed to provide an explanatory analysis of the types of questions posed above (Jordan, 2008).

3 The Spanish name for the Mexican Housing Corporation is *Sociedad Hipotecaria Federal* or SHF. For more information, see: www.shf.gob.mx/Paginas/default.aspx (accessed 13 August 2013).

4 The study also notes that '8.1 million earned above this cut-off, with a quarter of this group in the top two income deciles, suggesting that a lack of access to mortgage financing is also evident among higher income groups' (Herbert *et al.*, 2012: 10). This is an important aspect of study, but remains outside the scope of this analysis.

5 According to the UN-HABITAT, Housing's 'backward and forward linkages with other parts of the economy closely bond people's needs, demands and social processes with the supply of land, infrastructure, building materials, technology, labour, and housing finance. These linkages allow housing to act as an important engine for sustainable development and poverty reduction in both society and the economy' (UN-HABITAT, 2010a: 5).

6 Every enterprise, including agricultural, mining, industrial or other, is obliged to provide comfortable and hygienic housing for its workers. To meet this obligation, enterprises must pay the National Worker Housing Fund an amount equal to five percent of the amount paid in worker salaries. (Art. 136). The National Worker Housing Fund is intended to create financing systems that enable workers to obtain credit at low cost to acquire property or to construct, repair, or improve their housing (FLL Art. 137). The resources of the Fund shall be administered by a tripartite committee composed of representatives of the labour force, employers and the government (FLL Art. 138). United States Department of Labor. Minimum Employment Standards in Mexico. Available at: www.dol.gov/ilab/media/reports/nao/minemployment.htm#xxvii (accessed 3 March 2013).

7 This bank is referred to as the Banco Nacional de Fomento de la Vivienda y la Producción in Spanish.

8 Most of the social property can be further divided into two types: *ejidos*, which make up 83 percent of this form of property, and *communidades agrarias*, which comprise 17 percent (Inter-American Development Bank, 2011).

9 Given the expenses required to create legal ownership of land, and the pressing need for housing for the poor, the federal and municipal governments have turned a blind eye to this situation. Moreover, the benefits from holding formal or informal home ownership are somewhat unclear in many parts of Mexico. For instance, 'While a little more than half of homes without a title have water and sewage services in the home, it is also true that only about three quarters of homes with a title have these services' (Herbert *et al.*, 2012: 18).

10 In Spanish, CETES stands for *Certificados de la Tesorería*. More information is available at: www.banxico.org.mx/ayuda/temas-mas-consultados/cetes—mexican-federal-treasu. html (accessed 12 August 2013).

11 See Chapter 3 for the importance of monetarism to the neoliberal management of money and credit.

12 A SOFOL is limited purpose in that it may only lend to one sector only, such as housing, agri-industry, or manufacturing. The fastest growing and largest SOFOLS are those that specialise in mortgages (Emmond, 2005).

13 The Spanish name of this financial instrument is: *unidades de inversión*, or, UDIs, for short. For more information, see: www.banxico.org.mx/ayuda/temas-mas-consultados/udis--mexico_s-investment-uni.html (accessed 14 August 2013).

14 Habitat International Coalition (2006) 'State Support for Social Production of Housing?: Mexico's new Housing Law Exposes Planning Contradictions and Challenges'. Available at: www.gloobal.net/iepala/gloobal/fichas/ficha.php?entidad=Textos&id=5300&opcion= documento (accessed 9 August 2013).

15 The Mexican Federal Mortgage Company (SHF) was also to remove its 100 percent guarantee for funding mortgage securities in 2009. This was subsequently extended to 2013. As of January 2014, it is unclear if the SHF is actually implementing this decision, however (SHF, 2014). Available: www.pencom.gov.ng/download/.../Mortgage_Market_in_Mexico.ppt_ (accessed 15 January 2014).

16 'IDB to support expansion of CEMEX microfinance program for low-income families', *News Release*, 28 June 2011. Available: www.iadb.org/en/news/news-releases/2011-06-28/cemex-housing-microfinance,9413.html (accessed 28 June 2013).

CONCLUSION

In many ways, this book is a contribution to our understanding of the processes and paradoxes of neoliberalisation and its social reproduction. Drawing on a historical materialist lens, I examined the roles played by neoliberal states in deepening its class-based agenda through the social power of money. I also sought to explain how and why this configuration of class-led power has extended the privatisation of the commons, intensified the commodification of basic social services and normalised an overarching policy preference for hyper-individualised and marketised forms of self-help (responsibilisation) for the weak and corporate welfarism for the strong (Gill, 1995; Wacquant, 2009). I have also demonstrated how such strategies, framed by neoliberal states – and debtfarism in particular – have paved the way for the construction of the poverty industry in the United States and Mexico.

In so doing, the book sought to challenge conventional ways of thinking about the extension of privately created money in the form of consumer credit to the surplus population; that is, the poor who constitute an increasing segment of the world's population. In more specific terms, I wanted to contribute to the debates on neoliberalisation in a way that will facilitate a more rigorous and complete explanation regarding the origins of power, transformation and the social reproduction of the monetised relations of debt in the poverty industry.

I avoided using the fashionable, yet – as is often the case of trendy terms in academia – vacuous concept of 'financialisation'. Instead, I began my analysis where most debates about financialisation unfortunately end: taking seriously the social power of money as it relates to the wider dynamics and social relations of capital accumulation. In taking this step, I move beyond post-structuralist approaches that employ an economist's view of money and credit in capitalist society. These approaches, I argue, can only construct complementary fetishised understandings of the cultural and social dimensions of capitalism. As a corrective,

I suggest that we employ a historical materialist framework to locate the origins of the social power of money in the wider context of the dynamics of credit-led accumulation.

To understand the processes involved in the social reproduction of debtors, I have drawn analytical and concrete attention to the surplus population (under-employed and unemployed workers). This Marxian category of labour power is often portrayed as a dynamic, spatially specific and heterogeneous group of workers that are marginal to, but do not exist outside, the processes of capital accum-ulation. The surplus population, I argue, represents an integral feature of the expression of global capitalism since the early 1980s: namely, credit-led accumula-tion – or, accumulation via privately created money. The surplus population's significance to the processes of accumulation in neoliberalisation is two-fold. On the one hand, the low wages paid to surplus workers provides a competitive advantage for capitalists. To illustrate, the UN-HABITAT notes that slums facilitate the existence of a country's competitive advantage because they house the lowest-income worker. '[T]he lowest income worker becomes the "gold dust of the urban economy". And the place where they can afford to live becomes the "gold mine of the city economy"' (UN-HABITAT, 2006: 5). On the other hand, the surplus population has also come to represent a site for capitalists seeking to expand their interest-, fee- and commission-generating services ("the gold mine") to an increasing number of the surplus population. The latter have been sanitised in business language as the 'bottom of the pyramid', made victims of the dispossessive strategies of mainstream finance institutions that are veiled by the seemingly progressive, yet ambiguous, façade of financial inclusion strategies.

The dominance, power and contradictory nature of privately created money coupled with state retrenchment regarding social programmes in the face of the rise of the surplus population has fomented an institutional (legal and regulatory) and ideological (rhetorical) feature of state intervention: debtfarism. Sitting alongside other core modes of governance, such as workfare, monetarism, corporate welfare, the concept of debtfare promises to offer an important contribution to the debates of neoliberalisation. This new form of governance has facilitated the expansion of privately created money in the form of poverty industry and therewith has assisted in the social reproduction of the surplus population. At their base, the processes of social reproduction under debtfarism are aimed at constructing, both legally and ideologically, a dependence of the working poor on privately created money. Through the application of the social power of money and its attendant illusions of the community of money, debtfarism has assisted in underwriting a new social pact between corporations and surplus workers in which the former are entitled to state protection (e.g., private property) and welfare benefits (e.g., subsidisations, bailouts) while the latter are entitled to access formal credit channels to meet their basic subsistence needs in the name of financial inclusion and the democratisation of credit.

The illusions of democracy, equality and freedom underpinning the community of money are not only bolstered by the construction of the surplus population as a source of consumer citizens and/or clients. The distortion of the exploitative and disciplinary nature of the community of money is continually undergirded by those who insist on representing money and credit as economic categories that reside almost exclusively in the realm of exchange. As I have demonstrated, money has inherent social power. In capitalism, this expresses itself as a universal equivalent, a thing that has the capacity to expand abstract wealth independently of exploitation. Money also serves to destroy personal bonds of dependency and replace them with relations of objective dependency through which individuals relate to each other through 'things' (abstractions) such as interest rates, credit ratings, fees, consumer lender relations and so forth.

The illusionary powers of the community of money, including its ability to mask exploitation and individualise and commodify relations between people, is further amplified by the particular attributes of privately created money and its capacity to spatially and temporally displace contradictions – albeit only temporarily and only with the assistance of states and, in some cases, international organisations (e.g., G20). Extending privately created money to subprime borrowers in the United States and in Mexico, for example, represents a spatial fix in capitalists' interests of pursuing increasingly more lucrative outlets. The temporal displacement of these loans through sophisticated derivative-based instruments tied to asset-backed securitisation (i.e., the commodification of debt) cannot escape a fundamental tension of credit: no matter how far afield a privately contracted bill of exchange may circulate, it must always return to its place of origin for redemption (Harvey, 1999: 245–6).

The myriad of financial crises based on the paradoxes of privately created money – that is the expansion of credit beyond its monetary basis – has not meant the weakening of neoliberalisation. Instead, in many cases, neoliberalisation has been strengthened and deepened through these processes. From a Marxian perspective, crises are unpredictable but inevitable, providing moments in which the legitimacy of neoliberal-led capitalism can be questioned and contested across a wide variety of interests, constituencies and classes. Nonetheless, since the 1980s, the advent of each major financial crisis has been used to reimpose the power and discipline of money (e.g., fresh waves of fiscal austerity, especially for public sector workers and soft laws for corporations) by invoking and recreating the illusions of the community of money (Harvey, 1999).

Instead of guaranteeing living wages and public provisioning for basic social needs, the neoliberal pact in the new millennium is all about safeguarding market freedoms and equality to ensure that all *consumers* may benefit from standards of fairness, competition, transparency and accountability. These market freedoms guaranteed by debtfarism are continually framed in the illusions of the community of money and bolstered by the seeming neutrality of the legal obligation of debt and consumer protection. In this way, debtfarism mirrors new systems of governance in neoliberalism that has integrated states and corporate interests. A key feature of these new systems of neoliberal governance involves the social power of money. As David Harvey (2008: 38) observes, 'through the application of money power, [neoliberal states have] ensured that the disbursement of the surplus through the state apparatus favours corporate capital and the upper classes'.

My concept of debtfarism is designed to capture new modes of neoliberal governance in credit-led accumulation, specifically with regard to the personal indebtedness of impoverished workers. Implicit to these new modes of govern-ance are an unwritten, dynamic and informal compromise or pact that provides a foundational basis upon which neoliberalisation has come to rest. This pact, which I refer to here, out of convenience, as the 'corporate responsibilisation compact' is unique from previous compromises in that it is has emerged on an *ad hoc* basis since the early 1980s. I should also note that this compromise assumes different, differentiated, multi-scalar articulations and meanings over time and space.

Unlike the majority of compromises forged in the aftermath of World War II, the corporate responsibilisation pact does not involve either a tripartite agree-ment or a Keynesianist-inspired material basis, e.g., welfare protection. Instead, it involves an implicit, top-down relation between corporations and workers, which is undergirded by the rhetorical and regulatory powers of capitalist states. The compromise underpinning the corporate responsibilisation compact reflects some features of the Third Way solution, which was popularised by the Clinton Administration (1993–2001) in the United States and Tony Blair in the United Kingdom (1997–2007) and which also found itself reformulated in the Washington Consensus and the post-Washington Consensus (Giddens, 2000; Stiglitz, 2003). As many authors have rightfully argued, these features were largely rhetorical in nature and served to strengthen the foundations of neoliberalisation, prioritising individualised self-help as opposed to affect any meaningful form of social justice (Peck and Tickell, 2002; Wacquant, 2009). The connection between the Third Way and what might be referred to as the corporate responsibilisation compact is indeed an attempt to achieve economic growth through entrepreneurialism, market-led wealth creation and private consumption alongside greater social justice, which involves a major role for the state. However, the new system of neoliberal governance that has integrated state and corporate interests involves strategies that are not framed in legal or regulatory code; but instead remain less legible and very much top-down creations.

As Peck and Tickell (2002) argue, the continually changing forms of interven-tion of capitalist states and the deepening of the social power of money serves to deflect and even delegitimise alternatives to neoliberalisation – not least a return to public consumption and control over essential services, the protection of the weakest through basic safety standards and living wages and, more funda-mentally, the redistribution of wealth through progressive taxation, including corporations. The great irony and tragedy of our times is that, after several decades of continual neoliberal assaults, the meaning of the Third Way's insistence of a greater role for the state in achieving justice has translated into the institu-tionalisation and normalisation of corporations as both perpetrators against and providers of, protection against the social and environmental destruction of free-market growth. In this sense, the new pact driven by states and corporations has meant that all social and environmental concerns have been reconfigured into metrics that grant primacy to profit maximisation, individual responsibilisation and economic efficiency.

Debtfarism and its illusory powers of the community of money, manifest the corporate responsibilisation compact. There are many more articulations of this across the globe. The UN-HABITAT, as I noted in Chapter 9, has been actively seeking ways of implementing the corporate compact between capitalists and slum-dwellers through, for instance, its Slum Upgrading Housing Facility Programme (UN-HABITAT, 2006). This is an attempt to ensure that the surplus population ('the gold dust'), many members of which live in slum dwellings across the globe, are able to reproduce themselves through access to affordable housing. The solution to this dire social and environmental problem is not a turn to public housing and/or rent control. Instead, the role of the state and international organisations such as the UN-HABITAT, World Bank, Inter-American Development Bank and so forth is to connect global financial markets to slum dwellers, thereby creating a gold mine.

The state subsidised *Patrimonio Hoy* programme, financed by one of the world's largest cement corporations, Cemex, is a case in point. The former Canadian International Development Agency (CIDA) offers another example of a corporate responsibilisation compact.[1] Before its demise and takeover by the Canadian government's Department of Foreign Affairs and International Trade, CIDA was engaging in providing public funds to finance corporate social responsibility partnerships between development NGOs (e.g., World University Service of Canada and Plan Canada) and Canadian mining companies operating in the global South (MiningWatch Canada, 2012). In effect, the Canadian neoliberal state was not only engaging in corporate welfare for Canadian mining corporations; but also underwriting a compact between societal interests harmed by its extractive strategies. In other words, the Canadian state, along with large development NGOs – which are notoriously dependent on state and corporate financing – provide legitimacy to Canadian mining corporations to ensure the connection between the gold mine and the gold dust could be maintained in a free-market environment devoid of taxation, expensive reparations and or legal constraints.

This emerging corporate responsibilisation compact forces us to reflect critically on how we conceptualise new articulations of governance that undemocratically integrate state and corporate interests, while excluding all other voices and non-market based values. More work needs to be done in terms of thinking through and examining these new forms of governance, including debtfarism. In particular, we need to consider debtfarism against the backdrop of other debt relations – most notably sovereign debt and environmental debt – and across local, national and global scales of capitalism.

In closing, my contribution has not been to provide blueprints and roadmaps of how struggles should proceed. Instead, my aim has been to raise pertinent questions about how to radically re-think the meanings of the uncontested revolutionary power of money, the continued impoverishment of workers and neo-liberal modes of governance. In so doing, I have attempted to examine and theorise how these three sets of social relations are inextricably linked to the hegemony of credit-led accumulation – a form of accumulation that is charac-terised, as Marx warns, by unlimited forms of social power.

Note

1   CIDA was terminated in name and existing bureaucratic structure in 2013. Aid spending, however, continues through the Canadian government, but under the purview of the Department of Foreign Affairs and International Trade. For more information see, www.acdi-cida.gc.ca/acdi-cida/acdi-cida.nsf/eng/home (accessed 1 October 2013).

BIBLIOGRAPHY

ACA International (2010) *2010 Agency Benchmarking Survey*, Minneapolis, MN: ACA International (The Association of Credit and Collection Professionals).

Advance America (2010) *2010 Annual Report*, Spartanburg, SC: Advance America Cash Advance Centre.

—— (2012) *Groupo Elektra to Acquire Advance America for $10.50 Per Share*, 15 February. Available www.advanceamerica.net/press-details/grupo-elektra-to-acquire-advance-america-for-10.50-per-share (accessed 12 May 2012).

AFI (Alliance for Financial Inclusion) (2010) *Innovative Financial Inclusion: principles and report on innovative financial inclusion from the access through innovation sub-group of the G20 Financial Inclusion Experts Group*. Available: www.microfinancegateway.org/gm/document-1.9.44743/Innovative_Financial_Inclusion.pdf (accessed 15 July 2013).

—— (2011) *The G20 Principles for Innovative Financial Inclusion: bringing the principles to life – eleven country case studies*, Bangkok, Thailand: Alliance for Financial Inclusion.

—— (2012) *Strategy Development: organising for financial inclusion supporting strategic approaches to the AFI Network*. Available: www.afi-global.org/sites/default/files/publications/AFI_Strategy%20development_AW_low%20res.pdf (accessed 20 July 2013).

—— (2013) *Measuring Financial Inclusion in Mexico: CNBV's approach to obtaining better data for decision-makers*, Bangkok, Thailand: Alliance for Financial Inclusion.

Agarwal, S., Skiba, P. M. and Tobacman, J. (2009) 'Payday loans and credit cards: new liquidity and credit scoring puzzle?', *American Economic Review*, 99(2): 412–17.

Aitken, R. (2010) 'Regul(ariz)ation of Fringe Credit: payday lending and the borders of global financial practice', *Competition and Change*, 14(2): 80–99.

Albeda, R. (2012) 'Same single-mother poverty: fifteen years of welfare reform', *Dollars & Sense*, January/February: 11–17.

Albo, G. (1994) '"Competitive Austerity" and the impasse of capitalist employment policy', in L. Panitch and R. Milliband (eds) *Socialist Register*, London: Merlin Press.

Altbach, P. G., Reisberg, L. and Rumbley, L. (2007) *Trends in Global Higher Education: tracking an academic revolution*, Chestnut Hill, MA: Boston College Center for International Higher Education.

Altvater, E. (1993) *The Future of the Market: an essay on the regulation of money and nature after the collapse of 'actually existing socialism'*, London: Verso.

Altvater, E. (2009) *Privatisierung und Korruption: Zur Kriminologie von Globalisierung, Neoliberalismus und Finanzkrise.* Hamburg: Anders Verlag.

Altvater, E. and Hoffmann, J. (1990) 'The West German state derivation debate: The relation between economy and politics as a problem of Marxist state theory', *Social Text*, 24(2): 134–55.

Amin, S. (1974) *Accumulation on a World Scale: a critique of the theory of underdevelopment*, vol. 2, New York, NY: Monthly Review Press.

Angelucci, M., Karlan, D. and Zinman, J. (2013) *Win Some Lose Some? Evidence from a randomized microcredit programme placement experiment by Compartamos Banco*, Washington, DC: The National Bureau of Economic Research.

Anton-Diaz, P. (2013) 'Striking a balance between private and social interests: lessons from microfinance in Mexico', *Journal of International Affairs*, 66(2): npn. Available: http://jia.sipa.columbia.edu/striking-a-balance-between-private-and-social-interests (accessed 24 April 2013).

Arrieta Gonzales, G. M. (2005) 'Mortgage loans and assets to housing for low-income households in Latin America', *CEPAL Review*, 85: 111–24.

Arrighi, G. (1994) *The Long Twentieth Century: money, power and the origins of our times*, New York, NY: Verso.

Austin, R. (2004) 'Of predatory lending and the democratisation of credit: preserving the social safety net of informality in small-loan transactions', *American University Law Review*, 53(6): 1217–57.

Ausubel, L. M. (1997) 'Credit card defaults, credit card profits and bankruptcy', *American Bankruptcy Law Journal*, 71(Spring): 249–70.

Baars, G. (2011) 'Reform or revolt? Polanyian vs Marxian perspectives on the regulation of "the economic"', *Northern Ireland Legal Quarterly*, 24(4): 415–31.

Bakker, I. and Gill, S. (2003) *Power, Production and Social Reproduction*, London: Palgrave.

Ball, M. and Connolly, P. (1987) 'Capital and accumulation in the Mexican construction industry, 1930–1982', *International Journal of Urban and Regional Research*, 11(2): 153–71.

Banco de Mexico (2010) *Ley para la Transparencia y Ordenamiento de los Servicios Financieros LTOSF*. Available: www.banxico.org.mx/disposiciones/circulares/leyes/%7B24EF3EEB-A8A3-D421–2F2D-9FA43FA9850E%7D.pdf (accessed 15 July 2013).

—— (2011) *Financial System Report*, Mexico City, Mexico: Banco de Mexico.

—— (2013) *Mexico: the challenges of capital inflows*, Mexico City, Mexico: Banco de Mexico.

Bancomer (2011) *Mexico – Situación Inmobiliaria. Servicio de Estudios Económicos del Grupo BBVA*, Mexico City, Mexico: BBVA Bancomer.

—— (2013) *Real Estate Outlook – Mexico*, Mexico City, Mexico: BBVA Bancomer.

Bank for International Settlements (2006) 'The banking system in emerging economies: how much progress has been made?', *Monetary and Economic Department, Working Paper No. 28*, Basle, Switzerland: Bank for International Settlements.

—— (2010) *Country Review of Mexico. Peer Review Report*, Secretariat to the Financial Stability Board, Basel, Switzerland: Bank for International Settlements.

—— (2011) *The Joint Forum – report on asset securitisation incentives*, Basle, Switzerland: Bank for International Settlements.

—— (2013) *Statistical Release: OTC Derivatives Statistics at end-December 2012*, Basle, Switzerland: Bank for International Settlements.

Barkin, D. (2009) 'Welfare and well-being in Mexico', *Rethinking Marxism*, 12(3): 99–108.

Barry, C., Castañeda, G. and Lipscomb, J. B. (1994) 'The structure of mortgage markets in Mexico and prospects for their securitisation', *Journal of Housing Research*, 5(2): 173–204.

Bateman, M. (2010) *Why Doesn't Microfinance Work?*, London: Zed Books.

—— (2013) *The Age of Microfinance: destroying Latin American economies from the bottom up*, Vienna, Austria: Austrian Research Foundation for International Development/ Oesterreichische Forschungsstiftung fuer internationale Entwicklung.

BCP Securities LLC (2010) *Mexico's Consumer Finance Industry: three newcomers to the bond market offer attractive yields*, Greenwich, CT: BCP Securities LLC.

Beaver, W. (2012) 'Fraud in for-profit higher education', *Social Science and Public Policy*, 49(1): 274–8.

Bejar, A. (2006) 'Mexico's 2006 elections: the rise of populism and the end of neoliberalism?' *Latin American Perspectives*, 33(2): 17–32.

Bieler, A. and Lindberg, I. (eds) (2010) *Global Restructuring, Labour and the Challenges for Transnational Solidarity*, London: Routledge.

Bird, E. J., Hagstrom, P. A. and Wild, R. (1997) *Credit Cards and the Poor*, University of Wisconsin-Madison: Institute for Research on Poverty, Discussion Paper No. 1148–97.

Birdwell, M. G. (1978) 'Student loan bankruptcies', *Washington University Law Review*, 6(3): 593–621.

Bivens, J. and Mishel, L. (2013) 'The pay of corporate executives and financial professionals as evidence of rents in top 1 percent of incomes', *Journal of Economic Persectives*, 27(3): 58–78.

Bond, P. (2013) 'Debt, uneven development and capitalist crisis in South Africa: from Moody's macroeconomic monitoring to Marikana microfinance mashonistas', *Third World Quarterly*, 34(4): 569–92.

Bonefeld, W. (1995) 'Money, equality and exploitation: an interpretation of Marx's treatment of money', in W. Bonefeld and J. Holloway (eds) *Global Capital, National State and the Politics of Money*, New York, NY: St. Martin's Press.

Bonefeld, W. and Holloway, J. (eds) (1995) *Global Capital, National State and the Politics of Money*, New York, NY: St. Martin's Press.

Bourdieu, P. (1991) *Language and Symbolic Power*, Cambridge, MA: Harvard University Press.

—— (1998) *Acts of Resistance: against the tyranny of the market*, New York, NY: The New York Press.

—— (2005) *The Social Structures of the Economy*, Cambridge: Polity Press.

—— (2009) *Outline of a Theory of Practice*, Cambridge: Cambridge University Press.

Braithwaite, J. and Drahos, P. (2000) *Global Business Regulation*, Cambridge: Cambridge University Press.

Breman, J. (2003) *The Labouring Poor in India; Patterns of Exploitation and Exclusion*, Delhi: Oxford University Press Delhi.

Breman, J. (2012) *Outcast Labour in Asia Circulation and Informalisation of the Workforce at the Bottom of the Economy*, Oxford: Oxford University Press.

Brenner, N., Peck, J. and Theodore, N. (2010) 'Variegated neoliberalisation: geographies, modalities, pathways', *Global Networks*, 10(2): 1470–2266.

Brookings Institute (2011) 'The suburbanization of poverty: trends in metropolitan America, 2000 to 2008', *Metropolitan Policy Programme at Brookings*, Washington, DC: Brookings Institute.

Brown, E. (2008) 'Credit default swaps: evolving financial meltdown and derivative disaster du jour', *Global Research*, 11 April. Available: www.webofdebt.com/articles/derivatives-disaster.php (accessed 19 July 2013).

Bruff, I. (2014) 'The rise of authoritarian neoliberalism', *Rethinking Marxism*, 26(1): 113–29.

Brummer, C. (2012) *Soft Law and the Global Financial System: rule making in the 21st Century*, Cambridge: Cambridge University Press.

Bryan, D. and Rafferty M. (2006) *Capitalism with Derivatives: a political economy of financial derivatives, capital and class*, London: Palgrave.

Burgess, R. A. and Ciolfi, M. A. (1986) 'Exportation or exploitation? A state regulator's view of interstate credit card transactions', *Business Law*, 42: 929–41.

Burkett, P. and Hart-Landsberg, M. (2003) 'A critique of "catch-up" theories of development', *Journal of Contemporary Asia*, 33(2): 147–71.

Burkey, M. L. and Simkins, S. P. (2004) 'Factors affecting the location of payday lending and traditional banking services in North Carolina', *The Review of Regional Studies*, 34(2): 191–205.

Burton, D. (2008) *Credit and Consumer Society*, London: Routledge.

Calder, L. (eds) (1999) *Financing the American Dream: a cultural history of consumer credit*, Princeton, NJ: Princeton University Press.

Carnoy, M. (1984) *The State and Political Theory*, Princeton, NJ: Princeton University Press.

Carrell, S. and Zinman, J. (2008) 'In harm's way? Payday loan access and military personnel performance', *Working Paper, No. 8–18*, Philadelphia, PA: Federal Reserve Bank of Philadelphia.

Carothers, T. (1998) 'The rule of law revival', *Foreign Affairs*, 77(2): 95–106.

CIDOC (2008) *Current Housing Situation in Mexico 2008*, Mexico City: Fundación Centro de Investigación y Documentación de la Casa (CIDOC).

—— (2011) *Current Housing Situation in Mexico 2011*, Mexico City, Mexico: Fundación Centro de Investigación y Documentación de la Casa (CIDOC).

—— (2012) *Current Housing Situation in Mexico*, Mexico City, Mexico: Fundación Centro de Investigación y Documentación de la Casa (CIDOC).

Casteñeda, G., Castellanos, S. G. and Hernandez, F. (2011) *Policies and Innovations for Improving Financial Access in Mexico*, Washington, DC: Centre for Global Development.

Cemex (2010) *Cemex Housing: affordable and sustainable communities*, San Pedro Garza García, Mexico: Cemex.

Center for Community Capitalism (2007) *North Carolina Consumers After Payday Lending: attitudes and experiences with credit options*, Chapel Hill, NC: University of North Carolina.

Centre for Financial Services Innovation (2008) *The CFSI Underbanked Consumer Study – underbanked consumer overview and market segments*, Washington, DC: Centre for Financial Services Innovation.

Centre for Responsible Lending (2010) *Mainstream Banks Making Payday Loans: regulators must put swift end to new trend*, Durham, NC: Centre for Responsible Lending.

—— (2011) *Big Bank Payday Loans: high-interest loans through checking accounts keep customers in long-term debt*, Durham, NC: Centre for Responsible Lending.

—— (2013) *Triple-Digit Danger: bank payday lending persists*, Durham, NC: Centre for Responsible Lending.

Cerny, P. G. (1997) 'Paradoxes of the competition state: the dynamics of political globalization', *Government and Opposition*, 32(2): 251–74.

CGAP (2006) *Mexico: Country-Level Savings Assessment, 3rd Edition*, Washington, DC: Consultative Group to Assist the Poor.

—— (2007a) *CGAP Reflections on the Compartamos Initial Public Offering: a case study on microfinance interest rates and profits*, Washington, DC: Consultative Group to Assist the Poor.

—— (2007b) *Focus Note*, June, Washington, DC: Consultative Group to Assist the Poor.

—— (2009a) *Financial Access: measuring access to financial services around the world*, Washington, DC: Consultative Group to Assist the Poor.

—— (2009b) *The Impact of the Financial Crisis on Microfinance Institutions and their Clients: results from CGAP's 2009 opinion survey*, Washington, DC: Consultative Group to Assist the Poor.

—— (2010a) *Financial Access 2010 Report*, Washington, DC: Consultative Group to Assist the Poor.

—— (2010b) *Securitisation: a technical guide*, Washington, DC: Consultative Group to Assist the Poor.

—— (2011) *Global Standard-Setting Bodies and Financial Inclusion for the Poor: toward proportionate standards and guidance. A white paper prepared by CGAP on Behalf of the G20's Global Partnership for Financial Inclusion*, Washington, DC: Consultative Group to Assist the Poor.

—— (2012a) *A Structured Approach to Understanding the Financial Service Needs of the Poor in Mexico*, Washington, DC: Consultative Group to Assist the Poor.

—— (2012b) *Measuring Financial Exclusion: how many people are unbanked?* Available: www.cgap.org/blog/measuring-financial-exclusion-how-many-people-are-unbanked (accessed 24 July 2013).

CGAP and Morgan, J. P. (2010) *All Eyes on Asset Quality: microfinance global valuation survey 2010, Occasional Report, No. 16*, Washington, DC: Consultative Group to Assist the Poor.

Chang, H.-J. (2002) *Kicking Away the Ladder: development strategy in historical perspective*, London: Anthem Press.

Chang, H.-J. and Grabel, I. (2004) *Reclaiming Development: an alternative economic policy manual*, London: Zed Books.

Charnock, G. (2005) 'The Crisis of Foxism: the political economy of fiscal reform in Mexico', *Capital & Class*, (2): 1–8.

Charnock, G., Purcell, T. and Ribera-Fumaz, R. (2014) *The Limits to Capital in Spain: Crisis and Revolt in the European South*, London: Palgrave MacMillan.

Chen, Z. A. (2007) 'Securitising microcredit: the implications of securitisation for microcredit institutions' human rights missions', *Columbia Human Rights Law Review*, 1(39): 757–94.

Chin, P. (2004) 'Payday loans: the case for federal legislation', *University of Illinois Law Review*, 3: 723–54.

Choitz, V. and Reimherr, P. (2013) *Mind the Gap: high unmet financial need threatens persistence and completion for low-income community college students*, Washington, DC: Center for Post-Secondary and Economic Success.

Clarke, S. (1978) 'Capital, fractions of capital and the state', *Capital & Class*, 5: 32–77.

—— (1988) *Keynesianism, Monetarism and the Crisis of the State*, Aldershot: Edward Elgar.

—— (1991) *The State Debate*, London: Palgrave MacMillian.

—— (1994) *Marx's Theory of Crisis*, London: Palgrave MacMillian.

Coco, L. (2012) 'The cultural logics of the bankruptcy abuse prevention and Consumer Protection Act of 2005: fiscal identities and financial failure', paper presented at the Repoliticising Debt Workshop, Queen's University, Kingston, Ontario, May 2012.

—— (2013) 'Mortgaging human potential: student indebtedness and the practices of the neoliberal state', *Southwestern Law Review*, 42: 565–603.

Collinge, A. (2009) *The Student Loan Scam: the most oppressive debt in US history and how we can fight back*, New York: Beacon Press.

Collins, J. L. and Mayer, V. (2010) *Both Hands Tied: welfare reform and the race to the bottom of the low-wage labor market*, Chicago, IL: University of Chicago Press.

Comisión Nacional Bancaria y de Valores (CNBV) (2010) *Microfinance Regulation in Mexico: lessons and challenges ahead*, Mexico City: Comisión Nacional Bancaria y de Valores.

Commission on Global Governance (1995) *Our Global Neighbourhood: The Report of the Commission on Global Governance*, Oxford: Oxford University Press.

CONAVI (2009) *Mexican Housing Outlook*, Mexico City, Mexico: Comisión Nacional de Vivienda (CONAVI).

CONEVAL (2012) *Informe de Evaluación de la Política de Desarrollo Social en México 2012*. Mexico City: CONEVAL.

Connolly, P. (2007) 'The Mexican construction industry at the start of the twenty-first century: trends and outlook', *Tecnología y Construcción*, 23(2): 120–38.

Consumer Federation of America (2004) *A Report on Devices Used by Payday Lenders to Evade State Usury and Small Loan Laws*, Washington, DC: Consumer Federation of America.

Consumer Financial Protection Bureau (CFPB) (2013) *Payday Loans and Deposit Advance Products – a white paper of initial data findings*, Washington, DC: Consumer Financial Protection Bureau.

Consumer Financial Protection Bureau (CFPB) and Education (2012) *Private Student Loans*, Washington, DC: US Department of Education.

Cooter, R. D. (1997) 'The rule of state law and the rule-of-law state: economic analysis of the legal foundations of development', *Annual World Bank Conference on Development Economics 1996*, Washington, DC: World Bank, 191–217.

Corbridge, S. (1993) *Debt and Development*, Oxford: Blackwell Publishers.

Corder, K. and Hoffman, S. (2001) 'Privatizing federal credit programs: Why Sallie Mae?' *6th National Public Management Conference*, Bloomington, IN.

Correa, E. (2006) 'Changing constraints of monetary policy', in L. Randall (ed.) *Changing Structure of Mexico: political, social and economic prospects*, New York, NY: M.E. Sharpe.

Cox, R. W. (1995) 'Gramsci, hegemony and international relations', in S. Gill (ed.) *Gramsci, Historical Materialism and International Relations*, Cambridge: Cambridge University Press.

Crane, E. M., Eichenseer, N. J. and Glazer, E. S. (2011) 'US consumer protection law: a federalist patchwork', *Defense Counsel Journal*, 78(3): 305–30.

CreditCards.com (2008) *Prepaid, Reloadable Payment Cards for Immigrants Roll Out: the 'no SSN' prepaid cards offer respite from high-cost fringe services*, 19 September. Available: www.creditcards.com/credit-card-news/immigrants-prepaid-credit-cards-social-security-1282.php#ixzz1MixDg13w (accessed 19 May 2011).

Crouch, C. (2011) *The Strange Non-Death of Neoliberalism*, Cambridge: Polity Press.

Cutler, C. (2003) *Private Power and Global Authority: transnational merchant law in the Global Political Economy*, Cambridge: Cambridge University Press.

Cypher, J. M. (2001) 'Developing disarticulation within the Mexican economy', *Latin American Perspectives*, 28(3): 11–37.

Cypher, J. M. and Delgado, R. W. (2010) *Mexico's Economic Dilemma: the development failure of neoliberalism*, Boulder, CO: Rowman & Littlefield Publishers.

Da Costa, D. (2013) 'The "Rule of Experts" in Making a Dynamic Micro-Insurance Industry in India', *Journal of Peasant Studies*, 40(5): 845–65.

Dahl, R. (1956) *A Preface to Democratic Theory*, Chicago, IL: University of Chicago Press.

Damar, E. H. (2009) 'Why do payday lenders enter local markets? Evidence from Oregon', *Review of Industrial Organisation*, 34(2): 173–91.

Danel, C. and Labarthe, C. (2008) *A Letter to our Peers*, 17 June. Available: www.compartamos.com/wps/wcm/connect/?MOD=PDMProxy&TYPE=personalization&ID=NONE&KEY=NONE&LIBRARY=%2FcontentRoot%2Ficm%3Alibraries&FOLDER=%2FAcerca+de+Compartamos%2FDocumentos+es%2F&DOC_NAME=%2FcontentRoot%2Ficm%33Alibraries%2FAcerca+de+Compartamos%2FDocumentos+es%2FAlettertoourpeers.pdf&VERSION (accessed 2 September 2013).

de Angelis, M. (2007) *The Beginning of History: value struggles and global capital*, London: Pluto Press.

de Brunhoff, S. (1976) *Marx on Money*, New York, NY: Urizen Books.

de Goede, M. (2005) *A Genealogy of Finance: virtue, fortune and faith*, Minneapolis, MN: University of Minnesota Press.

Delpechitre, D. and DeVaney, S. (2006) 'Credit card usage among White, African American and Hispanic households', *Consumer Interest Annual*, 52: 466–72.

Deming, D. J., Goldin, C. and Katz, L. F. (2012) 'The for-profit postsecondary school sector: nimble critters or agile predators?', *Journal of Economic Perspectives*, 26(1): 139–64.

Dēmos (2003) *Borrowing to Make Ends Meet: the growth of credit card debt in the 1990s*, New York: Dēmos.

Denning, M. (2010) 'Wageless life', *New Left Review*, 66 (November–December): 79–97.

Dickerson, A. M. (2008) 'Consumer over-indebtedness: a US perspective', *Texas International Law Journal*, 43(135): 135–60.

Diehl, J. (2009) 'Microfinance in emerging markets: the effects of the current economic crisis and the role of securitisation', *Business Law Brief*, Spring: 37–42.

Dogra, N. (2012) *Representations of Global Poverty: aid, development and international NGOs*, London: I.B. Tauris & Co. Ltd.

Domowitz, I. and Eovaldi, T. (1993) 'The impact of the Bankruptcy Reform Act of 1978 on consumer bankruptcy', *Journal of Law and Economics*, 36(2): 803–35.

Drainville, A. (1995) 'Monetarism in Canada and the world economy', *Studies in Political Economy*, 46(Spring): 7–42.

Draut, T. (2004) *Strapped: why America's 20- and 30-somethings can't get ahead*, New York, NY: Anchor Books.

—— (2011) 'Occupy college', *The Nation*, 26 October. Available: www.thenation.com/article/164209/occupy-college# (accessed 1 October 2012).

Drury, L. L. III (2009) 'Predatory lending and its impact on consumer credit', *Loyola Journal of Public Interest Law*, 10(2): 137–48.

Drysdale, L. and Keest, K. E. (2000) 'The two-tiered consumer financial services marketplace: the fringe banking system and its challenge to current thinking about the role of usury laws in today's society', *South Carolina Law Review*, 51: 589–669.

Duménil, G. and Lévy, D. (2011) *The Crisis of Neoliberalism*. Cambridge, MA: Harvard University Press.

Dworkin, R. (1985) *A Matter of Principle*. Cambridge, MA: Harvard University Press.

Dymski, G. A. (2009) 'Racial exclusion and the political economy of the subprime crisis', *Historical Materialism*, 17: 149–79.

—— (2010) 'From financial exploitation to global banking instability: two overlooked roots of the subprime crisis', in M. Konings (ed.) *The Great Credit Crash*, London: Verso, pp. 72–102.

Eagleton, T. (2007) *Ideology: an introduction*, London: Verso.

Economic Policy Institute (2001) *NAFTA at seven: its impact on workers in all three countries*. Washington, DC: Economic Policy Institute. Available: www.policyalternatives.ca/sites/default/files/uploads/publications/National_Office_Pubs/nafta_at_7.pdf (accessed 5 July 2013).

Edmiston, K. D. (2011) 'Could restrictions on payday lending hurt consumers?', *Federal Reserve Bank of Kansas City*, First Quarter: 63–93.

Eglin, J. J. (1993) 'Untangling student loans', *Society*, January/February: 51–9.

Elliehausen, G. and Lawrence, E.C. (2001) 'Payday advance credit in America: an analysis of customer demand', *Monograph 35*, Washington, DC: Credit Research Center, McDonough School of Business, Georgetown University.

Ellis, D. (1998) *The Effect of Consumer Interest Rate Deregulation on Credit Card Volumes, Charge-Offs and the Personal Bankruptcy Rate*, Federal Deposit Insurance Company, Bank Trends, No. 98–05, Washington, DC: Federal Deposit Insurance Corporation.

Elul, R. (2005) 'The economics of asset securitisation', *Business Review (Federal Reserve Bank of Philadelphia)*, Third Quarter: 16–25.

Elyachar, J. (2002) 'Empowerment money: the World Bank, non-governmental organisations and the value of culture in Egypt', *Public Culture*, 14(3): 493–513.

—— (2005) *Markets of Dispossession: NGOs, economic development and the state in Cairo*, Durham, NC: Duke University Press.

Emmund, K. (2005) 'Re-inventing Mexico's financial marketplace', *Business Mexico*, 15(9): 2.

Ergungor, O. E. and Hathaway, I. (2008) 'Trouble ahead for student loans?' *Federal Reserve Bank of Cleveland, Economic Commentary*, May: 1–4.

Euromonitor International (2013) *Passport – consumer lending in Mexico*, London: Euromonitor International.

Evans, P. B., Rueschmeyer, D. and Skocpol, T. (eds) (1985) *Bringing the State Back In*, Cambridge: Cambridge University Press.

Fabozzi, F. J. and Kothari, V. (2008) *Introduction to Securitisation*, Hoboken, NJ: Wiley & Sons.

FamiliesUSA: The Voice for Health Care Consumers (2013) *2013 Federal Poverty Guidelines*, Washington, DC: FamiliesUSA. Available: www.familiesusa.org/resources/tools-for-advocates/guides/federal-poverty-guidelines.html (accessed 13 June 2013).

Federal Deposit and Insurance Corporation (2006) *Affordable Small-Dollar Loan Guidelines*. Available: www.fdic.gov/news/news/press/2006/pr06107a.html (accessed 4 May 2012).

—— (2009) *National Survey of Unbanked and Underbanked Households*, Washington, DC: FDIC.

—— (2010) *Addendum to the 2009 FDIC National Survey of Unbanked and Underbanked Households*, Washington, DC: FDIC.

—— (2013) *FISCA Criticizes US Treasury for Needlessly Scaring Seniors, Vulnerable Populations into Electronic Forms of Government Payments*, Press Release. Available: www.fisca.org/Content/NavigationMenu/GovernmentAffairs/ChoiceCampaignPublicPage/FiSCA_Critical_of_Treasury_Position_on_Electronic_Payments_FINALwHEADER.pdf (accessed 14 July 2013).

Federal Reserve Bank of Boston (2010) *The 2010 Survey of Consumer Payment Choice*, Federal Reserve Bank of Boston. Available: www.bostonfed.org/economic/rdr/2013/rdr1302.pdf (accessed 15 July 2013).

Federal Reserve Bank of New York (2012) *Quarterly Report on Household Debt and Credit*, Research and Statistics Group – Microeconomic Studies (ed.) (February) New York, NY: Federal Reserve Bank of New York.

Federal Reserve Board (1983) *Panel Survey of Consumer Finances*, Washington, DC: Federal Reserve.

—— (1989) *Panel Survey of Consumer Finances*, Washington, DC: Federal Reserve.

—— (1998) Testimony of Chairman Alan Greenspan – The regulation of OTC derivatives Before the Committee on Banking and Financial Services, US House of Representatives July 24, 1998, Washington, DC: Federal Reserve. Available: www.federalreserve.gov/boarddocs/testimony/1998/19980724.htm (accessed 2 August 2013).

—— (2001) *Survey of Consumer Finances*, Washington, DC: Federal Reserve Board.

—— (2008) *Sandra F. Braunstein, Director, Division of Consumer and Community Affairs – The Community Reinvestment Act. Testimony before the Committee on Financial Services, US House of Representatives*, Board of Governors of the Federal Reserve System, Washington, DC: Federal Reserve Board.

—— (2010a) *2010 Survey of Consumer Finance Data*, Washington, DC: Federal Reserve Board.
—— (2010b) *Report to the Congress on Risk Retention, Submitted to the Congress Pursuant to Section 941 of the Dodd-Frank Wall Street Reform and Consumer Protection Act of 2010*, Washington, DC: Federal Reserve.
—— (2013) *Selected Interest Rates (Weekly) – H.15*, Release Date 24 June 2013. Available: http://federalreserve.gov/releases/h15/current (accessed 27 June 2013).
Ferry, M. (1995) 'Changes in student loan regulations', *The Business Lawyer*, 50: 1135–41.
Fine, B. (2002) *The World of Consumption: the material and cultural revisited*, London: Routledge.
—— (2006) 'The new development economics', in K. S. Jomo and B. Fine (eds) *The New Development Economics: after the Washington Consensus*, London: Zed.
—— (2010) 'Locating financialisation', *Historical Materialism*, 18(2): 97–116.
Foucault, M. (1980) *Power/Knowledge: selected interviews & other writings 1972–1977*, Ed. C. Gordon. Trans. C. Gordon L. Marshal J. Mepham and K. Sober, New York, NY: Pantheon.
FOVISSSTE (2012) *Mexico's new FOVISSSTE – Mexican housing day 2012*, Mexico City, Mexico: FOVISSSTE.
Francis, K. E. (2010) 'Rollover, rollover: a behavioural law and economics analysis of the payday-loan industry', *Texas Law Review*, 88:611–38.
Franco, I. (2010) 'Mexico consumer finance: beyond the crisis', *Latin American Chronicle*, 2 July. Available: www.latinbusinesschronicle.com/app/article.aspx?id=4319 (accessed 18 January 2014).
Francois, M. E. (2006) *A Culture of Everyday Credit: housekeeping, pawnbroking and governance in Mexico City, 1750–1920*, Lincoln, NE: University of Nebraska Press.
Fried, R.L. and Breheny, J.P. (2005) 'Tuition isn't the only thing increasing: the growth of the student loan ABS market', *The Journal of Structured Finance*, 40–5.
Friedman, M. (1993) *Why Government Is the Problem (Essays in Public Policy)*. Stanford, CA: Hoover Institution Press.
Friedman, M. (2002) *Capitalism and Freedom*, Chicago, IL: University of Chicago Press.
Froud, J., Erturk, I., Leaver, A., Williams, K. and Sukhdev, J. (2007) 'The democratisation of finance? Promises, outcomes, conditions', *Review of International Political Economy*, 14(4): 553–75.
Fusaro, M. A. (2008) 'Hidden consumer loans: an analysis of implicit interest rates on bounced checks', *Journal of Family and Economic Issues*, 29(1): 251–63.
Gallmeyer, A. and Wade, R. T. (2009) 'Payday lenders and economically distressed communities: a spatial analysis of financial predation', *The Social Science Journal*, 46(2): 521–38.
Geisst, C. R. (2009) *Collateral Damaged: the marketing of consumer debt to America*, New York, NY: Bloomberg Press.
Gelpern, A. (2007) 'Wal-Mart Bank in Mexico: money to the masses and the home-host hole', *Connecticut Law Review*, 39(4): 1513–38.
Germain, R. D. (1997) *The International Organisation of Credit: states in global finance in the world-economy*, Cambridge: Cambridge University Press.
Giddens, A. (2000) *The Global Third Way Debate*, Cambridge: Polity Press.
Gill, S. (1990) *American Hegemony and the Trilateral Commission*, Cambridge: Cambridge University Press.
—— (1995) 'Globalisation, market civilization and disciplinary neoliberalism', *Millennium: Journal of International Studies*, 24(3): 399–423.
Glasbeek, H. (2002) *Wealth by Stealth: corporate crime, corporate law and the perversion of democracy*, Toronto: Between the Lines.
GlobalLens (2006) *Cemex's Patrimonio Hoy: at the tipping point?* Ann Arbor, MI: William Davidson Institute, University of Michigan.

—— (2012) *Constructing the Base-of-the-Pyramid Business in a Multinational Corporation: CEMEX's Patrimonio Hoy looks to grow*, Ann Arbor, MI: William Davidson Institute, University of Michigan.

Gorski, E. (2010) 'Proposed federal rules target for-profit colleges', *Diverse Issues in Higher Education*, 27: 14.

Gorton, G. B. and Souleles, N. S. (2007) 'Special Purpose Vehicles and securitisation', in M. Carey and R. M. Stulz (eds) *The Risks of Financial Institutions*, Chicago, IL: University of Chicago.

Gotham, K. F. (2006) 'The secondary circuit of capital reconsidered: globalization and the US real estate sector', *American Journal of Sociology*, 112: 231–75.

—— (2009) 'Creating liquidity out of spatial fixity: the secondary circuit of capital and the subprime mortgage crisis', *International Journal of Urban and Regional Research*, 33(2): 355–71.

Government Accounting Office (2010) *Troubled Asset Relief – Treasury needs to strengthen its decision-making process on term asset-backed securities loan facility*, Report to Congressional Committees, February, Washington, DC: Government Accounting Office.

Gowan, P. (2010) 'The crisis in the heartland', in M. Konings (ed.) *The Great Credit Crash*, London: Verso, 46–71.

Grabel, I. (1999) 'Mexico redux? Making sense of the financial crisis of 1997–8?' *Journal of Economic Issues*, 33(2): 375–81.

Graeber, D. (2011) *Debt: the first 5,000 years*, Brooklyn, NY: Melville House Publishing.

Graffam, R. D. (2000) 'A case study in international securitisation', in L. T. Kendall and M. J. Fishman (eds.) *A Primer on Securitisation*, Cambridge, MA: MIT Press: 153–70.

Grameen Bank (2011) *What is Microcredit?*, Available: www.grameen-info.org/index.php?option=com_content&task=view&id=28&Itemid=108> (accessed 15 July 2013).

Grameen Foundation USA (2004) *Tapping the Financial Markets for Microfinance: Grameen Foundation USA's promotion of this emerging trend*, Working Paper Series, New York, NY: Grameen Foundation USA.

Gramsci, A. (1971) *Selections from Prison Notebooks*, New York, NY: International Publishers.

Granovetter, M. (1985) 'Economic action and social structure: The problem of embeddness, *American Journal of Sociology*, 91(3): 481–510.

Grant, K. L. (2011) 'Student loans in bankruptcy and the "undue hardships" exception: who should foot the bill?' *Brigham Young University Law Review*, 2011(3): 819–47.

Graves, S. M. and Peterson, C. L. (2005) 'Predatory lending and the military: the law and geography of "payday" loans in military towns', *Ohio State Law Journal*, 66(5): 653–832.

Greider, W. (1989) *Secrets of the Temple: how the Federal Reserve runs the country*, New York, NY: Simon & Schuster.

Gruffydd Jones, B. (2012) '"Bankable slums": the global politics of slum ugrading', *Third World Quarterly*, 33(5): 769–89.

Gumport, P. J., Iannozzi, M., Sharman, S. and Zemsky, R. (1997) *The United States Country Report: trends in higher education from massification to post-massification*, Stanford, CA: Stanford University, 1–50.

Grupo Compartamos (2012) *2012 Annual and Sustainable Report*, Mexico City, Mexico: Grupo Compartamos.

Haddad, C. A. (1999) 'The securitisation of assets in Mexico', *Mexico Law Journal*, 150(141): 141–50.

Haenn, N. (2006) 'The changing and enduring ejido: a state and regional examination of Mexico's land tenure counter-reforms', *Land Use Policy*, 23(1): 136–46.

Haller, M. H. and Alviti, J. V. (1977) 'Loansharking in American cities: historical analysis of a marginal enterprise', *The American Journal of Legal History*, 21: 125–56.

Halperin, S. (2013) *Global Development: a 'horizontal perspective'*, London: Routledge.

Harper, M. (2011) 'The commercializing of microfinance: resolution or extension of poverty?', in M. Bateman (ed.) *Confronting Microfinance: undermining sustainable development*, Sterling, VA: Kumarian Press: 49–64.

Hart-Landsberg, M. (2002) 'Challenging neoliberal myths: a critical look at the Mexican experience', *Monthly Review*, 54(7): 14–28.

Harvey, D. (1974) 'Class-monopoly rent, finance capital and the urban revolution', *Regional Studies*, 8(3–4): 239–55.

—— (1989) *The Urban Experience*, Baltimore, MD: The Johns Hopkins University Press.

—— (1999) *The Limits to Capital*, London: Verso.

—— (2001) *Spaces of Capital: Towards a Critical Geography*, New York: Routledge.

—— (2003) *The New Imperialism*, Oxford: Oxford University Press.

—— (2007) *A Brief History of Neoliberalism*, Oxford: Oxford University Press.

—— (2008) 'The Right to the City', *New Left Review*, 53 (Sept.–Oct.): 23–40.

—— (2010a) *A Companion to Marx's Capital*, London: Verso.

—— (2010b) *The Enigma of Capital and the Crises of Capitalism*, Oxford: Oxford University Press.

Helleiner, E. (1994) *States and the Reemergence of Global Finance*, Ithaca, NY: Cornell University Press.

Hellman, J. A. (1988) *Mexico in Crisis*, New York, NY: Holmes & Meier.

Herbert, C. E., Belsky, E. S. and DuBroff, N. (2012) *The State of Mexico's Housing – recent progress and continued challenges*, Cambridge, MA: Joint Centre for Housing Studies, Harvard University.

Hiltzik, M. (2011) *The New Deal: a modern history*, New York, NY: Free Press.

Hirsch, J. (1978) 'The state apparatus and social reproduction: elements of a theory of the bourgeois state', in J. Holloway and S. Piccioto (eds) *State and Capital: a Marxist debate*, London: Edward Arnold.

—— (1995) *Der Nationale Wettbewerbsstaat: staat, demokratie und politik im globalen kapitalismus*, Berlin: Edition ID-Archiv.

Holloway, J. (1994) 'Global capital and the national state', *Capital & Class*, 18(1): 23–49.

Holloway, J. and Picciotto, S. (eds) (1978) *State and Capital: a Marxist debate*, London: Edward Arnold.

—— (1991) 'Capital, crisis and the state', in S. Clarke (ed.) *The State Debate*, London: Palgrave Macmillian.

Huckstep, A. (2007) 'Payday lending: do outrageous prices necessarily mean outrageous profits?' *Fordham Journal of Corporate and Financial Law*, 12(1): 203–31.

Hudson, M. (1996) *The Merchants of Misery: how corporate America profits from poverty*, Monroe, ME: Common Courage Press.

Ingham, G. (2001) 'Fundamentals of a theory of money: untangling Fine, Lavapitsas and Zelizer', *Economy and Society*, 30(3): 304–23.

—— (2004) *The Nature of Money*, Cambridge: Polity.

Instituto Nacional de Estadística y Geografía (2012) *Mexico at a Glance*, Aguascaliente, Mexico: Instituto Nacional de Estadística y Geografía (INEGI).

Inter-American Development Bank (2001) *Microfinance: from village to Wall Street*, Washington, DC: Inter-American Development Bank.

—— (2006) *An Inside View of Latin American Microfinance*, Washington, DC: Inter-American Development Bank.

—— (2011) *Housing Finance in Mexico: current state and future sustainability*, Washington, DC: Inter-American Development Bank.

International Business Monitor (2011) *Mexico Infrastructure Report Q4 2011*, London, UK: Business Monitor International.

International Financial Corporation (2005) *Structured Finance – GMAC Financiera S. A. de CV*, Washington, DC: International Financial Corporation.

—— (2009) 'Financial innovations and developments in housing finance in Mexico', *IFC Bulletin*, Washington, DC: International Financial Corporation.

International Labour Organisation (2003) *Statistical Definition of Informal Employment: guidelines endorsed by the Seventeenth International Conference of Labour Statisticians*, Geneva, Switzerland: International Labour Organisation.

—— (2012) *Statistical Update on Employment in the Informal Economy*, Geneva, Switzerland: International Labour Organisation.

International Law Office (2008) *New Law Expands Credit Unions' Activities and Revises Governance Rules*. Available: www.internationallawoffice.com/newsletters/detail.aspx?g=e38a01c1-cc2e-4e09-a64e-264b3c4b56d5 (accessed 26 August 2011).

International Monetary Fund (1992) *Mexico: the strategy to achieve sustained economic growth*, Washington, DC: International Monetary Fund.

—— (2001) 'Securitisation of future flow receivables: a useful tool for developing countries', *Finance & Development*, 38(1): npn.

—— (2006) *Financial Sector Assessment Program Update – Mexico*, Washington, DC: International Monetary Fund.

—— (2008) *Housing Finance and Mortgage-Backed Securities in Mexico*, Monetary and Capital Markets Department, Washington, DC: International Monetary Fund.

—— (2010) *Mexico – selected issues*, Washington, DC: International Monetary Fund.

—— (2011) 'Mexico's rapid recovery attest to strong fundamentals', *IMF Survey Magazine: Countries & Regions*, Washington, DC: International Monetary Fund.

—— (2012a) 'Fixing the system', *Finance & Development*, June: 14–6, Washington, DC: International Monetary Fund.

—— (2012b) 'Mexico: detailed assessment of observance of International Organisation of Securities Commission (IOSCO) objectives and principles of securities regulation', *IMF Country Report No. 12/68 (March)*, Washington, DC: International Monetary Fund.

—— (2012c) 'Mexico: financial system stability assessment', *IMF Country Report No. 12/65*, Washington, DC: International Monetary Fund.

—— (2012d) *Staff Country Reports – Mexico*, Washington, DC: International Monetary Fund.

—— (2012e) *2012 Microfinance Americas – the top 100*, Washington, DC: Multilateral Investment Fund.

Itoh, M. and Lapavitsas, C. (1999) *Political Economy of Money and Finance*, London: MacMillan Press.

Jessop, B. (1993) 'Towards a Schumpeterian workfare state? Preliminary remarks on post-Fordist political economy', *Studies in Political Economy*, 40: 7–39.

Jobst, A. A. (2006) 'Sovereign securitisation in emerging markets', *Journal of Structured Finance*, 12(3): 2–13.

Johnston, A., Van Ostern, T. and While, A. (2012) *The Student Debt Crisis*, Washington, DC: Center for American Progress and Campus Progress.

Johnston, C. (2010) *Dear President Obama: you protected the troops; now fulfill your promise to protect all Americans from payday loans*. Available: http://works.bepress.com/creola_johnson/1 (accessed 4 April 2012).

Jonakin, J. (2006) 'Contradictions of neo-liberal reforms on Mexico's balance of payments and labour markets', *International Journal of Development Issues*, 5(2): 93–118.

Jordan, R. C. (2008) 'Will the bubble burst? Some subprime lessons for Mexico, Latin America's leader in asset securitisation', *International Law*, 42: 1181–97.

Jory, K. (2009) 'Mandatory arbitration clauses in payday lending loans: how the federal courts protect unfair lending practices in the name of anti-protectionism', *Ohio State Journal on Dispute Resolution*, 24(2): 315–80.

Karger, H. (2005) *Shortchanged: life and debt in the fringe economy*, San Francisco, CA: Berrett-Koehler.

Karim, L. (2011) *Microfinance and Its Discontents: women in debt in Bangladesh*, Minneapolis, MN: University of Minnesota Press.

Katz, C. (2001) 'Vagabond capitalism and the necessity of social reproduction', *Antipode: A Radical Journal of Geography*, 33(4): 709–28.

Kiely, R. (2010) *Rethinking Imperialism*, London: Palgrave.

Kirschner, J. A. and Volpin, P. F. (2009) *The Political Economy of Personal Bankruptcy Laws: Evidence from the 1978 Reform*, Social Science Research Network, Working Paper Series.

Knowledge@Wharton (2006) *The War Between Banks and 'Sofoles' Propels Mexican Real Estate*. Available: http://knowledge.wharton.upenn.edu/article/the-war-between-banks-and-sofoles-propels-mexican-real-estate/ (accessed 1 April 2013).

—— (2011) *The Home Truths about Non-Bank Mortgage Lending in Mexico*. Available: http://knowledge.wharton.upenn.edu/article/the-home-truths-about-non-bank-mortgage-lending-in-mexico/ (accessed 1 April 2013).

Konings, M. (2010) *The Great Credit Crash*, London: Verso.

Kopinak, K. (1994) 'The maquiladorization of the Mexican economy', in R. Grinspun and M. A. Cameron (eds) *The Political Economy of North American Free Trade*, New York, NY: St. Martin's Press.

Kothari, V. (2006) *Securitisation: the financial instrument of the future*, Singapore: Wiley & Sons.

Krippner, G. (2011) *Capitalizing on Crisis: the political origins of the rise of finance*, Cambridge, MA: Harvard University Press.

Kumar, L. (2013) 'Illusion of women empowerment in microfinance: a case study', *Economic and Political Weekly*, XLVIII(15): 70–6.

Lamoureaux, M. G. (2010) 'Financial regulatory reform – what you need to know', *Journal of Accountancy*, 30–33.

Langley, P. (2008) *The Everyday Life of Global Finance: saving and borrowing in Anglo-America*, Oxford: Oxford University Press.

Langley, P. and Leyshon, A. (2012) 'Financial subjects: culture and materiality', *Journal of Cultural Economy*, 5(4): 369–73.

Lapavitsas, C. (2013) *Profiting without Producing: how finance exploits us all*, London: Verso.

Lea, M. J. (2005) 'Privatizing a government sponsored enterprise: lessons from the Sallie Mae experience', Paper presented at the Conference on 'Fixing the Housing Finance System', Wharton School, University of Pennsylvania, 26–7 April 2005. Mimeo.

LeBaron, G. (2014) 'Debt As a Class-Based Form of Labor Discipline: Reconceptualising Debt Bondage', *Critical Sociology*, 40(5), forthcoming.

LeBaron, G. and Roberts, A. (2010) 'Toward a feminist political economy of capitalism and carcerality', *Signs: Journal of Women in Culture and Society*, 36(1): 19–44.

Lebowitz, M. (2003) *Beyond Capital: Marx's political economy of the working class*, Basingstoke: Palgrave.

Lefebvre, H. (1991a) *The Critique of Everyday Life*, vol. 1, London: Verso.

—— (1991b) *The Production of Space*, Oxford: Blackwell Publishing.

Lewis, J. C. (2008) 'Microloan sharks', *Stanford Innovation Review*, 6(3): 54–9.

Leyshon, A. and Thrift, N. (1997) *Money/Space: geographies of monetary transformation*, London: Routledge.

—— (1999) 'Lists come alive: electronic systems of knowledge and the rise of credit-scoring in retail banking', *Economy and Society*, 28(3): 434–66.

Li, T. M. (2009) 'To make live or let die? Rural dispossession and the protection of surplus populations', *Antipode*, 41(S1): 66–93.

Li, W., Parrish, L., Ernst, K. and Davis, D. (2009) *Predatory Profiling: the role of race and ethnicity in the location of payday lenders in California*, Durham, NC: Centre for Responsible Lending.

Logan, A. and Weller, C. E. (2009) *Who Borrows from Payday Lenders: an analysis of newly available data*, Washington, DC: Centre for American Progress.

Luccisano, L. (2006) 'The Mexican Oportunidades program: questioning the linking of security to conditional investments for mothers and children', *Canadian Journal of Latin American & Caribbean Studies*, 31: 53–85.

Luhmann, N. (2008) *Risk: a sociological theory*, New Brunswick, NJ: Aidine Transaction.

Lynch, M., Engle, J. and Cruz, J. L. (2010) *Subprime Opportunity: the unfilled promise of for-profit colleges and universities*, Washington, DC: The Education Trust.

Macartney, H. and Shields, S. (2011) 'Finding space in critical IPE: a scalar-relational approach', *Journal of International Relations and Development*, 14(3): 375–83.

MacKenzie, D. (2006) *An Engine, Not a Camera: how financial models shape markets*, Boston, MA: MIT Press.

McMichael, P. (2009) 'Contradictions in the global development project: geo-politics, global ecology and the "development climate"', *Third World Quarterly*, 30(1): 247–62.

—— (2012) *Development and Social Change: a global perspective*, 5th edn, Thousand Oaks, CA: Sage.

McNally, D. (2011) *Global Slump: the economics and politics of crisis and resistance*, Winnipeg, PM Press.

Madrid, R. (2002) 'The politics and economics of pension privatization in Latin America', *Latin American Research Review*, 37(2): 159–82.

Mandel, E. (1968) *Marxist Economic Theory*, London: Merlin Press.

Mann, R. J. (2006) 'Bankruptcy reform and the 'sweat box' of credit card debt', *Illinois Law Review*, 375–403.

Mann, R. J. and Hawkins, J. (2007) 'Just until payday', *UCLA Law Review*, 54(4): 855–912.

Manning, R. D. (2000) *Credit Card Nation: the consequences of America's addiction to credit*, New York, NY, Basic Books.

Marier, P. (2008) 'The changing conception of pension rights in Canada, Mexico and the United States', *Social Policy and Administration*, 42(4): 418–33.

Marketwire.com (2013) *Alliance for Financial Inclusion Reaches 100 Member Institutions*, 20 March. Available: www.marketwire.com/press-release/alliance-for-financial-inclusion-reaches-100-member-institutions-1769906.htm (accessed 15 July 2013).

Marois, T. (2012) *States, Banks and Crisis: emerging finance capitalism in Mexico and Turkey*, Cheltenham: Edward Elgar.

Marois, T. (2014) 'Historical precedents, contemporary manifestations: Crisis and the socialization of financial risk in neoliberal Mexico', *Review of Radical Political Economics*, 46 (3), forthcoming.

Marron, D. (2007) 'Lending by numbers: credit scoring and the constitution of risk within American consumer credit', *Economy and Society*, 36(1): 103–33.

Martin, R. (2002) *Financialisation of Daily Life*, Philadelphia, PA: Temple University Press.

Marx, K. and Engels, F. (1974) *The German Ideology*. New York, NY: International Publishers.

Marx, K. (1990) *Capital*, vol. 1, London: Penguin Classics.

—— (1991) *Capital*, vol. 3, London: Penguin Books.

—— (2005) *Grundrisse*, London: Penguin.

Mas, I. and Almazan, M. (2011) 'Banking the poor through everyday stores', *Innovations*, 6(1): 119–28.

Mattie, U. and Nader, L. (2008) *Plunder: when the rule of law is illegal*, Oxford: Blackwell Publishing.

Mauss, M. (1967) *The Gift: forms and functions of exchange in archaic societies*. New York, NY: Norton & Company.

May, C. (2012) 'The rule of law: what is it and why is it "constantly on people's lips"?', *Political Studies Review*, 9(3): 357–65.

—— (2014) *The Rule of Law: the common sense of global politics*, Cheltenham: Edward Elgar.

Melzer, B. T. and Morgan, D. P. (2009) 'Competition and adverse selection in the small-dollar loan market: overdraft versus payday credit', *Federal Reserve Bank of New Staff Report No. 391*, New York, NY: Federal Reserve Bank of New York.

Michelman, I. S. (1970) *Consumer Finance: a case history in American business*, New York, NY: August M. Kelley Publishers.

MicroRate (2011) *The State of Microfinance Investment 2011*, Arlington, VA: MicroRate.

—— (2012) *The State of Microfinance Investment 2012: MicroRate's 7th annual survey and analysis of MIVs*, Arlington, VA: MicroRate.

Minns, R. (2001) *The Cold War: stock markets versus pensions*. London: Verso.

MiningWatch Canada (2012) 'CIDA's partnership with mining companies fails to acknow-ledge and address the role of mining in the creation of development deficits'. A brief prepared for the House of Commons Standing Committee on Foreign Affairs and International Development's Study on the Role of the Private Sector in Achieving Canada's International Development Interests. Ottawa: MiningWatch Canada. Available: www.miningwatch.ca/sites/www.miningwatch.ca/files/Mining_and_Development_FAAE_2012.pdf (accessed 2 April 2013).

Minton, M. (2008) *The Community Reinvestment Act's Harmful Legacy: how it hampers access to credit*, Washington DC: Competitive Enterprise Institute.

Mishal, L. and Bernstein, J. (1994) *The State of Working America: 1994–1995*, Armonk, NY: M. E. Sharpe.

Mitchell, T. (2008) 'Rethinking economy', *Geoforum*, 39(6): 1116–11121.

Mohanty, Chandra. (1995) 'Under Western eyes: feminist scholarship and colonial dis-courses', in C. T. Mohanty, A. Russo and L. Torres (eds) *Third World Women and the Politics of Feminism*, Bloomington, IN: University of Indiana Press.

Monkonnen, P. (2011a) 'Housing finance reform and increasing socioeconomic segregation in Mexico', *International Journal of Urban and Regional Research*, 85(1): 1468–2427.

—— (2011b) 'The housing transition in Mexico: expanding access to housing finance', *Urban Affairs Review*, 47(1): 672–95.

Moody, K. (1997) *Workers in a Lean World: unions in the international economy*, London: Verso.

—— (2007) *US Labor in Trouble and Transition*, London: Verso.

Moore, K. M. (2009) 'The pending credit card debt meltdown: what's happening in your wallet?', *St. Thomas Law Review*, 21(420): 420–40.

Montgomerie, J. (2009) 'The pursuit of (past) happiness? Middle-class indebtedness and American financialisation', *New Political Economy*, 14(1): 1–24.

—— (2010) 'Neoliberalism and the making of subprime borrowers', in M. Konings (ed.) *The Great Credit Crash*, London: Verso.

Moreno-Brid, J. C., Carpizo, P., Ernesto, J. and Bosch Ros, J. (2009) 'Economic develop-ment and social policies in Mexico', *Economy and Society*, 38(1): 154–76.

Morgan, D. P. (2007) 'Defining and detecting predatory lending', *Federal Reserve Bank of New York Staff Reports No. 273*, New York, NY: Federal Reserve Bank of New York.

Morgan, D. P. and Strain, M. R. (2008) 'Payday holiday: how households fare after payday credit bans', *Federal Reserve Bank of New York Staff Reports, No. 39*, New York, NY: Federal Reserve Bank of New York.

Morse, A. (2009) *Payday Lenders: heroes or villains?'*, Chicago, IL: Booth School of Business, University of Chicago.

Morton, A. D. (2011) *Revolution and State in Modern Mexico: the political economy of uneven development*, Lanham, MD: Rowman & Littlefield Publishers.

Moyo, S. and Yeros, P. (eds) (2005) *Reclaiming the Land: the resurgence of rural movements in Africa, Asia and Latin America*, London: Zed.

National Bankruptcy Research Centre (2011) *February 2011 Bankruptcy Report*, Burlingame, CA: National Bankruptcy Research Centre.

National Centre for Education Statistics (2012) *Digest of Educational Statistics – table 223, total fall enrolment in degree-granting institutions, by control and level of institution: 1970 through 2011*. Available: http://nces.ed.gov/programs/digest/d12/tables/dt12_223.asp (accessed 28 June 2013).

—— (2012) *Digest of Education Statistics – table 381, average undergraduate tuition and fees and room and board rates charged for full-time students in degree-granting institutions, by level and control of institutions: 1969–70 through 2011–12*. Available: http://nces.ed.gov/programs/digest/d12/tables/dt12_381.asp (accessed 28 June 2013).

National People's Action (2010) *American Profiteers: how the mainstream banks finance the payday lending industry*. Available: www.npa-us.org (accessed 14 July 2013).

—— (2012) *Profiting from Poverty: how payday lenders strip wealth from the working-poor for record profits*, Chicago, IL: National People's Action.

National Poverty Centre (2012) *Extreme Poverty in the United States, 1996–2011*, Ann Arbor, MI: National Poverty Centre, University of Michigan.

Nugent, R. (1941) 'The Loan-Shark Problems', *Law & Contemporary Problems*, 3(4): 3–13.

Nun, J. (2000) 'The end of ork and the "marginal mass" thesis', *Latin American Perspectives*, 27(1): 6–32.

OECD (2009) *Pension Markets in Focus*, Paris: OECD.

OECD (2012) 'Mexico: better policies for inclusive development', *OECD "Better Policies" Series*, Paris: Organisation for Economic Cooperation and Development.

O'Rourke, K. H. and Williamson, J. G. (1999) *Globalization and History: the evolution of a nineteenth century atlantic*, Cambridge, MA: MIT.

Ocampo, J., Kregel, J. and Griffith-Jones, S. (eds) (2007) *International Finance and Development*, London: Zed.

Occupy Student Debt Campaign. Available: www.occupystudentdebtcampaign.org/our-principles (accessed 1 June 2013).

Office of the (US) Press Secretary (2009) *Reforms to Protect American Credit Card Holders. President Obama signs Credit Card Accountability, Responsibility and Disclosure Act*, Office of the Press Secretary, Washington, DC: Office of the Press Secretary.

Otero, M. (2005) 'A commercial future for microfinance: opportunities and challenges', *Microfinance Matters*, 17 (October): 25–8.

Panitch, L. and Gindin, S. (2012) *The Making of Global Capitalism: the political economy of American empire*, London: Verso.

Pashman, S. (2001) 'Discharge of student loan debt under 11 U.S.C. 523(a)(b): reassessing "undue hardship" after the elimination of the seven-years exception', *New York Law School Law Review*, 44: 605–21.

Pastor, M. J. (1999) 'Globalization, sovereignty and policy choice: lessons from the Mexican Peso crisis', in D. Smith, J. Solinger and S. C. Topik (eds) *States and Sovereignty in the Global Economy*, London: Routledge.

Peck, J. (2001) *Workfare States*, New York, NY: Guilford.

—— (2010) *Constructions of Neoliberal Reason*, Oxford: Oxford University Press.

Peck, J. and Tickell, A. (2002) 'Neoliberalising space', *Antipode: A Radical Journal of Geography*, 34(3): 380–404.

Peters, E. D. (2000) *Polarizing Mexico: the impact of liberalization strategy*, Boulder, CO: Lynne Rienner.

Peterson, C. L. (2007) 'Usury law, payday loans and statutory sleight of hand: an empirical analysis of American credit pricing limits', *Selected Words of Christopher L. Peterson*, Gainsville, FL: University of Florida.

Peterson, S. V. (2003) *A Critical Rewriting of Global Political Economy: integrating reproductive, productive and virtual economies*, London: Routledge.

Petras, J. and Veltmeyer, H. (2001) *Globalization Unmasked: imperialism in the 21st century*, London: Zed Books.

Pew Research Centre (2009) 'Still waiting: "unfair or deceptive" credit card practices continue as American wait for new reforms to take effect', *The Pew Charitable Trusts*, October. Available: www.pewtrusts.org/our_work_detail.aspx?id=630 (accessed 26 May 2011).

—— (2011) *A New Equilibrium: after passage of landmark credit card reform, interest rates and fees have stabilized*, Washington, DC: Pew Research Centre.

Picciotto, S. (2011) *Regulating Global Corporate Capitalism*, Cambridge: Cambridge University Press.

Pickering, N. (2000) 'The Mexican mortgage boom, bust and bail out: determinants of borrower default and loan restructure after the 1995 currency crisis', *Joint Center for Housing Studies*, Cambridge, MA: Harvard University.

Piven, F. F. and Cloward, R. A. (1993) *Regulating the Poor: the functions of the welfare state*, New York, NY: Vintage Books.

Plunkett, L. A. and Hurtado, A. L. (2011) 'Small dollar loans, big problems: how states protect consumers from abuses and how the federal government can help', *Suffolk University Law Review*, XLIV(31): 31–88.

Poindexter, G. C. and Vargas-Cartaya, W. (2002–2003) 'En ruta hacia el desarrollo: the emerging secondary mortgage market in Latin America', *George Washington International Law Review*, 34: 257–86.

Porter, T. (2005) *Globalization and Finance*, Cambridge: Polity Press.

—— (2007) 'Compromises of embedded knowledge: standards, codes and technical authority in global governance', in S. Bernstein and L. W. Pauly (eds) *Global Liberalism and Political Order: toward a new compromise?*, Albany, NY: SUNY Press: 109–31.

Pradash, V. (2007) *The Darker Nations: a people's history of the Third World*, New York, NY: The New Press.

—— (2013) *The Poorer Nations: a possible history of the Global South*, London: Verso.

Project on Student Debt (2012) *Student Debt and the Class of 2012*, Washington, DC: The Institute for College Access and Success.

Puyana, A. (2010) *The Impact of Trade Liberalization and the Global Economic Crisis on the Productive Sectors, Employment and Incomes in Mexico*, vol. 15, Geneva, Switzerland: International Center for Trade and Sustainable Development.

Raccanello, K. and Romero, D. G. (2011) 'Predatory credit and credit law in Mexico', *International Journal of Microfinance*, 1(1): 48–56.

Rankin, K. (2001) 'Governing development: neoliberalism, microcredit and rational economic woman', *Economy and Society*, 30(1): 18–37.

—— (2013) 'A critical geography of poverty finance', *Third World Quarterly*, 34(4): 547–68.

Rankin, K. and Shakya, Y. B. (2008) 'The politics of subversion in development practice: microfinance in Nepal and Vietnam', *Journal of Development Studies*, 44(8): 1214–35.

Reddy, R. (2007) 'Microfinancing cracking the capital markets II', *InSight*, Washington, DC: Centre for Financial Inclusion.

Reimherr, P., Harmon, T., Strawn, J. and Chitz, V. (2013) *Reforming Student Aid: how to simplify tax aid and use performance metrics to improve college choices and completion*, Washington, DC: Center for Postsecondary and Economic Success.

Reinert, E. S. (2008) *How Rich Countries Got Rich and Why Poor Countries Stay Poor*, London: Constable.

Rivlin, G. (2010) *Broke, USA – from pawnshops to Poverty, Inc. – how the working poor became big business*, New York, NY: HarperCollins.

Roberts, A. (2013) 'Financing social reproduction: the gendered relations of debt and mortgage finance in twenty-first-century America', *New Political Economy*, 18(1): 21–45.

Roberts, A. and Soederberg, S. (2012) 'Gender equality as smart economics? A critique of the 2012 World Development Report', *Third World Quarterly*, 33(5): 949–68.

Roberts, B., Povich, D. and Mather, M. (2013) *Low-Income Working Families: the growing economic gap*, Silver Spring, MD: The Working Poor Families Project.

Robinson, J. (1962) *Economic Philosophy*, Piscataway, NJ: Transaction Publishers.

Rodolsky, R. (1977) *The Making of Marx's Capital*, London: Pluto Press.

Rodriguez, D. (2007) 'Left behind: the impact of the Bankruptcy Abuse Prevention and Consumer Protection Act of 2005 on economic, social and racial justice', *Berkeley La Raza Law*, 65(18): npn.

Rodriguez, M. and Heurga, A. 'A study of four listed microfinance institutions', presented at the International Conference on Industrial Engineering and Industrial Management, Vigo, Spain, 18–20 July 2012.

Roodman, D. (2006) 'Creditor initiatives in the 1980s and 1990s', in C. Jochnick and A. Fraser (eds.) *Sovereign Debt at the Crossroads: challenges and proposals for resolving the Third World debt crisis*, New York, NY: Oxford University Press.

—— (2011) 'Does Compartamos charge 195% interest?', *David Roodman's Microfinance Open Book Blog*, Washington, DC: Centre for Global Development.

Roy, A. (2010) *Poverty Capital: micro-finance and the making of development*, London: Routledge.

Rutledge, S. L. (2010) *Consumer Protection and Financial Literacy: lessons from nine country studies. Policy Research Working Paper No. 5326*, Washington, DC: World Bank Group.

Saez, E. (2013) *Striking it Richer: the evolution of top incomes in the United States (updated with 2012 preliminary estimates)*, Berkeley, CA, Department of Economics: University of California Berkeley.

Sallie Mae (2013) *Sallie Mae Reports Fourth-Quarter and Full-Year 2012 Financial Results*, Newark, Delaware: Sallie Mae. Available: http://opennet.salliemae.com (accessed 1 June 2012).

Sanchez, M. (2010) 'Financial innovation and the global crisis', *International Journal of Business and Management*, 5(11): 26–31.

Sandoval, R. (2005) 'Block by block: how one of the world's largest companies builds loyalty among Mexico's poor', *Stanford Innovation Review*, Summer: 34–7.

Sanyal, K. K. (2007) *Rethinking Capitalist Development: primitive accumulation, governmentality and post-colonial capitalism*, New Dehli: Routledge.

Sassen, S. (2006) *Territory, Authority, Rights: from medieval to global assemblages*, 2nd edn, Princeton, NJ: Princeton University Press.

—— (2008) 'Mortgage capital and its particularities: A new frontier for global finance', *Journal of International Affairs*, 62(1): 187–212.

—— (2009) 'When local housing becomes an electronic instrument: the global circulation of mortgages – a research note', *International Journal of Urban and Regional Research*, 33(2): 411–26.

—— (2010) 'A savage sorting of winners and losers: contemporary versions of primitive accumulation', *Globalizations*, 7(1–2): 23–50.

Schwartz, D. S. (1997) 'Enforcing small print to protect big business: employee and consumer rights claims in an age of compelled arbitration', *Wisconsin Law Review*, 33(1): 36–132.

Schwartz, H. M. (2009) *Subprime Nation: American power, global capital and the housing bubble*, Ithaca, NY: Cornell University Press.

Secretariat of the Commonwealth (2013) *Financial Inclusion in the Commonwealth and Francophonie. A paper for the Commonwealth-Francophonie-G20 Development Working Group Meeting*, 21 April. Available: www.thecommonwealth.org/files/254284/FileName/FinancialInclusionintheCommonwealthandFrancophonie-11April2013.pdf (accessed 22 July 2013).

Sengupta, R. and Aubuchon, C. P. (2008) 'The microfinance revolution: an overview', *Review, Federal Reserve Bank of St. Louis*, 90(1): 9–30.

SHF (2008) *Current Housing Situation in Mexico 2008*. Mexico City: SHF.

SHF (2011) *Outlook for Mexican Housing Industry and SHF Role and Perspectives*, Mexico City: SHF. Available: www.shf.gob.mx/Paginas/default.aspx (accessed 13 August 2013).

SHF (2014) *Mortgage Market in Mexico*, Mexico City: SHF. Available: www.pencom.gov.ng/download/seminars/Mortgage_Market_in_Mexico.ppt (accessed 15 January 2014).

Shragge, E. (ed.) (1997) *Workfare: ideology for a new underclass*, Toronto: Garamond Press.

Simkovic, M. (2009) 'The effect of BAPCPA on credit card industry profits and prices', *American Bankruptcy Law Journal*, 83(1): 1–27.

—— (2013, in press) 'Risk-based student loans', *Washington and Lee Law Review*, 70(1).

Simmel, G. (2004) *The Philosophy of Money*. London: Routledge.

Slivinski, S. (2007) *The Corporate Welfare State: how the federal government subsidizes US businesses*, Washington, DC: CATO Institute.

SEDESOL (2009) *Mercado Formal y Informal de Suelo: análisis de ocho ciudades*, Mexico City, Mexico: Secretaria de Desarrollo Social (SEDESOL).

Soederberg, S. (2004) *The Politics of the New International Financial Architecture: reimposing neoliberal domination in the Global South*, London; New York: Zed Books.

—— (2006) *Global Governance in Question: empire, class and the new common sense in managing North-South relations*, London; Ann Arbor, MI: Pluto Press.

—— (2010a) 'Cannibalistic capitalism: the paradoxes of neoliberal pension securitisation', in L. Pantich, G. Albo and V. Chibber (eds) *Socialist Register 2011: the crisis this time*, vol. 47, London: Merlin Press, pp. 224–41.

—— (2010b) *Corporate Power and Ownership in Contemporary Capitalism: the politics of resistance and domination*, London: Routledge.

—— (2010c) 'The Mexican competition state and the paradoxes of managed neoliberalism', *Policy Studies*, 31(1): 77–94.

—— (2010d) 'The politics of representation and financial fetishism: the case of the G20 summits', *Third World Quarterly*, 31(4): 523–40.

Soederberg, S., Menz, G. and Cery, P. G. (2005) *Internalizing Globalization: the rise of neoliberalism and the decline of national varieties of capitalism*, Basingstoke, UK; New York, NY: Palgrave Macmillan.

Stafford Loans (2013) 'Unsubsidized Stafford Loan' Available: www.staffordloan.com/stafford-loan-info/unsubsidized-student-loan.php (accessed 4 May 2013).

Standard & Poor's (2006) 'Mexican RMBS market finds keys to success', *Ratings Direct Research*, New York, NY: Standard & Poor's.

Standing, G. (2011) *The Precariat: the new dangerous class*, London: Bloomsbury Academic.

Stanford, J. (2008) *Economics for Everyone: a short guide to the economics of capitalism*, Halifax: Fernwood Publishing.

Stegman, M. (2007) 'Payday lending', *Journal of Economic Perspectives*, 21(1): 169–90.

Stegman, F. and Faris, R. (2005) 'Welfare, work and banking: the use of consumer credit by current and former TANF recipients in Charlotte, North Carolina', *Journal of Urban Affairs*, 27(4): 379–402.

Stehl, R. L. (1999) 'The failings of the credit counseling and debtor education requirements of the proposed Consumer Bankruptcy Reform Legislation of 1998', *American Bankruptcy Law Journal*, 7: 133–54.

Stieber, S. (2007) 'Is securitisation right for microfinance?', *Innovations: technology, governance, globalization*, 2(1–2): 202–13.

Strange, S. (1988) *States and Markets: an introduction to International Political Economy*, 2nd edn, New York, NY: Basil Blackwell.

Sullivan, T. A., Warren, E. and Westbrook, J. L. (2006) 'Less stigma or more financial distress: an empirical analysis of the extraordinary increase in bankruptcy findings', *Stanford Law Review*, 59(4): 213–56.

Taylor, M. (2006) *From Pinochet to the Third Way: neoliberalism and social transformation in Chile*, London: Pluto.

—— (2008) *Global Economy Contested: power and conflict across the international division of labor*, London, New York, NY: Routledge.

—— (2011) 'Freedom from poverty is not for free: rural development and the microfinance crisis in Andhra Pradesh, India', *Journal of Agrarian Change*, 11(4): 484–504.

Thompson, E. P. (1991) *The Making of the English Working Class*, London: Penguin.

Tokman, V. E. (2007) 'The informal economy, insecurity and social cohesion in Latin America', *International Labour Review*, 146(1–2): 81–107.

Traub, A. (2013) *Discredited*, New York, NY: Dēmos.

Traub, A. and McGhee, H. C. (2013) *State of the American Dream: economic policy and the future of the middle class*, New York, NY: Dēmos.

Traub, A. and Ruetschlin, C. (2012) *The Plastic Safety Net: findings from the 2012 National Survey on Credit Card Debt of Low- and Middle-Income Households*, New York, NY: Dēmos.

Traub, A., Draut, T. and Callahan, D. (2012) *The Contract for College*, New York, NY: Dēmos.

United Nations (2003) 'General Assembly greenlights programme for the International Year of Microcredit 2005', *Press Release DEV/2452*, New York, NY: United Nations.

—— (2010a) 'To what extent are Bangladesh's recent gains in poverty reduction different from the past?', *Policy Research Working Paper 5199*, Washington, DC: World Bank Group.

—— (2010b) *World Economic and Social Survey 2010 – retooling development*, New York, NY: United Nations.

—— (2011) *World Economic Situation and Prospects 2011*, New York, NY: United Nations.

—— (2012) *World Economic Situation and Prospects 2012: update as of mid-2012*, New York, NY: United Nations.

UN-HABITAT (2006) *An Approach to Financial Action Planning for Slum Upgrading and New Low-Income Residential Neighbourhoods*, The SUF Handbook, vol. 1, Nairboi, Kenya: UN-HABITAT.

—— (2010a) *A Practical Guide for Conducting: housing profiles*, Nairobi, Kenya: UN-HABITAT.

—— (2010b) 'Homes, neighbourhoods, happiness: building prosperity through development', *Urban Finance*, Nairobi, Kenya: UN-HABITAT.

—— (2011) *Housing Finance Mechanisms in Mexico*, Nairobi, Kenya: UN-HABITAT.

USAID (2009) 'Will the bottom of the pyramid hit bottom? The effects of the global credit crisis on the microfinance sector', *MicroReport, No. 150*, Washington, DC: USAID.

US Department of Commerce and Bureau of the Census (2012) 'Income, poverty and health insurance coverage in the United States: 2011', *US Census*, Washington, DC: US Census.

—— (2013) *Preliminary Estimate of Weighted Average Poverty Thresholds for 2012*, Washington, DC: US Census. Available: www.census.gov/hhes/www/poverty/data/threshld/index.html (accessed 10 June 2013).

US Congressional Budget Office (2011) *Reducing the Deficit: spending and revenue options*, March, Washington, DC: Congressional Budget Office.

—— (2013a) *Report on the Troubled Asset Relief Program*, May. Available: www.cbo.gov/publication/44256 (accessed 3 July 2013).

—— (2013b) February 2013 Baseline Projections for the Student Loan Program. Available: www.cbo.gov/sites/default/files/cbofiles/attachments/43913_StudentLoans.pdf (accessed 12 June 2013).

US Congressional Research Service (2010) *NAFTA and the Mexican Economy*, Washington, DC: US Congressional Research Service.

US Department of Commerce (2010) *Middle Class in America – for the Vice President of the United States Middle Class Task Force*, Department of Commerce Economics and Statistic Administration, Washington, DC: Government Printing Office.

US Department of Defense (2006) *Report on Predatory Lending Practices Directed at Members of the Armed Forces and their Dependents*, Washington, DC: Department of Defense.

US Department of Education (2011) *Student Loans Overview – fiscal year 2011 budget request*, Washington, DC: US Department of Education.

—— (2012) *Digest of Education Statistics – 2011*, Department of Education, Washington DC: US Department of Education.

US Department of Housing (2001) *Curbing Predatory Home Mortgage Lending*, Washington DC: Department of Housing and the Treasury Task Force on Predatory Lending.

US Department of Labor (2002) *Consumer Spending: an engine for U.S. job growth*, Washington, DC: US Department of Labor.

—— (2009) *How the Government Measures Unemployment*, Washington, DC: US Government Printing Office.

—— (2010) *Occupational Outlook Handbook, 2010–11 Edition*, Bureau of Labor Statistics, Washington, DC: Government Printing Office.

—— (2012) *Employment Projections: 2010–2020 summary*, Department of Labor, Washington, DC: US Department of Labor.

US Department of Treasury (2006) *Lessons Learned from the Privatization of Sallie Mae*, March, Washington, DC: US Department of Treasury, Office of Sallie Mae Oversight.

van Apeldoorn, B. de Graaff, N. and Overbeek, H. (eds) (2012) 'The rebound of the capitalist state: the rearticulation of the state-capital nexus in the global crisis' (Special Issue), *Globalizations*, 9(4): 467–622.

van Gelder, J.-L. (2013) 'Paradoxes of urban housing informality in the developing world', *Law & Society*, 47(3): 493–522.

van Wayenberg, E. (2006) 'From Washington to Post-Washington Consensus: illusions of development', in K. S. Jomo and B. Fine *The New Development Economics: after the Washington Consensus*, London: Zed, pp. 22–45.

von Braunmuehl, C. (1973) *Probleme einer materiallistischen staatstheorie*, Frankfurt am Main, Germany: Suhrkamp Verlag.

von Hayek, F. A. (2011) *Der Weg zur Knechtschaft*. Munich: Olzog.

von Mises, L. (2009) *The Anti-Capitalistic Mentality*. Eastford, CT: Martino Fine Books.

Wacquant, L. (2009) *Punishing the Poor: the neoliberal government of social insecurity*, Durham, NC: Duke University Press.

—— (2010) 'Crafting the neoliberal state: workfare, prisonfare and social insecurity', *Sociological Forum*, 25(2): 197–220.

Walsh, E. (2008) 'Asset backed alert and Wachovia Capital Markets LLC', in B. P. Lancaster, G. M. Schultz and F. J. Fabozzi (eds) *Structured Products and Related Credit Derivatives: a comprehensive guide for investors*, Hoboken, NJ: John Wiley & Sons.

Warren, E. and Warren Tyagi, A. (2004) *The Two-Income Trap: why middle-class parents are going broke*, New York, NY: Basic Books.

Waterford, C. (2008) *Explanation of Compartamos Interest Rates*. Available: www.micro financetransparency.com/evidence/PDF/5.6%20Explanation%20of%20Compartamos%20 Interest%20Rates.pdf (accessed 17 July 2013).

Weber, H. (2002) 'The imposition of a global development architecture: the example of microcredit', *Review of International Political Economy*, 28(3): 537–55.

—— (2006) 'A political analysis of the PRSP initiative: social struggles and the organisation of persistent relations of inequality', *Globalizations*, 3(2): 187–206.

Weller, C., Morzuch, B. J. and Logan, A. (2008) 'Desperate vs. deadbeat: can we quantify the effect of the bankruptcy abuse prevention and Consumer Protection Act of 2005', *Working Paper Series, No. 185*, Amherst, MA: Political Economy Research Centre, University of Massachusetts Amherst.

Wennerlind, C. (2011) *Casualties of Credit: the English financial revolution, 1620–1720*, Cambridge, MA: Harvard University Press.

White, B. N. F., Borras Jr, S. M., Hall, R., Scoones, I. and Worlford, W. (2012) 'The new enclosures: critical perspectives on corporate land deals', *Journal of Peasant Studies*, 39(3–4): 619–47.

Whitfield, D. (2001) *Public Services of Corporate Welfare: rethinking the nation state in the global economy*, London: Pluto Press.

Wicks-Lim, J. (2013) 'Undercounting the Poor: the US's new, but only marginally improved, poverty measure', *Dollars & Sense*, May/June: npn.

Wiese, K. (1984) 'Discharging student loans in bankruptcy: the bankruptcy court tests of "undue hardship"', *Arizona Law Review*, 26: 445–59.

Williams, B. (2004) *Debt for Sale: a social history of the credit trap*, Philadelphia, PA: University of Pennsylvania Press.

Williams, H. (2001) 'Of free trade and debt bondage: fighting banks and the state in Mexico', *Latin American Perspectives*, 28(4): 30–51.

Woo-Cummings, M. (1999) *The Developmental State*, Ithaca, NY: Cornell University Press.

Woolston, A.S. (2010) 'Neither borrower nor lender be: the future of payday lending in Arizona', *Arizona Law Review*, 52(3): 853–87.

World Bank (1993) *Housing: Enabling Markets to Work*. Washington, DC: World Bank.

—— (1994) *Averting the Old Age Crisis: policies to protect the old and promote growth*, Washington, DC: World Bank Group.

—— (2000/2001) *World Development Report: Attacking Poverty*, Washington, DC: World Bank Group.

—— (2001) *The Microfinance Revolution*, Washington, DC: World Bank Group.

—— (2002a) *World Development Report 2002: building institutions for markets*, Washington, DC: World Bank Group.

—— (2002b) *Mexico: low income housing: issues and options*, Mexico Country Management Unit, Washington, DC: World Bank Group.

—— (2004a) *Integrating the Poor into the Mainstream Financial System: the BANSEFI and AGARPA Programs in Mexico*, Washington, DC: World Bank Group.

—— (2004b) *Mortgage Securities in Emerging Markets*, Washington, DC: World Bank Group.

—— (2004c) *Poverty in Mexico: an assessment of conditions, trends and government strategies*, Washington, DC: World Bank Group.

—— (2005a) *Credit and Loan Reporting Systems in Mexico*, Washington, DC: World Bank Group.

—— (2005b) in M. Fay (ed.) *The Urban Poor in Latin America*, Washington, DC: World Bank Group.

—— (2006) 'The urban unbanked in Mexico and the United States', *World Bank Policy Research Working Paper 3835*, Washington, DC: World Bank Group.

—— (2007a) *Economic Opportunities for Indigenous Peoples in Latin America and Mexico*, Washington, DC: World Bank Group.

—— (2007b) *Financing of the Private Sector in Mexico, 2000–2005: evolution, composition and determinants*, Washington, DC: World Bank Group.

—— (2008) *Finance for All? Policies and pitfalls in expanding access*, Washington, DC: World Bank Group.

—— (2009a) 'Microfinance tradeoffs: regulation, competition and financing', *Policy Research Working Paper No. 5086*, Washington, DC: World Bank Group.

—— (2009b) L. Chiquier and M. Lea (eds) *Housing Finance Policy in Emerging Markets*, Washington, DC: World Bank Group.

—— (2009c) *The Economic Impact of Banking the Unbanked: evidence from Mexico*, Washington, DC: World Bank Group.

—— (2010a) *Global Development Finance: external debt of developing countries*, Washington, DC: World Bank Group.

—— (2010b) *To What Extent Are Bangladesh's Recent Gains In Poverty Reduction Different From The Past?* Washington, DC: World Bank Group.

—— (2012a) *Findex Notes*. Available: http://siteresources.worldbank.org/EXTGLOBAL FIN/Resources/8519638–1332259343991/N2savingsENG.pdf (accessed 15 July 2013).

—— (2012b) *Global Development Finance 2012: external debt of developing countries*, Washington, DC: World Bank Group.

—— (2012c) *Mexico Policy Note 1*, Washington, DC: World Bank Group.

—— (2012d) *Report to the International Bar Association: meeting of the World Bank Working Group on Insolvency of National Persons*, Washington, DC: World Bank Group.

—— (2012e) *World Development Report 2012: gender equality and development*, Washington, DC: World Bank Group.

—— (2013a) *International Debt Statistics*, Washington, DC: World Bank Group.

—— (2013b) *World Development Report on Jobs*, Washington, DC: World Bank Group.

—— (2014) *Global Finance Development Report – financial inclusion*. Washington, DC: World Bank Group.

Wyly, E., Moos, M., Hammel, D. and Kabahizi, E. (2009) 'Cartographies of race and class: mapping the class-monopoly rents of American subprime rents of American subprime mortgage capital', *International Journal of Urban and Regional Research*, 33(2): 323–54.

Yanes, P. (2011) 'Mexico's targeted and conditional transfers: between Oportunidades and rights', *Economic & Political Weekly*, XLVI(21): 49–54.

Zapata, F. (2006) 'Mexico labour in context of political, social and economic change', in L. Randall (ed.) *Changing Structure of Mexico: political, social and economic prospectives*, New York, NY: M.E. Sharpe.

Zelizer, V. A. (1997) *The Social Meaning of Money: money, paychecks, poor relief and other currencies*, Princeton, NJ: Princeton University Press.

Zinman, J. (2010) 'Restricting consumer credit access: household survey evidence on effects around Oregon rate cap', *Journal of Banking & Finance*, 34(1): 546–56.

INDEX

Locators to plans and tables are in *italics*; the letter 'n' refers to an end note.